Principles of object-oriented software development

INTERNATIONAL COMPUTER SCIENCE SERIES

Consulting Editor **A D McGettrick** University of Strathclyde

2nd Edition

Principles of
Object-Oriented
Software Development

Anton Eliëns

An imprint of **Pearson Education**

Harlow, England · London · New York · Reading, Massachusetts · San Francisco · Toronto · Don Mills, Ontario · Sydney
Tokyo · Singapore · Hong Kong · Seoul · Taipei · Cape Town · Madrid · Mexico City · Amsterdam · Munich · Paris · Milan

Pearson Education Ltd
Edinburgh Gate
Harlow
Essex CM20 2JE
England

and Associated Companies around the World.

Visit us on the World Wide Web at:
www.pearsoneduc-ema.com

First edition 1994
Second edition 2000

ISBN 0201-39856-7

British Library Cataloguing-in-Publication Data
A catalogue record for this book can be obtained from the British Library

10 9 8 7 6 5 4 3 2 1
04 03 02 01 00

Typeset by the author with the LATEX Documentation System
Printed in Great Britain by Henry Ling Limited at the Dorset Press, Dorchester, Dorset.

Foreword

What an unusual book! I have certainly seen many books on object-oriented software development and even some that have similar coverage, but Anton Eliëns's book is in a different category entirely. As so many books in our field, this one has also had its roots in the development of lecture notes. However, Eliëns took a surprising deviation from the established path of developing notes into books. Instead of inflating the notes, reorganizing the material, and creating the traditional textbook, Eliëns decided to keep the essence of his notes alive.

By condensing the key points into "slides" and keeping these slides as visual anchors all over his text, the reader's experience is truly different. There is a fast track where we just follow the slides: this is what students to with handouts on first encounter. Then there are the deeper modes of reading where we focus in and follow Eliëns's full-text explanations; explanations that are thorough enough where that is important and shallow enough where overwhelming detail wouldn't pay back. Reading through this book and working with it to enhance our understanding is a pleasure.

For a breakdown of the book's structure, I refer to the preface and the foreword to the first edition. However, it is worth noting that Eliëns has improved his text substantially over the first edition. A theme close to my heart has been woven into the text: components. Software architecture, a closely related theme of quickly growing importance, has also found coverage.

The style and didactic quality of the presentation are matched by a wide-ranging selection of topics. Living in times of rapid change and extremely broad diversification of our discipline, we have to value the few books that span significant ranges in an integrative fashion. After all, it is the reader's key challenge to use books like Eliëns's to reconstruct and integrate the vast sea of knowledge fragments out there; and it is with the help of books like Eliëns's that the reader has a chance of achieving this formidable goal. Instructors and lecturers will equally appreciate this book as readily usable for teaching and lecturing tasks.

In the end, for the software developer to be, as well as for the established software developer or the computer scientist with an eye on software development, there is a lot to know from a spectrum of subdisciplines, before we can feel even half-confident about what we are actually doing when developing software. To get there, we need to understand everything from modeling and design techniques, over architecture and components, to implementation detail expressed in specific programming languages. This book is a good starting point for doing so from an object-oriented perspective. (Keep your eyes open for other perspectives and approaches, though!)

Clemens Szyperski
November 1999

Foreword to the first edition

This book is an important contribution to object-oriented literature, bridging the gap between the language and software engineering communities. It covers language design issues relating to inheritance, types, polymorphism, and active objects as well as software design paradigms such as the object modeling technique (OMT), the model-view-controller paradigm (MVC) and responsibility-driven design. Its four-part subdivision of the subject matter into design, languages and systems, foundations, and application frameworks nicely balances practice and theory, covering both practical design techniques and foundational models. Its use of C++ as the primary application language, with Smalltalk and Eiffel as additional languages, allows the book to be used in courses with programming assignments in mainstream object-oriented languages.

The overall sense of balance and perspective is matched by an engaging style and a modern treatment of an exceptionally broad range of topics in the body of the book. The conceptually challenging questions at the end of each chapter (with answers in an appendix) are sometimes humorous. For example, the question 'Why do you need friends?', which invites the reader to examine the value of this C++ language construct, is nicely answered by pointing out tradeoffs between efficiency and safety, ending with the admonition 'treat friends with care'.

Object-oriented programming started as a language framework for single-user systems, but is maturing into a technology for heterogeneous, distributed network systems that focus on interoperability and glue for the composition of heterogeneous modules. The notion of structure in object-oriented programming is analogous to, but more complex than, the structure of structured programming. This book reflects the maturation process from single-user to distributed systems technology and provides a bridge from object-oriented concepts of single-user programming to distributed software design concepts.

Basic object-oriented concepts are introduced from the viewpoint of design, thereby motivating language concepts by their role in the software life cycle. The first four chapters provide a gentle introduction to fundamental concepts that yields unexpected insights for the seasoned reader. Chapter 1 examines paradigms of programming and provides a distinctive object-oriented view of the software life cycle, while chapter 2 presents C++, examines its benefits and pitfalls, and compares it to Smalltalk and Eiffel. Chapter 3 on object-oriented design includes an insightful discussion of models, contracts, and specifications that provides a comparative overview and synthesis of alternative approaches to the conceptual foundations of design. Chapter 4 rounds out the section on design with a discussion of testing and metrics for software validation that provides a practical counterpoint to the conceptual focus of earlier chapters.

The topics in the first four chapters are well chosen to provide a foundation for later topics. The chapter on language design principles includes an up-to-date review of models of inheritance and delegation, the chapter on concurrency examines inheritance anomalies, concurrent object models, and principles of distributed programming, while the chapter on composition and collaboration explains callbacks, window management, and event-driven computation. The three chapters on foundations examine, in a substantive but relaxed way, algebraic models for abstract data types, calculi for type polymorphism, and behavioral refinement through subtyping. The two final chapters provide an account of interoperability, standards, library design, requirements engineering, hypermedia links, and heterogeneous systems.

This book covers an unusually broad range of topics in an eminently readable fashion and is unique in its balance between theory and practice and its multifaceted approach. Anton Eliëns demonstrates an up-to-date mastery of the literature and the rare ability to compare, evaluate, and synthesize the work of different software research and development communities. He is to be commended on his skill and versatility in weaving a sequential expository thread through a heterogeneous, distributed domain of subject matter.

Peter Wegner
October 1994

Preface

This is a book about object-oriented software development. It reflects the contents of an upper-level undergraduate course on Object-Oriented Programming, given at the Vrije Universiteit Amsterdam.

This was the beginning of the preface of the first edition. It still holds true. However, OO is a rapidly evolving field. As a consequence my book, published in 1994, may have been considered to be outdated from the start. As an example, right after its publication, patterns came into the focus of public interest. As another example, think of the Java wave that has come over us. Clearly, a revised edition was needed in which those subjects, and other subjects, are covered, or, as in the case of CORBA, are covered in more detail.

Another reason is that the field of OO itself has matured considerably. The acceptance of UML as a modeling standard is one example. The increased utilization of CORBA for business-critical applications is another sign that (distributed) object technology is being considered as sufficiently robust.

The availability of new topics in itself is not enough to justify a second edition, since new books have been published in which these topics are covered. You only have to think of the enormous number of books on Java ... A revised second edition of the book is justified however, in my opinion, since the book distinguishes itself from the competition by its approach. Set up as a series of lectures, organized around so-called slides, the book covers a large number of topics, some in depth, some more casually. From an educational point of view, the advantage of this approach is the direct availability of educational material, including the slides to be presented in classroom. For the average reader, moreover, the slides provide an overview which facilitates comprehension and recall.

Finally, another more personal reason for bringing out a revised edition is that both in research and teaching my experience with OO has become more extensive, and I may even dare say that my own thoughts about OO have matured to some extent. In particular, in my group we have developed a multi-paradigm OO framework, which was already introduced in chapter 12 of the first edition, that has been applied in, for example, business process reengineering and collective improvisation on the Web. Although I do not plan to treat any of this material extensively, it does provide a basis for the examples and, moreover, the material (including articles, software and examples) will be available on the accompanying CDROM.

Features of this book

- The book provides an introduction to object-oriented programming, covering design, languages, and foundational issues. It pays attention to issues such as reuse, component technology, design patterns and in particular the application of object technology in Web applications.

- It contains guidelines for developing object-oriented applications. Apart from practical examples it provides an overview of development methods as well as an introduction to UML, the standard for object-oriented modeling. In particular *design patterns* will act as a recurrent theme, or rather as a perspective from which examples and solutions will be discussed.

- Distributed object technology will be a major theme. The book provides an introduction to CORBA that allows the student to gain hands-on experience with developing CORBA applications. It also provides a discussion of competing technologies, and in particular it will elucidate the distinction between component technology and distributed objects. Examples in Java and C++ will be included.

- Another major theme of the book is to establish precisely the relation between the guidelines and prescriptions emerging from software engineering practice on the one hand, and the constraints and insights originating from theoretical research. In the book attention will be paid to foundational issues as well as the pragmatical solutions the designers of object-oriented languages have chosen to realize their ideas.

- Many of the notions introduced and problems discussed are clarified by short programs, mostly in Java, some in C++. The examples cover GUI development, business process reengineering and Web applications. No extensive knowledge of the programming languages used is required since a brief tutorial on a number of object-oriented programming languages, including C++, Smalltalk, Eiffel and Java, is given in the appendix.

- The material is organized around *slides*. The slides occur in the text in reduced format, but are also available in Powerpoint and Netscape Presentation format. Each slide captures some important notion or concept which is explained and commented upon in the accompanying text. An online Instructor's Guide is available that provides hints for presenting the slides and answers to the questions posed at the end of each chapter.

- The entire book, including the software from the examples and the *Instructor's Guide* is available electronically, on the accompanying CDROM as well as on the Internet. The electronic version contains links to other material on the Internet. The electronic version may be accessed also in *slide mode* that allows for presenting the material in a classroom equipped with a beamer.

Intended readers The book will primarily address an academic audience, or IT professionals with an academic interest. Nevertheless, since I am getting more and more involved in joint research with business partners and the development of extra-academic curricula, examples are included that are of more relevance to IT in business. In particular, it contains a section on the deployment of (object-oriented) simulation for business process redesign, and a section on the 3D visualisation of business data using object technology.

This book may be used as the primary text for a course on OO or independently as study or reference material. It may be used by the following categories of readers:

- *students* – as a textbook or as supplementary reading for research or project papers.

- *software engineers* – as (another) text on object-oriented software development.

- *professional teachers* – as ready-made material for a course on object-oriented software development.

Naturally, this is not meant to exclude other readers. For instance, researchers may find the book useful for its treatment of foundational issues. Programmers may benefit from the hints and example programs in Java and C++. Another reason for using this book may be its compact representation of already familiar material and the references to other (often research) literature.

The book is meant to be self-contained. As prior knowledge, however, a general background in computer science (that is, computer languages and data structures as a minimum) is required. To fully understand the sections that deal with foundational issues or formal aspects, the reader must also have some knowledge of elementary mathematical logic.

Organization The book is divided into four parts. Each part presents the issues involved in object-oriented programming from a different perspective, which may be characterized respectively as *software engineering and design*, *languages and system development*, *abstract data types and polymorphism*, and *applications and frameworks*.

Part I: Designing Object-Oriented Systems

1. *Introduction*: This chapter gives an introduction to the area of object-oriented software development. It gives a global view on the object-oriented life cycle and discusses object orientation as a paradigm of programming. It discusses a number of trends and technologies that have come into the focus of public attention and indicates their relevance to 'object-orientation'.

2. *Idioms and patterns**: This chapter introduces *idioms* and *design patterns* as means to capture recurrent structures and solutions in object-oriented programming. It distinguishes between idioms as solutions tied to a particular language and patterns which are the product of rational design. This chapter contains numerous examples, in Java.

3. *Software engineering perspectives*: This chapter discusses the process of software development and the various modeling perspectives involved in analysis and design. It explains the issues involved in arriving at a proper object model and introduces the notion of *contract* as an instrument to capture the relationships between object classes. In addition, it proposes a method for validation and testing based on *contracts*.

4. *Application development**: In this chapter we develop a complete application and discuss the issues involved in its design and realization. It presents guidelines for (individual) class design, and gives an example of how to derive an implementation from a formal specification.

Part II: Object-Oriented Languages and Systems

5. *Object-oriented languages*: This chapter provides a comparison between object-oriented languages, including Smalltalk, Eiffel, C++ and Java. It further discusses a number of alternative languages, included Self and Javascript, each with their own object model, and treats issues such as dynamic inheritance by delegation. synchronous active objects, and meta-level architectures for class-based languages.

6. *Component technology**: This chapter discusses the relation between component technology and distributed object technology, and will give a brief overview of the solutions that are available on the market, including Microsoft COM/ActiveX, JavaBeans, Java RMI and CORBA. It also presents a simple workgroup application and an example of integrating CORBA with an existing software library.

7. *Software architecture**: In this chapter we explore how software architecture affects design and implementation. It treats design patterns for distributed object systems, and looks at the technical issues involved in developing multi-lingual systems. As an example we show how to employ the native interface to embed an existing framework in Java.

Part III: Foundations of Object-Oriented Modeling

8. *Abstract data types*: This chapter considers the notion of abstract data types from the perspective of *types as constraints*. It presents an algebraic approach in which objects may be characterized as algebras. Further, it explains the difference between the classical approach of realizing abstract data types in procedural languages and the realization of abstract data types in object-oriented languages. The implications of a more pragmatic conception of types is also discussed.

9. *Polymorphism*: This chapter discusses inheritance from a declarative perspective, and gives a precise characterization of the subtype relation. It further discusses the various flavors of polymorphism and presents a type theoretical treatment of genericity and overloading. Also, type calculi that capture data hiding and self-reference are given. These insights are related to the realization of polymorphism in Eiffel, C++ and Java.

10. *Behavioral refinement*: This chapter extends the notion of types as constraints to include behavioral properties. It presents an assertion logic for the verification of programs and discusses the operational model underlying the verification of object behavior based on traces. It further gives precise guidelines to determine whether classes that are syntactical subtypes satisfy the behavioral refinement relation. Finally, an overview is given of formal approaches to characterize the behavior of collections of objects.

Part IV: Object-Oriented Application Frameworks

11. *Business process redesign**: In this chapter we look at the opportunities IT offers in (re)designing business processes. In particular, we look at (object-oriented) simulation as a means to capture the logistical aspects involved in business process modeling, and in addition we look at how simulation models can be made available as to allow decision making, by deploying visualisation and dissemination over the Web.

12. *Web applications**: In this chapter we look at how object technology may be applied to the Web. We will look both at client-side extensions and server-side solutions. In particular, we look at systems that employ CORBA in addition to other Web technologies. We also briefly look at another new trend in computing, intelligent, mobile agents, and we argue that agents are a direct derivation from object technology.

Appendices The appendices contain brief tutorials on Smalltalk, Eiffel, C++, Java and the distributed logic programming language DLP. They also contain an overview of UML, an overview of CORBA IDL, a tutorial on programming CORBA applications with Orbacus, and suggestions for small and medium-term projects.

Tracks For those developing a course on object-oriented programming, the book offers a choice between various tracks, for which the ingredients are sketched below. Also, an indication is given of the sections that contain more advanced material.

	regular	extended	advanced
programming	2, 4, 5, 12	6, 11	7, 8
software engineering	1, 3, 4, 11	8.1-2, 10.1	9.1-3, 10.2
theoretical	1, 3, 8	5, 9.1-4	9.5-6, 10

The *programming track*, consisting of chapters 2, 4, 5 and 12, may be augmented with material from the appendices and chapters 6 and 11. The *software engineering track*, consisting of chapters 1, 3, 4 and 11, may be augmented with material from the theoretical track as indicated. The *theoretical track*, consisting of chapters 8, 9 and 10, may need to be augmented with more general information concerning OOP provided in the other tracks.

Differences with respect to the first edition For clarity I have marked the chapters that have been substantially changed with an asterisks.

Adding new topics is one thing, eliminating parts of the book, naturally, is quite another thing. Yet I have chosen to remove the chapters on C++ (previously chapter 2), software engineering issues (chapter 4), concurrency in C++ (chapter 6), composition mechanisms (chapter 7), software libraries (chapter 11) and hypermedia (chapter 12). Some of this material, for example parts of the hypermedia chapter (12), composition mechanisms (7), and software engineering issues (4), will reappear elsewhere. Nevertheless, since some of it is obsolete, and other material does not function well in classroom, it is better to remove it, and allow its space to be taken by other topics.

Background and motivations My own interest in object-oriented languages and software development stems from my research on the language DLP, a language integrating logic programming with object-oriented features and parallelism (Eliëns, 1992). When looking for material for a course on object-oriented programming, I could not find a book that paid sufficient attention to foundational and formal aspects. Most of the books were written from a perspective on OOP that did not quite suit my purposes. What I was looking for could to some extent only be found in research papers. As a consequence, I organized my OOP course around a small number of papers, selecting the papers that, to my mind, can be considered as *landmark papers*, papers that have become known as originally presenting some significant notion or insight. The apparent disadvantage of basing a course on OOP on papers is the obvious lack of a unified view, and of a consistent use of terminology. The advantage of such an approach, however, is that students are encouraged to assess the contribution of each paper and to form their own view by comparing critically the different viewpoints expressed in the papers. Personally, I favor the use of original papers, since these somehow show more clearly how the ideas put forward originated. Later, more polished, renderings of these same ideas often lack this quality of 'discovery'.

The idea of organizing a book around slides came quite naturally, as the result of structuring the growing collection of slides, and the wish to maintain the compact representation offered by the slides.

The choice of material reflects my personal preference for foundational issues, in other words, papers that are focused on concepts rather than (mal)practice. The choice of material has also been colored by my interest in (distributed) hypermedia systems, the Web and, to some extent, by my previous work on distributed logic programming. Although the book is certainly not focused on language constructs, modeling issues as well as foundational issues are generally related to existing or conceivable language constructs, and (whenever possible) illustrated by working examples developed for that purpose.

The choice for Java as the main vehicle for presenting the program fragments and examples is motivated simply by the popularity of Java. The presentation of some of the other examples in C++ reflects my belief that C++ must still be considered as a valid programming language for object-oriented software development. However, I also believe that in the (near) future multi-paradigm approaches (extending Java and C++) will play a significant role.

The approach taken in this book may be characterized as *abstract*, in the sense that attention is paid primarily to concepts rather than particular details of a solution or implementation language. By chance, in response to a discussion in my class, I looked up the meaning of *abstract* in a dictionary, where to my surprise I learned that one of its meanings is *to steal, to take away dishonestly*. Jokingly, I remarked that this meaning sheds a different light on the notion of *abstract data types*, but at a deeper level I recognized the extent to which the ideas presented in this book have profited from the ideas originally developed by others. My rendering of these ideas in a more abstract form is, however, not meant to appropriate them in a dishonest way, but rather to give these ideas the credit they deserve by fitting them in a context, a framework encompassing both theoretical and pragmatical aspects of object-oriented computing. As one of the meanings of the adjective *abstract*, the dictionary also lists the word *abstruse* (not easy to understand). There is no need to say that, within the limits of my capabilities, I have tried to avoid becoming abstruse.

Finally, in presenting the material, I have tried to retain a sufficient degree of objectivity. Nevertheless, whenever personal judgments have slipped in, they are meant rather to provoke a discussion than provide a final answer.

Information The electronic version can be found at

http://*www.cs.vu.nl/~eliens/online/oo*

For any questions or comments you may contact the author at eliens@cs.vu.nl by electronic mail, or at Dr A. Eliëns, Vrije Universiteit, Faculty of Sciences, Division of Mathematics and Computer Science, De Boelelaan 1081, 1081 HV Amsterdam, The Netherlands.

Contents of the CDROM The CDROM contains a complete online version of the book, including additional lectures, software and links to resources on the Internet. This online version may be used for presentation in the classroom, using the Netscape Presentation Format, which is supported by Netscape Navigator 4.x or better and by Internet Explorer 4.x or better. For each chapter, the CDROM also provides a Powerpoint presentation, that may be adapted by the lecturer. For additional information, see README file on the CDROM.

Acknowledgements In writing this book [1] , I have profited from the enthusiasm and criticism of numerous students and colleagues. In the latter years it has been Jacco van Ossenbruggen, Bastiaan Schönhage and Martijn van Welie, my PhD students, who have been unrelenting in their advice, criticism and quest for conceptual clarity.

Some of the material in this book has been taken from jointly written papers. The material on the handle/body idiom in chapter 2 is due to Jacco van Ossenbruggen. The workgroup application in chapter 6 has been written by John Caspers. The section on architectural styles in chapter 7 is due to Bastiaan Schönhage. And the material in chapters 11 and 12 has been developed in close cooperation with Jacco van Ossenbruggen, Bastiaan Schönhage, Martijn van Welie, Frank Niessink, Dirk Bolier, Sam Megens and Paul Nash. I also thank my colleague Hans de Bruin for providing me with the material on software architectures; Thiel Chang, principal manager of ASZ Research and Development, and the ASZ/SanFrancisco team, consisting of Arne Bultman, Joris Kuipers, Ard van der Scheer, Remco van de Woestijne and Irmen de Jong, for their enthusiastic collaboration in an interesting project; and last but not least my students, who gave a fresh look on object orientation in their term papers.

For the first edition I owe thanks moreover to, in arbitrary order, Hans van Vliet, Henri Bal, Dick Grune, Cees Visser, Ira Pohl, John Caspers, and Matthijs van Doorn. Also, I thank Chris Dollin for his detailed and constructive comments on the first edition. And finally, my editors, Sally Mortimore, who got me the contract for the second edition, Keith Mansfield, who took over where Sally left off, Alison Birtwell and Karen Sutherland, for their assistance, Hedwig van Lier (from Pearson Education), for providing me with nice books, Julie Knight, who guided me through the production phase, Karen Mosman with whom I discussed the possibilities of an online version on a number of successive Web conferences, not forgetting Simon Plumtree and Andrew McGettrick for, as they will surely understand, 'playing it by ear'.

The short musical phrases appearing at the beginning of each chapter are taken from *The Notebook for Anna Magdalena Bach*. Although other composers contributed to the 'notebook', these phrases occur in a selection of pieces, composed by Johann Sebastian Bach, which are intended primarily for young players. Despite their apparent simplicity, however, they are acknowledged by experienced pianists as being hard to play properly, yet they are among the standard exercises for learner pianists. In a way this reflects the problem of teaching object-oriented programming. The concepts underlying object-oriented programming may at first seem deceptively simple (and not require the complexity of C++ or a type-theoretical analysis). However, in developing object-oriented models and applications some intrinsically difficult questions remain, for which we have no

---

[1]The picture on the cover is from Louis Soutter, Souplesse, 1939, Peinture au doigt, 44 x 58 cm, Musée cantonal des Beaux-Arts, Lausanne. Photo J.-C. Ducret, Musée cantonal des Beaux-Arts, Lausanne.

definite answer and which may even require extensive expertise and technology to come up with a partial solution. Returning to the music, I often find myself improvising, leaving the written music for what it is, a starting point.

Anton Eliëns
Januari 2000

Contents

Part I

Designing Object-Oriented Systems

1

Introduction

To gain an understanding of some new area, it is virtually unavoidable to be immersed in the material for a while without exactly understanding where it will lead.

Principles of Object-Oriented Software Development   ☐ 1   *1-1*

- themes and variations – *object speak*
- abstraction – *paradigms of programming*
- software development – *the OO life-cycle*
- object technology – *trends*

Additional keywords and phrases: *object, data abstraction, analysis, design, implementation, distribution*

Slide 1-1: Introduction

This first chapter will give a preliminary characterization of object-oriented software development, sketch some of its history and give an outline of the main themes of this book. The dominant theme may be summarized by the phrase that object-orientation provides the software developer with the *right* abstractions for the analysis, design, implementation, and perhaps even the testing of complex software systems. The underlying theme of the book, however, is to indicate the technological requirements that must be satisfied to employ these abstractions effectively in actual software development. Yet another theme of the book is based on the observation that what OO offers is not altogether new. So, we will relate the solutions offered by OO to their precedents in the history of computer programming and software design. The reader may then establish whether OO is just another toy for software developers or a significant contribution to both software engineering and programming.

1.1   Themes and variations

Nowadays, many have at least some notion of object orientation. Undergraduate courses teaching programming in Java are becoming standard practice. And, in industry and business, object-oriented technology is being adopted on an increasingly large scale. Nevertheless, to some extent, object orientation is still an emerging technology with many open questions. So, we will start with a brief survey of what object orientation is about, what solutions it offers and what is needed to put these solutions effectively into practice. We will also briefly review some *object terminology*, reflect on the notion of *object computation*, and discuss *design by contract*.

Themes and variations   *1-2*

- abstraction – *the object metaphor*
- modeling – *understanding structure and behavior*
- software architecture – *mastering complexity*
- frameworks – *patterns for problem solving*
- components – *scalable software*

Slide 1-2: Themes and variations

Object metaphor In an object-oriented approach, objects are our primary abstraction device. Objects provide a metaphor that helps us in each phase of the software life-cycle. During analysis, we may partition the domain into objects, that have properties, possibly responsibilities, and relations among each other.

In design, objects are our primary unit of decomposition. In our design, objects may reflect real life entities, such as *Employer* and *Employee*, but may also represent system artefacts, such as *stacks* or *graphics*.

In actual development, that is in the implementation, objects are our unit of implementation. Each object itself may be regarded as a collection of functions. But it is the collection of functions, and the behavior that they describe, that we take as our unit; not the individual function.

Modeling Taking objects as the unit of analysis, design and implementation, allows us to define the structure and behavior of a software system in a natural way. Nevertheless, although this may at first sight seem to simplify our task, it does actually become more difficult to develop software. Why? Simply, because it takes more effort to find the right kinds of objects! It is difficult to arrive at stable abstractions, to define the corresponding objects, to define the objects' interfaces and to define the appropriate relations between the objects, and to implement them so that everything works.

A consequence of adopting an object-oriented approach is that we have to spend more time in describing and understanding the structure and behavior of the system, and to learn the formalisms and tools that enable us to do so.

Software architecture Objects not only provide a metaphor. Objects also define a computational platform. Computation in an object-oriented system consists of objects sending messages to one another. This may give rise to very complicated sequences of instructions, in particular when the system is dependent on events from the outside, for example the window or network environment.

To master this complexity, we need to think about how objects can be made to fit together. To benefit from an object-oriented approach, we need to design a software architecture that defines and regulates the interactions between objects.

Frameworks When does an object-oriented approach pay off? It does pay off when we have arrived at (more or less) stable abstractions for which we have good implementations, that may be reused for a variety of other applications.

A framework is a kind of library of reusable objects. However, in contrast with ordinary software libraries, frameworks may at times take over control. The best-known examples of frameworks are in the GUI domain; frameworks in other domains (e.g. the business process domain) are emerging.

Using a framework may simplify your life, since a framework provides generic solutions for a particular application domain. But the price you pay is twofold. You have to understand what (patterns of) solutions the framework provides, and you have to comply with the rules of the game imposed by the framework.

Components Frameworks consist of components. Simplistically, components correspond to objects in a one-to-one way. However, life is more complicated. Components usually consist of a collection of objects that provide additional functionality that allows components to interact together. A typical example of components are distributed objects, objects that may be accessed over a network. These objects must have, preferably in a non-visible way, all the functionality needed to make a network connection and send data (arguments and results) over a network.

1.1.1   Object terminology

Object-orientation originally grew out of research in programming languages. The first object-oriented language was Simula. However, Smalltalk may be held responsible for the initial popularity of the object-oriented approach. The terminology Smalltalk introduced was at the time unfamiliar and, for many, somewhat hard to grasp. Nowadays, students and IT specialists, have at least heard the object-oriented jargon. Let's briefly look at it. See slide 1-3.

Objects provide the means by which to structure a system. In Smalltalk (and most other object-oriented languages) objects are considered to be grouped in classes. A *class* specifies the behavior of the objects that are its instances. Also, classes act as templates from which actual objects may be created. Inheritance is defined for classes only. From the perspective of design, inheritance is primarily meant to promote the reuse of specifications.

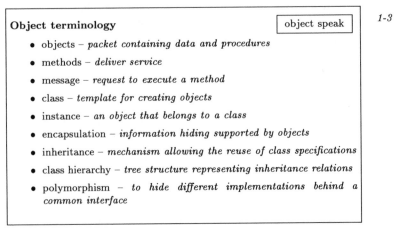

Slide 1-3: Object terminology

The use of inheritance results in a class hierarchy that, from an operational point of view, determines the dispatching behavior of objects, that is what method will be selected in response to a message. If certain restrictions are met (see sections 3.3, 9.2 and 10.4), the class hierarchy corresponds to a type hierarchy, specifying the subtype relation between classes of objects.

Finally, an important feature of object-oriented languages is their support for polymorphism. Polymorphism is often incorrectly identified with inheritance. Polymorphism by inheritance makes it possible to hide different implementations behind a common interface. However, other forms of polymorphism may arise by overloading functions and the use of generic (template) classes or functions. See sections 2.1.2 and 9.3.

Features and benefits of OOP Having become acquainted with the terminology of OOP, we will briefly review what are generally considered features and benefits from a pragmatic point of view. This summary is based on Pokkunuri (1989). I do expect, however, that the reader will take the necessary caution with respect to these claims. See slide 1-4.

Both *information hiding* and *data abstraction* relieve the task of the programmer using existing code, since these mechanisms mean that the programmer's attention is no longer distracted by irrelevant implementation details. On the other hand, the developer of the code (i.e. objects) may profit from information hiding as well, since it gives the programmer the freedom to optimize the implementation without interfering with the client code. Sealing off the object's implementation by means of a well-defined message interface moreover offers the opportunity to endow an object with (possibly concurrent) autonomous behavior.

Features of OOP   *1-4*

information hiding: state, autonomous behavior

data abstraction: emphasis on *what* rather than *how*

dynamic binding: binding at runtime, polymorphism

inheritance: incremental changes (specialization), reusability

---

Slide 1-4: Features of OOP

The flexible dispatching behavior of objects that lends objects their polymorphic behavior is due to the dynamic binding of methods to messages. Polymorphic object behavior is effected by using methods, or in C++ jargon *virtual functions*, for which, in contrast to ordinary functions, the binding to an actual function takes place at runtime and not at compile-time. In this way, inheritance provides a flexible mechanism by which to reuse code since a derived class may specialize or override parts of the inherited specification.

Encapsulation and inheritance Object-oriented languages offer *encapsulation* and *inheritance* as the major abstraction mechanisms to be used in program development. See slide 1-5.

Encapsulation promotes *modularity*, meaning that objects must be regarded as the building blocks of a complex system. Once a proper modularization has been achieved, the implementor of the object may postpone any final decisions concerning the implementation at will. This feature allows for quick prototyping, with the risk that the 'quick and dirty' implementations will never be cleaned up. However, experience with constructing object-oriented libraries and frameworks has shown that the modularization achieved with objects may not be very stable.

Another advantage of an object oriented approach, often considered to be the main advantage, is the reuse of code. Inheritance is an invaluable mechanism in this respect, since the code that is reused seldom offers all that is needed. The inheritance mechanism enables the programmer to modify the behavior of a class of objects without requiring access to the source code.

Although an object-oriented approach to program development indeed offers great flexibility, some of the problems it addresses are intrinsically difficult and cannot really be solved by mechanisms alone. For instance, modularization is recognized to be a notoriously difficult problem in the software engineering literature. Hence, since some of the promises of OOP depend upon the stability of the chosen modularization, the real advantage of OOP may be rather short-lived. Moreover,

---

Benefits of OOP   *1-5*

- OO = encapsulation + inheritance
- *modularity* – autonomous entities, cooperation through exchanges of messages
- *deferred commitment* – the internal workings of an object can be redefined without changing other parts of the system
- *reusability* – refining classes through inheritance
- *naturalness* – object-oriented analysis / design, modeling

---

Slide 1-5: Benefits of OOP

despite the optimistic claims about 'tuning' reused code by means of inheritance, experience shows that often more understanding of the inherited classes is needed than is available in their specification.

The probability of arriving at a stable modularization may increase when shifting focus from programming to design. The mechanisms supported by OOP allow for modeling application oriented concepts in a direct, natural way. But this benefit of OOP will only be gained at the price of increasing the design effort.

1.1.2 Object computation

Programming is, put briefly, to provide a computing device with the instructions it needs to do a particular computation. In the words of Dijkstra: *'Programming is the combination of human reasoning and symbol manipulation skills used to develop symbol manipulators (programs). By supplying a computer to such a symbol manipulator it becomes a* concrete *one.'* Although we are by now used to quite fashionable computing devices, including graphic interfaces and multimedia peripherals, the abstract meaning of a computing device has not essentially altered since the original conception of the mathematical model that we know as the Turing machine (see below).

Despite the fact that our basic mathematical model of a computing device (and hence our notion of computability) has not altered significantly, the development of high level programming languages has meant a drastic change in our conception of programming. Within the tradition of imperative programming, the introduction of objects, and object-oriented programming, may be thought of as the most radical change of all. Indeed, at the time of the introduction of Smalltalk, one spoke of a true revolution in the practice of programming.

The object model introduced by Smalltalk somehow breaks radically with our traditional notion of computation. Instead of regarding a computation as the execution of a sequence of instructions (changing the state of the machine), object-based computation must be viewed as sending messages between objects. Such a notion of computation had already been introduced in the late 1960s in the programming language Simula (see Dahl and Nygaard, 1966). Objects were

---

The object model   *1-6*

- computation is sending messages between objects

Message

- *object method arguments*

Encapsulation

- objects encapsulate data and procedures

Protocol

- the collection of messages an object supports

Slide 1-6: The object model

introduced in Simula to simulate complex real-world events, and to model the interactions between real-world entities.

In the (ordinary) sequential machine model, the result of a computation is (represented by) the state of the machine at the end of the computation. In contrast, computation in the object model is best characterized as cooperation between objects. The end result then consists, so to speak, of the collective state of the objects that participated in the computation. See slide 1-6.

Operationally, an object may be regarded as an abstract machine capable of answering messages. The collection of messages that may be handled by an object is often referred to as the *protocol* obeyed by the object. This notion was introduced in the Smalltalk programming environment originally to provide the means to group the messages to which an object may respond. For instance, the distinction between methods for initialization and methods for modification or processing may be convenient in developing or using a program. The notion of *protocol* may also be given a more formal interpretation, as has been done for instance in the notion of *contracts* (introduced in Eiffel) stating the requirements that must be adhered to in communicating with an object.

Structurally, an object may be regarded as a collection of data and procedures. In principle, the data are invisible from the outside and may be manipulated only by invoking the right procedure. In a pure object-oriented language such as Smalltalk and Eiffel, sending a message to an object is the only way of invoking such a procedure. Combined, *data-hiding* and *message interface abstraction* will be referred to as *encapsulation*. Actually, object-oriented languages, while in some way supporting objects as collections of data and procedures, may differ subtly in the degree and way in which they support data-hiding and abstraction.

Computability and complexity Mathematically, a computing device consists of a finite table of instructions and a possible infinite memory in which to store intermediate results. In order to perform a computation the device also needs an input and some means by which to display the results.

For now, we need not be concerned with the precise mathematical details of our model of a computing device. For a very much more precise and elaborate description of the Turing machine, the interested reader is referred to Hopcroft and Ullman (1979). What is important, however, is that this model captures in a very precise sense the notion of computation, in that it allows us to characterize what can be computed, and also what a computation will cost, in terms of computing time and memory usage.

An interesting, but perhaps somewhat distressing, feature of the Turing machine model is that it is the strongest model we have, which means that any other model of computation is at best equivalent to it. Parallel computation models in effect do extend the power of (sequential) Turing machines, but only in a linear relation with the number of processors. In other words, the Turing machine defines what we may regard as *computable* and establishes a measure of the complexity of a computation, in space and time. The awareness of the intrinsic limitations imposed by a precise mathematical notion of computability has, for example, led us to regarding the claims of artificial intelligence with some caution, see Rabin (1974). However, the theoretical insight that a problem may in the worst case not be solved in finite time or space should not hinder us in looking for an optimal, approximate solution that is reachable with bounded resources.

An equally important feature of the Turing machine model is that it gives us an illustration of what it means to program a computing device, that is to instruct the machine to perform actions dependent on its input and state. As an extension to the model, we can easily build a *universal* computing device, into which we may feed the description of some particular machine, in order to mimic the computation of that machine. Apparently, this gives us a more powerful machine. However, this has proven not to be the case. Neither does this universal device enlarge the class of computable problems, nor does it affect in any significant sense the computational complexity of what we know to be computable. See slide 1-7.

1-7

Computing devices

- mathematical model – *Turing machine*

- universal machine – machines as programs

- computability & complexity – time/space bounded

Object-oriented programming does not enlarge the class of computable problems, nor does it reduce the computational complexity of the problems we can handle.

Slide 1-7: Computing devices

Interestingly, there is an extension of the (basic and universal) Turing machine model that allows us to extend the narrow boundaries imposed by a mathematical characterization of computability. This extension is known as an *oracle* machine, and as the name suggests, the solution to an (otherwise) intractable problem must come from some external source, be it human, machine-like or divine (which is unlikely). Partly, this explains why *intelligent* systems (such as automatic translation systems) are, to a certain extent, intrinsically interactive, since only the human user can provide the (oracle) information needed to arrive at a solution.

Our model of a computing device does quite precisely delimit the domain of computable problems, and gives us an indication of what we can expect the machine to do for us, and what not. Also, it illustrates what means we have available to program such a device, in order to let it act in the way we want. Historically, the Turing machine model may be regarded as a mathematical description of what is called the Von Neumann machine architecture, on which most of our present-day computers are based. The Von Neumann machine consists of a memory and a processor that fetches data from the memory, does some computation and stores the data back in memory. This architecture has been heavily criticized, but no other model has yet taken its place. This criticism has been motivated strongly by its influence on the practice of programming. Traditionally, programs for the Von Neumann architecture are conceived as sequences of instructions that may modify the state of the machine. In opposition to this limited, machine-oriented view of programming a number of proposals have been made that are intended to arrive at a more abstract notion of programming, where the machine is truly at the service of the programmer and not the other way around.

One of these proposals to arrive at a more abstract notion of programming is advocated as the *object-oriented approach*. Before studying the intrinsics of the object-oriented approach, however, it may be useful to reflect on what we may expect from it. Do we hope to be able to solve more problems, or to solve known problems better? In other words, what precisely is the contribution of an object-oriented approach?

Based on the characterization of a computing device, some answers are quite straightforward. We cannot expect to be able to solve more problems, nor can we expect to reduce the computational complexity of the problems that we can solve. What an object-oriented approach can contribute, however, is simply in providing better means with which to program the machine. Better means, to reduce the chance of (human) errors, better means, also, to manage the complexity of the task of programming (but not to reduce the computational complexity of the problem itself). In other words, by providing abstractions that are less machine oriented and more human oriented, we may enlarge the class of problems that we can tackle in the reality of software engineering. However, we simply cannot expect that an object-oriented approach may in any sense enlarge our notion of what is computable.

Some history In the last few decades, we have been able to witness a rapid change in the technology underlying our computer systems. Simultaneously, our ideas of how to program these machines have changed radically as well.

The history of programming languages may be regarded as a progression from low level constructs towards high level abstractions, that enable the programmer to specify programs in a more abstract manner and hence allow problem-related abstractions to be captured more directly in a program. This development towards high level languages was partly motivated by the need to be able to verify that a program adequately implemented a specification (given in terms of a formal description of the requirements of an application). Regarded from this perspective, it is then perhaps more appropriate to speak of a progression of *paradigms of programming*, where a paradigm must be understood as a set of mechanisms and guidelines telling us how to employ these mechanisms.

The first abstraction mechanism beyond the level of assembler language and macros is provided by *procedures*. Procedures play an important role in the method of *stepwise refinement* introduced by the school of *structured programming*. Stepwise refinement allows the specification of a complex algorithm gradually in more and more detail. Program verification amounts to establishing whether the implementation of an algorithm in a programming language meets its specification given in mathematical or logical terms. Associated with the school of structured programming is a method of verification based on what has become known as *Hoare logic*, which proceeds by introducing *assertions* and establishing that procedures meet particular pre- and post-conditions.

Other developments in programming language research are aimed at providing ways in which to capture the mathematical or logical meaning of a program more directly. These developments have resulted in a number of functional programming languages (e.g. ML, Miranda) and logic programming languages, of which Prolog is the best-known. The programming language Lisp may in this respect also be regarded as a functional language.

The history of object-oriented programming may be traced back to a concern for *data abstraction*, which was needed to deal with algorithms that involved complex data structures. The notion of *objects*, originally introduced in Simula (Dahl and Nygaard, 1966), has significantly influenced the design of many subsequent languages (e.g. CLU, Modula and Ada). The first well-known *object-oriented language* was Smalltalk, originally developed to program the *Dynabook*, a kind of machine that is now familiar to us as a laptop or notebook computer. In Smalltalk, the data-hiding aspect of objects has been combined with the mechanism of inheritance, allowing the reuse of code defining the behavior of objects. The primary motivation behind Smalltalk's notion of *objects*, as a mechanism to manage the complexity of graphic user interfaces, has now proven its worth, since it has been followed by most of the manufacturers of graphic user interfaces and window systems.

Summarizing, from a historical perspective, the introduction of the object-oriented approach may be regarded as a natural extension to previous developments in programming practice, motivated by the need to cope with the complexity of new applications. History doesn't stop here. Later developments, represented by Eiffel, C++ (to a certain extent) and Java, more clearly reflect the concern with abstraction and verification, which intrinsically belongs to the notion of *abstract data types* as supported by these languages.

1.1.3   Design by Contract

After this first glance at the terminology and mechanisms employed in object-oriented computation, we will look at what I consider to be the contribution of an object-oriented approach (and the theme of this book) in a more thematic way. The term 'contract' in the title of this section is meant to refer to an approach to design that has become known as *design by contract*, originally introduced in Meyer (1988), which is closely related to *responsibility-driven design* (see Wirfs-Brock, 1989). Of course, the reader is encouraged to reflect on alternative interpretations of the phrase *responsibilities in OOP*.

The approach captured by the term *contract* stresses the importance of an abstract characterization of what services an object delivers, in other words what responsibilities an object carries with respect to the system as a whole. Contracts specify in a precise manner the relation between an object and its 'clients'.

Objects allow one to modularize a system in distinct units, and to hide the implementation details of these units, by packaging data and procedures in a record-like structure and defining a message interface to which users of these units must comply. *Encapsulation* refers to the combination of packaging and hiding. The formal counterpart of encapsulation is to be found in the theory of *abstract data types*. An abstract data type (ADT) specifies the behavior of an entity in an abstract way by means of what are called *operations* and *observations*, which operationally amount to procedures and functions to change or observe the state of the entity. See also section 8.3.

Abstract data types, that is elements thereof, are generally realized by employing a hidden *state*. The state itself is invisible, but may be accessed and modified by means of the observations and operations specified by the type. See slide 1-8.

Encapsulation   *1-8*

  • Abstract data types

$$ADT = state + behavior$$

Object-oriented modeling

  • data oriented

Slide 1-8: Abstract data types – encapsulation

Complex applications involve usually complex data. As observed by Wirfs-Brock (1989), software developers have reacted to this situation by adopting more data oriented solutions. Methods such as semantic information modeling and object-oriented modeling were developed to accommodate this need. See also sections 3.1 and 4.3.1.

Objects may be regarded as embodying an (element of an) abstract data type. To use an object, the client only needs to know *what* an object does, not (generally speaking) *how* the behavior of the object is implemented. However, for a client to profit from the data hiding facilities offered by objects, the developer of the object must provide an interface that captures the behavior of the object in a sufficiently abstract way. The (implicit) design guideline in this respect must be to regard an object as a *server* that provides high level services on request and to determine what services the application requires of that particular (class of) object(s). See slide 1-9.

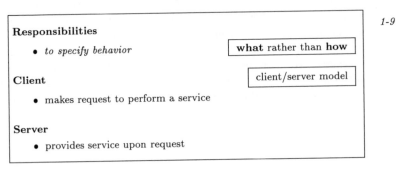

Slide 1-9: Responsibilities in OOP

Naturally, the responsibilities of an object cannot be determined by viewing the object in isolation. In actual systems, the functionality required is often dependent on complex interactions between a collection of objects that must cooperate in order to achieve the desired effect. However, before trying to specify these interactions, we must indicate more precisely how the communication between a server and a single client proceeds.

From a language implementation perspective, an object is nothing but an advanced data structure, even when we fit it in a client-server model. For design, however, we must shift our perspective to viewing the object as a collection of high level, application-oriented services. Specifying the behavior of an object from this perspective, then, means to define what specific information the object is responsible for and how it maintains the integrity of that information. See slide 1-10.

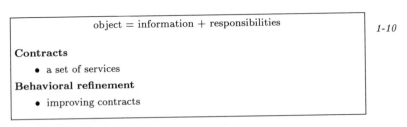

Slide 1-10: Contracts and behavioral refinement

The notion of *contracts* was introduced by Meyer (1988) to characterize in a precise manner what services an object must provide and what requirements clients of an object must meet in order to request a service (and expect to get a good result). A contract specifies both the requirements imposed on a client and the obligations the server has, provided the requirements are met. When viewed from the position of a client, a contract reveals what the client can count on when the requirements are fulfilled. From the position of the server, on the other hand, when a client does not fulfill the requirements imposed, the server has no obligation whatsoever.

Formally, the requirements imposed on the client and the obligations of the server can be specified by means of pre- and post-conditions surrounding a method. Nevertheless, despite the possibility of formally verifying these conditions, the designer must specify the right contract for this approach to work at all. A problem of a more technical nature the designer of object-oriented systems faces is how to deal with inheritance.

Inheritance, as a mechanism of code reuse, supports the refinement of the specification of a server. From the perspective of abstract data types, we must require that the derived specification refines the behavior of the original server. We must answer the following two questions here. What restrictions apply, when we try to refine the behavior of a server object? And, ultimately, what does it mean to improve a contract?

Behavioral refinement Inheritance provides a very general and powerful mechanism for reusing code. In fact, the inheritance mechanism is more powerful than is desirable from a type-theoretical perspective.

Conformance – *behavioral refinement*   *1-11*

     if B refines A then   B may be used   wherever A is allowed

---

Slide 1-11: Behavioral refinement

An abstract data type specifies the behavior of a collection of entities. When we use inheritance to augment the definition of a given type, we either specify new behavior in addition to what was given, or we modify the inherited behavior, or both. The restriction that must be met when modifying behavior is that the objects defined in this way are allowed to be used at all places where objects of the given type were allowed. This restriction is expressed in the so-called *conformance rule* that states that *if* B *refines* A *then* B *may be used wherever* A *is allowed.* Naturally, when behavior is added, this condition is automatically fulfilled. See slide 1-11.

The conformance rule gives a very useful heuristic for applying inheritance safely. This form of inheritance is often called 'strict' inheritance. However, it is not all that easy to verify that a class derived by inheritance actually refines the behavior specified in a given class. Partly, we can check for syntactic criteria such as the signature (that is, type) of the individual methods, but this is definitely not sufficient. We need a way in which to establish that the behavior (in relation to a possible) client is refined according to the standard introduced above. In other words we need to know how to improve a *contract*.

Recall that from an operational point of view an object may be regarded as containing data attributes storing information and procedures or methods representing services. The question *'how to improve a contract?'* then boils down to two separate questions, namely: (1) *'how to improve the information?'* and (2) *'how to improve a service?'*. To provide better *information* is, technically speaking, simply to provide more information, that is more specific information. Type-theoretically, this corresponds to narrowing down the possible elements of the set that represents the (sub) type. To provide a better *service* requires either relieving the restrictions imposed on the client or improving the result, that is tightening the obligations of the server. Naturally, the *or* must be taken as non-exclusive. See slide 1-12.

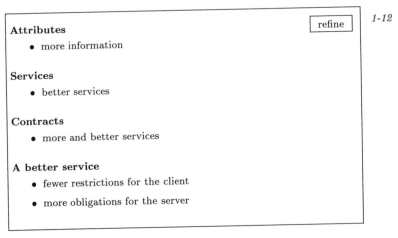

Slide 1-12: Improving services

To improve a *contract* thus simply means adding more services or improving the services that are already present. As a remark, Meyer (1988) inadvertently uses the term *subcontract* for this kind of refinement. However, in my understanding, subcontracting is more a process of delegating parts of a contract to other contractors whereas refinement, in the sense of improving contracts, deals with the contract as a whole, and as such has a more competitive edge.

Summarizing, at a very high level we may think of objects as embodying a *contract*. The contract is specified in the definition of the class of which that object is an instance. Moreover, we may think of inheritance as a mechanism to effect *behavioral refinement*, which ultimately means to improve the contract defining the relation between the object as a server and a potential client.

To warrant the phrase *contract*, however, the designer of an object must specify the functionality of an object in a sufficiently abstract, application-oriented way. The (implicit) guideline in this respect is to construct a *model* of the application domain. See slide 1-13.

Object-oriented modeling   *1-13*

- prototyping, specification, refinement, interactions

OOP = Contracts + Refinements

Slide 1-13: Object-oriented modeling

The opportunity offered by an object-oriented approach to model concepts of the application domain in a direct way makes an object-oriented style suitable for incremental prototyping (provided that the low-level support is available).

The metaphor of contracts provides valid guidelines for the design of objects. Because of its foundation in the theory of abstract data types, contracts may be specified (and verified) in a formal way, although in practice this is not really likely to occur.

Before closing this section, I wish to mention a somewhat different interpretation of the notion of *contracts* which is proposed by Helm *et al.* (1990). There contracts are introduced to specify the behavior of collections of cooperating objects. See section 10.5.

1.2   Paradigms of programming

In a landmark paper with the title *'What is object-oriented programming?'* Bjarne Stroustrup raises the question of when a language may be considered to support a particular style of programming, Stroustrup (1988). See slide 1-14.

Object-oriented programming   *1-14*

- *high tech synonym for good*

Styles of programming

- A language *supports* a style of programming if it provides facilities that make it convenient (easy, safe and efficient) to use that style

- compile/runtime checks

- clean interpretation/ orthogonal / efficient / minimal

Slide 1-14: Styles of programming

In general, one can say that a language supports a particular style of programming if it provides facilities, both syntactic and semantic, that makes it convenient (that is easy, safe and efficient) to use that style. The crucial distinction that must be made in this context is that between allowing a certain style and providing

support for that style. Allowing means that it is possible to program in that style.
To support a given style, however, requires in addition that suitable compile and
runtime checks are provided to enforce a proper use of the relevant language
constructs. With these considerations in mind, one could question the assertion
that *Ada is object-oriented* or that *Modula supports abstract data types*. Naturally,
this attitude backfires with C++. Does C++ support abstract data types and is
it really object-oriented?

1-15

Procedural programming
 • procedures, use the optimal algorithms

Modules
 • hide the data, provide functional abstractions

Data abstraction
 • types, provide a sufficiently complete set of operations

Object-oriented – *organize your types*
 • make commonality explicit

Slide 1-15: Paradigms of programming

It is equally important to establish whether a language allows a clean interpretation of the constructs introduced, whether the constructs supporting object
orientation are *orthogonal* to (that is independent of) the other constructs of the
language, whether an *efficient* implementation of these constructs is possible, and
whether the language is kept *minimal*, that is without superfluous constructs.

Before establishing what the main ingredients of object-orientation are, let
us briefly look at some of the styles of programming that may be considered as
leading to an object-oriented style. See slide 1-15.

In his article, Stroustrup (1988) stresses the continuity between the respective styles of programming pictured in slide 1-15. Each style is captured by a
short phrase stating its principal concern, that is guidelines for developing *good*
programs.

1.2.1   Procedural programming

The procedural style of programming is most closely related to the school of
structured programming, of which for instance Dijkstra (1976) and Gries (1981)
are important proponents. The procedural style supports a method of program
development that is known as *stepwise refinement*. Stepwise refinement is an
important heuristic for developing complex algorithms. Instead of writing out a
complex algorithm in all its detail, the method allows for refining the elementary
steps of the basic algorithm by means of increasingly detailed procedures.

1-16

```
while ( programming == art )  {

        incr( pleasure );
        decr( bugs );
        incr( portability );
        incr( maintainability );
        incr( quality );
        incr( salary );

}  // live happily ever after
```

Slide 1-16: Programming as an art

As a playful example of this style of programming, consider the fragment that may be found on the cover of Knuth (1992). See slide 1-16. Ignoring the contents, clearly the structure shows an algorithm that is conceived as the repeated execution of a number of less complex steps.

1.2.2   Data abstraction

When programs became larger and data more complex, the design of correct algorithms was no longer the primary concern. Rather, it became important to provide access to data in a representation independent manner. One of the early proponents of data hiding was, see Parnas (1972a) and Parnas (1972b), who introduced a precursor to the notion of *data abstraction* as it has become popular in object-oriented languages such as Smalltalk or C++.

As a language that supports data hiding, we may think of Modula-2 that offers strong support for modules and the specification of import and export relations between modules. Also the *package construct* of Ada provides support for data hiding. See slide 1-17.

Modules as provided by Modula-2 and Ada give a syntactic means for decomposing a program into more or less independent components. It is precisely the purely syntactic nature of modules that may be considered the principal defect of this approach to data hiding. Semantically, modules provide no guideline with respect to how to decompose a program into meaningful components.

To express the meaning of a module, we need the stronger notion of *types*, in the sense of *abstract data types* which are characterized by a set of operations. The notion of types as for example supported in CLU, Liskov and Zilles (1974), enables us to determine whether our decomposition satisfies certain formal criteria. For instance, we may ask whether we have defined sufficiently many operations for a given type and whether we have correctly done so. An important advantage of using abstract data types is that we can often find a mathematical model that formally characterizes the behavior of that type. From the perspective of formal

Support for data abstraction
- Abstract Data Types – *encapsulation*

Encapsulation
- initialization
- protection
- coercions

Slide 1-17: Data abstraction

methods, data abstraction by means of abstract data types may be considered as one of the principal means for the specification and verification of complex software systems. See also sections 8.3 and 10.5.

From an implementation perspective, to support data abstraction a language must provide constructs to implement *concrete realizations* of abstract data types. Such support requires that means are provided to create and initialize elements of a concrete type in a safe way, and that vulnerable data is effectively protected.

Very important is the possibility of defining generic types, that is types which take a (type) parameter with which they are instantiated. For example, the definition of a *stack* does not differ for a stack of integers, a stack of strings or a stack of elements from an arbitrary user-defined type.

1.2.3 Object-oriented programming

There is a close similarity between the object model as presented earlier and the notion of abstract data types just described. Both objects and abstract data types define a set of applicable operations that completely determine the behavior of an object or an element of the data type. To relate an object to an abstract data type we need the notion of *class*, that serves as the description on an abstract level of the behavior of (a collection of) objects. (The objects are called the *instances* of the class.)

As noted in Stroustrup (1988), abstract data types as such, although mathematically satisfying, are rather inflexible and inconvenient for specifying complex software systems. To attain such flexibility, we need to be able to organize our types and express the commonality between them. The notion of class supports this by a mechanism called *inheritance*. When regarding classes as types, inheritance may be seen as introducing polymorphic types. A class that is derived from a particular class (the base class) may be treated by the compiler as a subtype of (the type of) that particular class. See slide 1-18.

Operationally, the power of inheritance comes from message dispatching. This mechanism is called *dynamic binding*. Message dispatching takes care of selecting the right method in response to a message or method call. In a hierarchy of (derived) classes, a method for an object may be either defined within the class

1-18

Support for OOP
- Polymorphism – *inheritance*

Inheritance
- dynamic binding
- protection
- multiple inheritance

Slide 1-18: Support for OOP

of the object itself or by one of the classes from which that class is (directly or indirectly) derived. Message dispatching is an essential mechanism for supporting polymorphism, since it allows to choose the most appropriate behavior for an object of a given type. This must occur at runtime, since the type of an object as determined at compile-time may be too general.

An important issue in determining whether a language supports object-oriented programming is whether it offers a protection mechanism to shield the vulnerable parts of a base class from the classes that derived from that class.

Another question of interest is whether a language must support multiple inheritance. Clearly, there is some disagreement on this issue. For example, Smalltalk-80 and Java do not support multiple inheritance. The Eiffel language, on the other hand, supported multiple inheritance from its first days. For C++, multiple inheritance was introduced at a later stage. At first, it was thought to be expensive and not really necessary. Closer analysis, however, revealed that the cost was not excessive. (See Ellis and Stroustrup, 1990.) The issue of multiple inheritance is still not resolved completely. Generally, it is acknowledged to be a powerful and at the same time natural extension of single inheritance. However, the inheritance mechanism itself seems to be under attack. Some doubt remains as to whether inheritance is a suitable composition mechanism when regarded from the perspective of reuse and reliability.

An elegant solution is provided by Java which offers multiple interface inheritance, by allowing multiple interfaces to be realized by an actual class.

1.3   The object-oriented software life-cycle

No approach to software development is likely to survive unless it solves some of the real problems encountered in software engineering practice. In this section we will examine how the object-oriented approach is related to the conceptions of the life-cycle of software and what factors may motivate the adoption of an object-oriented approach to software development.

Despite some variations in terminology, there is a generally agreed-on conception of the various phases in the development of a software product. Roughly, a distinction can be made between a phase of *analysis*, which aims at specifying the requirements a product must meet, a phase of *design*, which must result in a conceptual view of the architecture of the intended system, and a phase of *implementation*, covering coding, testing and, to some extent, also maintenance activities. See slide 1-19.

No such consensus exists with respect to the exact relation between these phases. More specifically, there is a considerable variation in methods and guidelines describing how to make the transition from one phase to another. Another important issue is to determine what the products are exactly, in terms of software and documentation, that must result from each phase.

The software life-cycle   *1-19*

  • Analysis – Conceptual Model, System Requirements

  • Design – System Design, Detailed Design

  • Implementation – Coding, Testing

  With an increase in the number of software products not satisfying user needs, prototyping has become quite popular!

Slide 1-19: The software life-cycle

The traditional conception of the software life-cycle is known as the *waterfall model*, which prescribes a strictly sequential transition between the successive phases, possibly in an iterative manner. Strict regulations with respect to validation of the products resulting from each phase may be imposed to avoid the risk of backtracking. Such a rigid approach, however, may cause severe problems, since it does not easily allow for modifying decisions taken earlier.

One important problem in this respect is that the needs of the users of a system may change over time, invalidating the requirements laid down in an earlier phase. To some extent this problem may be avoided by better techniques of evoking the user requirements in the analysis phase, for instance by developing a prototype. Unfortunately, the problem of accommodating changing user needs and adapting to changing circumstances (such as hardware) seems to be of a more persistent nature, which provides good reason to look at alternative software development models.

Software development models The software engineering literature abounds with descriptions of failing software projects and remedies proposed to solve the problem of software not meeting user expectations.

User expectations may be succinctly characterized by the RAMP requirements listed in slide 1-20. Reliability, adaptability, maintainability and performance are not unreasonable demands in themselves. However, opinions on how to satisfy these criteria clearly diverge.

Bersoff and Davis (1991) and Davis *et al.* (1988) explain how the choice of a particular software development model may influence the chances of successfully

---

Requirements – *user needs*   *1-20*

- **R**eliability – *incremental development, reuse, synthesis*
- **A**daptability – *evolutionary prototyping*
- **M**aintainability – *incremental development, synthesis*
- **P**erformance – *incremental development, reuse*

Slide 1-20: Requirements – RAMP

completing a software project. As already mentioned, *rapid throwaway proto-typing* may help to evoke user needs at an early stage, but does not help much in adapting to evolving user requirements. A better solution in this respect is to adopt a method of *evolutionary prototyping*. Dependent on the technology used, however, this may cause severe problems in maintaining the integrity and robustness of the system. Less flexible but more reliable is an approach of *incremental development*, which proceeds by realizing those parts of a system for which the user requirements can be clearly specified.

Another means of adapting to changing user requirements is to use a technique of *automated software synthesis*. However, such an approach works only if the user requirements can be formalized easily. This is not always very likely, unless the application domain is sufficiently restricted. A similar constraint adheres to the *reuse of software*. Only in familiar application domains is it possible to anticipate how user requirements may change and how to adapt the system appropriately. Nevertheless, the reuse of software seems a very promising technique with which to reduce the cost and time involved in software products without (in principle) sacrificing reliability and performance. See slide 1-21.

Software development models   *1-21*

- rapid throwaway prototyping – *quick and dirty*
- incremental development – *slowly evolving*
- evolutionary prototyping – *evolving requirements*
- reusable software – *reduces cost and time*
- automated software synthesis – *one level of abstraction higher*

Slide 1-21: Software development models

Two of the early advocates of object-oriented technology, Cox and Meyer, regard the reuse of software as the ultimate solution to the software crisis. However, the true solution is in my opinion not so straightforward. One problem is that tools and technologies are needed to store and retrieve reusable components. That simple solutions do not suffice is illustrated by an anecdote reported by Alan Kay telling how difficult it was to find his way in the Smalltalk class structure after a significant change, despite the browsing facilities offered by the Smalltalk system.

Another problem lies in the area of human factors. The incentives for programmer productivity have too long been directed at the number of lines of code to make software reuse attractive. This attitude is also encouraged in universities. Moreover, the reuse of other students' work is usually (not unjustifiably) punished instead of encouraged.

However, having a sufficiently large store of reusable software at our disposal will allow us to build software meeting the RAMP requirements stated above, only if we have arrived at sufficiently stable abstractions of the application domain.

In the following, we will explore how object-oriented technology is motivated by problems occurring in the respective phases of the software life-cycle and how it contributes to solving these problems.

1.3.1 Analysis

In academic environments software often seems to grow, without a clear plan or explicit intention of fulfilling some need or purpose, except perhaps as a vehicle for research. In contrast, industrial and business software projects are usually undertaken to meet some explicit goal or to satisfy some need.

One of the main problems in such situations, from the point of view of the developers of the software, is to extract the needs from the future users of the system and later to negotiate the solutions proposed by the team. The problem is primarily a problem of *communication*, of bridging the gap between two worlds, the world of domain expertise on the one hand and that of expertise in the craft of software development on the other.

In a number of publications (Coad and Yourdon, 1991a; Wirfs-Brock *et al.*, 1990; and Meyer, 1988) object-oriented analysis has been proposed as providing a solution to this problem of communication. According to Coad and Yourdon (1991a), object-oriented techniques allow us to capture the system requirements in a model that directly corresponds with a conceptual model of the problem domain. See slide 1-22.

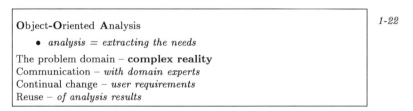

Slide 1-22: Object-oriented analysis

Another claim made by proponents of OOP is that an object-oriented approach enables a more seamless transition between the respective phases of the software life-cycle. If this claim is really met, this would mean that changing user requirements could be more easily discussed in terms of the consequences of these changes for the system, and if accepted could in principle be more easily propagated to the successive phases of development.

One of the basic ideas underlying object-oriented analysis is that the abstractions arrived at in developing a conceptual model of the problem domain will remain stable over time. Hence, rather than focusing on specific functional requirements, attention should be given to modeling the problem domain by means of high level abstractions. Due to the stability of these abstractions, the results of analysis are likely candidates for reuse.

The reality to be modeled in analysis is usually very complex. Coad and Yourdon (1991a) mention a number of principles or mechanisms with which to manage complexity. These show a great similarity to the abstraction mechanisms mentioned earlier.

Personally, I do not feel entirely comfortable with the characterization of the analysis phase given by Coad and Yourdon (1991a), since to my mind user needs and system requirements are perhaps more conveniently phrased in terms of functionality and constraints than in terms of a model that may simultaneously act as an architectural sketch of the system that is to be developed.

However, I do agree with Coad and Yourdon (1991a), and others, that the products of analysis, that is the documents describing user needs and system requirements, should as far as possible provide a conceptual model of the domain to which these needs and requirements are related.

Actually, I do consider the blurring of the distinction between analysis and design, and as we will see later, between design and implementation, as one of the attractive features of an object-oriented approach.

Analysis methods The phases of *analysis* and *design* differ primarily in orientation: during analysis the focus is on aspects of the problem domain and the goal is to arrive at a description of that domain to which the user and system requirements can be related. On the other hand, the design phase must result in an architectural model of the system, for which we can demonstrate that it fulfills the user needs and the additional requirements expressed as the result of analysis.

Analysis methods   *1-23*

- Functional Decomposition = Functions + Interfaces
- Data Flow Approach = Data Flow + Bubbles
- Information Modeling = Entities + Attributes + Relationships
- Object-Oriented = Objects + Inheritance + Message passing

Slide 1-23: Analysis methods

Coad and Yourdon (1991a) discuss a number of methods that are commonly used in analysis (see slide 1-23). The choice of a particular method will often depend upon circumstances of a more sociological nature. For instance, the experience of a team with a particular method is often a crucial factor for success. For this reason, perhaps, an eclectic method combining the various approaches may be preferable (see, for instance, Rumbaugh *et al.*, 1991). However, it is doubtful whether such an approach will have the same benefits as a purely object-oriented approach. See also section 3.1.

I will briefly characterize the various methods mentioned by Coad and Yourdon (1991a). For a more extensive description and evaluation the reader is referred to, for example, Jones (1990).

The method of *Functional Decomposition* aims at characterizing the steps that must be taken to reach a particular goal. These steps may be represented by functions that may take arguments in order to deal with data that is shared between the successive steps of the computation. In general, one can say that this method is not very good for data hiding. Another problem is that non-expert users may not be familiar with viewing their problem in terms of computation steps. Also, the method does not result in descriptions that are easily amenable to change.

The method indicated as the *Data Flow Approach* aims at depicting the information flow in a particular domain by means of arrows that represent data and bubbles that represent processes acting on these data.

Information Modeling is a method that has become popular primarily for developing information systems and applications involving databases. As a method, it aims at modeling the application domain in terms of *entities*, that may have attributes, and relations between entities.

An *object-oriented* approach to analysis is very similar in nature to the information modeling approach, at least with respect to its aim of developing a conceptual model of the application domain. However, in terms of their means, both methods differ significantly. The most important distinction between *objects*, in the sense of OOP, and *entities*, as used in information modeling, to my mind lies in the capacity of objects to embody actual behavior, whereas entities are of a more passive nature.

Concluding this brief exploration of the analysis phase, I think we may safely set as the goal for every method of analysis to aim at *stable abstractions*, that is a conceptual model which is robust with respect to evolving user requirements. Also, we may state a preference for methods which result in models that have a close correspondence to the concepts and notions used by the experts operating in the application domain.

With respect to notation UML (the Unified Modeling Language, see Appendix F) is the obvious choice. How to apply UML in the various phases of object-oriented software construction is an altogether different matter.

1.3.2   Design

In an object-oriented approach, the distinction between *analysis* and *design* is primarily one of emphasis; emphasis on modeling the reality of the problem domain versus emphasis on providing an architectural model of a system that lends itself to implementation.

One of the attractive features of such an approach is the opportunity of a seamless transition between the respective phases of the software product in development. The classical waterfall model can no longer be considered as appropriate for such an approach. An alternative model, the *fountain model*, is proposed by Henderson-Sellers (1992). This model allows for a more autonomous development of software components, within the constraints of a unifying framework. The end goal of such a development process may be viewed as a repository of reusable components. A similar viewpoint has originally been proposed by Cox (1986) and Meyer (1988).

Object-Oriented Design   *1-24*
  - design for maintenance and reuse!

Software quality
  - correctness, robustness, extensibility, compatibility

Design projects
  - IDA – Interior Design Assistant
  - MASS – Multi-user Agenda Support System

Slide 1-24: Object-oriented design

In examining the primary goals of design, Meyer (1988) distinguishes between *reusability, quality* and *ease of maintenance*. Naturally, reusable software presupposes quality, hence both quality and maintainability are important design goals. See slide 1-24. In Meyer (1988) a rough estimate is given of the shift in effort between the phases of the software life-cycle, brought about by an object-oriented approach. Essentially, these figures show an increase in the effort needed for design. This is an immediate consequence of the observation that the development of reusable code is intrinsically more difficult.

To my mind, there is yet another reason for the extra effort involved in design. In practice it appears to be difficult and time consuming to arrive at the appropriate abstract data types for a given application. The implementation of these structures, on the other hand, is usually straightforward. This is another indication that the unit of reuse should perhaps not be small pieces of code, but rather (the design of) components that fit into a larger framework.

From the perspective of software quality and maintenance, these mechanisms of *encapsulation* and *inheritance* may be characterized as powerful means to control the complexity of the code needed to realize a system. In Meyer (1988) it is estimated that maintenance accounts for 70% of the actual cost of software. Moreover, *adaptive maintenance*, which is the adaptation to changing requirements, accounts for a disproportionately large part of the cost. Of primary importance for maintenance, in the sense of the correction of errors, is the *principle of locality* supported by encapsulation, data abstraction and hiding. In contrast, inheritance is a feature that may interfere with maintenance, since it often breaks down the protection offered by encapsulation. However, to cope with changing requirements, inheritance provides both a convenient and relatively safe mechanism.

Design assignments

Actually designing systems is a complex activity, about which a lot can be said. Nevertheless, to get a good feeling for what is involved in designing a system it is best to gain some experience first. In the remainder of this subsection, you will find the descriptions of actual software engineering assignments. The assignments have been given, in subsequent years, to groups consisting of four or five CS2 students. The groups had to accomplish the assignments in five weeks, a total of 1000 man-hours. That includes formulating the requirements, writing the design specification and coding the implementation. (For the first of the assignments, IDA, C++ was used with the *hush* GUI library. For the second, MASS, Java with Swing was used.) In both cases we allowed for an iterative development cycle, inspired by a Rapid Application Development (RAD) approach. These assignments will be taken as a running example, in the sense that most examples presented in the book solve in one way or another the problems that may occur when realizing the systems described in the assignments.

IDA An *Interior Design Assistant* (IDA) is a tool to support an interior design architect. When designing the interior of a house or building, the architect proceeds from the spatial layout and a list of furniture items. IDA must allow for placing furniture in a room. It will check for constraints. For example placing a chair upon a table will be prohibited. For each design, IDA must be able to give information with respect to pricing and the time it takes to have the furniture items delivered. In addition to the design facilities, IDA must also offer a *showroom* mode, in which the various designs can be inspected and compared with respect to price and delivery time.

MASS An Agenda Support System assists the user in maintaining a record of important events, dates and appointments. It moreover offers the user various ways of inspecting his or her agenda, by giving an overview of important dates, an indication of important dates on a calendar, and (more advanced) timely notification.

A Multi-user Agenda Support System extends a simple Agenda Support System by providing facilities for scheduling a meeting, taking into account various constraints imposed by the agendas of the participants, as for example a special event for which a participant already has an entry in his or her agenda.

A minimal Multi-user Agenda Support System must provide facilities for registering important dates for an arbitrary number of users. It must, moreover, be able to give an overview of important dates for any individual user, and it must be possible to schedule a meeting between an arbitrary subset of users that satisfies the time-constraints for each individual in that particular group.

This minimal specification may be extended with input facilities, gadgets for presenting overviews and the possibility of adding additional constraints. Nevertheless, as a piece of advice, when developing a Multi-user Agenda Support System, follow the KISS principle: Keep It Simple ...

1.3.3   Implementation

In principle, the phase of implementation follows on from the design phase. In practice, however, the products of design may often only be regarded as providing a *post hoc* justification of the actual system. As noted, for instance, in Halbert and O'Brien (1987), an object-oriented approach may blur the distinction between design and implementation, even to the extent of reversing their actual order. The most important distinction between design and implementation is hence the level of abstraction at which the structure of the system is described. Design is meant to clarify the conceptual structure of a system, whereas the implementation must include all the details needed for the system to run. Whatever approach is followed, in the end the design must serve both as a *justification* and *clarification* of the actual implementation.

Design is of particular importance in projects that require long-term maintenance. Correcting errors or adapting the functionality of the system on the basis of code alone is not likely to succeed. What may help, though, are tools that extract explanatory information from the code.

Testing and maintenance Errors may (and will) occur during the implementation as well as later when the system is in operation. Apart from the correction of errors, other maintenance activities may be required, as we have seen previously.

In Knuth (1992), an amusing account is given of the errors Knuth detected in the TeX program over a period of time. These errors range from trivial typos to errors on an algorithmic level. See slide 1-25.

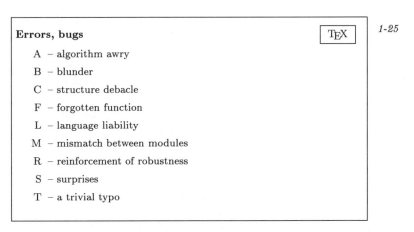

Slide 1-25: TeX errors and bugs

An interesting and important question is to what extent an object-oriented approach, and more specifically an object-oriented implementation language, is of help in avoiding and correcting such errors. The reader is encouraged to make a first guess, and to verify that guess later.

As an interesting aside, the TEX system has been implemented in a language system called Web. The Web system allows one to merge code and explanatory text in a single document, and to process that document as either code or text. In itself, this has nothing to do with object orientation, but the technique of documentation supported by the Web system is also suitable for object-oriented programs. We may note that the *javadoc* tool realizes some of the goals set for the Web system, for Java.

Object-oriented language support Operationally, *encapsulation* and *inheritance* are considered to be the basic mechanisms underlying the object-oriented approach. These mechanisms have been realized in a number of languages. (See slide 1-26. See also chapter 5 for a more complete overview.)

Historically, Smalltalk is often considered to be the most important object-oriented language. It has served as an implementation vehicle for a variety of applications (see, for instance, Pope, 1991). No doubt, Smalltalk has contributed greatly to the initial popularity of the object-oriented approach, yet its role is being taken over by C++ and Java, which jointly have the largest community of users. Smalltalk is a purely object-oriented language, which means that every entity, including integers, expressions and classes, is regarded as an object. The popularity of the Smalltalk language may be attributed partly to the Smalltalk environment, which allows the user to inspect the properties of all the objects in the system and which, moreover, contains a large collection of reusable classes. Together with the environment, Smalltalk provides excellent support for fast prototyping.

The language Eiffel, described by Meyer (1988), may also be considered as a pure object-oriented language, pure in the sense that it provides classes and inheritance as the main device with which to structure a program. The major contribution of Eiffel is its support for correctness constructs. These include the possibility to specify pre- and post-conditions for methods, as well as to specify a *class invariant*, that may be checked before and after each method invocation. The Eiffel system comes with a number of libraries, including libraries for graphics and window support, and a collection of tools for browsing and the extraction of documentation.

The C++ language (Stroustrup, 1991) has a somewhat different history. It was originally developed as an extension of C with classes. A primary design goal of C++ has been to develop a powerful but efficient language. In contrast to Smalltalk and Eiffel, C++ is not a pure object-oriented language; it is a *hybrid* language in the sense that it allows us to use functions in C-style as well as object-oriented constructs involving classes and inheritance.

The newest, and perhaps most important, object-oriented language around is Java, which owes its popularity partly to its tight connection with the Internet. Java comes with a virtual machine that allows for running Java programs (applets)

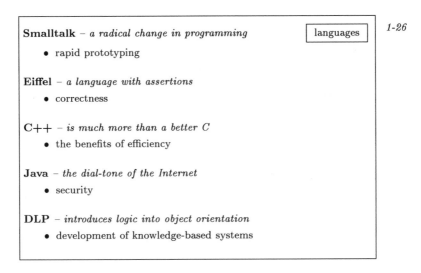

Slide 1-26: Object-oriented languages

in a browser, in a so-called sandbox, which protects the user from possibly malicious programs.

As the final language in this brief overview, I wish to mention the distributed logic programming language DLP (see Eliëns, 1992). The DLP language combines logic programming with object-oriented features and parallelism. I mention it, partly because the development of this language was my first involvement with OOP. And further, because it demonstrates that other paradigms of programming, in particular logic programming, may be fruitfully combined with OOP. The language DLP provides a high level vehicle for modeling knowledge-based systems in an object-oriented way.

A more extensive introduction to the Smalltalk, Eiffel, C++, Java and DLP languages is given in the appendix.

1.4 Beyond object-orientation?

No introduction to object orientation is complete without an indication of the trends and technologies that surround the field. The word trend should be understood in its positive meaning of set examples and emerging guidelines. And 'technologies', such as for example CORBA (the OMG Common Object Request Broker Architecture), as those that set the technological landscape which determines whether object-oriented approaches can be deployed effectively in practice.

At the design front, we may observe two dominant trends. The first may be called the *patterns* movement, which came into the forefront after the publication of *Design Patterns*, authored by a group of authors that is commonly known as the *'Gang of Four'*, Gamma *et al.* (1994). The design patterns published

---

Trends – *modeling*   *1-27*

- *patterns* – examples of design
- UML – Unified Modeling Language

Technologies – *components*

- Web – global infrastructure
- CORBA/DCOM - the software bus
- Java – the platform?

Challenges

- Applications $\rightarrow$ Frameworks $\leftarrow$ Patterns

---

Slide 1-27: Trends and technologies

there, and elsewhere e.g. Coplien and Schmidt (1995), may be regarded as the outcome of mining actual framework and application designs for valid solutions that may be generalized to broader classes of problems. Design patterns focus on understanding and describing structural and behavioral properties of (fragments of) software systems.

Equally focused on understanding structure and behavior, but more from a modeling perspective, is the Unified Modeling Language (UML), which has resulted from a common effort of leading experts in object-oriented analysis and design, Grady Booch, Ivar Jacobson and James Rumbaugh, also known as *'The Three Amigos'*. UML, indeed the second trend, aims at providing the full notational repertoire needed for modeling every conceivable structural and behavioral aspect of software systems. An excellent introduction to UML is given in Fowler (1997b). In Appendix F you will find a brief introduction to the UML.

With respect to technology, the field is still very much in flux. A dominant factor here is the rapid increase in Internet usage and, more in particular, the Web. The Web has boosted the interest of the IT business world in the deployment of distributed object or component technology to extend their range of business. Nevertheless, the very existence of this infrastructure is in itself somewhat embarrassing, in that the Web and the technology around which it is built is *not* object-oriented. Perhaps it should be, but it simply isn't. Our embarrassment is aggravated when we observe, following Szyperski (1997), that the technology which may change this, in casu component software, is in itself not object-oriented but, paraphrasing the subtitle of this excellent book, *'beyond object orientation'*. And even worse, object-oriented approaches at framework development have failed more often than they have succeeded, an observation which is confirmed by for example Cockburn (1997). Reading this you may think that object-orientation is in a deplorable state, and close the book. It isn't. First of all, because in terms of modeling and design there is *no* beyond object-orientation. And secondly, quoting Szyperski, 'object-technology, if harnessed carefully, is possibly one of the best ways to realize component technology ...'. Well, believe me, it is the best way. Whether it is CORBA, Microsof (D)COM or Java that will become the dominant component technology is quite another issue; component technology that ignores the object-lessons is doomed to fail!

Challenges Ignoring the component question for the moment, we may ask ourselves what the major challenges are that are confronting us as software developers. Briefly put, we still need to go a long way before we understand our applications well enough in terms of the (problem-solving) patterns underlying their construction that we can realize these patterns robustly in frameworks that are not only reusable conceptually, but that will also be (re)used in practice to develop cost-effective, competitive, economically viable applications.

More concretely, a major challenge for the next decade will be to develop and deploy frameworks that operate in areas such as finance, medical care, social welfare and insurance. This is explicitly not only a technical problem, but also a problem of coming to agreement with respect to the abstractions and corresponding standards that provide the computational infrastructure for these domains. Also on my wish-list is the separation of *logic* and *control*, by which I mean the decoupling of the more or less invariant functionality as may be provided by for example *business objects* and *business processes* and the more variable logic that controls these processes. In other words, it is necessary that the *business logic* is made explicit and that it is factored out of the code effectuating it.

Challenges in O-O   *1-28*

- vertical framework development – finance, medical care, insurance
- separation of 'logic' from 'control' – business rules
- distributed object technology – heterogeneous systems
- visualisation – structure and processes
- knowledge intensive applications – declarative
- heterogeneous systems – fragmented applications

Slide 1-28: Challenges

Another challenge is to integrate the various technologies into our frameworks and systems. In effect we will see more and more heterogeneous systems, composed of components from a variety of suppliers. These components may be implemented in every conceivable language, and may run on different platforms. How to connect these components in a reliable manner is still an open problem. And more generally, although there are solutions for crossing the various boundaries, the platform boundary and the language boundary, there are still a lot of problems to solve. In this book we will explore some of these problems, and get some experience with some of the solutions.

Both our hardware and software technology are improving rapidly. Yet, we are still stuck with the WIMP interfaces. In my opinion, it is time for a change. What I would like to see is an exploration of 3D user interfaces and 3D visualisations of the structure and processes underlying information-intensive applications. Although not specifically related to object-oriented software development, this is an area where object orientation can prove its worth.

When we think about real applications, for example information or business services on the Internet, they are usually the kind of applications that we may characterize as knowledge-intensive applications. In a somewhat idealistic vision, we may think of application development that consists of composing components from perhaps even a number of frameworks, so that we don't have to bother with the tiresome details of network access and GUI development. Then what remains to be done is to glue it all together, and provide the information and knowledge that enables our application to deliver its services. Partly we can rely on database technology for the storage and retrieval of information. But in addition we will need other declarative formalisms for expressing, for example, our business logic or, as another example, for expressing the synchronisation constraints of our multimedia presentation.

Considering Web applications, even as they are today, we see applications that consist of a mixture of code, tools and information. The phrase *fragmented applications* seems apt here. For example a store selling books on the Internet needs everything ranging from Javascript enabled webpages, to a secure CORBA-based accounting server. It is very likely that such applications will be developed partly by composing already existing components.

In his book, Szyperski (1997) argues that component-technology must be considered as the next stage, that is (as the subtitle of his book indicates) *beyond object orientation*. This is true to the extent that naive object orientation, characterized by weak encapsulation and white-box or implementation inheritance, has proven to be not entirely successful. What we need is a more robust specification of the behavioral properties of objects, for example by contractual specifications, and a stronger notion of encapsulation, in which not only the inner world of the object is protected from invasions from the outside, but where the outer world is also shielded from the object itself, so that the object cannot reach out into a world that might not even exist. More concretely, objects must be designed that allows them to be used in a distributed environment. They must observe, as Wegner puts it, the *distribution boundary*.

Summary

This chapter has given an outline of the major theme of this book, which may be characterized as the unification of a software engineering perspective and a foundational approach. The minor theme may be characterized by saying that a considerable amount of technology is involved.

In section 1 we looked at the terminology associated with object orientation, we studied the mechanisms underlying object computation and we discussed an approach to the development of software that centers around the identification of

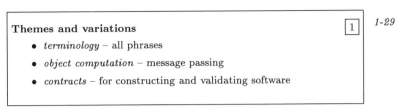

Slide 1-29: Section 1.1: Themes and variations

responsibilities and the definition of abstract data types embodying the mutual responsibilities of a client and a server object in terms of a *contract*. See slide 1-29.

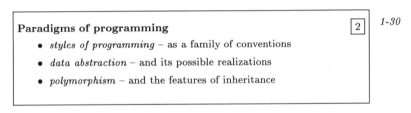

Slide 1-30: Section 1.2: Paradigms of programming

Then, in section 2, we looked at object-orientation as a paradigm of programming, extending an abstract data type approach with support for the organization of object types in a polymorphic type structure. See slide 1-30. Further, an overview was given of the literature available on OOP, including a number of landmark papers on which this book was originally based.

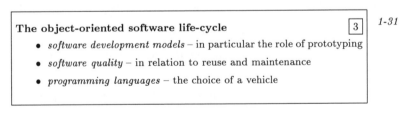

Slide 1-31: Section 1.3: The object-oriented software life-cycle

In section 3 we looked at the object-oriented software life-cycle, consisting of the phases of analysis, design and implementation. We discussed software development models and the role of prototyping, how an object-oriented approach may promote software quality and facilitate maintenance, and we looked at some programming languages as vehicles for the implementation of object-oriented code. See slide 1-31.

In section 4 we attempted to discern trends in the research and deployment of object-oriented technologies. We also tried to formulate the challenges we are

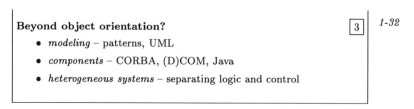

Slide 1-32: Section 1.4: Trends and technologies

faced with which concern the utilization of components for the development of knowledge-intensive heterogeneous systems, that allow to factor out the (business) logic in a declarative manner. See slide 1-32.

Questions

1. How would you characterize OOP and what, in your opinion, is the motivation underlying the introduction of OOP?

2. Characterize the most important features of OOP.

3. Explain the meaning of the phrase *'object orientation reduces the complexity of programming.'*

4. How would you characterize *contracts*? Why are *contracts* important?

5. How is OOP related to programming languages?

6. What classes of languages support OOP features? Explain.

7. What influence is an object-oriented approach said to have on the software life-cycle? What is your own opinion? Discuss the problem of maintenance.

8. How would you characterize *software quality*?

9. Mention a number of object-oriented programming languages, and give a brief characterization.

10. What do you see as the major challenges for research in object orientation?

Further reading

Nowadays there are many books that may serve as a starting point for reading about OO. Dependent on your interest, you may look at Cockburn (1997), which treats issues of OO project management, Meyer (1997), which gives an extensive introduction to design by contract and programming in Eiffel, or Fowler (1997b), which gives a succinct introduction to UML. Alternatively, you may take one of the introductory programming books for Java, from which you will almost certainly learn something about OO as well.

2

Idioms and patterns

Object orientation has brought about a radical shift in our notion of software development. The basic mechanisms of object-oriented programming, *encapsulation* and *inheritance*, have clear advantages when it comes to data-hiding and incremental development.

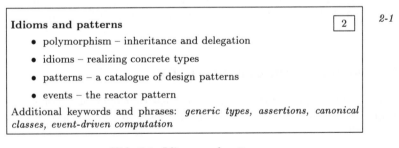

Slide 2-1: Idioms and patterns

However, these basic mechanisms alone do not suffice for the realization of more complex systems. In this chapter, we will look at idioms and patterns for object and class composition. Patterns, as originally introduced in Gamma *et al.* (1994), characterize a generic solution to a problem or dilemma in design. Idioms may be understood as the implementation techniques underlying the realization of (design) patterns.

First we will look at some examples in Java, illustrating the use of inheritance and delegation for the realization of some simple idioms and patterns. Then, we will briefly deal with polymorphism in C++, including the use of assertions that may be used to enforce contractual obligations. After discussing some of the idioms and patterns that have been employed in the *hush* framework, we will look more closely at the catalogue of design patterns introduced in Gamma *et al.* (1994). Finally, we will study the reactor pattern as introduced in Schmidt (1995) and briefly explore event-based software architectures.

2.1   Polymorphism

Polymorphism is an intriguing notion. Briefly put, polymorphism is the ability of a particular entity (which may be an object, a function, or a variable) to present itself as belonging to multiple types. Object-oriented languages are not unique in their support for polymorphism, but it is safe to say that polymorphism is an important feature of object-oriented languages. As explained in chapter 9, polymorphism comes in various flavors. With regard to object-oriented languages, we usually mean inheritance or *inclusion* polymorphism. Even within this restricted interpretation, we have to make a distinction between syntactic polymorphism, which requires merely that interfaces conform, and semantic polymorphism, where conformance requirements also include behavioral properties.

In this section, we will look at some simple examples in Java that illustrate how we may use the mechanisms of inheritance and (simple) delegation to define objects that have similar functionality but differ in the way that functionality is realized. These examples prepare the way for the more complex idioms and patterns presented later in this chapter.

In the rest of this section we will look briefly at the polymorphic constructs offered by C++. We will also study how behavioral conformance can be enforced in C++ by including invariants and assertions. These sections may be skipped on first reading.

2.1.1   Inheritance and delegation in Java

Consider the example below, an *envelope* class that offers a *message* method. In this form it is nothing but a variation on the *hello world* example presented in the appendix.

```
public class envelope {

public envelope() { }

public void message() {
        System.out.println("hello ... ");
        }
};
```

envelope

To illustrate the idea underlying idioms and patterns in its most simple form, we will refine the *envelope* class into the collection of classes depicted in slide 2-2.

We will proceed in three steps: (1) The *envelope* class will be redesigned so that it acts only as an interface to the *letter* implementation class. (2) Then we introduce a *factory* object, that is used to create *envelope* and *letter* instances. (3) Finally, we refine the *letter* class into a *singleton* class, that prevents the creation of multiple *letter* instances.

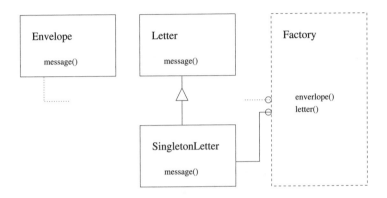

Slide 2-2: Envelope/Letter Factory

Envelope/Letter The *Envelope/Letter* idiom was introduced in Coplien (1992) as a means to separate interface aspects from implementation aspects. Here the call to *message* is simply forwarded to the *letter* object.

```
public class envelope {                                          envelope
letter impl;
public envelope() {
        impl = new letter();
        }

public void message() {
        impl.message();
        }
};


public class letter {                                            letter

public letter() { }

public void message() {
        System.out.println("Message in a letter");
        }
};
```

Admittedly, there is no need here to make such a distinction, but the idea speaks for itself. As you will see, this distinction allows us to change the implementation without modifying the *envelope* or interface class.

Factory In the next refinement, we introduce a *factory* object, that allows us to create *envelope* and *letter* instances without invoking a constructor.

```
public class factory {
                                                        factory

public factory() { }

letter letter() { return new letter(); }
envelope envelope() { return new envelope(); }
};
```

```
public class envelope {
                                                        envelope
letter impl;
public envelope() {
        factory f = new factory();
        impl = f.letter();   // obtained from factory
        }

public void message() {
        impl.message();
        }
};
```

The *factory* object is used in the *envelope* class to create a *letter*. The advantage here, as will be shown shortly, is that the *envelope* class does not need to have any information about the actual type of the *letter*.

Singleton letter Finally, we refine the *letter* class into a *singleton* class. When you inspect the implementation, you will see that only one instance of a *letter* will be created.

```
public class singleton extends letter {
                                                        singleton

static int number = 0;

protected singleton() { }

static letter instance() {
        if (number==0) {
                theletter = new letter();
                number = 1;
                }
        return theletter;
```

```
            }

    public void message() {
            System.out.println("Message in a letter");
            }

    static letter theletter;
    };
```

Note that the *factory* object must be modified so that the static method *instance* of *singleton* is invoked instead of the original constructor of *letter*.

Discussion This example, however simple, demonstrates the implementation of some of the idioms and patterns that will be discussed in the rest of this chapter. It shows that the basic mechanisms of inheritance and simple delegation or forwarding are sufficient to implement these idioms and patterns. We have not discussed yet why we need idioms and patterns, but this will hopefully become clear later on.

2.1.2   Polymorphism in C++

Polymorphism essentially characterizes the type of a variable, function or object. Polymorphism may be due to overloading, parametrized types or inheritance. Polymorphism due to inheritance is often considered as the greatest contribution of object-oriented languages. This may be true, but the importance of generic (template) types and overloading should not be overlooked.

In slide 2-3 some examples are given of declarations involving polymorphic types. The function *print* is separately defined for *int* and *float*. Also, a generic *list* class is defined by means by employing *templates*. The list may be used for any kind of objects, for example integers. Finally, a *shape* class is defined from which a *circle* class is derived. An instance of the *circle* may be referred to by using a *shape* pointer, because the type *shape* encompasses *circle* objects.

The Standard Template Library (STL)

The Standard Template Library for C++ provides a generic library of data structures to store, access and manipulate data. It is a generic library based on templates. In fact, it uses templates in such an aggressive way that the C++ standardization committee was forced to reconsider its definition of the generic template facility in C++. See Schildt (1999).

The Standard Template Library (STL) offers *containers*, to hold objects, *algorithms*, that act on containers, and *iterators*, to traverse containers. Algorithms, which are implemented as objects, may use *functions*, which are also defined as objects, overloading the application *operator*() method. In addition, STL offers *adaptors*, to transform objects, and *allocators*, for memory management.

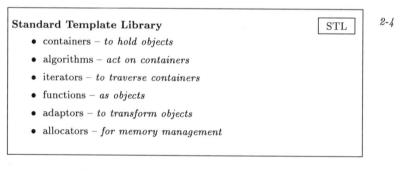

Slide 2-3: Polymorphic type declarations

Slide 2-4: The Standard Template Library

STL is supported by C++ compilers that adhere to the C++ standard, including Microsoft Visual C++ and the Cygnus/GNU C++ compilers. A more extensive discussion of STL is beyond the scope of this book, but the reader is advised to consult Schildt (1999), which gives an introduction to STL and its history, as well as a thorough course on programming with STL.

2.1.3 Assertions in C++

Whatever support a language may offer, reliable software is to a large extent the result of a disciplined approach to programming. The use of assertions has long since been recognized as a powerful way in which to check whether the functional behavior of a program corresponds with its intended behavior. In effect, many programming language environments support the use of assertions in some way.

For example, both C and C++ define a macro *assert* which checks for the result of a boolean expression and stops the execution if the expression is false.

In the example below, assertions are used to check for the satisfying of both the pre- and post-conditions of a function that computes the square root of its argument, employing a method known as Newton iteration.

```
double sqrt( double arg ) {
require ( arg >= 0 );
double r=arg, x=1, eps=0.0001;
while( fabs(r - x) > eps ) {
   r=x; x=r-((r*r-arg)/(2*r));
   }
promise ( r - arg * arg <= eps );
return r;
}
```

sqrt

In the example, the macro *assert* has been renamed *require* and *promise* to indicate whether the assertion serves as, respectively, a pre- or post-condition. As the example above shows, assertions provide a powerful means by which to characterize the behavior of functions, especially in those cases where the algorithmic structure itself does not give a good clue as to what the function is meant to do.

The use of assertions has been promoted in Meyer (1988) as a design method for object-oriented programming in Eiffel. The idea is to define the functionality of the various methods by means of pre- and post-conditions stating in a precise manner the requirements that clients of an object must meet and the obligations an object has when executing a method. Together, the collection of methods annotated with pre- and post-conditions may be regarded as a *contract* between the object and its potential clients. See section 3.3.

Whereas Eiffel directly supports the use of assertions by allowing access to the value of an instance variable before the execution of a method through the keyword *old*, the C++ programmer must rely on explicit programming to be able to compare the state before an operation with the state after the operation.

```
class counter {
public:
counter(int n = 0) : _n(n) {
        require( n >= 0 );
        promise( invariant() );         check initial state
        }

virtual void operator++() {
        require( true );                empty pre-condition
        hold();                         save the previous state
        _n += 1;
        promise( _n == old_n + 1 && invariant() );
        }
```

counter

```
int value() const { return _n; }                              no side effects

virtual bool invariant() { return value() >= 0; }

protected:
int _n;
int old_n;
virtual void hold() { old_n = n; }
};
```

The annotated *counter* above includes a member function *hold* to store the value of its instance variable. It is used in the *operator++* function to check whether the new value of the counter is indeed the result of incrementing the old value.

Assertions may also be used to check whether the object is correctly initialized. The pre-condition stated in the constructor requires that the counter must start with a value not less than zero. In addition, the constructor checks whether the class invariant, stated in the (virtual) member function *invariant*, is satisfied. Similarly, after checking whether the post-condition of the *operator++* function is true, the invariant is checked as well.

```
class bounded : public counter {                              bounded
public:
bounded(int b = MAXINT) : counter(0), max(b) {}
void operator++() {
        require( value() < max );                     to prevent overflow
        counter::operator++();
        }

bool invariant() {
        return value() <= max && counter::invariant();
        }

private:
int max;
};
```

When employing inheritance, care must be taken that the invariance requirements of the base class are not violated. The class *bounded*, given above, refines the class *counter* by imposing an additional constraint that the value of the (bounded) counter must not exceed some user-defined maximum. This constraint is checked in the *invariant* function, together with the original *counter :: invariant()*, which was declared virtual to allow for overriding by inheritance. In addition, the increment *operator++* function contains an extra pre-condition to check whether the state of the (bounded) counter allows it to perform the operation.

From a formal perspective, the use of assertions may be regarded as a way of augmenting the type system supported by object-oriented languages. More importantly, from a software engineering perspective, the use of assertions is a means to enforce contractual obligations.

2.1.4   Canonical class idioms

The multitude of constructs available in C++ to support object-oriented programming may lead the reader to think that object-oriented programming is not at all meant to reduce the complexity of programming but rather to increase it, for the joy of programming so to speak. This impression is partly justified, since the number and complexity of constructs is at first sight indeed slightly bewildering. However, it is necessary to realize that each of the constructs introduced (classes, constructors and destructors, protection mechanisms, type conversion, overloading, virtual functions and dynamic binding) may in some way be essential to support object-oriented programming in a type-safe, and yet convenient, way.

Having studied the mechanisms, the next step is to find proper ways, recipes as it were, to use these mechanisms. What we need, in the terminology of Coplien (1992), are *idioms*, that is established ways of solving particular problems with the mechanisms we have available. In his excellent book, Coplien discusses a number of advanced C++ idioms for a variety of problem domains, including signal processing and symbolic computing.

In this section, we will look at the concrete class idiom for C++, which states the ingredients that every class must have to behave as if it were a built-in type. Other idioms, in particular an improved version of the *handle/body* or *envelope/letter* idiom that may be used to separate interface from implementation, will be treated in the next section.

Concrete data types in C++ A concrete data type is the realization of an abstract data type. When a concrete data type is correctly implemented it must satisfy the requirements imposed by the definition of the abstract data type it realizes. These requirements specify what operations are defined for that type, and also their effects. In principle, these requirements may be formally specified, but in practice just an informal description is usually given. Apart from the demands imposed by a more abstract view of the functionality of the type, a programmer usually also wishes to meet other requirements, such as speed, efficiency in terms of storage and error conditions, to prevent the removal of an item from an empty stack, for example. The latter requirements may be characterized as requirements imposed by implementation concerns, whereas the former generally result from design considerations.

To verify whether a concrete data type meets the requirements imposed by the specification of the abstract data type is quite straightforward, although not always easy. However, the task of verifying whether a concrete data type is optimally implemented is rather less well defined. To arrive at an optimal implementation may involve a lot of skill and ingenuity, and in general it is hard to decide whether the right choices have been made. Establishing trade-offs

---

Canonical class in C++   *2-5*

  - default constructor

  - copy constructor

  - destructor

  - assignment

  - operators

Abstract data types must be indistinguishable from built-in types

---

Slide 2-5: Canonical class

and making choices, for better or worse, is a matter of experience, and crucially depends upon the skill in handling the tools and mechanisms available.

When defining concrete data types, the list of requirements defining the *canonical class* idiom given in slide 2-5 may be used as a check list to determine whether all the necessary features of a class have been defined. Ultimately, the programmer should strive to realize abstract data types in such a way that their behavior is in some sense indistinguishable from the behavior of the built-in data types. Since this may involve a lot of work, this need not be a primary aim in the first stages of a software development project. But for class libraries to work properly, it is simply essential.

2.2   Idioms in *hush*

The *hush* framework, developed by the author and his colleagues, aims at providing an easy-to-use and flexible, multi-paradigm environment for developing distributed hypermedia and web-based applications. Actually *hush*, which stands for *hyper utility shell*, is a part of the DejaVU framework which has been developed at the Free University in Amsterdam over the last five years. The DejaVU framework is meant as an umbrella for our research in object-oriented applications and architectures. Many of the examples in this book are in some way derived from *hush* or applications developed within the DejaVU project. The *hush* library was originally developed in C++, but parts of it have been ported to Java using the Java native runtime interface. You will see examples of *hush* in chapters 4, 6, 7, 11 and 12.

In this section a brief overview will be given of the basic concepts underlying *hush*. Then we will discuss the idioms used in realizing *hush* and its extensions, in particular an adapted version of the *handle/body* idiom originally introduced in Coplien (1992), the *virtual self-reference* idioms and the *dynamic role switching* idiom. At the end of this section we will discuss the implications these idioms have for developing *hush* applications. Readers not interested in *hush* may safely skip the introduction that follows and the discussion at the end of this section.

The *hush* framework is object-oriented in that it allows for a component-wise approach to developing applications. Yet, in addition to object class interfaces, it offers the opportunity to employ a script language, such as Tcl and Prolog, to develop applications and prototypes. The *hush* framework is a multi-paradigm framework, not only by supporting a multi-lingual approach, but also by providing support for distributed client/server solutions in a transparent (read CORBA) manner.

In this section we will look at the idioms employed for the realization of the framework. In developing *hush* we observed that there is a tension between defining a clean object model and providing the flexibility needed to support a multiparadigm approach. We resolved this tension by choosing to differentiate between the object model (that is class interfaces) offered to the average user of the framework and the object model offered to advanced users and system-level developers.

In this approach, idioms play a central role. We achieved the desired flexibility by systematically employing a limited number of basic idioms. We succeeded in hiding these idioms from the average user of the framework. However, the simplicity of our original object model is only apparent. Advanced or system-level developers who intend to define extensions to the framework must be well aware of the patterns underlying the basic concepts, that is the functionality requirements of the classes involved, and the idioms employed in realizing these requirements.

The *hush* framework – basic concepts

Application development generally encompasses a variety of programming tasks, including system-level software development (for example for networking or multimedia functionality), programming the user interface (including the definition of screen layout and the responsivity of the interface widgets to user actions), and the definition of (high-level) application-specific functionality. Each of these kinds of tasks may require a different approach and possibly a different application programming language. For example, the development of the user interface is often more conveniently done using a scripting language, to avoid the waiting times involved in compiling and linking. Similarly, defining knowledge-level application-specific functionality may benefit from the use of a declarative or logic programming language.

In developing *hush*, we decided from the start to support a multiparadigm approach to software development and consequently we had to define the mutual interaction between the various language paradigms, as for example the interaction between C++ and a scripting language, such as Tcl. Current scripting languages, including Python and Tcl, provide facilities for being embedded in C and C++, but extending these languages with functionality defined in C or C++ and employing the language from within C/C++ is rather cumbersome. The *hush* library offers a uniform interface to a number of script languages and, in addition, it offers a variety of widgets and multimedia extensions, which are accessible through any of the script interpreters as well as the C++ interface.

These concepts are embodied in (pseudo) abstract classes that are realized by employing idioms extending the *handle/body* idiom, as explained later on.

Programming a *hush* application requires the definition of an application class

---

Basic *hush* classes   *2-6*

- *session* – to manage (parts of) the application
- *kit* – to provide access to the underlying system and interpreter
- *handler* – to bind C++ functionality to events
- *event* – stores information concerning user actions or system events
- *widget* – to display information on a screen
- *item* – represents an element of a widget

Slide 2-6: Basic *hush* classes

derived from *session* to initialize the application and start the (window environment) main loop. In addition, one may bind Java or C+= *handler* objects to script commands by invoking the *kit::bind* function. Handler objects are to be considered an object realization of callback functions, with the advantage that client data may be accessed in a type-secure way (that is either by resources stored when creating the handler object or by information that is passed via events). When invoked, a handler object receives a pointer to an *event* (that is, either an X event or an event related to the evaluation of a script command). Both the *widget* and (graphical) *item* class are derived from *handler* to allow for declaring widgets and items to be their own handler.

Embedding script interpreters The *hush* framework offers a generic *kit* that may be used as the interface to any embedded interpreter. The public interface of the *kit* class looks as follows:

```
interface kit {                                              kit

        void eval(string cmd);
        string result();

        void bind(string name, handler h);
};
```

The function *eval* is used for evaluating (script) commands, and *result* may be used to communicate data back. The limitation of this approach, obviously, is that it is purely string based. In practice, however, this proves to be flexible and sufficiently powerful. The *bind* function may be used to define new commands and associate it with functionality defined in *handler* objects, which are introduced below.

Handler objects The problem of extending the script language with functionality defined by the application, is (as already indicated above) addressed by defining a generic *handler* object class. Handler objects may be regarded as a generalization of callback functions, in the sense that they are activated whenever the corresponding script command is evaluated. The advantage of using objects for callbacks instead of functions, obviously, is that we no longer need type-insecure casts, or static or global variables to pass information around. The public interface of the *handler* class looks as follows:

```
interface handler {                        handler
    int dispatch( event e );        // to dispatch events
    int operator();
};
```

The *dispatch* function is called by the underlying system. The *dispatch* function receives a pointer to an event which encodes the information relevant for that particular callback. In its turn *dispatch* calls the *operator()* function. Classes derived from *handler* need only redefine the *operator()* function. Information needed when activating a handler object must be provided when creating the object, or obtained from the event for which the handler is activated.

The use of handler objects is closely connected to the paradigm of event-driven computation. An *event*, conceptually speaking, is an entity that is characterized by two significant moments, the moment of its *creation* and the moment of its *activation*, its occurrence. Naturally, an event may be activated multiple times and even record a history of its activation, but the basic principle underlying the use of events is that all the information that is needed is stored at creation time and, subsequently, activation may proceed blindly. See section 2.4.1.

User actions Another use of handler objects (in *hush*) is for defining what must be done in response to user events, resulting from actions such as moving the mouse, or pressing a button, or selecting an entry from a menu. This is illustrated by the public interface of the generic *widget* class:

```
interface widget : handler {                    widget
    ...
    void bind( handler h );
    void bind( string action, handler h );
    ...
};
```

The first member function *bind* may be used for installing a handler for the default bindings of the widget, whereas the second *bind* function is to be used for overriding any specific bindings. (Recall that the class *widget* is derived from *handler* class to allow the widget to be its own handler. In this way inheritance or the delegation to a separate handler object may be used to define the functionality of a widget.)

In addition to the *widget* class, the *hush* library also provides the class *item*, representing graphical items. Graphical items, however, are to be placed within a canvas widget, and may be tagged to allow for the groupwise manipulation of a collection of items, as for example moving them in response to dragging the mouse pointer.

Programmer-defined events User interface events occur in response to actions by the user. They are scheduled by the underlying window system, which invokes the handler whenever it is convenient or necessary. When getting used to event-driven computation, system designers and programmers may feel the need to have events at their disposal that may be scheduled at will, under the programmer's control. It will come as no surprise that another use of handler objects is to allow for programmer-defined events. The public interface of the class *event* looks as follows:

```
interface event : handler {                                    event
    operator();
};
```

Actual event classes are derived from the generic class *event*, and a scheduler is provided to activate events at the appropriate time. (In effect, we provide a fully functional discrete event simulation library, including facilities for generating random distributions and analysing the outcome of experiments. Business process simulations done with this library are discussed in Chapter 11.) Note that there is an important difference between programmer-defined events and system-defined events. System-defined events are delivered to the user by activating a handler callback. In contrast, programmer-defined events are (directly) activated by a scheduler. They contain, so to speak, their own handler.

Discussion What benefits do we derive from employing handler objects and their derivatives? One advantage is that we have a uniform way to define the functionality of script commands, callbacks to user actions and programmer-controlled events. Another, less apparent advantage, is that it allows us to incorporate a variety of functionality (including sound synthesis facilities, digital video and active documents) in a relatively straightforward fashion.

2.2.1   The handle/body idiom

The handle/body class idiom, originally introduced in Coplien (1992), separates the class defining a component's abstract interface (the handle class) from its hidden implementation (the body class). All intelligence is located in the body, and (most) requests to the handle object are delegated to its implementation.

In order to illustrate the idiom, we use the following class as a running example:

```
class A {                                                      A − naive

public A() { }

public void f1() { System.out.println("A.f1"); f2(); }
```

```
public void f2() { System.out.println("A.f2"); }
};
```

The implementation of A is straightforward and does not make use of the handle/body idiom. A call to the f1() member function of A will print a message and make a subsequent call to f2().

Without any modification in the behavior of A's instances, it is possible to re-implement A using the handle/body idiom. The member functions of class A are implemented by its body, and A is reduced to a simple interface class:

```
class A {                                                          [ A ]

public A() { body = new BodyOfA(this); }
protected A(int x) {     }

public void f1() { body.f1(); }
public void f2() { body.f2(); }
public void f3() { System.out.println("A.f3"); }

private A body;
};
```

Note that the implementation of A's body can be completely hidden from the application programmer. In fact, by declaring A to be the superclass of its body class, even the existence of a body class can be hidden. If A is a class provided by a shared library, new implementations of its body class can be plugged in, without the need to recompile dependent applications:

```
class BodyOfA extends A {                           [ BodyOfA – naive ]

public BodyOfA() { super(911); }

public void f1() { System.out.println("A.f1"); f2(); }
public void f2() { System.out.println("A.f2"); }

};
```

In this example, the application of the idiom has only two minor drawbacks. First, in the implementation below, the main constructor of A makes an explicit call to the constructor of its body class. As a result, A's constructor needs to be changed whenever an alternative implementation of the body is required. The *Abstract Factory* pattern described in Gamma *et al.* (1994) may be used to solve this problem in a generic and elegant way. Another (aesthetic) problem is the need for the dummy constructor to prevent a recursive chain of constructor calls.

But the major drawback of the handle/body idiom occurs when deriving a subclass of A which partially redefines A's virtual member functions. Consider this definition of a derived class C:

```
class C extends A {                                          C
public void f2() { System.out.println("C.f2"); }
};
```

Try to predict the output of a code fragment like:

```
C c = new C; c.f1();
```

The behavior of instances of C does indeed depend on whether the hidden implementation of its base class A applies the handle/body idiom or not! If it does, the output will be `A.f1() A.f2().` because the indirect call to `f2()` in `f1()` will (unexpectedly) not call the redefined version of `f2()`. The original definition of A would of course yield `A.f1() C.f2().` but this can only be obtained by deriving C directly from the (hidden) body class.

Note that this is an illustration of one of the main drawbacks of the OOP paradigm: the inability to change base classes at the top of a hierarchy without introducing errors in derived classes.

Explicit invocation context In both implementations of A, the call to `f2()` in `f1()` is an abbreviation of `this.f2()`. However, in the first, naive implementation of A, the implicit `this` reference refers to the handle object (which can be an instance of a derived class). In contrast, `this` in the `BodyOfA` will refer to the body object. As a consequence, the body object is unable to make calls to functions redefined by classes derived from the base class A.

We use the term *invocation context* to denote a reference to the context in which the original request for a specific service is made, and represent this by a pointer to the handle object. In other words, the handle object needs a pointer to its body to be able to delegate its functionality, and, symmetrically, the body needs a pointer to the handle in order to be able to use any redefined virtual functions.

The body can be redefined as:

```
class BodyOfA extends A {                                   BodyOfA

public BodyOfA(A h) { super(911); handle = h; }

public void f1() { System.out.println("A.f1"); handle.f2(); }
public void f2() { System.out.println("A.f2"); }

A handle;                               reference to invocation context
};
```

The new body class is aware of the fact that it is implementing services which are accessed via the handle object. Consequently, it can use this information and is able to make calls to functions which might be redefined by descendants of A.

Note that this solution does require some programming discipline: all (implicit) references to the body object should be changed into a reference to the invocation context. Fortunately, this discipline is only required in the body classes of the implementation hierarchy.

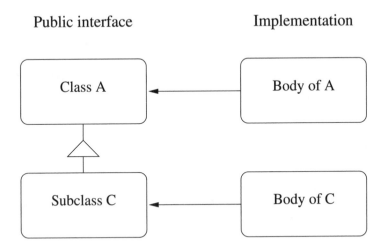

Slide 2-7: Separating interface hierarchy and implementation

Descendants of the handle classes in the public interface hierarchy can share and redefine code implemented by the hidden body classes in a completely transparent way, because all code sharing takes place indirectly, via the interface provided by the handle classes. However, even other body classes will typically share code via the handle classes. Also derived classes can use the handle/body idiom, as depicted in slide 2-7.

2.2.2 Virtual self-reference

A special feature of the *hush* widget class library is its support for the definition of new composite widgets, which provide to the application programmer the interface of a built-in (or possibly other composite) widget. To realize this flexibility, we introduced a *self()* function that adds another level of indirection to self-reference. For example, look at the *item* class below:

```
class item {

public item(String x) { _name = x; _self = null; }

String name() { return exists()?self().name():_name; }

public void redirect(item x) { _self = x; }

boolean exists() { return _self != null; }
```

item

```
public item self() { return exists()?_self.self():this; }

item _self;
String _name;
};
```

The *item* class has an instance variable _self, that can be set to an arbitrary instance of *item* by invoking *redirect*. Now, when we ask for the *name* of the *item*, it is checked whether a redirection *exists*. If so, the call is redirected to the instance referenced by self(), otherwise the name of the *item* itself is returned.

```
public class go {

    public static void main(String[] args) {
            item a = new item("a");
            item b = new item("b");
            a.redirect(b);
            System.out.println(a.name());                     indeed, b
    }

};
```

In combination with the *handle/body* idiom, we can create composites offering the interface of *item*, providing access to one or more (inner) items. This will be further illustrated in chapter 4.

Those well-versed in design patterns will recognize the *Decorator* patterns (as applied in the Interviews *MonoGlyph* class, Linton *et al.* (1989)).

2.2.3   Dynamic role-switching

For many applications, static type hierarchies do not provide the flexibility needed to model dynamically changing roles. For example we may wish to consider a person as an actor capable of various roles during his lifetime, some of which may even coexist concurrently. The characteristic feature of the *dynamic role switching* idiom underlying the *actor* pattern is that it allows us to regard a particular entity from multiple perspectives and to see that the behavior of that entity changes accordingly. We will look at a possible realization of the idiom below.

Taking our view of a person as an actor as a starting point, we need first to establish the repertoire of possible behavior.

```
class actor {                                               actor

    public static final int Person = 0;
    public static final int Student = 1;
    public static final int Employer = 2;
    public static final int Final = 3;
```

```
public void walk() { if (exists()) self().walk(); }
public void talk() { if (exists()) self().talk(); }
public void think() { if (exists()) self().think(); }
public void act() { if (exists()) self().act(); }

public boolean exists() { return false; }
public actor self() {   return this; }

public void become(actor A) { }
public void become(int R) { }
};
```

Apart from the repertoire of possible behavior, which consists of the ability to *walk, talk, think* and *act*, an actor has the ability to establish its own identity (*self*) and to check whether it exists as an actor, which is true only if it has become another self. However, an actor is not able to assume a different role or to become another self. We need a *person* for that!

Next, we may wish to refine the behavior of an actor for certain roles, such as for example the *student* and *employer* roles, which are among the many roles a person can play.

```
class student extends actor {                              │ student │
public void talk() { System.out.println("OOP"); }
public void think() { System.out.println("Z"); }
};
```

```
class employer extends actor {                             │ employer │
public void talk() { System.out.println("money"); }
public void act() { System.out.println("business"); }
};
```

Only a *person* has the ability to assume a different role or to assume a different identity. Apart from becoming a *Student* or *Employer*, a person may for example become an *adult_person* and in that capacity again assume a variety of roles.

```
class person extends actor {                               │ person │

public person() {
        role = new actor[ Final+1 ];
        for( int i = Person; i <= Final; i++ ) role[i]=this;
        become(Person);
        }

public boolean exists() { return role[_role] != this; }
```

```
public actor self() {
        if ( role[ Person ] != this ) return role[ Person ].self();
        else return role[_role];
        }

public void become(actor p) { role[ Person ] = p; }

public void become(int R) {

if (role[ Person ] != this) self().become(R);
else {
        _role = R;
        if ( role[_role] == this ) {
                switch(_role) {
                case Person: break;                     // nothing changes
                case Student: role[_role] = new student(); break;
                case Employer: role[_role] = new employer(); break;
                case Final: role[_role] = new actor(); break;
                default: break;                          // nothing happens
                }
        }
    }
}

int _role;
actor role[];
};
```

A person may check whether he exists as a *Person*, that is whether the *Person* role differs from the person's own identity. A person's *self* may be characterized as the actor belonging to the role the person is playing, taking a possible change of identity into account.

When a person is created, his repertoire is still empty. Only when a person changes identity by becoming a different actor (or person) or by assuming one of his (fixed) roles, is he capable of displaying actual behavior.

Assuming or 'becoming' a role results in creating a role instance if none exists and setting the _role instance variable to that particular role. When a person's identity has been changed, assuming a role affects the actor that replaced the person's original identity. (However, only a person can change roles!)

The ability to become an actor allows us to model the various phases of a person's lifetime by different classes, as illustrated by the *adult* class.

```
class adult extends person {                                    | adult |
public void talk() { System.out.println("interesting"); }
};
```

In the example code below we have a person talking while assuming different roles. Note that the person's identity may be restored by letting the person become its original self.

```
public class go {                                                    example

    public static void main(String[] args) {
            person p = new person(); p.talk();                       empty
            p.become(actor.Student); p.talk();                       OOP
            p.become(actor.Employer); p.talk();                      money
            p.become(new adult()); p.talk();                    interesting
            p.become(actor.Student); p.talk();                       OOP
            p.become(p); p.talk();                          old role: employer
            p.become(actor.Person); p.talk(); // initial state
            }
};
```

The *dynamic role switching* idiom can be used in any situation where we wish to change the functionality of an object dynamically. It may for example be used to incorporate a variety of tools in a drawing editor, as illustrated in chapter 4.

2.2.4 The art of *hush* programming

For the average user, programming in *hush* amounts (in general) to instantiating widgets and appropriate handler classes, or derived widget classes that define their own *handler*. However, advanced users and system-level programmers developing extensions are required to comply with the constraints resulting from the patterns underlying the design of *hush* and the application of their associated idioms in the realization of the library.

The design of *hush* and its extensions can be understood by a consideration of two basic patterns and their associated idioms, that is the *nested-component* pattern (which allows for nesting components that have a similar interface) and the *actor* pattern (which allows for attributing different modes or roles to objects). The realizations of these patterns are based on idioms that extend an improved version of the familiar *handle/body* idiom. Our improvement concerns the introduction of an *explicit invocation context* which is needed to repair the disruption of the virtual function call mechanism caused by the delegation to 'body implementation' objects.

In this section, we will first discuss the *handle/body* idiom and its improvement. Then we will discuss the two basic patterns underlying the design of *hush* and we will briefly sketch their realization by extensions of the (improved) *handle/body* idiom.

Invocation context The *handle/body* idiom is one of the most popular idioms. It underlies several other idioms and patterns (e.g. the envelope/letter idiom, Coplien (1992); the Bridge and Proxy patterns, Gamma *et al.* (1994)).

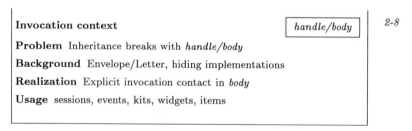

Slide 2-8: Invocation context

However, despite the fact that it is well documented there seems to be a major flaw in its realization. Its deficiency lies in the fact that the dynamic binding mechanism is disrupted by introducing an additional level of indirection (by delegating to the 'body' object), since it is not possible to make calls to member functions which are refined by subclasses of the (visible) handle class in the implementation of the (hidden) body class. We restored the working of the normal virtual function mechanism by introducing the notion of *explicit invocation context*. In this way, the handle/body idiom can be applied completely transparently, even for programmers of subclasses of the handle.

The (improved version of) the idiom is frequently used in the *hush* class library. The widget library is build of a stable interface hierarchy, offering several common GUI widgets classes like buttons, menus and scrollbars. The widget (handle) classes are implemented by a separate, hidden implementation hierarchy, which allows for changing the implementation of the widget library, without the need to recompile dependent applications. Additionally, the idiom helps us to ensure that the various widget implementations are used in a consistent manner.

The nested component pattern The *nested component* pattern has been introduced to support the development of compound widgets. It allows for (re)using the script and C++ interface of possibly compound widgets, by employing explicit redirection to an inner or primary component.

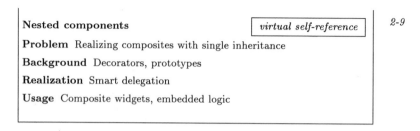

Slide 2-9: Nested components

Inheritance is not always a suitable technique for code sharing and object composition. A familiar example is the combination of a Text object and two

scrollbars into a ScrollableText object. In that case, most of the functionality of
ScrollableText will be equal to that of the Text object. This problem may be dealt
with by employing multiple inheritance. Using single inheritance, it may be hard
to inherit this functionality directly and add extra functionality by attaching the
scrollbars, especially when interface inheritance and implementation inheritance
coincide.

The *nested component* pattern is closely related to the Decorator pattern
treated in Gamma *et al.* (1994) and InterViews' notion of MonoGlyph, Linton *et
al.* (1989). Additionally, by using explicit delegation it provides an alternative
form of code sharing to inheritance, as can be found in languages supporting
prototypes or *exemplars*, see section 5.4.

The *nested component* pattern is realized by applying the *virtual self-reference*
idiom. Key to the implementation of that idiom is the virtual *self()* member of a
component. The *self()* member returns a reference to the object itself (e.g. *this*
in C++) by default, but returns the inner component if the outer object explicitly
delegated its functionality by using the *redirect()* method. Note that chasing for
self() is recursive, that is (widget) components can be nested to arbitrary depth.
The *self()* member must be used to access the functionality that may be realized
by the inner component.

The *nested component* pattern is employed in designing the *hush* widget hierarchy. Every (compound) widget can delegate part of its functionality to an inner
component. It is common practice to derive a compound widget from another
widget by using interface inheritance only, and to delegate functionality to an
inner component by explicit redirection.

The actor pattern The *actor* pattern provides a means to offer a multitude of
functional modes simultaneously. For example, a single *kit* object gives access to
multiple (embedded) script interpreters, as well as (possibly) a remote kit.

Actor pattern	*dynamic role switching*	*2-10*
Problem Static type hierarchies may be too limited		
Background State transitions, self-reference		
Realization Dynamic instantiation and delegation		
Usage Web viewer, kit – embedded logic		

Slide 2-10: Actor pattern

The characteristic feature of the actor pattern is that it allows us to regard a
particular entity as being attributed various roles or modes and that the behavior
of that entity changes accordingly.

Changing roles or modes can be regarded as some kind of state transition,
and indeed the actor pattern (and its associated *dynamic role-switching* idiom)
is closely related to the State pattern treated in Gamma *et al.* (1994). In both

cases, a single object is used to access the current role (or state) of a set of several
role (or state) classes. In combination with the *virtual self-reference* idiom, our
realization of the *actor* pattern allows for changing the role by installing a new
actor.

The realization of the actor pattern employs the *dynamic role-switching* idiom,
which is implemented by extending the handle class with a set of several bodies
instead of only one. To enable role-switching, some kind of indexing is needed.
Usually, a dictionary or a simple array of roles will be sufficient.

In the *hush* library the actor pattern is used to give access to multiple interpreters via the same interface class (i.e. the *kit* class). The pattern is essential
in supporting the multi-paradigm nature of the DejaVU framework. In our
description of the design of the Web components in section 12.2, we will show
how *dynamic role-switching* is employed for using various network protocols via
the same *(net)client* class. The actor pattern is also used to define a (single) viewer
class that is capable of displaying documents of various MIME-types (including
SGML, HTML, VRML).

2.3   A catalogue of design patterns

Why patterns, you may wonder. Why patterns and why not a method of object-
oriented design and an introduction in one or more object-oriented languages?
The answer is simple. Patterns bookmark effective design. They fill the gap
between the almost infinite possibilities of object-oriented programming languages
and tools and the rigor of methodical design. As Brian Foote expressed it in Martin *et al.* (1997), patterns are the footprints of design, paving the way for future
designs. They provide a common design vocabulary and are also helpful in
documenting a framework. And, as we will see later, patterns may also act as a
target for redesign, that is when the current design no longer offers the desired
functionality and flexibility.

A catalogue of design patterns   *2-11*

- a common design vocabulary

- documentation and learning aid

- an adjunct to existing methods

- a target for redesign

                                              Gamma *et al.* (1994)

Slide 2-11: A catalogue of design patterns

The Gang of Four book, *Design Patterns* by Gamma *et al.* (1994), was
immediately recognized as an important contribution to object-oriented software
development. Not only because of the actual patterns presented, but also because
of the style in which they were presented, crisp problem-oriented descriptions of
actual solutions to real design problems, written with scientific rigor and accuracy.

As Brian Foote remarked, actual design became a legitimate subject of computer science research.

The *pattern schema*, or rather a simplified version thereof, is depicted in slide 2-12. Each pattern must have a *name*, which acts as a handle in discussions about the design. Being able to speak about specific pattern solutions, such as a *factory*, greatly facilitates discussions about design.

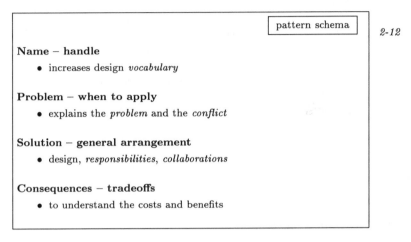

Slide 2-12: The pattern schema

Other important entries in the pattern schema are, the *problem* indicating what the patterns is all about, the *solution* describing the general arrangment of the classes and objects involved, and the *consequences* or tradeoffs that a particular solution entails.

The actual patterns presented in Gamma *et al.* (1994) are the result of the authors' involvement in developing various GUI toolkits, in particular Interviews, Linton *et al.* (1989), and ET++, Weinand *et al.* (1988), and applications such as, for example, interactive text and image editors. In the course of developing a toolkit or application there are many occasions for redesign. Reasons why you may need to redesign are listed in slide 2-13, along with an appropriate selection of patterns from Gamma *et al.* (1994).

Following Gamma *et al.* (1994), we may distinguish between *creational* patterns that govern the construction and management of objects, *structural* patterns that define the static relationships between objects, and *behavioral* patterns that characterize the dynamic aspects of the interaction between objects.

In this section we will look at a brief overview of the classification as originally presented in Gamma *et al.* (1994). The patterns themselves will be treated only briefly. The reader is invited to consult the original source and the many publications that followed: Coplien and Schmidt (1995), Vlissides *et al.* (1996), Martin *et al.* (1997).

```
┌─────────────────────────────────────────────────────────────────┐
│ Causes for redesign                    │ design for change │   2-13 │
│                                                                   │
│   • creating an object by specifying a class explicitly – Abstract│
│     Factory, Factory Method, Prototype                            │
│                                                                   │
│   • dependence on specific operations – Chain of Responsibilty, Com-│
│     mand                                                          │
│                                                                   │
│   • dependence on hardware & software platforms – Abstract Factory,│
│     Bridge                                                        │
│                                                                   │
│   • dependence on object implementation or representation –Abstract│
│     Factory, Bridge, Memento, Proxy                               │
│                                                                   │
│   • algorithm dependence – Iterator, Strategy, Template Method,   │
│     Visitor                                                       │
│                                                                   │
│   • extending functionality by subclassing – Bridge, Composite, Dec-│
│     orator, Observer                                             │
│                                                                   │
│   • tight coupling – Abstract Factory, Bridge, Chain of Responsibili-│
│     ties, Command, Facade, Mediator, Observer                    │
│                                                                   │
│   • inability to alter classes conveniently – Adaptor, Decorator, Visitor│
└─────────────────────────────────────────────────────────────────┘
```

Slide 2-13: Causes for redesign

2.3.1   Creational patterns

Design for change means to defer commitment to particular object implementations as long as possible. Due to inheritance, or rather subtyping, the client,
calling a particular method, can choose the most abstract class, highest in the
hierarchy. However, when it comes to creating objects, there seems to be no
other choice than naming the implementation class explicitly. Wrong. Creational
patterns are meant to take care of that, that is to hide the actual class used as
far away as possible.

```
┌─────────────────────────────────────────────────────────────────┐
│ Creational patterns                                         2-14  │
│                                                                   │
│   • Factory – hide concrete classes                               │
│                                                                   │
│   • Factory Method – virtual constructors                         │
│                                                                   │
│   • Prototype – dynamic creation by cloning                       │
│                                                                   │
│   • Singleton – one instance only                                 │
└─────────────────────────────────────────────────────────────────┘
```

Slide 2-14: Creational patterns

Creational patterns come in various flavors. In section 2.1.1 some example
realizations were presented. The *factory* class, for example, is a rather static way
of hiding the implementation classes. As an alternative, you may use a *factory
method*, similar to the *instance* method of the *singleton* class.

If you prefer a more dynamic approach, the *prototype* pattern might be better.

A *prototype* is an object that may be used to create copies or clones, in a similar way as instances are created from a class. However, cloning is much more dynamic, the more so if delegation is used instead of inheritance to share resources with some ancestor class. See section 5.4.

The advantage of using a *factory*, or any of the other creational patterns, is that exchanging product families becomes very easy. Just look for example at the Java Swing library. Swing is supported under Unix, Windows and MacOS. The key to multiple platform support is here, indeed, the use of factories to create widgets. Factories are also essential when using CORBA, simply because calling a constructor is of no use for creating objects on a remote site.

2.3.2 Structural patterns

Objects rarely live in isolation. In slide 2-15 a selection of the structural patterns treated in Gamma *et al.* (1994) is collected. Structural patterns indicate how classes and objects may be composed to form larger structures.

Structural patterns

2-15

- object and class composition

Pattern	Alias	Remarks
Composite	part/whole	collections of components
Flyweight	handle/body	extrinsic state, many objects
Adaptor	wrapper	resolve inconsistency between interfaces
Bridge	handle/body	relate abstraction to implementation
Decorator	handle/body	to introduce additional functionality
Facade	handle/body	provides unified interface
Proxy	handle/body	to defer ... remote, virtual, protection

Slide 2-15: Structural patterns

Imagine, for example, an application for interactive text processing. Now, the *Composite* pattern may be used to combine text, images and also compound components, that may itself consist of other components.

Closely related to the *Composite* pattern is the *Flyweight* pattern, which is needed when the number of components grows very large. In that case, the components themselves must for obvious reasons carry as little information as possible. Context or state information must then be passed as a parameter.

To give some more examples, suppose there exists a nice library for formatting text and images, but unfortunately with only a procedural interface. Then the *Adaptor* pattern may be used to provide a interface that suits you, by wrapping the original library.

The *Bridge* pattern is in some sense related to the *Factory*. In order to work with a platform-independent widget library, you need, as has been explained, a *factory* to hide the creation of widgets, but you also need to bridge a hierarchy of platform-dependent implementation classes to the more abstract platform-independent widget set.

When creating widgets to display text or images it may be very inconvenient to create a separate class, for example when adding scrolling functionality. The *Decorator* pattern allows you to insert additional functionality without subclassing.

Now think of a networked application, for example to be able to incorporate components that are delivered by a server. The library may provide a number of networking classes that deal with all possible communication protocols. To simplify access to these classes a *Facade* may be built, hiding the complexity of the original class interfaces.

Alternatively, remote components may be available through a *proxy*. The *Proxy* pattern describes how access may be regulated by an object that acts as a surrogate for the real object. Like *composites* and *decorators*, *proxies* may be used for recursive composition. However, *proxies* primarily regulate access, whereas *decorators* add responsibilities, and composites represent structure.

2.3.3 Behavioral patterns

Our final category of patterns, *behavioral patterns*, concern the construction of algorithms and the assignment of responsibilities to the objects that cooperate in achieving some goal.

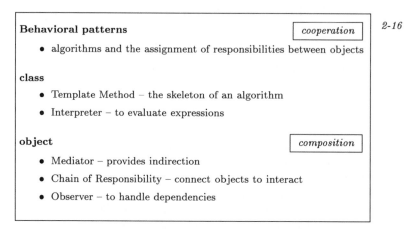

Slide 2-16: Behavioral patterns

A first distinction can be made between patterns that involve the composition of classes (using inheritance) and patterns that rely on object composition.

As an example of the *Template Method* pattern, think of a compiler class that offers methods for scanning and the creation of a parse tree. Each of these methods may be refined without affecting the structure of the compilation itself.

An *interpreter* allows for evaluating expressions, for example mathematical formula. Expressions may be organised in a hierarchy. new kinds of expressions can be inserted simply by filling in details of syntax and (semantic) evaluation.

Object composition, which employs the *handle/body* idiom and delegation, is employed in the *Mediator* pattern, the *Chain of Responsibility* pattern and the *Observer* pattern. The actual task, such as for example updating the display of information when the actual information has changed, is delegated to a more specialized object, to achieve a loose coupling between components. The difference between a *mediator* and *chain of responsibility* is primarily the complexity of co-ordinating the tasks. For example, changing the format of a single image component from one image type to another image type may be done simply by using an image converter (*mediator*), whereas exporting the complete document to a particular format such as HTML may involve delegating control to a specialized converter that itself needs access to the original components (*chain of responsibility*). We will discuss the *Observer* pattern in more detail later.

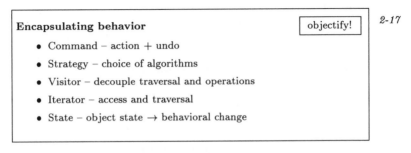

Slide 2-17: Encapsulating behavior

A common characteristic of the patterns listed in slide 2-17 is that functional behavior is realized as an object. Semantically, objects are more powerful than functions, since objects can carry a state. Hence, the imperative *objectify* pays off when we need functions that must know their invocation history.

As an example of the *Command* pattern, think of how you would realize insertion and deletion commands in an interactive editor, with undo! Turning these commands into an object in which the information necessary for undoing the command can be stored, for example having a snapshot of the state stored in a *Memento*, it suffices to stack the actual command objects. To undo a command, pop the stack and invoke the undo method.

The *Strategy* pattern may be used to hide the details of the various layout algorithms that are available. For example, you may use a straightforward algorithm that formats the text line by line, or you may use the much more advanced formatting algorithm of TEX, which involves the minimalization of penalties. These alternatives can be collected in a formatting *strategy* hierarchy, that hides the implementation details from the client by a common interface.

When doing the formatting, you may wish to separate the traversal of the component tree structure from the actual formatting operations. This may be accomplished by employing the *Visitor* pattern. In general it is recommended to abstract from the data structure and use a more abstract way, such as an *Iterator* or *Visitor* to access and traverse it.

The *State* pattern is similar to the *dynamic role switching* idiom that has been discussed in section 2.2.4. As an example, think of providing viewers for alternative document formats, such as VRML or PDF, in your application. Using the *State* pattern, it suffices to have a single viewer that changes itself according to the format of the document viewed.

The Observer pattern

The *Observer* pattern is a variant of the famous *Model-View-Control* (MVC) pattern, that governed the creation of the graphical user interface of the Smalltalk environment and many Smalltalk applications.

Observer   *2-18*

- one-to-many dependencies and notification

Consequences

- abstract coupling between subject and observer
- constraint propagation
- deals with unexpected updates

Slide 2-18: Observer pattern

The basic idea is simple, to decouple information management and the display of information. In other words, a distinction is made between the *model* or *subject*, that carries the information, and the *views* or *observers*, that present that information in some format. As a consequence, when a change occurs, the *viewers* or *observers* have only to be notified to update their presentation.

In effect, MVC or the *Observer* pattern can be regarded as a simple method for constraint propagation. An advantage is that unexpected updates can be easily dealt with.

The objects involved in realizing the *Observer* pattern are depicted in slide 2-19. The *subject* object must allow for *observers* to be attached and detached. Note that *observers* must also have a reference to the *subject*. In particular, concrete observers must know how to obtain information about the state of the *subject*, to be able to update their view. What the abstract *subject* and *observer* classes supply are the facilities for attachment and mechanisms for notification and updates.

In the implementation of the *Observer* pattern there are a number of problems and tradeoffs that must be considered. For example, do we allow one *observer* to be attached to more than one *subject*? Do we allow for alternative update semantics, for example observer-pull instead of subject-push? Do we provide facilities for specifying aspects of interest, so that updates only need to concern

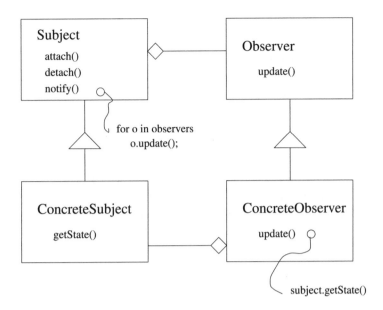

Slide 2-19: The Observer pattern

those aspects? And finally, how do we guarantee mutual consistency between subjects and observers when we do allow for alternative update semantics?

2.4   Event-driven computation

Event-driven computation underlies many applications, ranging from graphical user interfaces to systems for discrete event simulation and business process modeling. An important characteristic of event-driven computation is that control is relinquished to an environment that waits for events to occur. Handler function or handler objects are then invoked for an appropriate response.

In this section we will look at the *Reactor* pattern that explains the interaction between objects and the environment. We will also look at an event system, in which the event types are defined by the application programmer. In this application, events are used to maintain global consistency, similar to the *Observer* pattern.

2.4.1   The Reactor pattern

The *Reactor* pattern has been introduced in Schmidt (1995) as a general architecture for event-driven systems. It explains how to register handlers for particular event types, and how to activate handlers when events occur, even when events come from multiple sources, in a single-threaded environment. In other words, the *reactor* allows for the combination of multiple event-loops, without introducing additional threads.

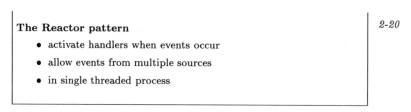

Slide 2-20: The Reactor pattern

The abstract layout of the software architecture needed to realize the pattern is depicted in slide 2-21. The *reactor* environment must allow for binding *handlers* to particular types of *events*. In addition, it must be able to receive events, and select a handler to which the event can be dispatched.

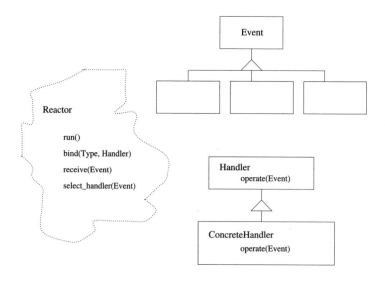

Slide 2-21: The Reactor pattern – structure

Events may be organized in a hierarchy. There are two possible choices here. Either the topmost event class has a fat interface, containing all the methods that an event may ever need to support, or the topmost event class can be lean, so that additional methods need to be added by the subclasses of event. The first solution is chosen for *hush*, because in C++ it is not possible to load new classes dynamically. The latter solution is the way Java does it. In Java new event types can be added at the *reactor* level without recompiling the system. In the Java AWT and Swing libraries, handlers are called *Listeners*.

Concrete handlers, derived from an abstract handler, must provide a method, such as **operate(Event)** that can be called by the *reactor* when the handler is selected after receiving an event.

The interaction between the application, its handlers, the *reactor* and the

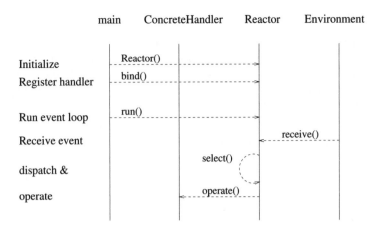

Slide 2-22: The Reactor Pattern - interaction

environment from which the events originate is depicted in slide 2-22. First, the *reactor* must be initialized, then one or more handlers can be registered, providing a binding for particular types of events. The *reactor* must then start to execute its eventloop. When it receives an event from the environment, it selects a handler and dispatches the event to that handler, by calling `operate(Event)`.

Consequences Modularity is one of the advantages of an event-driven software architecture. Handlers can be composed easily, since their invocation is controlled by the *reactor*. Another advantage is the decoupling of application-independent mechanisms from application-specific policies. In other words, handler objects need not be aware of how events are dispatched. This is the responsibility of the system or framework.

The fact that control is handed over to the environment has, however, also some disadvantages. First of all, as experience with student assignments shows, it is difficult to learn in the beginning. But even when mastered, applications may be hard to debug, since it is not always clear why a particular handler was invoked, and because it may be difficult to repeat the computation preceding the fault.

Applicability Some variant of the *reactor* pattern is used in Unix (X) Windows, (MS) Windows, and also GUI libraries such as Interviews, ET++ and *hush*. Another example is the Orbacus object request broker, that supports a *reactor* mode for server objects, which allows for receiving messages from multiple sources in a single thread. The Orbacus broker, however, also allows for multi-threaded servers.

2.4.2   Abstract event systems

To conclude this chapter about idioms and patterns, we will look at a somewhat more detailed example employing (user-defined) events to characterize and control the interaction between the objects. The example is taken from Henderson (1993). The *abstract system*, or repertoire of statements indicating the functionality of our application is depicted in slide 2-23.

```
th = new centigrade();
th = new fahrenheit();
th.set(f);
f = th.get();


For thermometer th, th1; float f;
```

2-23

Slide 2-23: Abstract system – thermometers

First, we will define the functional behavior of the system (in this case a collection of thermometers that record and display temperature values, as characterized above). Then we will introduce the user interface classes, respectively to update the temperature value of a thermometer and to display its value. After that we define a concrete event class (derived from an abstract event class) for each of the possible kinds of interactions that may occur. Then, after installing the actual objects comprising the system, we will define the dependencies between (actual) events, so that we can guarantee that interactions with the user will not result in an inconsistent state.

Functional behavior A thermometer must provide the means to store a temperature value and allow for the changing and retrieving of this value. The temperature values are assumed to be stored in degrees Kelvin.

```
class thermometer {                                        thermometer

protected thermometer( float v ) {  temp = v; }

public void set(float v) { temp = v; }
public float get() { return temp; }

protected float temp;
};
```

Since only derived classes can use the protected constructor, no direct instances of *thermometer* exist, so the class is abstract.

We will distinguish between two kinds of thermometers, measuring temperatures respectively in centigrade and fahrenheit.

```
class centigrade extends thermometer {                     centigrade
```

```
public centigrade() {  super(0);  }
public void set(float v) { temp = v + 273; }
public float get() { return temp - 273; }
};
```

The class *centigrade* redefines the methods *get* and *set* according to the measurement in centigrade, and in a similar way we may define the class *fahrenheit*.

```
class fahrenheit extends thermometer {
```
| fahrenheit |

```
public fahrenheit() { super(0); }
public void set(float v) { temp = (v - 32) * 5/9 + 273; }
public float get() { return temp * 9/5 + 32 - 273; }
};
```

Both the thermometer realization classes take care of performing the conversions necessary to store and retrieve the absolute temperature value.

User interface We will define two simple interface classes, of which we omit the implementation details. First, we define the interface of the *displayer* class, needed to *put* values to the screen.

```
class displayer extends window {
```
| displayer |

```
public displayer() { ... }
public void put(String s) { ... }
public void put(float f) { ... }
};
```

And secondly, we define a *prompter* class, which defines (in an abstract way) how we may get a value from the user (or some other component of the system).

```
class prompter extends window {
```
| prompter |

```
public prompter(String text) { ... }
public float get() { ... }
public String gets() { ... }
};
```

Together, the classes *displayer* and *prompter* define a rudimentary interface which is sufficient to take care of many of the interactions between the user and the system.

Events To define the interactions with the user (and their possible consequences) we will employ *events*, that is instances of realizations of the abstract event class, defined below.

```
abstract class event {                                          event
pubic void dependent(event e) { ... }
pubic void process() { ... }
public void operator(); // abstract method

private event[] dep;
};
```

Since a simple event (for example, the modification of a value) may result in a series of events (needed to keep the system in a consistent state), an event object maintains a set of dependent events, which may be activated using the *process* method. Further, each class derived from *event* is assumed to define the application operator, that is the actual actions resulting from activating the event.

The first realization of the abstract event class is the *update* event class, which corresponds to retrieving a new temperature value from the user.

```
class update extends event {                                    update

public update(thermometer th, prompter p) {
        _th =th;   _p = p;
        }
void operator()() {
        _th.set( _p.get() );
        process();
        }

thermometer _th;
prompter _p;
};
```

An update involves a thermometer and a prompter, which are stored when creating the update event object. Activating an update event instance results in retrieving a value from the prompter, setting the thermometer to this value and activating the dependent events.

In a similar way, we define the second realization of the abstract event class, the *show* event class, which corresponds to displaying the value of a thermometer.

```
class show extends event {                                      show

public show(thermometer th, displayer d) {
        _th = th;   _d = d;
        }
public void operator() {
        _d.put( _th.get() );
        process();
        }
```

```
thermometer _th;
displayer _d;
};
```

Activating a show event instance results in retrieving a value from the thermometer, putting that value on display and activating the events associated with this event.

The installation The next step we must take is to install the application, that is to create the objects comprising the functional behavior of the system, the user interface objects and (finally) the various event objects.

```
thermometer c = new centigrade();
thermometer f = new fahrenheit();

displayer cd = new displayer("centigrade");
displayer fd = new displayer("fahrenheit");

prompter cp = new prompter("enter centigrade value");
prompter fp = new prompter("enter fahrenheit value");

show sc = new show(c,cd);
show sf = new show(f,fd);

update uc = new update(c,cp);
update uf = new update(f,fp);
```

Having created the objects, we are almost done. The most important and perhaps difficult part is to define the appropriate dependencies between the respective event objects.

```
uc.dependent(sc);
uc.dependent(sf);
uf.dependent(sc);
uf.dependent(sf);
```

As shown above, we declare the event of showing the value of the centigrade thermometer (and also of the fahrenheit thermometer) to be dependent upon the event of updating the value of the centigrade thermometer. And we repeat this declaration for the event of updating the value of the fahrenheit thermometer.

We may now allow the user the choice between updating the centigrade or fahrenheit thermometer temperature value, for example by inserting these events in a menu, as indicated below

```
menu.insert(uc);
menu.insert(uf);
```

The reader is urged to do some mental processing to check that updating the value of one thermometer actually results in changing the value displayed for the other thermometer as well.

Discussion Organizing interactions with the user (and the other components of the system as well) by means of events provides a powerful way in which to control the consequences of one particular (kind of) interaction. The advantage of such an approach is that the repertoire of possible interactions can easily be extended or modified without affecting the other parts of the system (the parts realizing the functional behavior of the system and the particularities of the user interface). From the perspective of design, it is a good alternative for defining *behavioral compositions* (and its corresponding protocol of interaction) in a more or less formal way. See also section 10.5.

Summary

This chapter has introduced the idioms and patterns of object-oriented programming. We looked at a polymorphism in Java and C++, and discussed assertions in C++ and canonical class idioms.

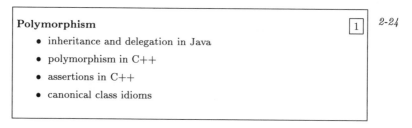

Slide 2-24: Section 2.1: Polymorphism

In section 2, we proceeded with a fairly detailed discussion of the idioms in *hush*, which illustrate basic solutions to problems occurring in the development of frameworks.

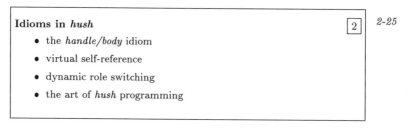

Slide 2-25: Section 2.2: Idioms in *hush*

Further, we looked at how these idioms are related to patterns that provide a solution on the level of design.

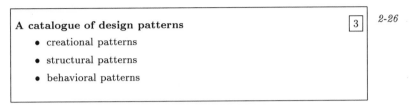

Slide 2-26: Section 2.3: A catalogue of design patterns

Following the treatment of idioms and patterns in *hush*, section 3 gave an overview of the catalogue of design patterns presented in Gamma *et al.* (1994). The catalogue includes *creational, structural* and *behavioral* patterns.

Slide 2-27: Section 2.4: Event-driven computation

In section 4, we discussed the *reactor* pattern, which provides a generalization of event-driven software architectures. We concluded with looking at an example of a simple temperature-monitoring system, implemented using events to maintain internal consistency.

Questions

1. How would you explain the *letter/envelope* idiom?

2. Characterize the notion of *polymorphism*. Give some examples.

3. What is a canonical class? Characterize its ingredients and give an example.

4. Give a brief description of the *handle/body* idiom, *virtual self-reference*, and *dynamic role switching*.

5. What kinds of patterns can you distinguish? Why do you consider patterns to be of relevance?

6. Give a detailed description of the *Factory* pattern and also of the *Observer* pattern.

7. Describe the *Reactor* pattern. Why is it useful?

8. Give an example of a system based on event-driven computation.

Further reading

For an introduction to Java, there is ample choice. An excellent online tutorial can be found on http://java.sun.com/docs/books/tutorial. As textbooks on C++ I recommend Lippman (1991), and for the more advanced reader Stroustrup (1998). For an extensive introduction to STL, read Schildt (1999). Coplien (1992) is the original introduction to idioms in C++. The by now classical book for patterns is Gamma *et al.* (1994). Well worth reading are the many articles in the POPL proceedings, Coplien and Schmidt (1995), Vlissides *et al.* (1996) and Martin *et al.* (1997).

3

Software engineering perspectives

In the previous chapter we looked at idioms and patterns that resulted from object-oriented software development. In this chapter we will focus on the software engineering of object-oriented systems and issues of design in particular, including the identification of objects and the specification of contractual obligations.

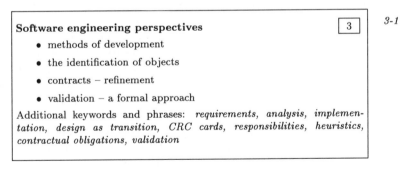

Slide 3-1: Software engineering perspectives

First we will explore what methods are available to guide us in the development of object-oriented systems. Then we will look more closely at the heuristics of actual design. After establishing what is involved in specifying contractual obligations, we will discuss what is needed for a more formal approach to object-oriented development.

3.1   Development methods

Object-oriented software development is a relatively new technology. Consequently, ideas with respect to methodologies supporting an object-oriented approach are still in flux. Nevertheless, a plethora of methods and tools does exist supporting object-oriented analysis and design. See slide 3-2.

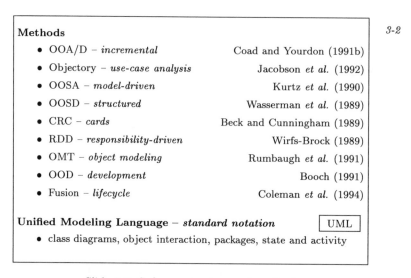

Methods   *3-2*

- OOA/D – *incremental*   Coad and Yourdon (1991b)
- Objectory – *use-case analysis*   Jacobson *et al.* (1992)
- OOSA – *model-driven*   Kurtz *et al.* (1990)
- OOSD – *structured*   Wasserman *et al.* (1989)
- CRC – *cards*   Beck and Cunningham (1989)
- RDD – *responsibility-driven*   Wirfs-Brock (1989)
- OMT – *object modeling*   Rumbaugh *et al.* (1991)
- OOD – *development*   Booch (1991)
- Fusion – *lifecycle*   Coleman *et al.* (1994)

Unified Modeling Language – *standard notation*   [UML]
- class diagrams, object interaction, packages, state and activity

Slide 3-2: Software development methods

Some of these methods (and corresponding tools) directly stem from a more conventional (read *structured*) approach to software development. Others are more radical and propose new tools to support the decomposition principles underlying object-oriented technology. Naturally, those who wish to make a gradual shift from conventional technology to adopting an object-oriented approach may benefit from methods that adapt familiar techniques to the new concepts.

In this section we will look at a variety of existing methods and the tools they offer. We do not discuss the tools and diagram techniques used in any detail. However, we will discuss the Fusion method in somewhat more detail. Fusion is a strongly systematic approach to object-oriented software development that integrates various concepts and modeling techniques from the other methods, notably OMT, Booch OOD, Objectory and CRC. We will discuss the process view underlying Fusion and sketch the models it supports in relation to the other methods. For the reader this section may supply an overview and references needed for a more detailed study of a particular method or tool.

A recent development is the Unified Modeling Language (UML), which has been approved as a standard in 1998. UML brings together the models and notations featured by the various methods. Jim Rumbaugh, Grady Booch and Ivar Jacobson, all leading experts in object-oriented development, joined forces to achieve this.

The importance of such a standardization can hardly be overemphasized. However, it must be noted that UML does not provide a method, in the sense of delineating the steps that must be taken in the development of a system. UML itself may be regarded as a toolbox, providing notations and modeling techniques that may be deployed when needed. A brief overview of UML is given in F. An excellent introduction to UML, including advice how to apply it in actual projects may be found in Fowler (1997b).

Structured methods Initially, structured methods (which were developed at the beginning of the 1970s) were primarily concerned with modeling processes in a modular way. Based on software engineering principles such as *module coupling* and *cohesion*, tools were developed to represent the structure of a design (within what we have previously called the procedural or modular paradigm); see, for example, Yourdon and Constantine (1979). Apart from diagrams to describe the modular architecture of a system (such as *structure charts* and *process specifications*), structured methods also employ *data flow diagrams* to depict processes and the flow of data between them, and *hierarchy diagrams* to model the structure of the data involved. See slide 3-3.

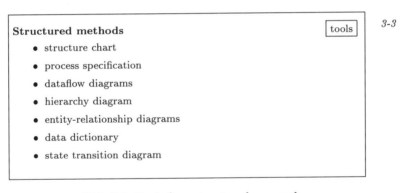

Slide 3-3: Tools for a structured approach

Later, structured methods were extended to encompass analysis, and the focus shifted to modeling the data by means of *entity-relationship diagrams* and *data dictionaries*. Also, *state transition diagrams* were employed to represent the behavioral aspects of a system.

As observed in Fichman and Kemerer (1992), in the late 1970s and early 1980s, planning and modeling of data began to take on a more central role in system development, culminating in data oriented methodologies, such as information engineering (which may be regarded as precursors to object-oriented methods). Information engineering, however, is primarily concerned with analysis and strategic planning. In addition to the modeling techniques mentioned, tools were developed to model the information needs of an enterprise and to perform risk analysis. Also, extensions to the *data dictionary* were proposed in order to have an integrated repository, serving all phases of the development. Currently, repository-based techniques are again of interest since, in combination with modern hypermedia technology, they may serve as the organizational basis for reuse.

3.1.1   Perspectives of modeling

Understanding a problem domain may be quite demanding. Understanding is even more difficult when the description of the domain is cast in some representation pertaining to the solution domain. An object-oriented approach is said to require less translation from the problem domain to the (software) solution domain, thus making understanding easier. Many proponents of an object-oriented approach, however, seem to be overly optimistic in their conception of the modeling task. From an epistemological point of view, modeling may be regarded as being essentially colored by the mechanisms that are available to express the model. Hence, rather than opposing the functional and object-oriented approach by claiming that an object-oriented approach aims at *modeling reality*, I would prefer to characterize the distinction in terms of (modeling from) a different vernacular, a different perspective due to different modeling mechanisms. In other words, a model is meant to capture some salient aspects of a system or problem domain. Dependent on what features are considered as most important, different means will be chosen to construct a model.

Even within the confines of an object-oriented approach, there appear to be radically different perspectives of the modeling required in the various phases of the software life-cycle.

Modeling reality – *vernacular*   *3-4*

- requirements – *use cases*

- analysis – *domain concepts*

- design – *system architecture*

- implementation – *language support*

Design model – *system oriented*

- provides a justification of the architecture

Slide 3-4: Perspectives of modeling

An important contribution of Jacobson *et al.* (1992) is the notion of *use cases* that describe the situations in which a user actually interacts with the system. Such a (use case) model is an important constituent of the *requirements* document, since it precisely describes what the system is intended for. For the purpose of analysis, it may be helpful to develop a more encompassing (conceptual) model of the problem domain. The advantage of such an approach is that the actual system may later easily be extended due to the generality of the underlying analysis model.

In contrast to the model used in analysis, both the design model and the implementation model are more *solution oriented* than *domain oriented*. The *implementation* model is clearly dependent on the available language support. Within a traditional life-cycle, the *design* model may be seen as a transition from analysis to implementation. The notion of *objects* may act as a unifying factor, relating the concepts described in the analysis document to the components around which the design model is built. However, as we have noted, object-oriented development does not necessarily follow the course of a traditional software life-cycle. Alternatively, we may characterize the function of the design document as a *justification* of the choices made in deciding on the final architecture of the system. This remark holds insofar as an object-oriented approach is adopted for both design and implementation. However, see Henderson-Sellers and Edwards (1990) for a variety of combinations of structured, functional and object-oriented techniques.

Dimensions of modeling When restricting ourselves to *design models*, we may again distinguish between different modeling perspectives or, which is perhaps more adequate in this context, *dimensions of modeling*.

In Rumbaugh *et al.* (1991), it is proposed to use three complementary models for describing the architecture and functionality of a system. See slide 3-5.

Dimensions of modeling – *OMT*   *3-5*

- object model – *decomposition into objects*

- dynamic model – *intra-object state changes*

- functional model – *object interaction* (data-flow)

Model of control

- procedure-driven, event-driven, concurrent

Slide 3-5: The OMT method

The OMT method distinguishes between an *object model*, for describing the (static) structure of object classes and their relations, a *dynamic model*, that describes for each object class the state changes resulting from performing operations, and a *functional model*, that describes the interaction between objects in terms of a *data-flow* graph.

An important contribution of Rumbaugh *et al.* (1991) is that it identifies a number of commonly used *control models*, including *procedure-driven* control, *event-driven* control and *concurrent* control. The choice for a particular control model may deeply affect the design of the system.

The OMT approach may be called a *hybrid method* since it employs non object-oriented techniques for describing intra-object dynamics, namely state-charts, and a functional approach involving data-flow diagrams, for describing inter-object communication.

Coherent models The OMT *object model*, however, only captures the static structure of the system. To model the dynamic and functional aspects, the object model is augmented with a *dynamic model*, which is given by state diagrams, and a *functional model*, which is handled by data flow diagrams. From a formal point of view this solution is rather unsatisfactory since, as argued in Hayes and Coleman (1991), it is hard to establish the consistency of the combined model, consisting of an object, dynamic and functional model.

Model criteria *– formal approach*   *3-6*

- *unambiguous* – single meaning

- *abstract* – no unnecessary detail

- *consistent* – absence of conflict

Slide 3-6: Coherent models – criteria

Consistency checking, or at least the possibility to do so, is important to increase our belief in the reliability (and reusability) of a model. To be able to determine whether a model is consistent, the model should be phrased in an unambiguous way, that is, in a notation with a clear and precise meaning. See slide 3-6. Also, to make the task of consistency checking manageable, a model should be as abstract as possible, by leaving out all irrelevant details. To establish the consistency of the combined model, covering structural, functional and dynamic aspects, the interaction between the various models must be clearly defined.

3.1.2   Requirements engineering – *Fusion*

The Fusion method is presented in Coleman *et al.* (1994) as a second generation object-oriented method. The phrase *second generation* is meant to indicate that the method transcends and incorporates the ideas and techniques employed in the early object-oriented methods.

Above all, the Fusion method focuses on a strongly systematic approach to object-oriented software development, with an emphasis on the *process* of development and the validation of the consistency between the models delivered in the various phases of a project.

The software life-cycle model underlying Fusion is the traditional waterfall model, consisting of the subsequent phases of analysis, design and implementation. Each phase results in a number of models describing particular aspects of the system. See slide 3-7. A *data dictionary* is to be kept as a means to unify the terminology employed in the various phases.

The models produced as the result of analysis, design and implementation serve to document the decisions made during the development. Each of the phases covers different aspects of the system. Analysis serves to document the system requirements from a user perspective. The Fusion method describes how

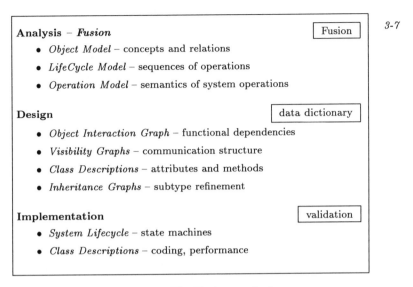

Slide 3-7: The Fusion method

to construct an *Object Model* that captures the basic concepts of the application domain. These concepts are represented as entities or objects and are connected by relations, similar to *entity-relationship* diagrams employed in semantic modeling. Analysis also results in an *Operation Model*, describing the semantics of the operations that may be performed by a user by means of pre- and post-conditions, in a formal manner. In addition, Fusion defines a *Lifecycle Model* that describes, by means of regular expressions, which sequences of operations are allowed.

Design may be considered as the transition between analysis and implementation. During design, decisions are made with respect to the realization of the system operations identified during analysis. Design according to the Fusion method results in an *Object Interaction Graph*, that for each system operation describes which objects are involved and which methods are invoked. Fusion also allows one to label the arrows representing method calls in the interaction diagram with sequencing information. In addition, design involves the construction of *Visibility Graphs*, indicating the attribute and method interface for each object, *Class Descriptions*, defining the attributes and methods of objects, and *Inheritance Graphs*, specifying the subtype refinement relation between classes.

Implementation is considered in the Fusion method as a phase in which to work out the details of the decisions taken during analysis and design. It results in a *System Lifecycle* description for each object identified in the *Object Model*, in the form of a finite state machine, and precise *Class Descriptions*, in the form of (preferably) efficient code.

Validation An important aspect of the Fusion method is the validation of the completeness and consistency of the collection of models. Completeness, obviously, is a relative matter and can only be established with respect to explicitly stated user requirements. However, the models developed in a particular phase impose additional requirements upon the efforts engaged in the later phases and in the end maintenance. Consistency involves verifying whether the various models are not contradictory. For both development and validation, the data dictionary plays an important role, as a common point of reference.

3.1.3   Methods for analysis and design – a comparative study

In Fichman and Kemerer (1992) a comparative review of a selected number of object-oriented analysis and design methods is given. Criteria for selection were the availability of documentation and acceptance in the object-oriented community, measured in terms of refereed articles.

Paraphrasing Fichman and Kemerer (1992) again: *As with traditional analysis, the primary goal of object-oriented analysis is the development of an accurate and complete description of the problem domain.*

The three analysis models described in Fichman and Kemerer (1992) share a number of diagram techniques with both structured methods and methods for object-oriented design. However, the method proposed in Shlaer and Mellor (1988) in particular reflects the domain-oriented focus of analysis.

A similar focus on domain requirements and analysis may be found in the Objectory method. See slide 3-8. Objectory is one of the methods that has inspired Fusion, in particular because it presents a systematic approach to the process of software development. The Objectory method centers around *use case* analysis. Use case analysis involves a precise description of the interaction between the user of a system and the components representing domain-specific functionality. The Objectory method gives precise guidelines on how to proceed from the identification of *use cases*, which include user interface aspects, to their realization in the subsequent phases of design and implementation. Objects are called blocks in Objectory. Use case analysis corresponds in a loose way with the identification of system operations in Fusion.

There is a close correspondence between the OMT object model and the analysis object model of Fusion. Both OMT and Fusion employ extended entity-relationship diagrams. Also, the dynamic model of OMT reoccurs in the Fusion method, albeit in a later phase. The functional model of OMT, which has the form of a dataflow diagram, is generally considered to be inappropriate for object-oriented analysis. Instead, Fusion employs a model in which the semantics of system operations are captured by means of formal pre- and post-conditions. In Coleman *et al.* (1994), OMT is characterized as a very loose method, giving few rules for discovering inconsistencies between the various models and lacking a clear view with respect to the process of development. OMT is strongly focused on analysis, giving nothing but heuristics to implement the models that result from analysis. However, what is called the *light-weight Fusion method* almost coincides with OMT.

A lack of detailed guidelines for the process of software development is also characteristic of the Booch OOD method. Booch offers a wealth of descriptive

---

3-8

Objectory – *systematic process*

- requirements – *use cases, domain object model, user interface*
- analysis – *subsystems*
- design, implementation – *block model, interaction diagrams*

OMT – *few rules for inconsistencies*

- analysis – *object model, dynamic model, functional model*
- design, implementation – *heuristics to implement analysis models*

Booch – *descriptive*

- diagrams – *class, object, timing, state, module, process*

CRC – *exploratory*

- analysis, design – *class, responsibilities, collaborators*

Formal methods

- operations – *pre- and post-conditions*

Slide 3-8: Comparison of methods (1)

diagrams, giving detailed information on the various aspects of a system, but offers merely heuristics for the actual process of development.

The CRC method must be regarded primarily as a means to explore the interaction between the various objects of a domain. It is powerful in generating ideas, but offers poor support for documenting the decisions with respect to the objects and how they interact.

Formal methods have been another important source of inspiration for the Fusion method. The description of system operations during analysis employs a characterization of the functionality of operations that is directly related to the specification of operations in model-based specification methods such as VDM and Z. See section 10.5.

The Fusion method may be regarded as being composed of elements of the methods mentioned above. It shares its object model with OMT, its approach to the characterization of system operations with formal methods, its focus on object interaction with CRC and its explicit description of classes and their relations with Booch. See slide 3-9.

In comparison with these methods, however, it provides a much more systematic approach to the process of development and, moreover, is explicitly concerned with issues of validation and consistency between models. In addition, Coleman *et al.* (1994) claim to provide explicit semantics for their various models, whereas the other methods fail to do so. However, it must be remarked that the Fusion method remains somewhat obscure about the nature of system operations. System operations are characterized as *asynchronous*. Yet, if they are to be taken as

Comparison – *as a systematic approach*				Fusion	3-9
	Objectory	OMT	Booch	CRC	Fusion
development	+	±	-	⊕	+
maintenance	+	±	+	-	+
structure	±	±	+	+	+
management	+	±	±	-	+
tool support	±	±	±	-	+

Slide 3-9: Comparison of methods (2)

methods, such operations may return a result, which is quite hard to reconcile with their asynchronous nature. The claim that the models have a precise semantics, which is essential for tool support, must be substantiated by providing an explicit semantics in a formal manner!

With regard to the process of development, both Objectory and Fusion provide precise guidelines. The CRC method may be valuable as an additional exploratory device. For maintenance, the extent to which a method enforces the documentation of design decisions is of utmost importance. Both the Objectory and Booch method satisfys this criterion, as does the Fusion method. OMT is lacking in this respect, and CRC is clearly inadequate.

Whether a method leads to a *good* object-oriented design of the system architecture, depends to a large extent upon the ability and experience of the development team. Apart from Fusion, both the Booch method and CRC may be characterized as purely object-oriented, whereas Objectory and OMT are considered to be impure.

A strongly systematic approach to the process of development is important in particular from the point of view of project management. Project management support entails a precise definition of the deliverables associated with each phase, as well as an indication of the timing of their deliverance and validation. Both the OMT method and Booch are lacking in this respect, since they primarily provide techniques to develop descriptive models. Clearly, CRC lacks any support for project management.

Tool support is dependent on the existence of a well-defined semantics for the models employed. For both Objectory and OMT commercial tools are available, despite their loosely specified semantics. The Fusion diagramming techniques are also supported. For CRC, tool support is considered to be useless. The success of the method depends upon flexibility, the ease with which new ideas can be tried, a flexibility which even hypertext cannot offer, according to its authors.

3.2   Identifying objects

Object-oriented design aims at describing a system in terms of objects (as the primary components) and the interaction between them. Motivated by the wish to arrive at stable abstractions, object-oriented design is often characterized as *modeling reality*, that is the application domain. However, many applications require, at least partly, a *system-oriented* view towards design, since they involve system artifacts for which there exist no clearly identifiable counterparts in the application domain. As an example, think of a window-based system. Many of the items (widgets) introduced in such a system belong to an artificial reality, which at best is only vaguely analogous with reality as we normally understand it.

Irrespective of whether the design is intended as a preliminary study before the implementation or as a *post hoc* justification of the actual system, the most important and difficult part of design is the *identification of objects* and the characterization of their role in the system and interaction with other objects.

As observed in McGregor and Sykes (1992), object-oriented design is best seen as *class oriented*, that is directed towards the *static* description of (classes of) objects, rather than a description of the dynamic interaction between actual objects. In section 5.4, we will discuss *class-less* languages which are well suited for exploratory programming. However, from the perspective of design, we are more interested in a (static) abstract specification of the components that constitute the system.

Object-oriented design – *decomposition into objects*   *3-10*

  • application/system/class oriented

Identifying objects – *responsibilities*

  • data/procedure oriented

Layers of abstraction

  • components, subsystems, frameworks

Slide 3-10: Object-oriented design

In comparison with a functional approach, object-oriented design is clearly *data oriented*. However, although a data-oriented approach may provide a first guideline in developing the system, the primary concern in object-oriented design should be the *responsibilities* of an object rather than how it acts as a *data manager*, so to speak.

For larger systems, the complexity of the design may necessitate the introduction of additional layers of abstraction. Apart from objects, which must be regarded as the basic components of a system, we may need to isolate subsystems, consisting of a number of related object classes. When we have developed a subsystem that can be used in a variety of contexts, such a subsystem may be used as a *framework*. A framework is generally not only a collection of classes but must also be seen as an approach or method in its own way, since it usually imposes additional constraints on the development. For example, most development environments for window-based applications provide a framework consisting of a number of predefined classes and functions, and guidelines or recipes that prescribe how to use or adapt these classes and functions. Also, most frameworks impose a specific control model, such as the *event-driven* control model imposed by window programming environments.

3.2.1 Modeling heuristics

Following Booch (1986), we may characterize objects as 'crisp' *entities* that *suffer* and *require* actions. From the perspective of system development, *objects* must primarily be regarded as *computational entities*, embodying the means by which we may express a computation. Modeling a particular problem domain, then, means defining abstractions in terms of *objects*, capturing the functional characteristics of that domain. The question is, how do we arrive at such a model?

Objects – *crisp entities*   *3-11*

  • *object* = an entity that *suffers* and *requires* actions

The method:

  • [1] Identify the objects and their attributes
  • [2] Identify operations suffered and required
  • [3, 4] Establish visibility/interface

Slide 3-11: The Booch method

In Booch (1986), a straightforward method of object oriented development is proposed, which consists of the successive identification of objects and their attributes, followed by a precise characterization of the interobject visibility relations. In Booch (1991), a shift of emphasis has occurred towards determining the semantics of an individual object and the interaction between collections of objects.

Heuristics   *3-12*

  • *model of reality* – balance *nouns* (objects) and *verbs* (operations)

Associations

  • *directed action* – drives, instructs
  • *communication* – talks-to, tells, instructs
  • *ownership* – has, part-of
  • *resemblance* – like, is-a
  • *others* – works-for, married-to

Slide 3-12: Heuristics for modeling

As a heuristic to arrive at the proper abstractions of the problem domain (in terms of object classes), Booch (1986) proposes scanning the requirements document for *nouns, verbs* and *adjectives*, and using these as initial suggestions for respectively *objects*, and *operations* and *attributes* belonging to objects (see slide 3-12). This technique has been adopted and augmented by a number of other authors, among which Wirfs-Brock *et al.* (1990) and Rumbaugh *et al.* (1991). For example, Wirfs-Brock *et al.* (1990) illustrate the technique in fine detail in several examples, including the design of an automated teller machine and a document processing system.

In addition to the interpretation of nouns as possible objects, verbs as possible operations on objects, and adjectives as possible attributes of objects, Rumbaugh *et al.* (1991) suggest this technique to determine other relations and associations between object classes as well. For instance, a model of control and object inter-action may be suggested by phrases indicating directed action or communication. Similarly, structural issues, such as whether an object owns another object or whether inheritance should be used, may be decided on the basis of resemblance or subordination relations.

Example – ATM (1) The example of an automated teller machine discussed in Wirfs-Brock *et al.* (1990) nicely illustrates a number of the notions that we have thus far looked at only in a very abstract way. A *teller* machine is a device, presumably familiar to everyone, that allows you to get money from your account at any time of the day. Obviously, there are a number of constraints that such a machine must satisfy. For instance, other people should not be allowed to withdraw money from your account. Another reasonable constraint is that a user cannot overdraw more than a designated amount of money. Moreover, each transaction must be correctly reflected by the state of the user's account.

Candidate classes   ATM   *3-13*

- *account* – represents the customer's account in the banks database
- *atm* – performs financial services for a customer
- *cardreader* – reads and validates a customer's bankcard
- *cashdispenser* – gives cash to the customer
- *screen* – presents text and visual information
- *keypad* – the keys a customer can press
- *pin* – the authorization code
- *transaction* – performs financial services and updates the database

---

Slide 3-13: The ATM example (1)

An initial decomposition into objects based on these requirements is shown in slide 3-13. In Wirfs-Brock *et al.* (1990), a fully detailed account is given of how one may arrive at such a decomposition by carefully reading (and re-reading) the requirements document. What we are interested in here, however, is how we may establish that we have not overlooked anything when proposing a design, and how we may verify that our design correctly reflects the requirements.

This particular example nicely illustrates the need for an analysis of the *use cases*. To develop a proper interface, we must precisely know what a user is expected to do (for instance, insert a bank card, key in a PIN code) and how the system must respond (what messages must be displayed, how to react to a wrong PIN code, etc.). Another decision that must be made is when the account will be changed as the result of a transaction. Also, we must decide what to do when a user overdraws.

A very important issue that we will look at in more detail in the next sections is how the collection of objects suggested above will interact. What means do we have to describe the cooperation between the objects, and how do we show that the proposed system meets all the requirements listed above? Moreover, can we verify that the system satisfies all the constraints mentioned in the requirements document?

Validation However, before examining these questions and trying out different scenarios, we may as well try to eliminate the spurious classes that came up in our initial attempt. In Rumbaugh *et al.* (1991), a number of reasons are summarized that may be grounds on which to reject a candidate class. See slide 3-14.

Eliminating spurious classes   *3-14*

  - *vague* – system, security-provision, record-keeping
  - *attribute* – account-data, receipt, cash
  - *redundant* – user
  - *irrelevant* – cost
  - *implementation* – transaction-log, access, communication

Good classes

  - our candidate classes

Slide 3-14: Eliminating spurious classes

For example, the notion underlying the candidate class may be too *vague* to be represented by a class, such as the notion of *system* or *record-keeping*. Another reason for rejecting a suggested class may be that the notion represents not so much a class, but rather a possible attribute of a class. Further, a proposed class may either be *redundant*, for example the class *user*, or simply *irrelevant*, as is the class *cost*. And finally, a class may be too *implementation* oriented, such as the class *transaction-log* or classes that represent the actual communication or access to the account.

Looking back, our choice of candidate classes seems to have been quite fortunate, but generally this will not be the case, and we may use the checklist above to prune the list of candidate classes.

An interesting architectural issue is, how may we provide for future extensions of the system? How easily can we reuse the design and the code for a system supporting different kinds of accounts, or different input or output devices? And how can we establish that the objects, as identified, interact as desired?

3.2.2 Assigning responsibilities

Design is to a large extent a matter of creative thinking. Heuristics such as performing a linguistic scan on the requirements document for finding objects (nouns), methods (verbs) and attributes (adjectives) may be helpful, but will hopelessly fail when not applied with good taste and judgement. Not surprisingly, one of the classical techniques of creative writing, namely the *shoe-box method*, has reappeared in the guise of an object-oriented development method. The shoe-box method consists of writing fragments and ideas on note cards and storing them in a (shoe) box, so that they may later be retrieved and manipulated to find a suitable ordering for the presentation of the material. To find a proper decomposition into objects, the method creates for each potential (object) class a so-called CRC card, which lists the *Class* name, the *Responsibilities* and the possible *Collaborators* of the proposed class. In a number of iterations, a collection of cards will result that more or less reflects the structure of the intended system.

According to the authors (see Beck and Cunningham, 1989), the method effectively supports the early stages of design, especially when working in small groups. An intrinsic part of the method consists of what the authors call *dynamic simulation*. To test whether a given collection of cards adequately characterizes the functionality of the intended system, the cards may be used to simulate the behavior of the system. When working in a group, the cards may be distributed among the members of the group, who participate in the simulation game according to their cards. See slide 3-15.

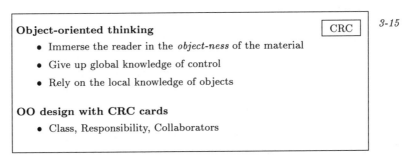

Slide 3-15: The CRC method

A number of authors have adopted this method, or developed a very similar method, for identifying objects and characterizing their functionality in an abstract way. It is doubtful, however, whether the method has any significance beyond the early stages of analysis and design. Without any more formal means to verify whether the responsibilities listed adequately characterize the intended functionality of the system, the method amounts to not much more than brainstorming. Clearly, the method needs to be complemented by more formal means to establish whether the (implicit) protocols of interaction between the objects satisfy the behavioral requirements of the system.

Nevertheless, the elegant simplicity of the method is appealing, and the card format lends itself to easy incorporation in an on-line documentation system. Moreover, since the method imposes no strict order, and has relatively little overhead, it is indeed a good way to get an initial idea of what objects the system will comprise.

Example – ATM (2) Actually, the ATM example is an interesting example for comparing the various approaches, since it is used by many authors to illustrate their methods. In Wirfs-Brock *et al.* (1990) the example is used for spelling out all the steps that must be taken. In Rumbaugh *et al.* (1991) it is extensively described to illustrate the various modeling techniques employed by the method. And in Beck and Cunningham (1989) the CRC cards method is illustrated by sketching the design of an automated teller machine.

The approaches presented in Beck and Cunningham (1989) and Wirfs-Brock *et al.* (1990) are actually very closely related. Both may be characterized as *responsibility-driven*, in that they concentrate on *responsibilities* and *collaboration* relations to model the interaction between objects. However, the method described in Wirfs-Brock *et al.* (1990) is much more detailed, and to some extent includes means to formally characterize the behavior of an object and its interaction with other objects. To this end it employs an informal notion of *contracts* as originally introduced in Meyer (1988).

In section 3.2.1 a number of candidate classes have been suggested for our ATM. Now, with the use of CRC cards, we will delineate the functionality of (a number of) these classes more precisely. Also we will establish how the various object classes must collaborate to perform their duties. At the highest level of the design, we may distinguish between two groups of classes: the classes representing the *banking model* (comprising the class *account* and the class *transaction*), and the classes that model the interaction with the user (comprising the class *cardreader* and the class *cash-dispenser*). At a lower level, we also need a class modeling the *database* that provides persistent storage for the user's account and the information needed for authorization. For each of these classes we will use a CRC card to indicate their responsibilities and the classes with which they need to collaborate.

The *banking model*, depicted in slide 3-16, consists of the classes *account* and *transaction*. The class *account* keeps a record of the actual *balance* of the *account* and must allow a user to *deposit* or *withdraw* money. However, for safety reasons, these operations are never carried out directly, but are performed by an intermediary *transaction* object.

The responsibilities of the *transaction* class may be summarized as: the validation of user requests and the execution of money transfers. The responsibility

```
┌─────────────────────────────────────────────────────────────┐
│                                                       ┌─────┐ │   3-16
│  Banking model                                        │ ATM │ │
│                                                       └─────┘ │
│   ┌────────────────────────────────┬──────────────────────┐  │
│   │ ┌─────────┐                    │  transaction         │  │
│   │ │ account │                    │  database            │  │
│   │ └─────────┘                    │                      │  │
│   │  keeps balance                 │                      │  │
│   │  deposit money                 │                      │  │
│   │  withdraw money                │                      │  │
│   ├────────────────────────────────┼──────────────────────┤  │
│ ─ │ ┌─────────────┐                │  card-reader         │  │
│   │ │ transaction │                │  cash-dispenser      │  │
│   │ └─────────────┘                │  account             │  │
│   │  validation                    │  database            │  │
│   │  performs transfer             │                      │  │
│   │  keeps audit info              │                      │  │
│   └────────────────────────────────┴──────────────────────┘  │
└─────────────────────────────────────────────────────────────┘
```

Slide 3-16: The ATM example (2a)

for maintaining audit information is also assigned to the *transaction* class. To act as required, a *transaction* object needs to communicate with a number of other objects. It must acquire information from both the *card-reader* and the *database* to check, for example, whether the user has entered the right PIN code. To validate a request, it must check whether the account will be overdrawn or not. To pay the requested money, it must instruct the *cash-dispenser* to do so. And it must contact the database to log the appropriate audit information. In contrast, an *account* only needs to respond to the requests it receives from a *transaction*. Apart from that, it must participate in committing the transaction to the bank's *database*. Note that the CRC method is non-specific about how the collaborations are actually realized; it is unclear which object will take the initiative. To model these aspects we will need a more precise notion of *control* that tells us how the potential behavior (or responsibility) of an object is activated.

The second group of classes may be called *interaction classes*, since these are meant to communicate with entities in the outside world, outside from the perspective of the system. Also the bank's *database* may be considered as belonging to the outside world, since it stores the information concerning the account and the authorization of customers in a system-independent manner. See slide 3-17.

Both the *card-reader* and the *cash-dispenser* rely on a class called *event*, which is needed to model the actions of the user. For example, when a user inserts a bankcard, we expect a transaction to start. For this to happen, we must presuppose an underlying system that dispatches the event to the *card-reader*, which in turn notifies the *teller machine* that a new transaction is to take place. The flow of control between a *transaction* object and the *cash-dispenser* is far more straightforward, since a *transaction* object only needs to issue the appropriate instruction. However, the actual interaction between the *cash-dispenser* and the underlying hardware, that turns out the money, may be quite intricate.

The *database* may either respond directly to the request coming from the *account* or *transaction* object or it may respond to *events* by taking the initiative to call the appropriate methods of the *account* and *transaction* objects. Whether the *database* may be accessed directly or will only react to events is actually dependent on the control model we assume when developing the system model.

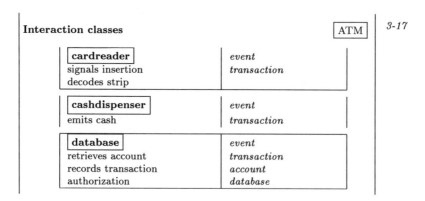

Slide 3-17: The ATM example (2b)

3.2.3   Object roles and interaction

Objects rarely live in isolation. In a system of some complexity, a number of different kinds of object classes may usually be distinguished. Each kind of class may be regarded as playing a specific role in the system. For example, when considering our ATM, classes such as *card-reader* and *cash-dispenser* are of a completely different kind, and play a completely different role, than the classes *account* and *database* for instance, or the classes *event* and *transaction*. Often it will take some experimentation to decide how control must be distributed among the objects comprising the system. Although the framework chosen for the development of the system may partly determine the control model, there will usually be ample choice left for the designer of the system to define the interactions between objects.

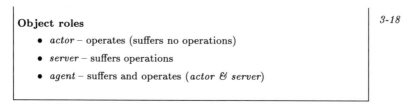

Slide 3-18: Object roles

An important function of the design document is to elucidate the role of each object class in the system, and to point out how the objects cooperate to complete the task. In Booch (1986), a distinction is made between objects that suffer no operations (actors), objects that only suffer operations (servers) and objects that both suffer and require operations (agents). Such a characterization in terms of *initiative* may give a first indication of the role an object plays in the system. For example, the *account* class in our ATM example is best characterized as a *server* class, whereas the *transaction class* may be regarded, in the terminology of Booch (1986), as an actor class, since it actively controls the computation. In many cases, the software control model adopted will also influence the way in which individual objects are supposed to behave. See slide 3-18.

With respect to a global view of the system, it is necessary to ensure that each object class is completely defined, that is to establish that each class provides a sufficiently complete method interface. In Booch (1986), a characterization is given of the kinds of methods that may occur in an interface. These include methods to create or destroy an object, methods to modify the state of an object and methods that only provide information on the state of an object, or parts thereof.

Before being able to make final decisions with respect to the functionality of a class, however, it is generally necessary to get a clear overall picture of the system first. This requires what Booch (1986) characterizes as *round trip gestalt* design, which in other words expresses the need to *analyze a little, design a little, implement a little, test a little* ... (The notion of *gestalt* comes from perception psychology, where it means a global perceptual configuration emerging from the background.)

3.3   Contracts

To establish the interaction between objects in a more precise way, we need a notion of *contracts*, specifying the requirements a client must comply with when requesting a service from a server object. Our notion of contracts will be based on the notion of *types*.

In the universe of programming, *types* are above all a means to create order and regularity. Also, in an object-oriented approach, types may play an important role in organizing classes and their relationships. As observed in Halbert and O'Brien (1987), the notion of types gives a natural criterion for *modularization*, perhaps not so much as a guideline to arrive at a particular object decomposition, but as a means to judge whether the modular structure of a system is consistently defined, that is technically well-typed.

Slide 3-19: Contractual obligations

The meaning of a type must be understood as a formal characterization of the behavior of the elements belonging to the type. A type consists of a (possibly infinite) collection of elements which is characterized by the definition of the type. For example, a *class* defines such a collection, namely the instances of the class, whose behavior is constrained by the specification of the class.

3.3.1   Specifying contractual obligations

A formal specification of the behavior of an object may be given by defining a *pre-condition* and *post-condition* for each method. The pre-condition of a method specifies in a logical manner what restrictions the client invoking a particular method is obliged to comply with. When the client fails to meet these requirements the result of the method will be undefined. In effect, after the violation of a pre-condition anything can happen. Usually, this means that the computation may be aborted or that some other means of error-handling may be started. For instance, when the implementation language supports exceptions an exception handler may be invoked.

The post-condition of a method states what obligations the server object has when executing the method, provided that the client's request satisfies the method's pre-condition.

Apart from specifying a pre-condition and post-condition for each method publicly supported by the class, the designer of the class may also specify a *class invariant*, to define the invariant properties of the state of each instance of the class.

A class annotated with an invariant and pre- and post-conditions for the methods may be regarded as a *contract*, since it specifies precisely (in an abstract way) the behavioral conformance conditions of the object and the constraints imposed on the interactions between the object and its clients. See slide 3-19.

Assertions – *formal specification*   *3-20*

- **require** – method call pre-condition
- **ensure, promise** – post-condition
- **invariant** – object invariance

Slide 3-20: Formal specification of contracts

Intuitively, *contracts* have a clear analogy to our business affairs in everyday life. For instance, when buying audio equipment, as a client you wish to know what you get for the price you pay, whereas the dealer may require that you pay in cash. Following this metaphor through, we see that the supplier may actually benefit from imposing a (reasonable) pre-condition and that the client has an interest in a well-stated post-condition. Most people are not willing to pay without knowing what they will get for their money.

Language support The use of *contracts* was originally proposed by Meyer (1988), and is directly supported by the language Eiffel, which offers the keywords *require* (to indicate a pre-condition), *ensure* (to indicate a post-condition) and *invariant* (to indicate the invariance condition). See slide 3-20. The Eiffel environment has options to dynamically check any of the three kinds of assertions, even selectively per class. The assertions, except for the invariance condition, are directly embedded in the code. Although less elegant, the same functionality can be achieved in C++ by using the *assert* macro defined in **assert.h** as explained in section 2.1.3, which also introduced the *require* and *promise* macros for C++.

For dynamically checking the invariance condition, a test should be executed when evaluating the constructor and before and after each method invocation. While a method is being executed, the invariant need not necessarily hold, but it is the responsibility of a method to restore the invariant when it is disrupted. In case object methods are recursively applied, the invariant must be restored when returning to the original caller.

An alternative approach to incorporating assertions in a class description is presented in Cline and Lea (1990), which introduces an extension of C++ called Annotated C++. Instead of directly embedding assertions in the code, Annotated C++ requires the user to specify separately the axioms characterizing the functionality of the methods and their effect on the state of the object.

Interfaces *Contracts* may be used to document the method interface of a class. Pre- and post-conditions allow the class designer to specify in a concise manner the functional characteristics of a method, whereas the use of natural language often leads to lengthy (and imprecise) descriptions. Below, an example is given of a contract specifying an account.

```
class account {                                          account
public:
account();
// assert( invariant() );

virtual float balance() { return _balance; }

void deposit(float x);                            to deposit money
// require( x ⩾ 0 );
// promise( balance() ≡ old_balance + x && invariant() );

void withdraw(float x);                           to withdraw money
// require( x ⩽ balance() );
// promise( balance() ≡ old_balance − x && invariant() );

bool invariant() { return balance() ⩾ 0; }
protected:
float _balance;
};
```

The interface for the *account* class specifies in an abstract way what the user expects of an account. From the perspective of design, the behavioral abstraction expressed by the axioms is exactly what we need, in principle. The implementation must guarantee that these constraints are met.

System development From the perspective of system development, the notion of contracts has some interesting consequences. Assertions may be used to decide who is responsible for any erroneous behavior of the system. See slide 3-21.

3-21

System development
- *violated pre-condition* – bug in client
- *violated post-condition* – bug in supplier

A pre-condition limits the cases that a supplier must handle!

Slide 3-21: System development with contracts

For example, imagine that you are using a software library to implement a system for financial transactions and that your company suffers a number of losses due to bugs in the system. How would you find out whether the loss is your own fault or whether it is caused by some bug in the library?

Perhaps surprisingly, the use of assertions allows you to determine exactly whether to sue the library vendor or not. Assume that the classes in the library are all annotated with assertions that can be checked dynamically at runtime. Now, when you replay the examples that resulted in a loss for your company with the option for checking pre- and post-conditions on, it can easily be decided who is in error. In the case that a pre-condition of a method signals violation, you, as a client of a library object, are in error. However, when no pre-condition violation is signaled, but instead a post-condition is violated, then the library object as the supplier of a service is in error; and you may proceed to go to court, or do something less dramatic such as asking the software vendor to correct the bug.

Realization The contract specified in the *account* class interface may actually be enforced in code as illustrated below.

```
class account {                                          account
public:
account() { _balance = 0; assert(invariant()); }

virtual float balance() { return _balance; }


void deposit(float x) {
        require( x >= 0 );                       check precondition
        hold();                                  to save the old state
        _balance += x;
        promise( balance() == old_balance + x );
        promise( invariant() );
        }
```

```
void withdraw(float x) {
        require( x <= _balance );                    check precondition
        hold();                                      to save the old state
        _balance -= x;
        promise( balance() == old_balance - x );
        promise( invariant() );
        }

virtual bool invariant() { return balance() >= 0; }
protected:
float _balance;
float old_balance;                                   additional variable
virtual void hold() { old_balance = _balance; }
};
```

The additional variable *old_balance* is needed to compare the state preceding
an operation with the state that results afterwards. The old state must explicitly
be copied by calling *hold*. In this respect, Eiffel offers better support than C++.

Whenever *balance()* proves to be less than zero, the procedure sketched above
can be used to determine whether the error is caused by an erroneous method
invocation, for example when calling *withdraw(x)* with $x \geqslant balance()$, or whether
the implementation code contains a bug.

For the developer of the software, pre-conditions offer a means to limit the
number of cases that a method must be able to handle. Often, programmers
tend to anticipate all possible uses. For instance, many programs or systems
have options that may be learned only when inspecting the source code but are
otherwise undocumented. Rather than providing all possible options, for now
and the future, it is more sensible to delineate in a precise manner what input will
be processed and what input is considered illegal. For the developer, this may
significantly reduce the effort of producing the software.

3.3.2   Refining contracts

Contracts provide a means to specify the behavior of an object in a formal way by
using logical assertions. In particular, a contract specifies the constraints involved
in the interaction between a server object and a client invoking a method for that
object. When developing a refinement subtype hierarchy we need to establish
that the derived types satisfy the constraints imposed by the contract associated
with the base type.

To establish that the contract of a derived class refines the contract of the
base class it suffices to verify that the following rules are satisfied. See slide 3-22.

First, the invariant of the base class must apply to all instances of the derived
class. In other words, the invariance assertions of the derived class must be
logically equal to or stronger than the assertions characterizing the invariant
properties of the base class. This requirement may be verified by checking that the

---

Refining a contract – *state responsibilities and obligations*   3-22

- *invariance* – respect the invariants of the base class
- *methods* – services may be added or refined

Refining a method – *like improving a business contract*

```
class C : public P {
        virtual void m();
        }
```

- $pre(m_C) \geqslant pre(m_P)$ weaken pre-condition
- $post(m_C) \leqslant post(m_P)$ strengthen post-condition

Slide 3-22: Contracts and inheritance

invariance properties of the base class can be logically derived from the statement asserting the invariance properties of the derived class. The intuition underlying this requirement is that the behavior of the derived class is more tightly defined and hence subject to stronger invariance conditions.

Secondly, each method occurring in the base class must occur in the derived class, possibly in a refined form. Note that from a type-theoretical point of view it is perfectly all right to add methods but strictly forbidden to delete methods, since deleting a method would violate the requirement of behavioral conformance that adheres to the subtype relation. Apart from adding a method, we may also refine existing methods. Refining a method involves strengthening the post-condition and weakening the pre-condition. Suppose that we have a class C derived from a base class P, to verify that the method m_C refines the method m_P defined for the base class P, we must check, assuming that the signatures of m_C and m_P are compatible, that the post-condition of m_C is not weaker than the post-condition of m_P, and also that the pre-condition of m_C is not stronger than the pre-condition of m_P.

This rule may at first sight be surprising, because of the asymmetric way in which post-conditions and pre-conditions are treated. But reflecting on what it means to improve a service, the intuition underlying this rule, and in particular the contra-variant relation between the pre-conditions involved, is quite straightforward. To improve or refine a service, in our commonsense notion of a service, means that the quality of the product or the result delivered becomes better. Alternatively, a service may be considered as improved when, even with the result remaining the same, the cost of the service is decreased. In other words, a service is improved if either the client may have higher expectations of the result or the requirements on the client becomes less stringent. The *or* is non-exclusive. A derived class may improve a service while at the same time imposing fewer constraints on the clients.

Example As an example of improving a contract, consider the refinement of the class *account* into a class *credit_account*, which allows a consumer to overdraw an account to a limit of some *maximum* amount.

```
class credit_account : public account {                    credit_account
public:
credit_account(float x) { _maxcredit = x; _credit = 0; }

float balance() { return _balance + _credit; }

float credit(float x) {
        require( x + _credit <= _maxcredit );
        hold();
        _credit += x;
        promise( _credit = old_credit + x );
        promise( _balance = old_balance);
        promise( invariant() );
        }

void reduce(float x) {
        require( 0 <= x && x <= _credit );
        hold();
        _credit -= x;
        promise( _credit = old_credit - x );
        promise( _balance = old_balance );
        promise( invariant() );
        }


bool invariant() {
        return _credit <= _maxcredit && account::invariant();
        }
protected:
float _maxcredit, _credit;
float old_credit;
void hold() { old_credit = _credit; account::hold(); }
};
```

As a first observation, we may note that the invariant of *account* immediately follows from the invariant of *credit_account*. Also, we may easily establish that the pre-condition of *withdraw* has (implicitly) been weakened, since we are allowed to overdraw the *credit_account* by the amount given by *credit*. Note, however, that this is implied by the virtual definition of *balance*(). To manage the *credit* given, the methods *credit* and *reduce* are supplied. This allows us to leave the methods *deposit* and *withdraw* unmodified.

3.3.3   Runtime consistency checking

Debugging is a hopelessly time-consuming and unrewarding activity. Unless the testing process is guided by clearly specified criteria on what to test for, testing in the sense of looking for errors must be considered as ordinary debugging, that is running the system to see what will happen. Client/server contracts, as introduced in section 3.3 as a method for design, do offer such guidelines in that they enable the programmer to specify precisely the restrictions characterizing the legal states of the object, as well as the conditions that must be satisfied in order for legal state transitions to occur. See slide 3-23.

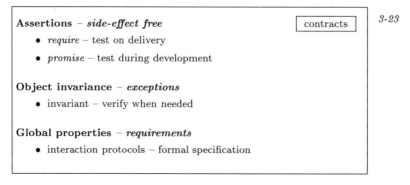

Slide 3-23: Runtime consistency checking

The Eiffel language is the first (object-oriented) language in which assertions were explicitly introduced as a means to develop software and to monitor the runtime consistency of a system. Contracts as supported by Eiffel were primarily influenced by notions concerning the construction of correct programs. The unique contribution of Meyer (1988) consists of showing that these notions may be employed operationally by specifying the pragmatic meaning of pre- and post-conditions defining the behavior of methods. To use assertions operationally, however, the assertion language must be restricted to side-effect free boolean expressions in the language being used.

Combined with a bottom-up approach to development, the notion of contracts gives rise to the following guidelines for testing. Post-conditions and invariance assertions should primarily be checked during development. When sufficient confidence is gained in the reliability of the object definitions, checking these assertions may be omitted in favor of efficiency. However, pre-conditions must be checked when delivering the system to ensure that the user complies with the protocol specified by the contract.

When delivering the system, it is a matter of contractual agreement between the deliverer and user whether pre- and/or post-conditions will be enabled. The safest option is to enable them both, since the violation of a pre-condition may be caused by an undetected violated post-condition.

In addition, the method of testing for identity transitions may be used to cover higher level invariants, involving multiple objects. To check whether the conditions with respect to complex interaction protocols are satisfied, explicit consistency checks need to be inserted by the programmer. See also section 10.5.

3.4   Towards a formal approach

Reliability is the cornerstone of reuse. Hence, object-oriented implementation, design and analysis must first and foremost support the development of reliable software, should the original claim to promote the reuse of software ever come true.

Validating software by means of testing alone is clearly insufficient. As argued in Backhouse (1986), the probability of finding an error is usually too small to view testing as a reliable method of detecting the error.

The fallacy of any empirical approach to validating software, which includes quantitative measurements based on software metrics, is that in the end we just have to wait and see what happens. In other words, it is useless as a design methodology.

Formal specification – *contracts*   *3-24*

  - type specification – local properties

  - relational specification – structural properties, type relations

  - functional specification – requirements

Verification – *as a design methodology*

  - reasoning about program specification/code

Runtime consistency – *invariance*

  - behavioral types specify test cases

  - invariants and assertions monitor consistency

Slide 3-24: Formal specification and verification

Verification should be at the heart of any design method. In addition to allowing us to reason about the specification and the code, the design process should result in an architectural description of the system as well as in a proof that the system meets its requirements. Looking at the various approaches to the specification and verification of software, we can see that the notion of *invariance* plays a crucial role in developing provably correct solutions for a variety of problems (cf. Gries, 1981; Backhouse, 1986; Apt and Olderog, 1991; Dahl, 1992).

Invariance, as we observed when discussing object test methods, also play an important role in testing the runtime consistency of a system. Hence, from a pragmatic point of view, studying formal approaches may help us become aware of the properties that determine the runtime consistency of object-oriented systems.

In part III (chapter 10), we will explore what formal methods we have available
for developing object-oriented software. Our starting point will be the foundations
underlying the notion of *contracts* as introduced in Meyer (1988). We will take a
closer look at the relation between *contracts* and the specification of the properties
of abstract data types. Also, we will look at methods allowing us to specify
structural and functional relations between types, as may occur in behavioral
compositions of objects. More specifically, we will study the means available to
relate an abstract specification of the properties of a data type to a concrete
implementation. These studies are based on an analysis of the notion of abstract
data types, and the relation between inheritance and subtyping. In particular, we
will look at rules to determine whether a subclass derived by inheritance conforms
to the subtype relation that we may define in a formal approach to object types.

However, before we delve into the formal foundations of object-oriented modeling, we will first look at an example of application development and explore the
design space of object-oriented languages and system implementation techniques.
These insights will enable us to establish to what extent we may capture a design in
formal terms, and what heuristics are available to accomplish the tasks remaining
in object-oriented development.

Summary

This chapter presented an overview of the issues involved in the design and
software engineering of object-oriented software. The approach taken may be
characterized as eclectic, in that various methods are referred to when illustrating
design issues without commitment to a particular method or approach.

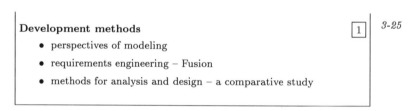

Slide 3-25: Section 3.1: Development methods

In section 1, we discussed perspectives of modeling and requirements engineering. We looked at the second-generation development method Fusion and
made a comparative study of analysis and design methods. We then discussed
the differences between functional and object-oriented development approaches.

In section 2, we discussed the issues that arise in defining an object model.
We looked at heuristics for identifying objects, based on a linguistic analysis of
the requirements document, and discussed the evaluation criteria that may be
used for eliminating spurious classes. Also, the CRC method, which approaches
class design by delineating responsibilities and collaborations, was illustrated with
some examples.

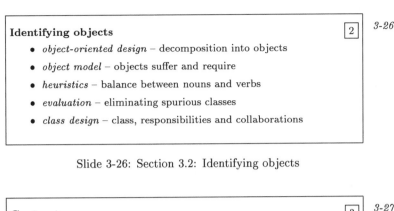

Slide 3-26: Section 3.2: Identifying objects

Contracts   3   *3-27*

- *types* – as an organizing principle
- *contracts* – obligations and benefits
- *subtyping* – the substitutability requirement
- *partial types* – designed to have subtypes

Slide 3-27: Section 3.3: Contracts

The object model resulting from an initial exploration may be formalized by employing types. In section 3, we discussed the notion of *contracts* as a means to characterize the behavioral aspects of types, specifying the restrictions and obligations of an object and its clients. We also looked at the requirements for subtype refinement and the refinement of contractual obligations.

Slide 3-28: Section 3.4: Towards a formal approach

Finally, in section 4, we reflected on the possible contribution of formal methods to the software engineering of object-oriented systems, and concluded that the notion of *contracts* may play an invaluable role, both as a design methodology and as a means to establish the runtime consistency of a system.

Questions

1. Describe the Fusion method. How does Fusion compare with other methods

of OO analysis and design?

2. Give an outline of the steps required in object-oriented design. What heuristics can you think of for identifying objects?

3. What criteria may be used to eliminate spurious classes from an initial object model?

4. Explain the methods of CRC cards. Give an example.

5. Explain how you may characterize the behavior of an object by means of a contract.

6. What benefits may design by contract have for system developers? And for users?

7. Give a detailed account of the issues that arise in refining a contract.

8. How may contracts be employed to test object behavior?

9. Discuss how a formal approach may contribute to OO software development.

Further reading

Fowler (1997b) is not only a good introduction to UML, but contains also many useful insights on the process of object-oriented development. Additionally, Fowler (1997a) may be read as a source on *analysis patterns*, which are reusable elements of analysis and design. For more information on Fusion, consult Coleman *et al.* (1994). As earlier references on object-oriented methods, I recommend Booch (1994), Wirfs-Brock *et al.* (1990) and Rumbaugh *et al.* (1991). Also worthwhile are Henderson (1993) and Champeaux *et al.* (1993). An overview and comparative study of design representation methods is given in Webster (1988). Meyer (1997) is the ultimate reference on *contracts*. A more comprehensive article on *design by contract* is Meyer (1992b).

4

Application development

After studying general issues in the design and software engineering of object-oriented applications and frameworks, it is time to focus in somewhat more detail on actual application development.

In this chapter we will look at the *drawtool* application, as a representative of a broader category of interactive editing tools.

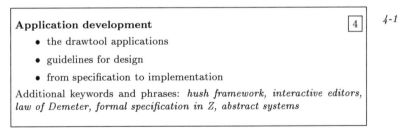

4-1

Slide 4-1: Application development

The *drawtool* application is a Java application using the multiparadigm *hush* framework. However, in discussing its development, we will concentrate on specifying the requirements and issues of design.

After that we will treat some miscellaneous issues in the design of classes. This chapter will be concluded with a case study, a concise, yet detailed, example of a more formal approach to the development of an object-oriented application.

4.1   The *drawtool* **application**

Interactive editors are an interesting category of applications. Interactive editors, which include word processors and drawing tools, are the kind of applications the average (end) user is most familiar with. From a software engineering perspective, interactive editors are interesting because they combine interactive and functional features. See also Gamma *et al.* (1994), which provides many patterns for interactive editors.

In the Software Engineering curriculum at the Vrije Universiteit, we have repeatedly used interactive editors as a medium-term assignment for CS2 students (five weeks for groups of four or five students). One example of such an assignment is the *Interactive Design Assistant* discussed in section 1.3.2. Another example is the musical score editor (see appendix I), which has been chosen by a selected group of CS3 and CS4 students as a practical assignment for the Object-Oriented Software Development course.

In this section we will look at the *drawtool* application, which is a representative realization of a (rather simple) drawing editor. The implementation of *drawtool* presented here is realized in the Java version of the *hush* framework. The *hush* C++ framework has been used for a number of years in the Software Engineering curriculum, but has recently been replaced by Java with Swing. The *drawtool* application is nevertheless interesting because it acted for many years as the basic example of an interactive editor for quite a number of students.

Before studying *drawtool*, we will first look at the realization of a drawing canvas in *hush*

A simple drawing canvas in *hush*

The Tcl/Tk toolkit provides a very powerful scripting environment for realizing graphical user interfaces, Ousterhout (1991). The *hush* Java/C++ library gives convenient access to the Tcl/Tk toolkit in an object-oriented style. See also Eliëns (1995).

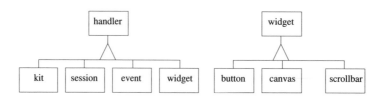

Slide 4-2: The *hush* class hierarchy

The *hush* library provides three kinds of classes, namely (a) the widget classes, which mimic the functionality of Tk, (b) the handler and event classes, which are involved in the handling of events and the binding of Java/C++ code to Tcl commands, and (c) the classes *kit* and *session*, which encapsulate the embedded interpreter and the window management system,

In the widget class hierarchy depicted on the right in slide 4-2, the *widget* class represents an abstract widget, defining the commands that are valid for each of the descendant concrete widget classes. The *widget* class, however, is not an abstract class in Java or C++ terms. It may be used for creating references to widgets defined in Tcl. In contrast, employing the constructor of one of the concrete widget classes results in actually creating a widget.

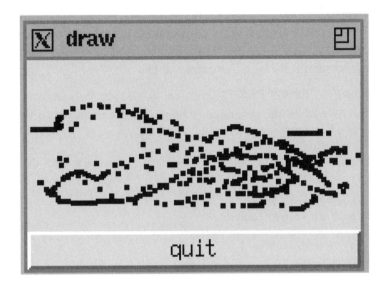

Slide 4-3: Drawing canvas

Widgets are the elements from which a GUI is made. They appear as windows on the screen to display text or graphics and may respond to events such as motioning the mouse or pressing a key by calling an action associated with that event. The interface of the *widget* class may be defined by the (pseudo) interface below.

```
public interface widget {

public String path();

public void eval(String cmd);

public void pack(String s);

public void bind(handler h,String s);
public void bind(String p, handler h,String s);

public void configure(String cmd);
public void geometry(int x, int y);

public void xscroll(widget w);
```

widget

```
public void yscroll(widget w);

public widget self();                    to define compound widgets
public void redirect(widget inner);
};
```

The function *path* delivers the path name of a widget object. Each widget created by Tk actually defines a Tcl command associated with the path name of the widget. In other words, an actual widget may be regarded as an object which can be asked to evaluate commands. For example a widget '.b' may be asked to change its background color by a Tcl command like

```
.b configure -background blue
```

The function *eval* enables the programmer to apply Tcl commands to the widget directly, as does the *configure* command. The function *geometry* sets the width and height of the widget.

As an example look at the code for the drawing canvas widget depicted in slide 4-3.

```
import hush.dv.api.event;
import hush.dv.widgets.canvas;

class draw extends canvas {                              draw
boolean dragging;

public draw(String path) {
        super(path);
        dragging = false;
        bind(this);
        }

public void press(event ev) {
        dragging = true;
        }

public void release(event ev) {
        dragging = false;
        }

public void motion(event ev) {
        if (dragging)
                circle(ev.x(),ev.y(),2,"-fill black");
        }
};
```

The class *draw* has an instance variable *dragging*, that reflects whether the user is actually drawing a figure. If *dragging* is true, motions with the mouse will result in small dots on the screen.

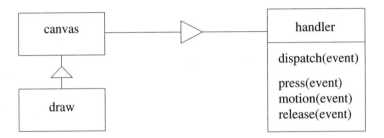

Slide 4-4: Drawing canvas

A structural view of the *draw* class is given in slide 4-4. The *draw* class is derived from a *canvas*, which is itself (indirectly) derived from a *handler* class. The *handler* class dispatches events to predefined handler methods, such as *press*, *motion* and *release*.

For the *draw* class we must distinguish between a *handler* and a *canvas* part. The *handler* part is defined by the methods *press*, *release* and *motion*. The *canvas* part allows for drawing figures, such as a small circle.

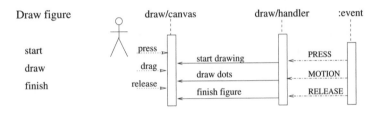

Slide 4-5: Drawing canvas

In slide 4-5 it is depicted how these two parts interact when the user draws a figure. Actions of the user result in events that activate the handler. Note that the UML sequence diagrams are not completely adequate here, since it is difficult to express information concerning the events and the state of the *draw* instance.

Widgets may respond to events. To associate an event with an action, an explicit binding must be specified for that particular widget. Some widgets provide default bindings. These may, however, be overruled.

The function *bind* is used to associate handlers with events. The first string parameter of *bind* may be used to specify the event type. Common event types are, for example, *ButtonPress*, *ButtonRelease* and *Motion*, which are the default events for canvas widgets. Also keystrokes may be defined as events, for example *Return*, which is the default event for the *entry* widget.

The function *bind(handler, String)* may be used to associate a handler object with the default bindings for the widget. Concrete widgets may not override the *bind* function itself, but must define the protected function *install*. Typically, the install function consists of calls to *bind* for each of the event types that is relevant to the widget.

In addition, the widget class offers two functions that may be used when defining compound or mega widgets. The function *redirect(w)* must by used to delegate the invocation of the *eval, configure* and *bind* functions to the widget *w*. The function *self()* gives access to the widget to which the commands are redirected. The function *path* will still deliver the path name of the outer widget. Calling *redirect* when creating the compound widget class suffices for most situations. However, when the default events must be changed or the declaration of a handler must take effect for several component widgets, the function *install* must be redefined to handle the delegation explicitly.

The *drawtool* application

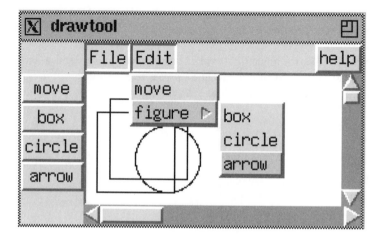

Slide 4-6: The *drawtool* interface

In this section we will look at the realization of simple drawing tool. The example illustrates how to use the *hush* library widgets, and serves to illustrate in particular how to construct compound widgets.

A structural view of the *drawtool* application is given in slide 4-7.

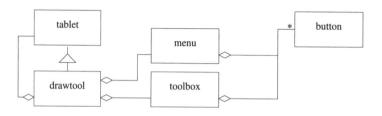

Slide 4-7: A (partial) class diagram

Usually, the various widgets constituting the user interface are (hierarchically) related to each other, such as in the *drawtool* application which contains a canvas to display graphic elements, a button toolbox for selecting the graphic items and a menubar offering various options such as saving the drawing in a file.

Widgets in Tk are identified by a *path name*. The path name of a widget reflects its possible subordination to another widget. See slide 4-8.

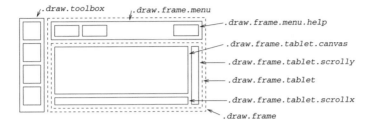

Slide 4-8: Widget containment

Pathnames consist of strings separated by dots. The first character of a path must be a dot. The first letter of a path must be lower case. The format of a path name may be expressed in BNF form as

$$path ::= \text{'.'} \mid \text{'.'} string \mid path \text{'.'} string$$

For example '.' is the path name of the root widget, whereas '.quit' is the path name of a widget subordinate to the root widget. A widget subordinate to another widget must have the path name of that widget as part of its own path name. For example, the widget '.f.m' may have a widget '.f.m.h' as a subordinate widget. Note that the widget hierarchy induced by the path names is completely orthogonal to the widget class inheritance hierarchy. With respect to the path name hierarchy, when speaking of ancestors we simply mean superordinate widgets.

Our drawing tool consists of a *tablet*, which is a canvas with scrollbars to allow for a large size canvas of which only a part is displayed, a *menubar*, having a *File* and an *Edit* menu, and a *toolbox*, which is a collection of buttons for selecting from among the drawing facilities. In addition, a help facility is offered.

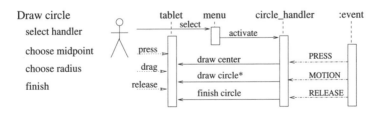

Slide 4-9: An interaction diagram

A typical interaction (or *use case*) with *drawtool* is depicted in slide 4-9. On selecting the *circle* menu entry (or toolbox button), the *circle handler* is activated to assist in the drawing of a circle. Details will be given when discussing the *tablet* widget.

The *toolbox* component As the first component of *drawtool*, we will look at the *toolbox*. The *toolbox* is a collection of buttons packed in a frame.

```
import hush.dv.api.*;
import hush.dv.widgets.frame;

public class toolbox extends frame {                          toolbox

tablet tablet;

public toolbox(widget w, tablet t) {
    super(w,"toolbox");
    tablet = t;
    new toolbutton(this,"draw");
    new toolbutton(this,"move");
    new toolbutton(this,"box");
    new toolbutton(this,"circle");
    new toolbutton(this,"arrow");
}

public int operator() {
        tablet.mode(_event.arg(1));              reset tablet mode
        return OK;
        }

};
```

Each button is an instance of the class *toolbutton*.

```
import hush.dv.api.*;
import hush.dv.widgets.button;

public class toolbutton extends button {              toolbutton
public toolbutton(widget w, String name) {
        super(w,name);
        text(name);
        bind(w,name);
        pack("-side top -fill both -expand 1");
        }
};
```

When a toolbutton is created, the actual button is given the name of the button as its path. Next, the button is given the name as its text, the ancestor widget *w* is declared to be the handler for the button and the button is packed. The function *text* is a member function of the class *button*, whereas both *handler* and *pack* are common widget functions. Note that the parameter *name* is used as a path name, as the text to display, and as an argument for the handler, that will be passed as a parameter when invoking the handler object.

The *toolbox* class inherits from the *frame* widget class, and creates a frame widget with a path relative to the widget parameter provided by the constructor. The constructor further creates the five toolbuttons.

The *toolbox* is both the superordinate widget and handler for each *toolbutton*. When the *operator*() function of the *toolbox* is invoked in response to pressing a button, the call is delegated to the *mode* function of the *tablet*. The argument given to *mode* corresponds to the name of the button pressed.

The definition of the *toolbutton* and *toolbox* illustrates that a widget need not necessarily be its own handler. The decision, whether to define a subclass which is made its own handler or to install an external handler depends upon what is considered the most convenient way in which to access the resources needed. As a guideline, exploit the regularity of the application.

The *menubar* component The second component of our drawing tool is the *menubar*.

```
import hush.dv.api.widget;

public class menubar extends hush.dv.widgets.menubar {      menubar

public menubar(widget w, tablet t, toolbox b)  {
    super(w,"bar");
    configure("-relief sunken");

    new FileMenu(this,t);
    new EditMenu(this,b);
    new HelpButton(this);
    }
};
```

The class *menubar*, given above, is derived from the *hush* widget *menubar*. Its constructor requires an ancestor widget, a *tablet* and a *toolbox*. The tablet is passed as a parameter to the *file_menu*, and the *toolbox* to the *edit_menu*. In addition, a *help_button* is created, which provides online help in a hypertext format when pressed.

A menubar consists of menubuttons to which actual menus are attached. Each menu consists of a number of entries, which may possibly lead to cascaded menus.

The second button of the *menubar* is defined by the *EditMenu*. The *EditMenu* requires a *toolbox* and creates a menubutton. It configures the button and defines a menu containing two entries, one of which is a cascaded menu. Both the main menu and the cascaded menu are given the *toolbox* as a handler. This makes sense only because for our simple application the functionality offered by the *toolbox* and *EditMenu* coincide.

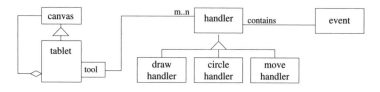

Slide 4-10: Tablet

The *tablet* component The most important component of our *drawtool* application is defined by the *tablet* widget class given below.

```
import hush.dv.api.*;
import hush.dv.widgets.*;

public class tablet extends canvas {                              tablet

int _mode;
canvas canvas;
handler[] handlers;

final int DRAW = 0;
final int MOVE = 1;
final int CIRCLE = 2;
final int BOX = 3;
final int ARROW = 5;

public tablet(widget w, String name, String options) {

        super(w,name,"*");

        handlers = new handler[12];

        init(options);

        redirect(canvas); // to delegate to canvas
        bind(this); // to intercept user actions

        handlers[DRAW]   = new DrawHandler(canvas);
        handlers[MOVE]   = new MoveHandler(canvas);
        handlers[BOX]    = new BoxHandler(canvas);
        handlers[CIRCLE] = new CircleHandler(canvas);
        handlers[ARROW]  = new ArrowHandler(canvas);

        _mode = 0; // drawmode.draw;
        }

public int operator() {
        handlers[_mode].dispatch(_event);
        return OK;
```

```
        }

public int mode(String s) {
        int m = -1;
        if ("draw".equals(s))   m = DRAW;
        if ("move".equals(s))   m = MOVE;
        if ("box".equals(s))    m = BOX;
        if ("circle".equals(s)) m = CIRCLE;
        if ("arrow".equals(s))  m = ARROW;
        if (m >= 0) _mode = m;
        return _mode;
        }

void init(String options) {

        widget root = new frame(path(),"-class tablet");

        canvas = new canvas(root,"canvas",options);
        canvas.configure("-relief sunken -background white");
        canvas.geometry(200,100);

        scrollbar scrollx = new Scrollbar(root,"scrollx");
        scrollx.orient("horizontal");
        scrollx.pack("-side bottom -fill x -expand 0");

        scrollbar scrolly = new Scrollbar(root,"scrolly");

        scrolly.orient("vertical");
        scrolly.pack("-side right -fill y -expand 0");

        canvas.pack("-side top -fill both -expand 1");

        canvas.xscroll(scrollx);  scrollx.xview(canvas);
        canvas.yscroll(scrolly);  scrolly.yview(canvas);
        }

};
```

The various modes supported by the drawing tool are enumerated as final constants. The *tablet* class itself inherits from the *canvas* widget class. This has the advantage that it offers the full functionality of a canvas. In addition to the constructor and *operator*() function, which delegates the incoming event to the appropriate handler according to the _mode variable, it offers a function *mode*, which sets the mode of the canvas as indicated by its string argument, and a function *init* that determines the creation and geometrical layout of the component widgets. As instance variables, it contains an integer _mode variable and an array of handlers that contains the handlers corresponding to the modes supported.

Although the *tablet* must act as a canvas, the actual *tablet* widget is nothing but a *frame* that contains a canvas widget as one of its components. This is reflected in the invocation of the canvas constructor (*super*). By convention, when the options parameter is ∗ instead of the empty string, no actual widget is created but only an abstract widget, as happens when calling the *widget* class constructor. Instead of creating a canvas right away, the *tablet* constructor creates a top frame, initializes the actual component widgets, and redirects the *eval*, *configure* and *bind* invocations to the subordinate *canvas* widget. It then binds itself to be its own handler, which results in binding itself to be the handler for the canvas component. Note that reversing the order of calling *redirect* and *bind* would be disastrous. After that it creates the handlers for the various modes and sets the initial mode to *move*.

The *operator*() function takes care of dispatching calls to the appropriate handler. The *dispatch* function must be called to pass the *tk*, *argc* and *argv* parameters.

The *drawtool* class Having taken care of the basic components of the drawing tool, that is the *toolbox*, *menubar* and *tablet* widgets, all that remains to be done is to define a suitable *file_handler*, appropriate handlers for the various drawing modes and a *help_handler*.

We will skip these, but look at the definition of the *drawtool* class instead. In particular, it will be shown how we may grant the *drawtool* the status of a veritable Tk widget, by defining a *drawtool* handler class and a corresponding *drawtool* widget command.

```
import hush.dv.api.*;
import hush.dv.widgets.frame;
import hush.dv.widgets.canvas;
```

public class drawtool extends canvas { | *drawtool* |

```
widget root;
tablet tablet;
```

public drawtool() { System.out.println("meta handler created"); }

public drawtool(String p, String options) {
        super(p,"*");   // *create empty tablet*
        init(options);
        }

public int operator() {
        System.out.println("Calling drawtool:" + _event.args(0));
        String[] argv = _event.argv();
        if ("self".equals(argv[1])) tk.result(self().path());
        else if ("drawtool".equals(argv[0]))
                create(argv[1],_event.args(2));
        else if ("path".equals(argv[1])) tk.result(path());

```
            else if ("pack".equals(argv[1])) pack(_event.args(2));
            else self().eval( _event.args(1) );   // send through
            return OK;
            }

    void create(String name, String options) {
            drawtool m = new drawtool(name,options);
            }

    void init(String options) {
            root = new frame(path(),"-class Meta");

            frame frame = new frame(root,"frame");

            tablet = new tablet(frame,"tablet",options);

            toolbox toolbox = new toolbox(frame,tablet);
            menubar menubar = new menubar(root,tablet,toolbox);

            toolbox.pack("-side left -fill y -expand 0");
            tablet.pack("-side left -fill both -expand 1");

            menubar.pack();
            frame.pack("-expand 1 -fill both");


            redirect( tablet );   // the widget of interest
            }
    };
```

Defining a widget command involves three steps: (I) the declaration of the
binding between a command and a handler, (II) the definition of the *operator*()
function, which actually defines a mini-interpreter, and (III) the definition of the
actual creation of the widget and its declaration as a Tcl/Tk command.

Step (I) is straightforward. We need to define an empty handler, which will
be associated with the *drawtool* command when starting the application. The
functionality offered by the interpreter defined by the *operator*() function in (II)
is kept quite simple, but may easily be extended. When the first argument of
the call is *drawtool*, a new *drawtool* widget is created as specified in (III), except
when the second argument is *self*. In that case, the virtual path of the widget is
returned, which is actually the path of the *tablet*'s canvas. It is the responsibility
of the writer of the script that the *self* command is not addressed to the empty
handler. If neither of these cases apply, the function *eval* is invoked for *self*(),
with the remaining arguments flattened to a string. This allows for using the
drawtool almost as an ordinary canvas.

```
            Canvas c = new DrawTool("draw","");
            tk.bind("drawtool",c);
```

```
c.circle(20,20,20,"-fill red");
c.rectangle(30,30,70,70,"-fill blue");
c.pack();
```

In the program fragment above, the Tcl command *drawtool* is declared, with an instance of *drawtool* as its handler. (It is assumed that the *tk* variable refers to an instance of *kit*.) In this way, the *drawtool* widget is made available as a command when the program is used as an interpreter. In this case, the actual *drawtool* widget is made the handler of the command, to allow for a script to address the *drawtool* by calling *drawtool self*.

4.2   Guidelines for design

Computing is a relatively young discipline. Despite its short history, a number of styles and schools promoting a particular style have emerged. However, in contrast to other disciplines such as the fine arts (including architecture) and musical composition, there is no well-established tradition of what is to be considered as *good taste* with respect to software design. There is an on-going and somewhat pointless debate as to whether software design must be looked at as an *art* or must be promoted into a *science*. See, for example, Knuth (1992) and Gries (1981). The debate has certainly resulted in new technology but has not, I am afraid, resulted in universally valid design guidelines.

The notion of *good design* in the other disciplines is usually implicitly defined by a collection of examples of good design, as preserved in museums or (art or music) historical works. For software design, we are still a long way from anything like a museum, setting the standards of good design. Nevertheless, a compendium of examples of object-oriented applications such as Pinson and Wiener (1990) and Harmon and Taylor (1993), if perhaps not setting the standards for good design, may certainly be instructive.

Development process – *cognitive factors*   *4-11*

  • model → realize → refine

Design criteria – *natural, flexible, reusable*

  • abstraction – *types*

  • modularity – *strong cohesion* (class)

  • structure – *subtyping*

  • information hiding – *narrow interfaces*

  • complexity – *weak coupling*

Slide 4-11: Criteria for design

The software engineering literature abounds with advice and tools to measure the quality of good design. In slide 4-11, a number of the criteria commonly found in software engineering texts is listed. In software design, we evidently strive for a high level of abstraction (as enabled by a notion of types and a corresponding notion of *contracts*), a modular structure with strongly cohesive units (as supported by the class construct), with units interrelated in a precisely defined way (for instance by a client/server or subtype relation). Other desirable properties are a high degree of information hiding (that is narrowly defined and yet complete interfaces) and a low level of complexity (which may be achieved with units that have only weak coupling, as supported by the client/server model). An impressive list, indeed.

Design is a human process, in which *cognitive factors* play a critical role. The role of cognitive factors is reflected in the so-called *fractal design process model* introduced in Johnson and Foote (1988), which describes object-oriented development as a triangle with bases labeled by the phrases *model, realize* and *refine*. This triangle may be iterated at each of the bases, and so on. The iterative view of software development does justice to the importance of human understanding, since it allows for a simultaneous understanding of the problem domain and the mechanisms needed to model the domain and the system architecture.

Good design involves taste. My personal definition of good design would certainly also involve cognitive factors (*is the design understandable?*), including subjective criteria such as *is it pleasant to read or study the design?*

4.2.1   Individual class design

A class should represent a faithful model of a single concept, and be a reusable, plug-compatible component that is robust, well-designed and extensible. In slide 4-12, we list a number of suggestions put forward by McGregor and Sykes (1992).

```
Class design – guidelines                                        4-12

   • only methods public – information hiding

   • do not expose implementation details

   • public members available to all classes – strong cohesion

   • as few dependencies as possible – weak coupling

   • explicit information passing

   • root class should be abstract model – abstraction
```

Slide 4-12: Individual class design

The first two guidelines enforce the principle of *information hiding*, advising that only methods should be public and all implementation details should be hidden. The third guideline states a principle of *strong cohesion* by requiring that classes implement a single protocol that is valid for all potential clients. A principle of *weak coupling* is enforced by requiring a class to have as few dependencies as possible, and to employ explicit information passing using messages instead of inheritance (except when inheritance may be used in a type consistent fashion). When using inheritance, the root class should be an abstract model of its derived classes, whether inheritance is used to realize a partial type or to define a specialization in a conceptual hierarchy.

The properties of classes, including their interfaces and relations with other classes, must be laid down in the design document. Ideally, the design document should present a complete and formal description of the structural, functional and dynamic aspects of the system, including an argument showing that the various models are consistent. However, in practice this will seldom be realized, partly because object-oriented design techniques are as yet not sufficiently matured to allow a completely formal treatment, and partly because most designers will be satisfied with a non-formal rendering of the architecture of their system. Admittedly, the task of designing is already sufficiently complex, even without the additional complexity of a completely formal treatment. Nevertheless, studying the formal underpinnings of object-oriented modeling based on types and polymorphism is still worthwhile, since it will sharpen the intuition with respect to the notion of behavioral conformance and the refinement of contracts, which are both essential for developing reliable object models. And reliability is the key to reuse!

4.2.2   Inheritance and invariance

When developing complex systems or class libraries, reliability is of critical importance. As shown in section 3.3, assertions provide a means by which to check the runtime consistency of objects. In particular, assertions may be used to check that the requirements for behavioral conformance of derived classes are met.

Invariant properties are often conveniently expressed in the form of algebraic laws that must hold for an object. Naturally, when extending a class by inheritance (to define a specialization or refinement) the invariants pertaining to the base class should not be disrupted. Although we cannot give a general guideline to prevent disruption, the example discussed here clearly suggests that *hidden features* should be carefully checked with respect to the invariance properties of the (derived) class. The example is taken from Bar-David (1992).

In slide 4-13, we have defined a class *employee*. The main features of an *employee* are the (protected) attribute *sal* (storing the salary of an employee) and the methods to access and modify the salary attribute. For *employee* objects, the invariant (expressing that any amount k is equal to the salary of an employee whose salary has been set to k) clearly holds.

Now imagine that we distinguish between ordinary employees and managers by adding a permanent bonus when paying the salary of a manager, as shown in slide 4-14. The reader may judge whether this example is realistic or not.

Then, perhaps somewhat to our surprise, we find that the invariant stated for employees no longer holds for managers. From the perspective of predictable object behavior this is definitely undesirable, since invariants are the cornerstone

```
Invariant properties – algebraic laws                          4-13

    class employee {                        ┌──────────┐
                                            │ employee │
    public:                                 └──────────┘
    employee( int n = 0 ) : sal(n) { }
    employee* salary(int n) { sal = n; return
        this; }
    virtual long salary() { return sal; }
    protected:
    int sal;
    };


Invariant

        k == (e->salary(k))->salary()
```

Slide 4-13: Invariant properties as algebraic laws

```
Problem – hidden bonus                                         4-14

    class manager : public employee {       ┌─────────┐
                                            │ manager │
    public:                                 └─────────┘
    long salary() { return sal + 1000; }
    };


Invariant

        k =?= (m->salary(k))->salary()
```

Slide 4-14: Violating the invariant

of reliable software. The solution to this anomaly is to make the assignment of a
bonus explicit, as shown in slide 4-15.

   Now, the invariant pertaining to managers may be strengthened by including
the effects of assigning a bonus. As a consequence, the difference in salary no
longer occurs as if by magic but is directly visible in the interaction with a manager
object, as it should be.

4.2.3   An objective sense of style

The guidelines presented by Lieberherr and Holland (1989) were among the first,
and they still provide good advice with respect to designing class interfaces.

4-15

Solution – *explicit bonus*

```
class manager : public employee {        manager'
public:
manager* bonus(int n) { sal += n; return this;
    }
};
```

Invariant – *restored*

$$k + n == ((m->salary(k))->bonus(n))->salary()$$

Slide 4-15: Restoring the invariant

4-16

Good Object-Oriented Design

- *organize and reduce dependencies between classes*

Client – A method m is a client of C if m calls a method of C

Supplier – If m is a client of C then C is a supplier of m

Acquaintance – C is an acquaintance of m if C is a supplier of m but not (the type of) an *argument* of m or (of) an *instance variable* of the object of m

- C is a *preferred acquaintance* of m if an object of C is created in m or C is the type of a global variable

- C is a *preferred supplier* of m if C is a supplier and C is (the type of) an instance variable, an argument or a preferred acquaintance

Slide 4-16: Clients, suppliers and acquaintances

In slide 4-16, an explicit definition of the dual notions of *client* and *supplier* has been given. It is important to note that not all of the potential suppliers for a class may be considered *safe*. Potentially *unsafe* suppliers are distinguished as *acquaintances*, of which those that are either created during a method call or stored in a global variable are to be preferred.

Although this may not be immediately obvious, this excludes *suppliers* that are accessed in some indirect way, for instance as the result of a method call to some *safe* supplier. As an example of using an unsafe supplier, consider the call

```
screen->cursor()->move();
```

which instructs the cursor associated with the screen to move to its home position. Although *screen* may be assumed to be a safe supplier, the object delivered by *screen* → *cursor*() need not necessarily be a safe supplier. In contrast, the call

```
screen->move_cursor();
```

does not make use of an indirection introducing a potentially unsafe supplier.

The guideline concerning the use of *safe* suppliers is known as the *Law of Demeter*, of which the underlying intuition is that the programmer should not be bothered by knowledge that is not immediately apparent from the program text (that is the class interface) or founded in well-established conventions (as in the case of using special global variables). See slide 4-17.

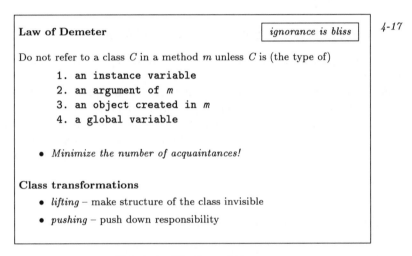

Slide 4-17: The Law of Demeter

To remedy the use of unsafe suppliers, two kinds of program transformation are suggested by Lieberherr and Holland (1989). First, the structure of a class should be made invisible for clients, to prohibit the use of a component as (an unsafe) supplier. This may require the *lifting* of primitive actions to the encompassing object, in order to make these primitives available to the client in a safe way. Secondly, the client should not be given the responsibility of performing (a sequence of) low-level actions. For example, moving the cursor should not be the responsibility of the client of the screen, but instead of the object representing the screen. In principle, the client need not be burdened with detailed knowledge of the cursor class.

The software engineering principles underlying the *Law of Demeter* may be characterized as representing a *compositional approach*, since *the law* enforces the use of immediate parts only. As additional benefits, conformance to *the law* results in hiding the component structure of classes, reduces the coupling of control and, moreover, promotes reuse by enforcing the use of localized (type) information.

4.3   From specification to implementation

Designing an object-oriented system requires the identification of object classes and the characterization of their responsibilities, preferably by means of *contracts*.

In addition, one must establish the relationships between the object classes constituting the system and delineate the facilities the system offers to the user. Such facilities are usually derived from a requirements document and may be formally specified in terms of abstract operations on the system.

In this section we will look at the means we have available to express the properties of our object model, and we will study how we may employ abstract specifications of system operations to arrive at the integration of user actions and the object model underlying a system in a seamless way. The approach sketched may be characterized as event-centered.

4.3.1   Structural versus behavioral encapsulation

Object-oriented modeling has clearly been inspired by or, to be more careful, shows significant similarity to the method of *semantic modeling* that has become popular for developing information systems. In an amusing paper, King (1989) discusses how semantic modeling and object-oriented modeling are related. Apart from a difference in terminology, semantic modeling differs from object-oriented modeling primarily by its focus on *structural aspects*, whereas object-oriented modeling is more concerned with *behavioral* aspects, as characterized by the notion of *responsibilities*.

Structural versus behavioral encapsulation   *4-18*

	semantic model	object-oriented
abstraction	structural	behavioral
inheritance	subtypes	subclasses

Semantic modeling – *constructing types*

  - *aggregation, grouping by association*

Slide 4-18: Semantic modeling

Typically, semantic modeling techniques provide a richer repertoire for constructing types, including a variety of methods for aggregation and a notion of grouping by association. See slide 4-18. The object-oriented counterpart of aggregation may be characterized as the *has-a* or *part-of* relation, that is usually expressed by including the (part) object as a data member.

Associations between objects cannot be expressed directly in an object-oriented framework. On an implementation level, the association relation corresponds to membership of a common collection, or being stored in the same container. However, the absence of an explicit association relation makes it hard to express general *m-n relations*, as, for example, the relation between students and courses.

Object-oriented modeling   *4-19*

- *is-a* – inheritance
- *has-a, uses* – delegation
- *uses* – templates

Slide 4-19: Relations between objects

The influence of a semantic modeling background can be clearly felt in the OMT method. The object model of OMT is a rather direct generalization of the *entity-relationship* model. Entities in the *entity-relationship* model may only contain (non-object) data members, which are called attributes.

In contrast, *objects* (in the more general sense) usually hide object and non-object data members, and instead provide a method interface. Moreover, object-oriented modeling focuses on behavioral properties, whereas semantic modeling has been more concerned with (non-behavioral) data types and (in the presence of inheritance) data subtypes.

Relations, as may be expressed in the *entity-relationship* model, can partly be expressed directly in terms of the mechanisms supported by object-oriented languages. For instance, the *is-a* relation corresponds closely (although not completely) with the inheritance relation. See slide 4-19. Both the *has-a* and *uses* relation is usually implemented by including (a pointer to) an object as a data member. Another important relation is the *is-like* relation, which may exist between objects that are neither related by the inheritance relation nor by the subtype relation, but yet have a similar interface and hence may be regarded as being of analogous types. The *is-like* relation may be enforced by parametrized types that require the presence of particular methods, such as a *compare* operator in the case of a generic list supporting a *sort* method.

4.3.2   Model-based specification

Several development methods, including Responsibility Driven Design and Fusion (see section 3.1.2), allow for the specification of user interactions in a semi-formal way by means of pre- and post-conditions. These approaches have been inspired by model-based specification methods such as VDM and Z, which offer a formal framework for specifying the requirements of a system. Model-based specification methods derive their name from the opportunity to specify a mathematical model capturing the relevant features of the system. Operations, which may correspond to user actions, can then be specified in a purely logical way.

In the following, an outline of the specification language Z will be given. More importantly, the specification of a simple library system will be discussed, illustrating how we may specify user actions in an abstract way. (The use of the Z specification language is in this respect only of subsidiary importance.) In the subsequent section, we will look at the realization of the library employing an

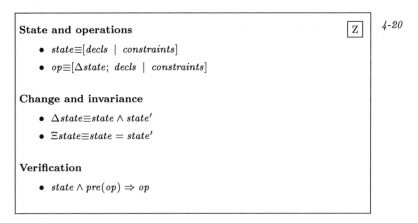

Slide 4-20: Model-based specification

abstract system of objects and events corresponding to the user actions, which reflects the characterization given in the formal specification.

The specification language Z is based on classical (two-valued) logic and set theory. It has been used in a number of industrial projects, Hayes (1992), and to specify the architecture of complex intelligent systems, Craig (1991). The central compositional unit of specification in Z is the *schema*. A schema may be used to specify both states and operations in a logical way. The logic employed in Z is a typed logic. The specification of a *schema* consists of a number of *declarations* followed by *constraints* specifying conditions on the variables introduced in the declarations. Declarations may include other schemas, as in the example specification of the operation *op*. The schema $\Delta state$ itself is a compound schema that results from the logical conjunction of the schema *state* and its primed version *state'*, which denotes *state* after applying *op*.

Both schema inclusion and schema conjunction are examples of the powerful schema calculus supported by Z, which enables the user to specify complex systems in Z.

Moreover, schemas may be decorated to specify the effects of an operation. Invariance may be specified as in $\Xi state$, which expresses that the *state* before applying the operation is the same as the state (denoted by *state'*) after applying the operation.

Since schemas are specified in a logical manner, both pre- and post-conditions are implicitly specified by the constraints included in the schema. Hence, to verify that an operation *op* is legal for a state it is merely required to verify that the conditions specified for *state* hold, and that, together with the pre-conditions (which are implicitly specified by the schema for *op*), they imply the logical formula characterizing *op*. See slide 4-20.

An important property of Z is that it allows for a graphical layout of schemas, as illustrated in the specification of a *Counter* given in slide 4-21. The state of a *Counter* is given by the *Counter* schema declaring an integer variable n,

State

$Counter$

___ $Counter$ _____

$n : \mathbb{N}$

_____

$n \geq 0$

_____

Operations

___ $Incr$ _____

$\Delta\,Counter$

_____

$n' = n + 1$

_____

___ $Decr$ _____

$\Delta\,Counter$

_____

$n > 0$

$n' = n - 1$

_____

Slide 4-21: The specification of a $Counter$ in Z

which is constrained by the condition $n \geq 0$. The operations $Incr$ and $Decr$ are specified by defining the state following the operation by, respectively, $n' = n + 1$ and $n' = n - 1$. Both operations require the declaration $\Delta\,Counter$ to indicate that the state specified by $Counter$ will be modified. In addition, the operation $Decr$ requires as a pre-condition that $n>0$, needed to prevent the violation of the invariant, which would happen whenever n became less than zero.

An alternative specification of the $Counter$ is given in slide 4-22. To emphasize that we may regard the $Counter$ as an object, the operations have been prefixed by $Counter$ in a C++-like manner. This is only a syntactic device, however, carrying no formal meaning. In addition, both the operations $Incr$ and $Decr$ declare an integer variable $v?$ which acts, by convention, as an input parameter. Similarly, the integer variable $v!$ declared for the operation $value$ acts, again by convention, as an output parameter.

Since Z allows the inclusion of other schemas in the declaration part of a schema, we may easily mimic inheritance as illustrated in the specification of $Bounded :: Counter$, which is a $Counter$ with a maximum given by an integer constant Max.

Similarly, we may specify the operations for the $Bounded :: Counter$ by including the corresponding operations specified for the $Counter$, adding conditions if required.

Counter $\boxed{\text{Z}}$ *4-22*

- $Counter == [n : \mathbb{N} \mid n \geq 0]$

- $Counter :: Incr == [\Delta Counter, v? : \mathbb{N} \mid n' = n + v?]$

- $Counter :: Decr == [\Delta Counter \mid n{>}0; \; n' = n - 1]$

- $Counter :: Value == [\Xi Counter; \; v! : \mathbb{N} \mid v! = n]$

Bounded counter

- $Bounded :: Counter == [Counter \mid n \leq Max]$

- $Bounded :: Incr == [Counter :: Incr \mid n{<}Max]$

Slide 4-22: An alternative specification of the *Counter*

From a schema we may easily extract the pre-conditions for an operation by removing from the conditions the parts involving a primed variable. Clearly, the post-condition is then characterized by the conditions thus eliminated.

For example, the pre-condition of the *Counter :: Incr* operation is $v? \geq 0$, whereas the post-condition is $n' = n{+}v?$ which corresponds to the implementation requirement that the new value of the *Counter* is the old value plus the value of the argument $v?$. In a similar way, the pre-condition for applying the *Bounded :: Incr* operation is $n{+}v? \leq Max$. Note, however, that this pre-condition is stronger than the original pre-condition $v? \geq 0$, hence to conform with the rules for refinement we must specify what happens when $n + v?{>}Max$ as well. This is left as an exercise for the reader.

Clearly, although Z lacks a notion of objects or classes, it may conveniently be employed to specify the behavior of an object. In Stepney *et al.* (1992), a number of studies are collected which propose extending Z with a formal notion of classes and inheritance. The reader interested in these extensions is invited in particular to study Object-Z, OOZE and Z++. As an historical aside, we may note that Z has been of significant influence in the development of Eiffel (see Meyer, 1992b). Although the two approaches are quite divergent, they obviously still share a common interest in correctness.

In contrast to Eiffel, which offers only a semi-formal way in which to specify the behavior of object classes, Z allows for a precise formal specification of the requirements a system must meet. To have the specification reflect the object structure of the system more closely, one of the extensions of Z mentioned above may be used. An example of using (plain) Z to specify the functionality of a library system is given below.

The specification of a library Imagine that you must develop a program to manage a library, that is keep a record of the books that have been borrowed.

Before developing a detailed object model, you may well reflect on what user services the library must provide. These services include the borrowing of a book,

$$
\begin{array}{|l r|}
\hline
\textbf{State} & \textit{4-23} \\
& \boxed{\textit{Library } (1)} \\
& \\
\text{\quad\_\_ Library _____} & \\
\hline
\end{array}
$$

State   4-23

                                        $\boxed{\textit{Library } (1)}$

    Library ————————————————————
     $books : \mathbb{P}\, Book$
     $borrowed : Book \nrightarrow Person$
    ————————————————————————
     $\text{dom } borrowed \subseteq books$

Slide 4-23: The specification of a library

returning a book and asking whether a person has borrowed any books, and if so which books. These operations are specified by the schemas *Borrow*, *Return* and *Has* in slide 4-24.

Operations   *4-24*

                                        $\boxed{\textit{Library } (2)}$

    Borrow ————————————————————
     $\Delta Library;\ b? : Book;\ p? : Person$
    ————————————————————————
     $b? \notin \text{dom } borrowed$
     $b? \in books$
     $borrowed' = borrowed \cup \{b? \mapsto p?\}$

    Return ————————————————————
     $\Delta Library;\ b? : Book;\ p? : Person$
    ————————————————————————
     $b? \in \text{dom } borrowed$
     $borrowed' = borrowed \setminus \{b? \mapsto p?\}$

    Has ————————————————————
     $\Xi Library;\ p? : Person;\ bks : \mathbb{P}\, Book$
    ————————————————————————
     $bks! = borrowed^{-1} (\!|\ \{p?\}\ |\!)$

Slide 4-24: The library operations

Don't be frightened of the mathematical notation in which these operations are specified. The notation is only of secondary importance and will be explained as we go along.

Since we are only interested in the abstract relations between people and books, we may assume *Book* and *Person* to be primitive types. The specification given in slide 4-23 specifies an abstract state, which is actually a partial function delivering the person that borrowed the book if the function is defined for the book. The function is partial to allow for the situation where a book has not been borrowed, but still lies on the shelves. The invariant of the library system states that the domain of the function *borrowed* must be a subset of the books available in the library.

Given the specification of the state, and some mathematical intuition, the specification of the operations is quite straightforward.

When a *Borrow* action occurs, which has as input a book $b?$ and a person $p?$, the function *borrowed'* is defined by extending *borrowed* with the association between $b?$ and $p?$, which is expressed as the mapping $b? \mapsto p?$. As a pre-condition for *Borrow*, we have that *borrowed* must not be defined for $b?$, otherwise some person would already have borrowed the book $b?$.

The *Return* action may be considered as the reverse of the *Borrow* action. Its pre-condition states that *borrowed* must be defined for $b?$ and the result of the operation is that the association between $b?$ and $p?$ is removed from *borrowed'*.

Finally, the operation *Has* allows us to query what books are in the possession of a person $p?$. The specification of *Has* employs the mathematical features of Z in a nice way. The output, which is stored in the output parameter $bks!$, consists of all the books related to the person $p?$. The set of books related to $p?$ is obtained by taking the relational image of the inversion of *borrowed* for the singleton set consisting of $p?$, that is, each book x for which an association $x \mapsto p?$ is in *borrowed* is included in the set $bks!$. Again, it is not the notation that is important here, but the fact that the specification defines all top-level user interactions.

4.3.3 Abstract systems and events

User actions may require complex interactions between the objects constituting the object model of a system. Such interactions are often of an *ad hoc* character in the sense that they embody one of the many possible ways in which the functionality of objects may be used. What we need is a methodology or paradigm that allows us to express these interactions in a concise yet pragmatically amenable way. In Henderson (1993), a notion of *abstract systems* is introduced that seems to meet our needs to a large extent. See slide 4-25.

Abstract systems – *design methodology*   *4-25*

    • abstract system = abstract data types + protocol

Events – *high level glue*

    • realization of the interaction protocol

Slide 4-25: Abstract systems and events

Abstract systems extend the notion of abstract data types to capture the (possible) interactions between collections of objects. The idea underlying the notion of an *abstract system* is to collect the commands available for the client or user of the *system*. The collection of commands comprising an abstract system are usually a (strict) subset of the commands available in the combined interface of the abstract data types involved. In other words, an abstract system provides a restricted interface, restricted to safeguard the user from breaking the protocol of interaction implicitly defined by the collection of abstract data types of which the system consists.

An abstract system in itself merely provides a guideline on how a collection of objects is to be used, but does not offer a formal means to check whether a user plays by the rules. After presenting an example of an abstract system, we will look at how *events* may be used to protect the user against breaking the (implicit) laws governing the interaction.

Example – the library The abstract system comprising a library may be characterized as in slide 4-26. In essence, it provides an exemplary interface, that is, it lists the statements that are typically used by a client of the library software. We use typical identifiers to denote objects of the various types involved.

4-26

```
Abstract system – exemplary interface                    library

        p = new person();
        b = new book();
        p = b->borrower;
        s = p->books;
        tf = b->inlibrary();
        b->borrow(p);
        p->allocate(b);
        p->deallocate(b);
        b->_return(p);

For person* p; book* b; set<book>* s; bool tf;
```

Slide 4-26: The library system

The commands available to the user of the library software are constructors for a *person* and a *book*, an instruction to get access to the *borrower* of a particular book, an instruction to ask what books a particular person has borrowed, an instruction to query whether a particular book is in the library, and instructions for a person to *borrow* or *return* a book.

To realize the abstract system *library*, we evidently need the classes *book* and *person*. The class *book* may be defined as follows.

```
class book {                                              book
public:
```

```
person* borrower;
book() {}
void borrow( person* p ) { borrower = p;   }
void _return( person* p ) { borrower = 0; }
bool inlibrary() { return !borrower; }
};
```

It consists of a constructor, functions to *borrow* and *return* a book, a function to test whether the book is in the library and an instance variable containing the *borrower* of the book. Naturally, the class *book* may be improved with respect to encapsulation (by providing a method to access the borrower) and may further be extended to store additional information, such as the title and publisher of the book.

```
class person {                                          person
public:
person() { books = new set<book>(); }
void allocate( book* b ) { books->insert(b); }
void deallocate( book* b ) { books->remove(b); }
set<book>* books;
};
```

The next class involved in the *library* system is the class *person*, given above. The class *person* offers a constructor, an instance variable to store the set of books borrowed by the person and the functions *allocate* and *deallocate* to respectively insert and remove the books from the person's collection. A typical example of using the library system is given below.

```
book* Stroustrup = new book();                          example
book* ChandyMisra = new book();
book* Smalltalk80 = new book();

person* Hans = new person();
person* Cees = new person();

Stroustrup->borrow(Hans);
Hans->allocate(Stroustrup);
ChandyMisra->borrow(Cees);
Cees->allocate(ChandyMisra);
Smalltalk80->borrow(Cees);
Cees->allocate(Smalltalk80);
```

First, a number of books are defined, then a number of persons, and finally (some of) the books that are borrowed by (some of) the persons.

Note that lending a book involves both the invocation of *book* :: *borrow* and *person* :: *allocate*. This could easily be simplified by extending the function *book* :: *borrow* and *book* :: *_return* with the statements $p \rightarrow allocate(this)$ and $p \rightarrow deallocate(this)$ respectively. However, I would rather take the opportunity to illustrate the use of *events*, providing a generic solution to the interaction problem noted.

Events Henderson (1993) introduces *events* as a means by which to control the complexity of relating a user interface to the functionality provided by the classes comprising the library system. The idea underlying the use of events is that for every kind of interaction with the user a specific event class is defined that captures the details of the interaction between the user and the various object classes. Abstractly, we may define an event as an entity with only two significant moments in its life-span, the moment of its *creation* (and initialization) and the moment of its *activation* (that is when it actually happens). As a class we may define an *event* as follows.

```
class Event {                                          Event
public:
virtual void operator()() = 0;
};
```

The class *Event* is an abstract class, since the application operator that may be used to activate the event is defined as zero.

```
class Borrow : public Event {                          Borrow
public:
Borrow( person* _p, book* _b ) { _b = b; _p = p; }
void operator()() {
        require( _b && _p );                           _b and _p exist
        _b->borrow(p);
        _p->allocate(b);
        }
private:
person* _p; book* _b;
};
```

For the *library* system defined above we may conceive of two actual events (that is, possible refinements of the *Event* class), namely a *Borrow* event and a *Return* event.

The *Borrow* event class provides a controlled way in which to effect the borrowing of a book. In a similar way, a *Return* event class may be defined.

```
class Return : public Event {                          Return
public:
Return( person* _p, book* _b ) { _b = b; _p = p; }
void operator()() {
        require( _b && _p );
        _b->_return(p);
        _p->deallocate(b);
        }
```

```
private:
person* _p; book* _b;
};
```

The operation *Has* specified in the previous section has an immediate counterpart in the *person* :: *books* data member and need not be implemented by a
separate event.

Events are primarily used as intermediate between the user (interface) and the
objects comprising the library system. For the application at hand, using events
may seem to be somewhat of an overkill. However, events not only give a precise
characterization of the interactions involved but, equally importantly, allow for
extending the repertoire of interactions without disrupting the structure of the
application simply by introducing additional event types.

Summary

This chapter looked at application development. We started with a simple example and subsequently discussed guidelines for class design. We then looked at a
more formal approach, involving the transition from a formal specification to the
actual implementation based on a notion of abstract systems and events.

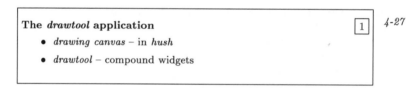

Slide 4-27: Section 4.1: The *drawtool* application

In section 1 we looked at how to develop applications in *hush*, as a typical
example of inplementing an interactive editor.

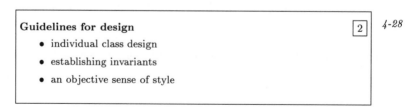

Slide 4-28: Section 4.2: Guidelines for design

In section 2, some guidelines for design were presented. We looked at issues
that may arise when attempting to establish class invariants. Finally, we discussed
the rules imposed by the *Demeter* method.

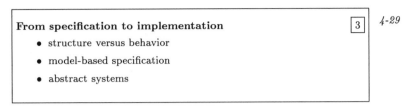

Slide 4-29: Section 4.3: From specification to implementation

In section 3, we discussed the distinction between structural and behavioral aspects of a system. We looked at the application of formal methods to specify the requirements for a system, and we studied an implementation based on abstract systems and events which was derived from the original formal specification.

Questions

1. Give an example of your choice to describe OO application development.

2. Discuss possible guidelines for individual class design.

3. Discuss how inheritance may affect class invariants.

4. What would be your rendering of the Law of Demeter? Can you phrase its underlying intuition? Explain.

5. Define the notions of client, supplier and acquaintance. What restrictions must be satisfied to speak of a preferred acquaintance and a preferred supplier?

6. Characterize the differences between semantic modeling and object-oriented modeling.

7. How would you characterize the notion of abstract systems?

8. Explain how events may be employed to maintain system integrity. Give an example!

Further reading

The original paper on *hush* is Eliëns (1995). A veritable catalogue of object-oriented applications can be found in Harmon and Taylor (1993). A classical paper on class design is Johnson and Foote (1988). For the *Law of Demeter*, consult Lieberherr and Holland (1989). The notion of *abstract systems* was introduced in Henderson (1993), which also gives a good account of a formal approach to object-oriented design. For an introduction to formal methods and Z, consult Diller (1994). For object-oriented extensions of Z, see Stepney *et al.* (1992).

Part II

Object-Oriented Languages and Systems

5

Object-oriented programming languages

When developing an object-oriented system, at some time a choice has to be made for an actual programming language or environment. It goes without saying that the optimal environment will be one that is in accord with the method chosen for design. Naturally, other desiderata (involving efficiency, portability or client-imposed constraints) may play an equally significant role.

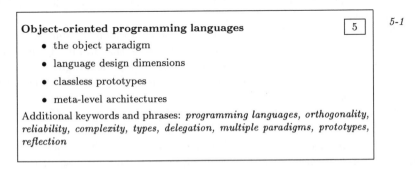

Slide 5-1: Object-oriented programming languages

This chapter will present an overview of the numerous languages that exist for object-oriented development. A comparison of Smalltalk, Eiffel, C++ and Java will be given, and we will look at the considerations underlying the design of the various object-oriented (extensions of) programming languages. Also, some possible modifications and alternatives to the traditional class-based object model will be discussed, including active objects, prototypes and meta-level architectures.

5.1   The object paradigm

The object paradigm is embodied in numerous programming languages. Saunders (1989) presents a survey of 88 object-oriented languages, of which 69 are *standalone* and 19 incorporated into either multi-paradigm or database systems. (A multi-paradigm system, in this context, means a system embedding an environment for window programming or knowledge-based reasoning.)

In this section, we will first look at the classification of object-oriented languages (as given in Saunders, 1989). Most of the languages mentioned are based on a distinction between classes and objects. However, alternative object models (without classes) are also being employed. Finally, we will review a number of object extensions of the languages Lisp, C and Prolog.

On the notion of object Before our comparative study of object-oriented programming languages, we may well reflect on some issues of language design (specifically the motivations underlying the development of a programming language) and in particular on the notion of object underlying our conception of object oriented programming languages.

Language design is an intricate issue. The motivation to develop a programming language may come from the desire for experimentation (as it has been for the author, Eliëns (1992)), from governmental policy (in the case of Ada), corporate policy (as for PL-1), the wish to improve programming habits (which lies at the basis of Pascal and Modula, Wirth (1983)), the wish to provide more adequate programming constructs (as, for instance, C++ was originally meant to be a better C), the efficient implementation of a theoretically interesting model of computing (as has been the case for Prolog), or circumstantial forces (of which Java may be considered an example).

Whatever motivation lies behind the development of a programming language, every language is meant to serve some purpose. Whether implicitly or explicitly stated, a programming language is characterized by its design goals and the applications it is intended to support. *A fortiori* this holds for object-oriented programming languages.

The impetus to research in object-oriented programming may be traced back to the development of Simula, which was originally intended for discrete event simulation. As observed in Taivalsaari (1993), Simula has since served as a valuable source of ideas in several research areas in computer science. See slide 5-2.

These areas include *abstract data types* (that play a prominent role in software engineering, Parnas (1972b); Liskov and Zilles (1974)), *frames* in artificial intelligence (which have become an invaluable mechanism for knowledge repre-

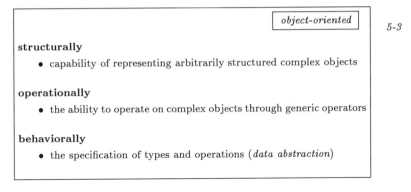

Slide 5-2: The heritage of Simula

sentation, Fikes and Kehler (1985) and Minsky (1975)), *semantic data models* (which are widely used to develop information systems, Hammer and McLeod (1978)), and *capability-based computing* (that plays a prominent role in distributed computer systems, Levy (1984)).

The research efforts in these areas in their turn have had a strong impact on our conception of object-oriented computing. With regard to object-oriented programming we may differentiate between three (partially distinct) viewpoints from which to characterize the notion of an object.

Slide 5-3: Perspectives of object orientation

From a *structural* viewpoint, object-oriented means the capability of representing arbitrarily complex objects. This viewpoint is of importance for implementing object-oriented languages and the development of adequate runtime models of object-oriented computing. From this perspective, an object is (in the end) a structure in memory.

From an *operational* viewpoint, object-oriented means the ability to operate on complex objects through generic operators. This viewpoint is closely related to the notion of semantic data models, and is of particular importance for conceptual modeling. From this perspective, an object represents (an element of) a conceptual model.

From a *behavioral* viewpoint, object-oriented means the support to specify abstract polymorphic types with associated operations. This viewpoint is primarily of importance for software engineering and the development of formal methods of specification and verification. From this perspective an object is like a module, to be used for data abstraction.

From the inception of Simula, there has been a close relation between object-orientation and modeling, that is a tendency to regard a program as a physical model simulating the behavior of either a real or imaginary part of the world, see Knudsen and Madsen (1988). However, as observed in Taivalsaari (1993), there seems to be a division between the European interpretation of object orientation (which remains close to the original notion of conceptual modeling) and the American interpretation (which is of a more pragmatic nature as it stresses the importance of data abstraction and the reusability of program components).

5.1.1   A classification of object-oriented languages

To be characterized as *object-oriented*, a language must minimally support an *object creation* facility and a *message-passing* facility (message-passing in the sense of method invocation). In addition, many languages provide a mechanism to define *classes* together with some form of *inheritance*. See slide 5-4.

Objects – language characteristics   *5-4*

- object creation facility
- message-passing capability
- class capability
- inheritance features

Classification

- hybrid – *C, Lisp, Pascal, Prolog*
- frame-based – *knowledge-based reasoning*
- distributed, concurrent, actor – *parallel computing*
- alternative object models – *prototypes, delegation*

Slide 5-4: A classification of languages

Actually, as we will see in section 5.3, one may have a lively debate on the proper design dimensions of object-oriented programming languages. An important issue in this respect is what makes a language object-oriented as opposed to object-based. Other issues in this debate are whether an object-oriented language must support classes (in addition to a mechanism to create objects) and whether (static) inheritance should be preferred above (dynamic) delegation. This debate is reflected in a number of research efforts investigating alternative object models and object communication mechanisms. See section 5.4.

Of the 69 (standalone) object-oriented languages surveyed, 53 were research projects and only 16 were commercial products. Of these, 14 were extensions of either Lisp (10) or C (4). Among the remaining languages, quite a number were derived from languages such as Pascal, Ada or Prolog.

There is a great diversity between the different object-oriented languages. However, following Saunders (1989), they may be divided among subcategories reflecting their origin or the area of application for which they were developed (as shown above).

Hybrid languages These, having originated out of (an object-oriented extension of) an already existing language, are likely to be applied in a similar area to their ancestor. In practice, this category of languages (which includes C++ and CLOS) seems to be quite important, partly because their implementation support is as good as the implementation support for their base languages and, more importantly, they allow potential software developers a smooth transition from a non object-oriented to an object-oriented approach.

Frame-based languages in contrast to the previous category, these were explicitly developed to deal with one particular application area, knowledge-based reasoning. A *frame* is a structure consisting of *slots* that may either indicate a relation to other frames or contain the value of an attribute of the frame. In fact, the early frame-based languages such as FRL, Bundy (1986), and KRL, Bobrow and Winograd (1977), may be considered as object-oriented *avant la lettre*, that is before object orientation gained its popularity. Later frame-based systems, such as KEE, Kunz *et al.* (1984), and LOOPS, Stefik and Bobrow (1986), incorporated explicitly object-oriented notions such as classes and (multiple) inheritance.

Concurrent, distributed and actor languages To promote the use of parallel processing architectures a number of parallel object-oriented languages have been developed, among which are the language *Hybrid* (which supports active objects with their own thread of control, Nierstrasz (1987)), Concurrent Smalltalk (a concurrent extension of Smalltalk), Orient-K (a language for parallel knowledge processing) and POOL-T (which may be characterized as a simplified version of Ada), see Yonezawa and Tokoro (1987). More recently sC++, an extension of C++ with synchronous active objects has been proposed in PetitPierre (1998). A realisation of the same concept in Java has also been proposed, albeit without compiler support, in PetitPierre (1999).

POOL-T also supports the notion of *active objects*. Active objects have a body which allows them to execute their own activity in parallel with other active objects. To answer a request to execute a method, an active object must explicitly interrupt its activity (by means of an answer or *accept* statement as in Ada). POOL-T is interesting, primarily, because it is complemented by extensive theoretical research into the semantical foundations of parallel object-oriented computing. See de Bakker *et al.* (1990) and also section 10.3.

The idea of simultaneously active objects leads in a natural way to the notion of distributed object-oriented languages that support objects which may be located on geographically distinct processors and which communicate by means of (actual) message passing. Examples of such languages are *Distributed Smalltalk* (a distributed extension of Smalltalk that introduces so-called *proxy objects* to deal with communication between objects residing on different processors, Bennett (1987)) and *Emerald* (that supports primitives to migrate objects across a processor network, Black and Hutchinson (1986)).

All parallel/distributed object-oriented languages introduced thus far are based on a traditional object model insofar as an object retains its identity during its lifetime. In contrast, the so-called *actor* languages support a notion of object whereby the parallel activity of an object is enabled by *self-replacement* of the object in response to a message. Self-replacement proceeds as follows. Each *actor* object has a mail-queue. When a message arrives for the *actor* object, the object invokes the appropriate method and subsequently creates a successor object (which basically is a copy of itself with some modifications that may depend upon the contents of the message). Message handling occurs asynchronously. This scheme of asynchronous message passing enables an *actor* system to execute in parallel, since during the execution of a method the replacement object may proceed to handle other incoming messages.

In *actor* systems, object identity is replaced by what may be called mail-queue or address identity. From a theoretical viewpoint this allows us to treat *actor* objects as functions (in a mathematical sense) that deliver an effect and another object in response to a message. However, pragmatically this leads to a complicated and quite low-level object model which is hard to implement in a truly parallel way.

5.1.2 Alternative object models

Since the introduction of Smalltalk, the predominant notion of objects has been based on the distinction between classes and objects. Classes serve to describe the functionality and behavior of objects, while objects are instance of classes. In other words, classes serve as templates to create objects. Inheritance, then, may be regarded as a means by which to share (descriptions of) object behavior. It is generally defined on classes in terms of a derivation mechanism, that allows one to declare a class to be a subclass of another (super) class.

The distinction between classes and objects leads to a number of difficulties, both of a pragmatic and theoretical nature. (See also sections 5.3 and 5.5 for a discussion of the theoretical problems.) For example, the existence of *one-of-a-kind* classes, that is classes which have only one instance, is often considered unnatural. An example of a class-less language is the language *Self*. Self has a Smalltalk-like syntax, but in contrast to Smalltalk only supports *objects* (containing slots) and *messages*, and hence no classes. Slots may be designated to be parent-slots which means that messages that cannot be handled by the object itself are delegated to the parent object. In contrast to inheritance, which is static since the inherited functionality is computed at object creation time, delegation to parent objects as in Self is dynamic, since parent slots may be changed during the lifetime of an object.

Objects in Self may themselves be used to create other objects (as copies of the original object) in a similar way as classes may be used to create instances.

However, the changes made to an object are propagated when cloning object copies. Single objects, from which copies are taken, may in other words be regarded as prototypes, approximating in a dynamic way the functionality of their offspring, whereas classes provide a more static, so to speak universal, description of their object instances. Self employs runtime compilation, which is claimed to result in an efficiency comparable to C in Ungar and Smith (1987). In section 5.4 we will discuss the use of prototypes and the distinction between inheritance and delegation.

Alternative object models may also be encountered in object-oriented database managements systems and in systems embedding objects such as hypertext or hypermedia systems.

5.1.3   Object extensions of Lisp, C and Prolog

The notion of object is to a certain extent orthogonal to, that is independent of, language constructs around which programming languages may be constructed, such as expressions, functions and procedures. Hence, it should come as no surprise that a number of (popular) object-oriented programming languages were originally developed as extensions of existing languages or language implementations. See slide 5-5.

Object extensions   *5-5*

- Lisp – LOOPS, FLAVORS, CLOS, FOOPS
- C – Objective C, C++
- Prolog – SPOOL, VULCAN, DLP

Commercial products – *languages*

- Smalltalk, Eiffel, C++, Objective C, Object Pascal, Java

Slide 5-5: Object-oriented languages

The advantage of extending an existing language with object-oriented constructs, from the point of view of the user, is that the object-oriented approach can be gradually learned. However, at the same time this may be a disadvantage, since a hybrid approach to software development may give rise to sloppy design. Many proponents of an object-oriented approach, therefore, believe that learning to use object-oriented constructs is best done in an environment as offered by Smalltalk, where classes and objects are the sole means of developing an application.

It is noteworthy that, with the exception of Smalltalk, Eiffel and Java, many commercially available languages are actually extensions of existing languages such as Lisp, C and (to some extent) Prolog.

Lisp-based extensions In Saunders (1989), ten Lisp-based object-oriented languages are mentioned, among which are LOOPS (introducing a variety of object-oriented constructs, see Stefik and Bobrow (1986)), Flavors (which extends Lisp by adding generic functions that operate on objects, see Moon (1986)), and CLOS (which is actually a standardization effort of the ANSI X3J13 group to define the Common Lisp Object Standard). CLOS is a widely used system containing some non-trivial extensions to the object model and the way in which polymorphic methods may be defined.

C-based extensions Another very important class of object extensions is those of C-based object-oriented languages, of which the most well-known are Objective-C and C++.

The concepts underlying these two extensions are radically different. Objective-C introduces objects as an add-on to the constructs (including *structs*) available in C, whereas C++ realizes a close (and efficient) coupling between the *struct* (record) notion of C and the concept of a class.

In other words, in Objective-C there is a clear distinction between conventional C values and data types such as *int, float* and *struct* on the one hand, and objects on the other hand. Objects have a special data type (*id*) which allows them to be treated as first class elements. To define an object class, both an *interface* and *implementation* description must be given. These descriptions are preceded by a special sign to designate Objective-C specific code. Also, method declarations (in the interface description) and method definitions (which are to be put in the implementation section) must be preceded by a special sign to designate them as methods available for clients of object instances of that class.

The object model of Objective-C is similar to the object model of Smalltalk. In contrast, C++ quite radically departs from this object model in order to achieve an as efficient as possible implementation of objects. The key to an efficient implementation lies in the integration of the *struct* (record) construct originally provided by C with the class concept, by allowing functions to be members of a *struct*.

As explained in Stroustrup (1991), the equivalences depicted in slide 5-6 hold.

```
┌─────────────────────────────────────────────────────────────────┐          5-6
│  Object structure – efficient mapping              ┌──────┐        │
│                                                    │ C++  │        │
│                                                    └──────┘        │
│      struct A { ... }  ==  class  A { public:  ... }              │
│      class  A { ... }  ==  struct A { private: ... }              │
│                                                                   │
└─────────────────────────────────────────────────────────────────┘
```

Slide 5-6: The equivalence between *class* and *struct*

This interpretation allows an efficient mapping of object structures to the memory of a computer, provided that the compiler is clever enough.

Nevertheless, the efficiency of C++ comes at a price. C++ does support micro-efficiency but does not necessarily lead to the design of efficient code. In particular, hand-crafted memory management will not necessarily offer the most efficient solution when compared with built-in support, but is almost certainly detrimental to the quality of the code.

Prolog-based extensions A quite different class of object-oriented extensions, used primarily in research laboratories, consists of attempts to incorporate object-oriented features in (high-level) logic-based languages, such as Prolog. Among these are languages such as SPOOL (developed in the context of the Japanese fifth-generation computing project, see Fukanaga (1986)), Vulcan (that provides a preprocessor giving syntactic support for embedding objects in concurrent logic programming languages, see Kahn *et al.* (1986)) and DLP (a language combining logic programming with object-oriented features and parallelism developed by the author, see appendix E). The list of research articles covering the subject of combining logic programming and object-oriented programming is quite extensive. An overview and discussion of the various approaches is given in Davison (1993) and also in Eliëns (1992).

5.1.4   Script languages – integration with Java

Scripting has become a popular way to create applications, in particular GUI-based applications and Web applications. Tcl/Tk and Python are extensively used for GUI-based applications. For Web applications, scripting may be used at the client-side, for example to customize HTML pages using Javascript, or at the server-side, for writing CGI-scripts in (for example) Perl.

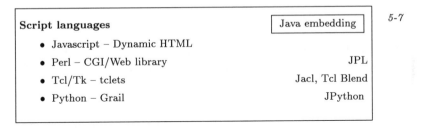

Script languages	Java embedding	*5-7*
• Javascript – Dynamic HTML		
• Perl – CGI/Web library	JPL	
• Tcl/Tk – tclets	Jacl, Tcl Blend	
• Python – Grail	JPython	

Slide 5-7: Script languages

Most of the scripting languages, including Tcl/Tk, Perl and Python, have an extensive library for creating (server-side) Web applications. For Tcl/Tk, there exists a Netscape plugin which allows for the inclusion of so-called *tclets* (pronounce *ticklets*), applets written in Tcl/Tk, in a HTML Web page.

Scripting has clear advantages for rapid prototyping. Disadvantages of scripting concern the lack of efficiency, and the absence of compile-time checks.

Script languages may be extended using C/C++, and more recently Java. The impact of Java becomes evident when considering that there exists a Java implementation for almost each scripting language, including Tcl/Tk, Perl and Python. JPython, which is the realization of Python in Java, even offers the possibility to integrate Python classes with Java classes, and is announced as a candidate scripting platform for Java in van Rossum (1998).

Java has also in other respects stimulated programming language research, since it appears to be an ideal platform for realising higher level programming languages.

Objects in Javascript

Originally, objects were not part of the languages Tcl/Tk and Perl. For these languages, objects have been added in an ad hoc fashion. In contrast, Python has been developed as an object-oriented language from its inception.

Javascript is a somewhat special case, since it allows for the use of built-in objects, in particular the objects defined by the Document Object Model (DOM), and its precursors. Nevertheless, due to its dynamic nature, Javascript also allows for creating user-defined objects, as indicated in the example below.

```
<script language=Javascript>                      javascript
function object_display(msg) {                    object method
        return msg + ' (' + this.variable++ + ')';
        }

function object() {                               object constructor
this.variable=0;
this.display = object_display;
return this;
}

var a = new object();                             create object

document.write(a.display("a message"));
document.write(a.display("another message"));
</script>
```

The trick is to define a function that allocates the storage for instance variables, which may include references to functions. Using the keyword *new*, a new structure is created that may be used as an object.

Which objects are available as built-in objects depends on the environment in which Javascript programs are executed. In the example, there is an invocation of the *write* method for a *document* object. The *document* object, as well as other objects corresponding to the browser environment and the contents of the page loaded, are part of the *Document Object Model*, which is discussed in more detail in section 12.2.1.

As an aside, Javascript has become surprisingly popular for writing dynamic HTML pages, as well as for writing server-side scripts. It is also supported by many VRML (Virtual Reality Modeling Language) browsers to define script nodes. See section 11.4.2. A reference implementation of Javascript is available, for embedding Javascript in C/C++ applications.

5.2   Comparing Smalltalk, Eiffel, C++ and Java

The languages Smalltalk, Eiffel, C++ and Java may be regarded as the four most important (and popular) representatives of classical object-oriented languages, classical in the sense of being based on a class/object distinction.

Criteria for comparison   *5-8*

- class libraries

- programming environment

- language characteristics

Slide 5-8: Criteria for comparison

In this section we will compare these languages with respect to what may be called their intrinsic language characteristics. Before that, however, we will indicate some other (more external) criteria for comparison such as the availability of class libraries and the existence of a programming environment. See slide 5-8. Our discussion is based on (but in some respects disagrees with and extends) Blaschek *et al.* (1989).

5.2.1   Criteria for comparison

When choosing a particular programming language as a vehicle for program development a number of factors play a role, among which are the availability of a class library, the existence of a good programming environment, and, naturally, the characteristics of the language itself.

Class libraries An important criterion when selecting a language may be the availability of sufficient class library support. A general class library, and preferably libraries suitable for the application domain one is working in, may drastically reduce development time. Another important benefit of using (well-tested) class libraries is an improvement of the reliability of the application.

Smalltalk (that is Smalltalk-80 of ParcPlace Systems) comes with a large collection of general purpose and graphics programming classes, that are identical for both MS-DOS and Unix platforms. Also Eiffel comes with a standard collection of well-documented libraries containing common data structures, container classes and classes for graphics programming. For both Smalltalk and Eiffel, the accompanying classes may almost be considered to be part of the language definition, in the sense that they provide a standard means to solve particular problems.

In contrast, for C++ there is almost no standard library support (except for IO stream classes). Even worse, the various C++ compiler vendors disagree considerably in what functionality the standard class libraries of C++ must offer. Fortunately, however, there is an increasingly large number of third party libraries (commercially and non-commercially) available. The burden of choosing the appropriate libraries is, however, placed on the shoulders of a user or a company, which has the advantage that a more optimal solution may be obtained than possible within the confines of standard libraries.

Java, on the other hand, offers an overwhelming amount of APIs, including a Reflection API, for meta programming, APIs for networking, communication, and APIs for multimedia and 3D. Perhaps the greatest benefit of Java is the effort put into the standardization of these APIs.

Programming environments Another selection criterion in choosing a language is the existence of a good programming environment. What constitutes a *good* programming environment is not as simple as it may seem, since that depends to a large extent upon the experience and preferences of the user. For example, with respect to operating systems, many novice users favor a graphical interface as originally offered by the Apple Macintosh computers, while experienced users often feel constrained by the limitations imposed by such systems. In contrast, experienced users may delight in the terseness and flexibility of the command-based Unix operating system, which leads to outright bewilderment with many novice users.

Of the object-oriented programming languages we consider, Smalltalk definitely offers the most comprehensive programming environment (including editors, browsers and debuggers). Eiffel comes with a number of additional tools (such as a graphical browser, and a program documentation tool) to support program development (and maintenance).

In contrast, C++ usually comes with nothing at all. However, increasingly many tools (including browsers and debuggers) have become available.

For Java there are a number of IDEs (Integrated Development Environments) available, most of which run only on the PC platform.

Language characteristics Despite the commonality between Smalltalk, Eiffel, C++ and Java (which may be characterized by saying that they all support *data abstraction, inheritance, polymorphism* and *dynamic binding*), these languages widely disagree on a number of other properties, such as those listed in slide 5-9.

These characteristics were used in Blaschek *et al.* (1989) to compare Smalltalk, Eiffel and C++ with the language Oberon, which offers what may be called a minimal (typed) object-oriented language. We will, however, limit our discussion here to Smalltalk, Eiffel, C++, and, additionally, Java.

5.2.2   Language characteristics

Smalltalk, Eiffel, C++ and Java differ with respect to a number of language characteristics. An indication of the differences between these languages is given slide 5-10.

This characterization conforms to the one given in Blaschek *et al.* (1989), with which I think the majority of the object-oriented community will agree. It is further motivated below. However, the places indicated by an asterisk deserve

5-9

Language characteristics

- uniformity of data structures

- documentation value

- reliability

- inheritance mechanisms

- efficiency

- memory management

- language complexity

Slide 5-9: Language characteristics

5-10

	Smalltalk	Eiffel	C++	Java
uniformity	high	medium	low	medium
documentation	medium	high	medium	high
reliability	medium	medium	low*	high*
protection	no	no	yes	yes
inheritance	no	yes	yes	no*
efficiency	low	medium	high	low
garbage	yes	yes	no*	yes
complexity	low*	medium	high	medium

Slide 5-10: Comparing Smalltalk, Eiffel, C++ and Java

some discussion. In particular, I wish to stress that I disagree with characterizing the reliability of C++ as *low*. (See below.)

Uniformity In Smalltalk, each data type is described by a class. This includes booleans, integers, real numbers and control constructs. In Eiffel there is a distinction between elementary data types (such as boolean, integer and real) and (user-defined) classes. However (in the later versions of Eiffel) the built-in elementary types behave as if declared by pre-declared classes. For C++, the elementary data types and simple data structures (as may be defined in C) do not behave as objects. To a certain extent, however, programmers may deal with this non-uniformity by some work-around, for example by overloading functions and operators or by embedding built-in types in a (wrapper) class. Java may be regarded as a simplified version of C++. Due to its restrictions, such as the absence of operator overloading and type casts, the language appears to be more uniform for the programmers.

Documentation value Smalltalk promotes a consistent style in writing programs, due to the assumption that *everything is an object*. One of perhaps the most important features of Eiffel is the use of special keywords for constructs to specify the correctness of programs and the behavioral properties that determine the external interface of objects. Moreover, Eiffel provides a tool to extract a description of the interface of the method classes (including pre- and post-conditions associated with a method) which may be used to document (a library of) classes. To my taste, however, the Eiffel syntax leads to somewhat verbose programs, at least in comparison with programs written in C++.

The issue of producing documentation from C++ is still open. A number of tools exist (including a WEB-like system for C++ and a tool to produce manual pages from C++ header files) but no standard has yet emerged. Moreover, some people truly dislike the terseness of C/C++. Personally, I prefer the C/C++ syntax above the syntactical conventions of both Eiffel and Smalltalk, provided that it is used in a disciplined fashion.

Java programs may be documented using *javadoc*. The *javadoc* program may be regarded as the standard C++ has been waiting for, in vain.

Reliability Smalltalk is a dynamically typed language. In other words, type checking, other than detecting runtime errors, is completely absent. Eiffel is generally regarded as a language possessing all characteristics needed for writing reliable programs, such as static type checking and constructs for stating correctness assertions (which may be checked at runtime). Due to its heritage from C, the language C++ is still considered by many as unreliable. In contrast to C, however, C++ does provide full static type checking, including the signature of functions and external object interfaces as arise in independent compilation of module files. Nevertheless, C++ only weakly supports type checking across module boundaries.

Contrary to common belief, Eiffel's type system is demonstrably inconsistent, due to a feature that enables a user to dynamically define the type of a newly created object in a virtual way (see section 9.6). This does not necessarily lead to type-insecure programs though, since the Eiffel compiler employs a special algorithm to detect such cases.

The type system of C++, on the other hand, is consistent and conforms to the notion of subtype as introduced informally in the previous part. Nevertheless, C++ allows the programmer to escape the rigor of the type system by employing casts.

An important feature of Eiffel is that it supports assertions that may be validated at runtime. In combinations with exceptions, this provides a powerful feature for the development of reliable programs.

At the price of some additional coding (for example, to save the current state to enable the use of the *old* value), such assertions may be expressed by using the assert macros provided for C++.

In defense of C++, it is important to acknowledge that C++ offers adequate protection mechanisms to shield classes derived by inheritance from the implementation details of their ancestor classes. Neither Smalltalk nor Eiffel offer such protection.

Java was introduced as a more reliable variant of C++. Java's reliability comes partly from the shielded environment offered by the Java virtual machine, and partly from the absence of pointers and the availability of built-in garbage collection. Practical experience shows that for the average student/programmer Java is indeed substantially less error-prone than C++.

Inheritance Smalltalk offers only single inheritance. In contrast, both Eiffel and C++ offer multiple inheritance. For statically typed languages, compile-time optimizations may be applied that result in only a low overhead. In principle, multiple inheritance allows one to model particular aspects of the application domain in a flexible and natural way.

As far as the assertion mechanism offered by Eiffel is concerned, Meyer (1988) gives clear guidelines prescribing how to use assertions in derived classes. However, the Eiffel compiler offers no assistance in verifying whether these rules are followed. The same guidelines apply to the use of assertions in C++, naturally lacking compiler support as well.

The Java language offers only single (code) inheritance, but allows for multiple interface inheritance. The realization of (multiple) interfaces seems to be a fairly good substitute for multiple (implementation) inheritance.

Efficiency Smalltalk, being an interpreted language, is typically slower than conventionally compiled languages. Nevertheless, as discussed in section 5.4.2, interpreted object-based languages allow for significant optimizations, for example by employing runtime compilation techniques.

The compilation of Eiffel programs can result in programs having adequate execution speed. However, in Eiffel dynamic binding takes place in principle for all methods. Yet a clever compiler can significantly reduce the number of indirections needed to execute a method.

In contrast to C++, in Eiffel all objects are created on the heap. The garbage collection needed to remove these objects may affect the execution speed of programs.

C++ has been designed with efficiency in mind. For instance, the availability of inline functions, and the possibility to allocate objects on the runtime stack (instead of on the heap), and the possibility to declare *friend* functions and classes that have direct access to the private instance variables of a class allow the programmer to squeeze out the last drop of efficiency. However, as a drawback, when higher level functionality is needed (as in automatic garbage collection) it must be explicitly programmed, and a similar price as when the functionality would have been provided by the system has to be paid. The only difference is that the programmer has a choice.

At the time of writing there does not exist a truly efficient implementation of the Java language. Significant improvements may be expected from the JIT (Just In Time) compilers that produce native code dynamically, employing techniques as originally developed for the Self language, discussed in section 5.4.2.

Language complexity Smalltalk may be regarded as having a low language complexity. Control is primarily effected by message passing, yet, many of the familiar conditional and iterative control constructs reappear in Smalltalk programs emulated by sending messages. This certainly has some elegance, but does not necessarily lead to easily comprehensible programs.

Eiffel contains few language elements that extend beyond object-oriented programming. In particular, Eiffel does not allow for overloading method names (according to signature) within a class. This may lead to unnecessarily elaborate method names. (The new version of Eiffel (Eiffel-3) does allow for overloading method names.)

Without doubt, C++ is generally regarded as a highly complex language. In particular, the rules governing the overloading of operators and functions are quite complicated. The confusion even extends to the various compiler suppliers, which is one of the reasons why C++ is still barely portable. Somewhat unfortunately, the rules for overloading and type conversion for C++ have to a large extent been determined by the need to remain compatible with C. Even experienced programmers need occasionally to experiment to find out what will happen.

According to Blaschek *et al.* (1989), C++ is too large and contains too much of the syntax and semantics inherited from C. However, the validity of their motto *small is beautiful* is not as obvious as it seems. The motivations underlying the introduction of the various features incorporated in C++ are quite well explained in Stroustrup (1997). The main problem, to my mind, in using C++ (or any of the object-oriented languages for that matter) lies in the area of design. We still have insufficient experience in using abstract data types to define a complete method and operator interface including its relation to other data types (that is its behavior under the various operators and type conversions that apply to a particular type). The problem is hence not only one of language design but of the design of abstract data types.

Java is certainly less complex than C++. For example, it offers no templates, no operator overloading and no type coercion operators. However, although Java is apparently easier to use, it is far less elegant than C++ when it comes to creating user-defined types. Class interfaces in Java are usually much more verbose than similar interfaces in C++. And, due to the absence of templates, type casts are necessary in many places. On the other hand, casts in Java are type safe.

5.3   Design dimensions of object-oriented languages

Despites the widespread adoption of object-oriented terminology in the various areas of computer science and software development practice, there is considerable confusion about the precise meaning of the terms employed and the (true) nature of object-oriented computing. In an attempt to resolve this confusion, Wegner (1987) (in the landmark paper *Dimensions of object-based language design*) introduces the distinction between *object-based* and *object-oriented*. See slide 5-11. This distinction comes down to, roughly, the distinction between languages providing only encapsulation (object-based) or encapsulation plus inheritance (object-oriented). See section 5.3.1. Another issue in the debate about object-orientation is the relation between *classes* and *types*. Wegner (1987) concludes that the notions of objects, classes and inheritance (that constitute the classical object model) are highly interrelated, and instead proposes an orthogonal approach by outlining the various dimensions along which to design an object-oriented language. These dimensions may be characterized by the phrases: *objects*, *types*, *delegation* and *abstraction*.

Object-oriented language design   *5-11*

- **object**: state + operations
- **class**: template for object creation
- **inheritance**: super/base and subclasses

```
object-oriented =
          objects + classes + inheritance
```

data abstraction – *state accessible by operations*

strong typing – *compile time checking*

Slide 5-11: Object-based versus object-oriented

In this section we will look at the arguments presented in Wegner (1987) in somewhat more detail. Also, we will look at the viability of combining seemingly disparate paradigms (such as the logic programming paradigm) with the object-oriented language paradigm. In the sections that follow, we will discuss some alternatives and extensions to the object model.

5.3.1   Object-based versus object-oriented

How would you characterize Ada83? See Barnes (1994). Is Ada object-oriented? And Modula-2? See Wirth (1983). The answer is no and no. And Ada9X and Modula-3? See Barnes (1994) and Cardelli *et al.* (1989). The answer is yes and yes. In the past there has been some confusion as to when to characterize a language as *object-oriented*. For example, Booch (1986) characterizes Ada as object-oriented and motivates this by saying that Ada can be used as an implementation language in an object-oriented approach to program development.

Clearly, Ada supports some notion of objects (which are defined as *packages*). However, although Ada supports objects and generic descriptions of objects (by generic packages), it does not support code sharing by inheritance. In a later work, Booch (1991) revises his original (faulty) opinion, in response to Wegner (1987), who proposed considering *inheritance* as an essential characteristic of *object orientation*.

Similarly, despite the support that Modula-2 offers for defining (object-like) abstract data types, consisting of an interface specification and an implementation (which may be hidden), Modula-2 does not support the creation of derived (sub)types that share the behavior of their base (super)type. See also section 8.3.

Classes versus types Another confusion that frequently arises is due to the ill-defined relationship between the notion of a class and the notion of a type.

The notion of *types* is already familiar from procedural programming languages such as Pascal and (in an ill-famed way) from C. The type of variables and functions may be profitably used to check for (syntactical) errors. Strong static type checking may prevent errors ranging from simple typos to using undefined (or wrongly defined) functions.

The notion of a class originally has a more operational meaning. Operationally, a class is a template for object creation. In other words, a *class* is a description of the collection of its instances, that is the objects that are created using the class description as a recipe.

Related to this notion of a class, *inheritance* was originally defined as a means to share (parts of) a description. Sharing by (inheritance) derivation is, pragmatically, very convenient. It provides a more controlled way of code sharing than, for example, the use of macros and file inclusion (as were popular in the C community).

Since Wegner (1987) published his original analysis of the dimensions of object-oriented language design, the phrase *object-oriented* has been commonly understood as involving *objects*, *classes* and *inheritance*. This is the traditional object model as embodied by Smalltalk and, to a large extent, by Eiffel, C++ and Java. However, unlike Smalltalk, both Eiffel and C++ have also been strongly influenced by the *abstract data type* approach to programming. Consequently, in Eiffel and C++ classes have been identified with types and derivation by inheritance with subtyping.

Unfortunately, derivation by inheritance need not necessarily result in the creation of proper subtypes, that is classes whose instances conform to the behavior specified by their base class. In effect, derived classes may be only distantly related to their base classes when inheritance is only used as a code sharing device. For example, a window manager class may inherit from a list container class (an idiom used in Meyer, 1988).

5.3.2   Towards an orthogonal approach – type extensions

According to Wegner (1987), much of the confusion around the various features of object-oriented programming languages arises from the fact that these features are largely interdependent, as for instance the notion of object and class on the one hand, and the notion of class and inheritance on the other.

To resolve this confusion, Wegner (1987) proposes a more orthogonal approach to characterize the various features of object-oriented languages, according to dimensions that are to a large extent independent. See slide 5-12.

The features that constitute an object-oriented programming language in an orthogonal way are, according to Wegner (1987): *objects*, *types*, *delegation* and *abstraction*.

Orthogonal approach   *5-12*

- **objects** – *modular computing agents*
- **types** – *expression classification*
- **delegation** – *resource sharing*
- **abstraction** – *interface specification*

Slide 5-12: Orthogonal dimensions

Objects are in essence *modular computing agents*. They correspond to the need for encapsulation in design, that is the construction of modular units to which a principle of locality applies (due to combining data and operations).

Object-oriented languages may, however, differ in the degree to which they support encapsulation. For example, in a distributed environment a high degree of encapsulation must be offered, prohibiting attempts to alter global variables (from within an object) or local instance variables (from without). Moreover, the runtime object support system must allow for what may best be called *remote method invocation*.

As far as parallel activity is concerned, only a few languages provide constructs to define concurrently active objects. See section 5.3.4 for a more detailed discussion.

Whether objects support *reactiveness*, that is sufficient flexibility to respond safely to a message, depends largely upon (program) design. Meyer (1988), for instance, advocates a *shopping list approach* to designing the interface of an object, to allow for a high degree of (temporal) independence between method calls.

Types may be understood as a mechanism for *expression classification*. From this perspective, Smalltalk may be regarded as having a dynamic typing system: dynamic, in the sense that the inability to evaluate an expression will lead to a runtime error. The existence of types obviates the need to have classes, since a type may be considered as a more abstract description of the behavior of an object. Furthermore, subclasses (as may be derived through inheritance) are more safely defined as subtypes in a polymorphic type system. See section 9.3.

At the opposite side of the type dimension we find the statically typed languages, which allow us to determine the type of the designation of a variable at compile-time. In that case, the runtime support system need not carry any type information, except a dispatch table to locate virtual functions.

Delegation (in its most generic sense) is a mechanism for *resource sharing*. As has been shown in Lieberman (1986), delegation subsumes inheritance, since the resource sharing effected by inheritance may easily be mimicked by delegating messages to the object's ancestors by means of an appropriate dispatching mechanism.

In a narrower sense, delegation is usually understood as a more dynamic mechanism that allows the redirection of control dynamically. In addition, languages supporting dynamic delegation (such as Self) do not sacrifice dynamic self-reference. This means that when the object executing a method refers to itself, the actual context will be the delegating object. See section 5.4 for a more detailed discussion.

In contrast, inheritance (as usually understood in the context of classes) is a far more static mechanism. Inheritance may be understood as (statically) copying the code from an ancestor class to the inheriting class (with perhaps some modifications), whereas delegation is truly dynamic in that messages are dispatched to objects that have a life-span independent of the dispatching object.

Abstraction (although to some extent related to types) is a mechanism that may be independently applied to provide an *interface specification* for an object. For example, in the presence of active objects (that may execute in parallel) we may need to be able to restrict dynamically the interface of an object as specified by its type in order to maintain the object in a consistent state. Also for purely sequential objects we may impose a particular protocol of interaction (as may, for example, be expressed by a *contract*) to be able to guarantee correct behavior.

Another important aspect of abstraction is *protection*. Object-oriented languages may provide (at least) two kinds of protection. First, a language may have facilities to protect the object from illegal access by a client (from without). This is effected by annotations such as *private* and *protected*. And secondly, a language may have facilities to protect the object (as it were from within) from illegal access through delegation (that is by instances of derived object classes). Most languages support the first kind of protection. Only few languages, among which are C++ and Java, support the second kind too.

The independence of abstraction and typing may further be argued by pointing out that languages supporting strong typing need not enforce the use of abstract data types having a well-defined behavior.

5.3.3 Multi-paradigm languages – logic

Object-oriented programming has evolved as a new and strong *paradigm of programming*. Has it? Of the languages mentioned, only Smalltalk has what may be considered a radically new language design (and to some extent also the language Self, that we will discuss in the next section). Most of the other languages, including Eiffel, C++ (and for that matter also CLOS and Oberon), may be considered as object-oriented extensions of already existing languages or, to put it more broadly, language paradigms. Most popular are, evidently, object-oriented extensions based on procedural language paradigms, closely followed by the (Lisp-based) extensions of the functional language paradigm. Less well-known are extensions based on the logic programming paradigm, of which DLP is my favorite example.

In Wegner (1992), it is argued that the logic programming paradigm does not fit in with an object-oriented approach. I strongly disagree with this position.

However, the arguments given in Wegner (1992) to defend it are worthwhile, in that they make explicit what desiderata we may impose on object-oriented languages.

Remaining within the confines of a classical object model, the basic ingredients for an object-oriented extension of any language (paradigm) are: *objects, classes* and *inheritance*. Although the exact meaning of these notions is open for discussion, language designers seem to have no difficulty in applying these concepts to extend (or design) a programming language.

5-13

Open systems

- reactive – *flexible (dynamic) choice of actions*
- modular – *(static) scalability*

Dimensions of modularity

- encapsulation boundary – *interface to client*
- distribution boundary – *visibility from within objects*
- concurrency boundary – *threads per object, synchronization*

Slide 5-13: Dimensions of modularity

According to Wegner (1992), the principal argument against combining logic programming and object-oriented programming is that such a combination does not support the development of open systems without compromising the logical nature of logic programming. Openness may be considered as one of the prime goals of object orientation. See slide 5-13.

A software system is said to be *open* if its behavior can be easily modified and extended. Wegner (1992) distinguishes between two mechanisms to achieve openness; dynamically through *reactiveness*, and statically through *modularity*.

Reactiveness allows a program to choose dynamically between potential actions. For sequential object-oriented languages, *late binding* (that is, the dispatching mechanism underlying virtual function calls) is one of the mechanisms used to effect the dynamic selection of alternatives. Concurrent object-oriented languages usually offer an additional construct, in the form of a *guard* or *accept* statement, to determine dynamically which method call to answer. In both cases, the answer depends upon the nature of the object and (especially in the latter case) the state of the object (and its willingness to answer).

Openness through modularity means that a system can safely be extended by adding (statically) new components. The issue of openness in the latter sense is immediately related to the notion of *scalability*, that is the degree to which a particular component can be safely embedded in a larger environment and extended to include new functionality. At first sight, classes and inheritance strongly contribute to achieving such (static) openness. However, there is more to modularity than the encapsulation provided by classes only.

From a modeling perspective, encapsulation (as provided by objects and classes) is the basic mechanism to define the elements or entities of a model. The declarative nature of an object-oriented approach resides exactly in the opportunity to define such entities and their relations through inheritance. However, encapsulation (as typically understood in the context of a classical object model) only provides protection from illegal access from without. As such, it is a one-sided boundary.

The other side, the extent to which the outside world is visible for the object (from within), may be called the *distribution boundary*. Many languages, including Smalltalk and C++, violate the distribution boundary by allowing the use of (class-wide) global variables. (See also section 5.5.) Evidently, this may lead to problems when objects reside on distinct processors, as may be the case in distributed systems.

Typically, the message passing metaphor (commonly used to characterize the interaction between objects) contains the suggestion that objects may be physically distributed (across a network of processors). Also (because of the notion of encapsulation), objects are often regarded as autonomous entities, that in principle may have independent activity. However, most of the languages mentioned do not (immediately) fulfill the additional requirements needed for actual physical distribution or parallel (multi-threaded) activity.

Object-oriented logic programming Logic programming is often characterized as *relational* programming, since it allows the exhaustive exploration of a search space defined by logical relations (for instance, by backtracking as in Prolog). The advantage of logic programming, from a modeling point of view, is that it allows us to specify in a logical manner (that is by logical clauses) the relations between the entities of a particular domain.

A number of efforts to combine logic programming with object-oriented features have been undertaken, among which is the development of the language Vulcan. Vulcan is based on the Concurrent Prolog language and relies on a way of implementing objects as perpetual processes. Without going into detail, the idea (originally proposed in Shapiro and Takeuchi, 1983) is that an object may be implemented as a process defined by one or more (recursive) clauses. An object may accept messages in the form of a predicate call. The state of an object is maintained by parameters of the predicate, which are (possibly modified by the method call) passed to the recursive invocation of one of the clauses defining the object.

To communicate, an object (defined as a process) waits until a client asks for the execution of a method. The clauses defining the object are then evaluated to check which one is appropriate for that particular method call. If there are multiple candidate clauses, one is selected and evaluated. The other candidate clauses are discarded. Since the clauses defining an object are recursive, after the evaluation of a method the object is ready to accept another message.

The model of (object) interaction supported by Concurrent Prolog requires fine-grained concurrency, which is possible due to the side-effect free nature of logical clauses. However, to restrict the number of processes created during the evaluation of a goal, Concurrent Prolog enforces a *committed choice* between candidate clauses, thus throwing away alternative solutions.

Wegner (1992) observes, rightly I think, that the notion of committed choice is in conflict with the relational nature of logic programming. Indeed, Concurrent Prolog absolves logical completeness in the form of backtracking, to remain within the confines of the process model adopted. Wegner (1992), however, goes a step further and states that *reactiveness* and *backtracking* are irreconcilable features.

That these features may fruitfully be incorporated in a single language framework is demonstrated by the language DLP. However, to support backtracking and objects, a more elaborate process model is needed than the process model supported by Concurrent Prolog (which in a way identifies an object with a process). With such a model (sketched in appendix E), there seems to be no reason to be against the marriage of logic programming and object orientation.

5.3.4 Active objects – synchronous Java/C++

When it comes to combining *objects* (the building blocks in an object-oriented approach) with *processes* (the building blocks in parallel computing), there are three approaches conceivable. See slide 5-14.

Object-based concurrency   *5-14*

- add processes – *synchronization*
- multiple active objects – *rendezvous*
- asynchronous communication – *message buffers*

Slide 5-14: Objects and concurrency

One can simply add *processes* as an additional data type. Alternatively, one can introduce *active objects*, having activity of their own, or, one can employ *asynchronous communication*, allowing the client and server object to proceed independently.

Processes The first, most straightforward approach, is to simply add *processes* as a primitive data type, allowing the creation of independent threads of processing. An example is Distributed Smalltalk (see Bennett, 1987). Another example is Java, which provides support for threads, synchronized methods and statements like *wait* and *notify* to protect re-entrant concurrent methods. The disadvantage of this approach, however, is that the programmer has full responsibility for the most difficult part of parallel programming, namely the synchronization between processes and the avoidance of common errors such as simultaneously assigning a value to a shared variable. Despite the fact that the literature, see Andrews (1991), abounds with primitives supporting synchronization (such as semaphores, conditional sections and monitors), such an approach is error-prone and means a heavy burden on the shoulders of the application developer.

Active objects A second, and in my view preferable, approach is to introduce explicitly a notion of *active objects*. Within this approach, parallelism is introduced by having multiple, simultaneously active objects. An example of a language supporting active objects is POOL, described in America (1987). Communication between active objects occurs by means of a (synchronous) rendezvous. To engage in a rendezvous, however, an active object must interrupt its own activity by means of an (Ada-like) *accept statement* (or *answer statement* as it is called in POOL), indicating that the object is willing to answer a message. The advantage of this approach is, clearly, that the encapsulation boundary of the object (its message interface) can conveniently be employed as a monitor-like mechanism to enforce mutual exclusion between method invocations.

Despite the elegance of this solution, however, unifying objects and processes in *active objects* is not without problems. First, one has to decide whether to make all objects active or allow both passive and active objects. Logically, passive objects may be regarded as active objects that are eternally willing to answer every message listed in the interface description of the object. However, this generalization is not without penalty in terms of runtime efficiency. Secondly, a much more serious problem is that the message-answering semantics of active objects is distinctly different from the message-answering semantics of passive objects with respect to self-invocation. Namely, to answer a message, an active object must interrupt its own activity. Yet, if an active object (in the middle of answering a message) sends a message to itself, we have a situation of *deadlock*. Direct self-invocation, of course, can be easily detected, but indirect self-invocations require an analysis of the complete method invocation graph, which is generally not feasible.

Asynchronous communication Deadlock may come about by synchronous (indirect) self-invocation. An immediate solution to this problem is provided by languages supporting asynchronous communication, which provide message buffers allowing the caller to proceed without waiting for an answer. Asynchronous message passing, however, radically deviates from the (synchronous) message passing supported by the traditional (passive) object model. This has the following consequences. First, for the programmer, it becomes impossible to know when a message will be dealt with and, consequently, when to expect an answer. Secondly, for the language implementor, allocating resources for storing incoming messages and deciding when to deal with messages waiting in a message buffer becomes a responsibility for which it is hard to find a general, yet efficient, solution. Active objects with asynchronous message passing constitute the so-called *actor* model, which has influenced several language designs. See Agha (1990).

Synchronous C++/Java

In PetitPierre (1998), an extension of C++ is proposed that supports active objects, method calls by rendez vous and dynamic checks of synchronization conditions. The concurrency model supported by this language, which is called sC++, closely resembles the models supported by CCS, CSP and Ada.

An example of the declaration of an active object in sC++ is given in slide 5-15.

```
                                                        sC++       5-15
    active class S {
    public:
        m () { ... }
    private:
        @S () {                              pseudo-constructor
            select {
                01 -> m();                        external call
                instructions ...
            ||
                accept m;           accept internal method
                instructions ...
            ||
                waituntil (date);                 time-out
                instructions ...
            ||
                default                             default
                instructions ...
            }
        }
    }
```

Slide 5-15: Synchronization conditions in sC++

The synchronization conditions for instances of the class are specified in a *select* statement contained in a constructor-like method, which defines the active body of the object. Synchronization may take place in either (external) calls to another active object, internal methods that are specified as acceptable, or time-out conditions. When none of the synchronization conditions are met, a default action may take place. In addition to the synchronization conditions mentioned, a *when* guard-statement may occur in any of the clauses of *select*, to specify conditions on the state of the object or real-time constraints.

The sC++ language is implemented as an extension to the GNU C++ compiler. The sC++ runtime environment offers the possibility to validate a program by executing random walks, which is a powerful way to check the various synchronization conditions. The model of active objects supported by sC++ has also been realized as a Java library, see PetitPierre (1999). There is currently, however, no preprocessor or compiler for Java supporting synchronous active objects.

As argued in PetitPierre (1998), one of the advantages of synchronous active objects is that they allow us to do away with event-loops and callbacks.

Another, perhaps more important, advantage is that the model bears a close relationship with formal models of concurrency as embodied by CCS and CSP, which opens opportunities for the verification and validation of concurrent object-oriented programs. In conclusion, in my opinion, the active object model discussed deserves to become a standard for both C++ and Java, not because it unifies the concurrency model for these languages, which is for example also done by JThreads++ described in Orbacus (1998), but because it offers a high level of abstraction suitable for concurrent object-oriented software engineering.

5.4   Prototypes – delegation versus inheritance

The classical object model (which is constituted by classes, objects and inheritance) not only has its theoretical weaknesses (as outlined in the previous section) but has also been criticized from a more pragmatic perspective because of its inflexibility when it comes to developing systems.

Code sharing has been mentioned as one of the advantages of inheritance (as it allows incremental development). However, alternative (read more flexible) forms of *sharing* have been proposed, employing prototypes and delegation instead of inheritance.

5.4.1   Alternative forms of sharing

A *class* provides a generic description of one or more objects, its instances. From a formal point of view, classes are related to types, and hence a class may be said to correspond to the set of instances that may be generated from it. This viewpoint leads to some anomalies, as in the case of *abstract* classes that at best correspond to partially defined sets. As another problem, in the context of inheritance, behavioral compatibility may be hard to arrive at, and hence the notion of *subtype* (which roughly corresponds with the subset relation) may be too restrictive. In practice, we may further encounter *one-of-a-kind* objects, for which it is simply cumbersome to construct an independent class.

In a by now classical paper, Lieberman (1986) proposes the use of *prototypes* instead of classes. The notion of prototypes (or *exemplars*) has been used in cognitive psychology to explain the incremental nature of concept learning. As Lieberman (1986) notes, the philosophical distinction between prototypes (which provide a representative example of an object) and classes (which characterize a set of similar objects) may have important pragmatical consequences as it concerns the incremental definition of (hierarchies of) related objects. First, it is (claims Lieberman, 1986) more natural to start from a concrete example than to start from an abstract characterization as given by a class. And secondly, sharing information between prototypes and clones (that is, modified copies) thereof is far more flexible than the rather static means of sharing code as supported by the class inheritance mechanism.

Code sharing by inheritance may be characterized as *creation time* sharing, which in this respect is similar to creating a copy of the object by cloning. In addition, prototypes may also support *lifetime* resource sharing by means of delegation. In principle, delegation is nothing but the forwarding of a message. However, in contrast to the forwarding mechanism as described in sections 2.1.1 and 2.2, delegation in the context of prototypes does not change implicit self-reference to the forwarding object. In other words, when delegating a message to a *parent* object, the context of answering the message remains the same, as if the forwarding object answers the request directly. See slide 5-16.

Slide 5-16: Prototypes

An almost classical example used to illustrate *prototypical* programming is the example of a *turtle* object that delegates its request to move itself to a *pen* object (which has *x* and *y* coordinate attributes and a *move* method). The flexibility of delegation becomes apparent when we define a number of *turtle* objects by cloning the *pen* object and adding an *y* coordinate private to each *turtle*. In contrast to derivation by inheritance, the *x* coordinate of the *pen* object is shared dynamically. When changing the value of *x* in one of the *turtle* objects, all the *turtle* objects will be affected. Evidently, this allows considerable (and sometimes unwished for) flexibility. However, for applications (such as multimedia systems) such flexibility may be desirable.

Design issues Strictly speaking, prototype-based delegation is not stronger than forwarding in languages supporting classes and inheritance. In Dony *et al.* (1992), a taxonomy of prototype-based languages is given. (This taxonomy has been partly implemented in Smalltalk. The implementation, however, employs so-called class-variables, which are not unproblematic themselves. See section 5.5.)

One of the principal advantages of prototype-based languages is that they offer a consistent yet simple model of programming, consisting of objects, cloning and delegation. Yet, when designing a prototype-based language, a number of design decisions must be made (as reflected in the taxonomy given in Dony *et al.*, 1992). These issues concern the representation of the state of an object, how objects are created and the way in which delegation is handled. See slide 5-17.

The basic prototype model only features *slots* which may store either a value or a piece of code that may be executed as a method. Alternatively, a distinction may be made between variables and methods. In both cases, late binding must be employed to access a value. In contrast, instance variable bindings in class-based languages are usually resolved statically.

When creating a new object by cloning an existing object, we have the choice between deep copying and shallow copying. Only shallow copying, however, allows

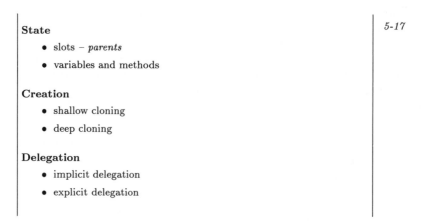

State
- slots – *parents*
- variables and methods

Creation
- shallow cloning
- deep cloning

Delegation
- implicit delegation
- explicit delegation

Slide 5-17: Prototypes – state, creation, delegation

lifetime sharing (since deep copying results in a replica at creation time). Shallow copying is thus the obvious choice.

Finally, delegation is usually handled implicitly, for instance by means of a special *parent* slot, indicating the ancestor of the object (which may be changed dynamically). Alternatively, it may be required to indicate delegation explicitly for each method. This gives a programmer more flexibility since it allows an object to have multiple ancestors, but at the price of an increase in notational complexity. Explicit delegation, by the way, most closely resembles the use of forwarding in class-based systems.

One of the, as yet, unresolved problems of delegation-based computing is how to deal with what Dony *et al.* (1992) call *split* objects. An object may (internally) consist of a large number of (smaller) objects that are linked to each other by the delegation relation. It is not clear how to address such a complex object as a single entity. Also, the existence of a large number of small objects that communicate by message passing may impose severe performance penalties.

5.4.2   Implementation techniques – Self

A major concern of software developers is (often) the runtime efficiency of the system developed. An order of magnitude difference in execution speed may, indeed, mean the difference between acceptance and rejection.

There are a number of ways in which to improve on the runtime efficiency of programs, including object-oriented programs. For example, Ungar *et al.* (1992) mention the reliance on special-purpose hardware (which thus far has been rapidly overtaken by new general-purpose processor technology), the use of hybrid languages (which are considered error-prone), static typing (which for object-oriented programming provides only a partial solution) and dynamic compilation (which has been successfully applied for Self). See slide 5-18.

As for the use of hybrid languages, of which C++ is an example, the apparent

```
┌──────────────────────────────────────────────────────────┬─────────┐
│                                                          5-18      │
│  Improving performance                                            │
│        • special-purpose hardware                                 │
│        • hybrid languages                                         │
│        • static typing                                            │
│        • dynamic compilation                                      │
│                                                                   │
└───────────────────────────────────────────────────────────────────┘
```

Slide 5-18: Improving performance

impurity of such an approach may (to my mind) even be beneficial in some cases. However, the programmer is required to deal more explicitly with the implementation features of the language than may be desirable.

In general, both with respect to reliability and efficiency, statically typed languages have a distinct advantage over dynamically typed (interpreted) languages. Yet, for the purpose of fast prototyping, interpreted languages (like Smalltalk) offer an advantage in terms of development time and flexibility. Moreover, the use of (polymorphic) virtual functions and dynamic binding necessitate additional dynamic runtime support (that is not needed in strictly procedural languages). Clever compilation reduces the overhead (even in the case of multiple inheritance) to one or two additional indirections.

Dynamic compilation The language Self is quite pure and simple in design. It supports objects with *slots* (that may contain both values and code, representing methods), shallow cloning, and implicit delegation (via a designated *parent* slot). Moreover, the developers of Self have introduced a number of techniques to improve the efficiency of prototype-based computing.

```
┌──────────────────────────────────────────────────────────┬─────────┐
│                                                          5-19      │
│  Self – prototypes                                                │
│        • objects, cloning, delegation                             │
│                                                                   │
│  Dynamic compilation – type information                           │
│        • customized compilation                                   │
│        • message inlining                                         │
│        • lazy compilation                                         │
│        • message splitting                                        │
│                                                                   │
└───────────────────────────────────────────────────────────────────┘
```

Slide 5-19: Dynamic compilation – Self

The optimization techniques are based on dynamic compilation, a technique that resembles the partial evaluation techniques employed in functional and logic programming. Dynamic compilation employs the type information gathered during the computation to improve the efficiency of message passing.

Whenever a method is repeatedly invoked, the address of the recipient object may be backpatched in the caller. In some cases, even the result may be inlined to replace the request. Both techniques make it appear that message passing takes place, but at a much lower price. More complicated techniques, involving lazy compilation (by delaying the compilation of infrequently visited code) and message splitting (involving a dataflow analysis and the reduction of redundancies) may be applied to achieve more optimal results.

Benchmark tests have indicated a significant improvement in execution speed (up to 60% of optimized C code) for cases where type information could be dynamically obtained. The reader is referred to Ungar *et al.* (1992) for further details.

5.5   Meta-level architectures

Another weakness of the classical object model (or perhaps one of its strengths) is that the concept of a class easily lends itself to being overloaded with additional meanings and features such as *class variables* and *metaclasses*. These notions lead to extensions to the original *class/instance* scheme that are hard to unify in a single elegant framework. In this section we will study a proposal based on a reflexive relation between classes and objects.

Depending on one's perspective, a class may either be regarded as a kind of abstract data type (specifying the operational interface of its object instances) or, more pragmatically, as a template for object creation (that is, a means to generate new instances).

The class concept   *5-20*

   • abstract data type – *interface description*

   • object generator – *template for creation*

   • repository – *for sharing resources*

   • object – *instance of a metaclass*

Slide 5-20: The concept of class

In addition, however, in a number of systems a class may be used as a repository for sharing class-wide resources. For example, the Smalltalk language allows the definition of *class variables* that are accessible to all instances of the class. See slide 5-20.

Class variables Clearly, the use of class variables violates what we have called the *distribution boundary* in section 5.3.3, since it allows objects to reach out of their encapsulation borders. Class variables may also be employed in C++ and Java by defining data members as *static*. Apart from class variables, Smalltalk also supports the notion of *class methods*, which may be regarded as routines having the class and its instances as their scope. Class methods in Smalltalk are typically used for the creation and initialization of new instances of the class for which they are defined. In C++ and Java, creation and initialization is taken care of by the constructor(s) of a class, together with the (system supplied) *new* operator. Class methods, in C++ and Java, take the form of static member functions that are like ordinary functions (apart from their restricted scope and their calling syntax, which is of the form *class :: member*(...) in C++ and *class.member*(...) in Java).

Contrary to classes in C++ and Java, classes in Smalltalk have a functionality similar to that of objects. Classes in Smalltalk provide encapsulation (encompassing class variables and class methods) and message passing (for example for the creation and initialization of new instances). To account for this object-like behavior, the designers of Smalltalk have introduced the notion of *metaclass* of which a class is an instance.

Metaclasses In the classical object model, two relations play a role when describing the architectural properties of a system. The first relation is the *instance* relation to indicate that an object *O* is an instance of a class *C*. The second (equally important) relation is the *inheritance* relation, which indicates that a class *C* is a subclass (or derived from) a given (ancestor) class *P*.

When adopting the philosophy *everything is an object* together with the idea that *each object is an instance of a class* (as the developers of Smalltalk did), we evidently get into problems when we try to explain the nature (and existence) of a class.

To be an object, a class itself must be an instance of a class (which for convenience we will call a *metaclass*). Take, for example, the class *Point*. This class must be an instance of a (meta)class (say *Class*) which in its turn must be an instance of a (meta) class (say *MetaClass*), and so on. Clearly, following the instance relation leads to an infinite regress. Hence, we must postulate some system-defined *MetaClass* (at a certain level) from which to instantiate the (metaclasses of) actual classes such as *Point*.

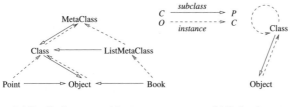

(a) Smalltalk meta architecture   *(b) Reflective meta architecture*

Slide 5-21: Meta architectures

The figure in slide 5-21(a) is a (more or less) accurate rendering of the solution provided by Smalltalk. We may add additional flexibility by allowing user-defined metaclasses that may refine the behavior of the system-defined metaclass *Class*. This is the solution chosen for Loops, see Stefik and Bobrow (1986).

Thus far we have traced the instance relation which leads (following the reversed arrows) from top to bottom, from metaclasses to actual object instances. As pictured in the diagram (a) above, the inheritance relation (followed in the same manner) goes in exactly the opposite direction, having the class *Object* at the root of the inheritance hierarchy. For example, the class *Point* (while being an instance of the metaclass *Class*) is derived by inheritance from the class *Object*. Similarly, the (meta)class *Class* itself inherits from the class *Object*, and in its turn the system-defined metaclass *MetaClass* inherits from *Class*. As for the user-defined metaclasses, these may be thought of as inheriting from the system-defined metaclass *Class*. Apart from being slightly confusing, Smalltalk's meta-architecture is rather inelegant due to the magic (that is system-defined) number of meta levels. In the following, we will study a means to overcome this inelegancy.

Reflection   Cointe (1987) proposes an architecture that unifies the notions of object, class and metaclass, while allowing metaclasses to be defined at an arbitrary level. The key to this solution lies in the postulates characterizing the behavior of an object-oriented system given in slide 5-22.

Postulates – *class-based languages*   *5-22*

  - everything is an object

  - every object belongs to a class

  - every class inherits from the class *Object*

  - class variables of an object are instance variables of its class

---

Slide 5-22: Class-based languages – postulates

The first three postulates are quite straightforward. They agree with the assumptions underlying Smalltalk. The last postulate, however, stating that a class variable of an object must be an instance variable of the objects class (taken as an object), imposes a constraint of a self-recurrent or reflexive nature. This recurrence is pictured in slide 5-21(b), which displays the object *Class* as an instance of itself (that is the class *Class*). In other respects, the diagram is similar to the diagram depicting the (meta) architecture of Smalltalk and Loops.

To indicate how such a reflective relation may be implemented, Cointe (1987) introduces a representation of objects involving the attributes *name* (to indicate the class of the object), *supers* (to indicate its ancestor(s)), *iv* (to list the instance variables of the object) and *methods* (to store the methods belonging to the object).

In this scheme of representation, the system-defined metaclass *Class* is precisely the object reflecting its own structure in the values of its attributes, as depicted above. Every instance of *Class* may assign values to its instance variables (contained in *iv*) that are appropriate to the instances that will be created from it. In general, a metaclass is an object having at least the attributes of *Class* (and possibly more). See slide 5-23.

Reflective definition of *Class*   *5-23*

    name   *Class*

    supers   *(Object)*

    iv   *(name supers iv methods)*

    methods   *(new ...)*

Slide 5-23: A reflective definition of *Class*

Using this scheme, an arbitrary towering of metaclasses may be placed on top of concrete classes, thus allowing the software developer to squeeze out the last bit of differential programming. Elegant indeed, although it is doubtful whether many programmers will endeavor upon such a route. A nice example of employing (customized) metaclasses, however, is given in Malenfant *et al.* (1989), where metaclasses are used to define the functionality of distribution and communication primitives employed by concrete classes.

Summary

This chapter presented an overview of object-oriented programming languages. We discussed the heritage of Simula and the various areas of research and development the ideas introduced by Simula has generated.

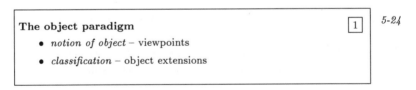

Slide 5-24: Section 5.1: The object paradigm

A overview of existing object-oriented languages was given in section 1 and we noted the prominence of hybrid languages derived from Lisp and C.

Comparing Smalltalk, Eiffel, C++ and Java   2   *5-25*

    • *criteria* – libraries, environments, language characteristics

    • *comparison* – language characteristics

Slide 5-25: Section 5.2: Comparing Smalltalk, Eiffel, C++ and Java

In section 2, we looked at a comparison of Smalltalk, Eiffel, C++ and Java, including criteria such as the availability of libraries, programming environments and language characteristics.

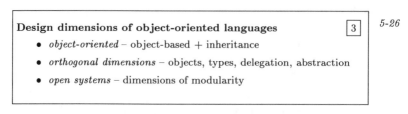

Slide 5-26: Section 5.3: Design dimensions of object-oriented languages

In section 3, we discussed the design dimensions of object-oriented languages and characterized an orthogonal set of dimensions consisting of objects, types, delegation and abstraction. We also discussed the notion of open systems and multi-paradigm languages combining logic programming with object-oriented features.

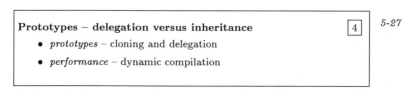

Slide 5-27: Section 5.4: Prototypes – delegation versus inheritance

In section 4, we dealt with classless prototype-based languages, supporting dynamic delegation instead of inheritance.

We also discussed performance issues and observed that dynamic compilation based on runtime type information may achieve good results.

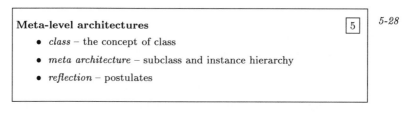

Slide 5-28: Section 5.5: Meta-level architectures

Finally, in section 5, we reflected on the concept of class and discussed a reflective architecture unifying the interpretation of a class as an object, capable of answering messages, and as a description of the properties of its instances.

Questions

1. What are the basic characteristics of object-oriented languages?

2. How would you classify object-oriented languages? Name a few representatives of each category.

3. What do you consider to be the major characteristic of the object model supported by C++? Explain.

4. Why would you need *friends*?

5. How would you characterize the difference between object-based and object-oriented?

6. Along what orthogonal dimensions would you design an object-oriented language? Explain.

7. Give a characterisation of *active objects*. In what situations may active objects be advantageous?

8. How would you characterize prototype-based languages?

9. What are the differences between inheritance and delegation? Does C++ support delegation? Explain. And Java?

10. How would you characterize the concept of a class?

11. Can you sketch the meta architecture of Smalltalk?

12. How would you phrase the postulates underlying class-based languages? Can you give a reflective version of these postulates?

Further reading

A concise treatment of programming languages is given in Bal and Grune (1994). For a collection of papers on object-oriented concepts, see Kim and Lochovsky (1989). Further, you may want to consult Wegner (1987), which contains the original presentation of the discussion concerning the distinction between *object-based* and *object-oriented*. Concurrency is studied in Agha *et al.* (1993). For Java, read the original white paper, Gosling and McGilton (1995). An interesting extension of C++ is described in PetitPierre (1998). At the corresponding web site, http://ltiwww.epfl.ch/sCxx , there is much additional material. Finally, for an account of the design and evolution of C++, read Stroustrup (1997). For more information on C++, visit http://www.accu.org , and for Java, http://www.javasoft.com.

6

Component technology

Many applications, for example in the area of telecomputing, banking and multimedia (but also in high performance computing and operating systems), require support for distribution and concurrency. Due to their complexity, these applications are likely candidates for an object-oriented approach. However, with regard to their distributed nature, some marriage between object-oriented computing and distributed computing must be realized.

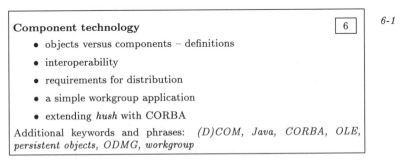

Slide 6-1: Component technology

In this chapter we will study component technology, which combines object-oriented features such as encapsulation and (interface) inheritance with (logical and/or physical) distribution. In reality, component technology is not a clear-cut category but rather, according to Szyperski (1997), a battlefield in action (with

(D)COM, CORBA and Java as the main players), from which eventually a winner will arise, or perhaps a merge of technologies. In this chapter, we will explore the forces at work, and in addition we will look at a case study deploying CORBA and Java for the creation of a workgroup application, and the integration of CORBA with an existing framework, *hush*.

6.1   Objects versus components

As observed in Szyperski (1997), there is some confusion between the notions of object and component. In this section we will look at the definition of *component* and compare it with what we know of objects. We will further explore the *technology matrix*, which classifies a selection of the available (component) technologies. Finally, we will discuss some of the software engineering issues involved in component-oriented development, and do away with some of the myths that surround component technology.

6.1.1   Definitions

Object orientation has not quite fulfilled its promise with respect to reuse. One of the reasons for this is that objects are generally not as modular as they might appear. Or, in the words of Szyperski (1997), objects are not a suitable *unit of deployment*.

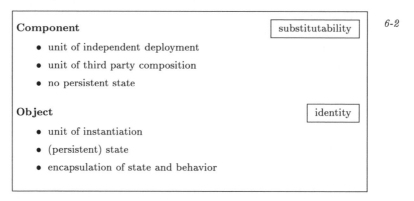

Slide 6-2: Definitions

Szyperski (1997) proposes components as a suitable unit of deployment instead, and advocates a *component-oriented* approach to deliver reusable *'off-the-shelf'* components for a composing large applications.

Let us look at the definition of *software component* given in Szyperski (1997):

> *A software component is a unit of composition with contractually specified interfaces and explicit context dependencies only. A software*

component can be deployed independently and is subject to composition by third parties.

This definition was the result of an ECOOP96 Workshop on Component-oriented Computing. Notice that the definition itself contains a reusability requirement, in mentioning *composition by third parties*. The requirements of explicit context dependencies, the absence of inherent state and contractually specified interfaces only strengthen this.

In contrast, an object is not a unit of deployment, but a *unit of instantiation*. Objects are not used in isolation. Objects, do have state and identity. Deploying an object or a collection of objects, moreover, is often subject to (implicit) assumptions concerning the interaction of objects.

Components as better objects From the characterization above it might appear that components are just better objects. To some extent this is true, but there are some important differences. First of all, in practice, there is a difference in granularity. Components are usually large grain, such as a text editor or database component. Objects, on the other hand, may be small grain, such as dates or text fields. Secondly, components are opaque, 'binary units' of functionality, interchangeable with units that deliver the same functionality. Objects, in contrast, carry a state and may be regarded as the living building blocks of an organic system.

Szyperski (1997) mentions that there is a debate whether inheritance is of relevance for component technology. No doubt, inheritance, although somewhat overrated, is an invaluable mechanism, both interface inheritance, to define hierarchies of types, and code reuse or implementation inheritance, to allow for incremental development.

Reconsidering the definitions given, I tend to think of the distinction between components and objects as a distinction between perspectives. From a deployment perspective we need components. From a developer's perspective we might prefer to speak about objects. Unfortunately, matters are not that easy. But we need to take a closer look at the technology to find out why.

6.1.2   The technology matrix

The component technology field is currently dominated by three players: Microsoft (D)COM, OMG CORBA, and (the youngest player) Sun Microsystems Java. When comparing these technologies with respect to attributes such as distribution, mobility, language and platform independence, and reflective capabilities, we see that there are many differences.

First of all, notice that component technology does not automatically mean distribution. For example, JavaBeans and Microsoft COM do not support distribution. Secondly, whereas language independence seemed to be of importance in the pre-Java era, that is for (D)COM and CORBA, it is not so for the Java-based solutions. Finally, platform independence is hard to achieve. But, fortunately, it is on the agenda of all three technologies, including (D)COM.

	distribution	mobility	language	platform	reflection
COM	–	–	*	–	+/–
DCOM	+	–	*	+/–	+/–
CORBA	+	–	*	*	+/–
Java/Beans	–	classes	Java	*	+
Java/RMI	+	classes	Java	*	+
Voyager	+	objects	Java	*	+

Slide 6-3: The technology matrix

It is worth mentioning that the three major technologies have a rather different origin. Microsoft (D)COM is primarily a desktop technology, with Office as its killer application, whereas CORBA originated from the need to have an enterprise-wide solution for distributed objects. Java is a special case. It started as a Web-based language, but rapidly took position in the desktop and enterprise world as well.

Java distinguishes itself from the other technologies both with respect to mobility and reflection. As a Web-based language, Java allows for downloading code dynamically, that is class descriptions for instantiating new objects. True mobile objects, that is instantiated objects that migrate themselves, are only possible when using a system such as Voyager, or any of the other Java-based agent ORBs. Java also provides a powerful Reflection API, which allows for various kinds of meta-programming, including the creation of new classes. In comparison, meta-programming facilities of the two other technologies are limited to querying the availability and functionality of interfaces, dynamic method invocation and some dynamic typing.

Trends – interoperability It is hard to predict the outcome of the 'battle of component technologies'. However, one can observe a convergence of technologies, that is bridges between Java and CORBA, CORBA and (D)COM, and Java and (D)COM/ActiveX. Each of these technologies sets a standard for interoperability. So, eventually some new standard may arise that encompasses them all. In the meantime, we may study the strengths of each of these technologies and establish what major challenges lie ahead. For example, Microsoft COM has demonstrated itself in an unescapable way in Microsoft Office. A related technology, OpenDoc, failed to gain a market position, but is nevertheless taken on by the OMG as document-oriented component technology.

An interesting project in this respect is the K-Office project, which aims at developing an Office Application Suite for the Unix/X11 desktop. It is built upon the KDE GUI environment, and employs a CORBA-based component technology, (nick)named *KOM*, to interconnect (embed and link) the various document components and their associated tools. See http://koffice.kde.com.

6.1.3   Component myths

Component software engineering may be characterized as an approach that relies on the availability of reusable 'off-the-shelf' components that may be composed into applications. This includes applications for banking, medical services, corporate management, entertainment, etcetera.

Components: myths and reality   *6-4*

- component-ware allows for combining components

  if semantical issues can be resolved

- component-ware simplifies software distribution and maintenance

  development becomes more complex

- component-ware supports mega applications

  it affects performance significantly

- component-ware is a revolution

  wrong, it is an evolution from OO and C/S

Slide 6-4: Components: myths and reality

From a market perspective, a successful component-based approach requires interoperability between components from different vendors, and standards with respect to the services components offer. Such standards are necessary to insulate clients (i.e. corporations) from vendor-specific, proprietary solutions. Clearly, on the technology side, this surpasses the mere wiring or plumbing standards that form part of (D)COM, ORBs and JavaRMI. In addition, suitable component standards are required for components to interact, as for example offered by ActiveX, JavaBeans or OpenDoc, as well as general services, as for example defined by the OMG, to manage such systems.

Software engineering perspectives From a software engineering perspective, we encounter a number of unsolved questions, as phrased in Szyperski (1997):

- How to describe the interaction between components?

- How to manage variety and flexibility?

- How to guarantee critical system-wide properties?

In addition, we need to deal with the practical aspects of developing component-oriented applications, that is master the distributed (object) technology involved, and manage multi-tier architectures.

And, as indicated in slide 6-4, do not underestimate the complexities of developing such applications. Given the failure of many OO projects, as described in Cockburn (1997), component-oriented solutions which involve client/server aspects are not likely to be better off, see Shimberg and Barnes (1997). Another area that needs to be studied is the performance of such systems, see for example Mowbray and Malveau (1997).

Yet, in conclusion, just as object orientation may be regarded as a natural evolution from data-oriented approaches, we may look at component-oriented approaches as a natural evolution from object orientation into the realm of distributed systems.

6.2   Standards for interoperability

The potential of an object-oriented approach, obviously, lies in the opportunities for *reuse*, both of code and design. However, reuse requires a common understanding of the basic principles underlying the technology and its application. More particularly, the reuse of code requires (a much more strict) agreement with respect to the components from which an application will be constructed and the language constructs used to implement them.

In this section, we will look at the object linking and embedding facilities offered by Microsoft OLE, and the standardization efforts undertaken by the OMG (Object Management Group) directed towards the interoperability of object components. In addition, we will look at the efforts of the ODMG (Object Database Management Group) undertaken to develop a standard for persistent objects.

6.2.1   Object linking and embedding – COM

Reuse is not necessarily code sharing. In effect, there seems to be a trend towards sharing components at a higher level of granularity, as possibly independent applications. This approach has, for example, been taken by the Microsoft object linking and embedding facility (OLE), which offers support for embedding (a copy) of a component in a (container) component, for including a link to another component, and for storing compound objects. See slide 6-5.

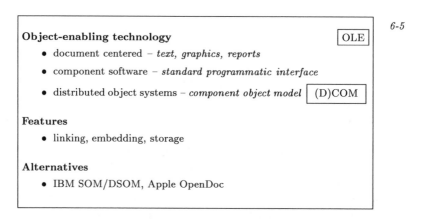

Slide 6-5: Object-enabling technology – OLE

The OLE technology, which builds upon (D)COM technology, is characterized by its developers as *object-enabling* technology, to contrast it with a more classical language-dependent object-oriented approach relying on inheritance.

The object-linking technology allows the user to maintain a link from one application to another, so that for example a text processor may directly employ the results of a spreadsheet. Moreover, object linking is dynamic and allows any updates in the spreadsheet application to be reflected directly in the outcome of the text processor. In contrast, object embedding works more as the traditional *cut and paste* techniques in that it results in including only a copy of the material. To be embedded or linked, applications must satisfy a standard programmatic interface. In effect, the interface must provide the facility to request an update of the display of the information contained in the application. In this respect, the OLE technology may be characterized as *document-centered.*

6.2.2 Object Request Brokers – CORBA

The ultimate goal of object technology may be phrased as the development of plug-compatible software that allows one to construct a particular application from off-the-shelf components. To achieve this goal, it is necessary to develop standards with respect to object interaction and communication interfaces that support *information sharing* between distinct components. Such standards are developed by the OMG (the Object Management Group, in which the leading vendors of software systems participate, including Digital Equipment Corporation, Hewlett-Packard Company, HyperDesk Corporation, NCR Corporation, Object Design Inc. and Sunsoft Inc.). The OMG aims at defining standards for information sharing in widely distributed, heterogeneous (multi-vendor) networks to support the reusability and portability of commercially available components, and more generally, to develop the technology and guidelines that allow the interoperability of applications. See slide 6-6.

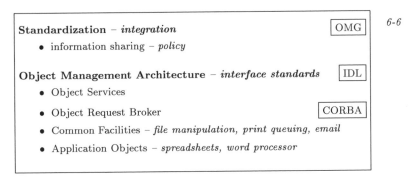

Slide 6-6: The OMG standardization effort

The OMG proceeds from the assumption that object technology (including encapsulation, polymorphism and inheritance) provides the mechanism necessary for language-, platform- and vendor-independent, *system integration.* The OMG has proposed an *abstract object model* and discusses technical and political objectives in the OMA Guide (Object Management Architecture Guide). The architecture specified in OMA provides a generic description of the components that constitute a system and defines the interface standards to which the components must comply.

An important aspect of OMA is the *interface description language* (IDL) that is introduced as a standard to describe object interfaces in a language-independent manner.

According to OMA, a system must support a number of *Object Services* (dealing with the lifecycle of objects, persistence, naming an event notification), and a so-called *Object Request Broker* (which is an intermediary between the object providing a service and the client requesting a service). Also a system will need, generally, *Common Facilities* (such as file manipulation and print queuing), and in addition will contain a number of *Application Objects* (such as a spreadsheet or word-processor) that constitute the proper application.

The OMG is primarily concerned with the adoption of technology by the producers and vendors of common facilities and application objects. Its contribution in this respect is the definition of a set of common object services and a standard interface to invoke such services by means of an object request broker. This standard has been adopted in CORBA (the Common Object Request Broker Architecture) which allows for the interaction between an application and distinct object request brokers.

The *object services* envisioned in OMA are intended to deal with objects in a language- and platform-independent manner. See slide 6-7.

Object Services   *6-7*

- life cycle – *creation and deletion*
- persistence – *management of storage*
- naming – *mapping to references*
- event notification – *registration*

Future

- transactions, concurrency, relationships, ... ,time

Slide 6-7: The OMG Object Services

These services encompass the creation and deletion of objects, the management of object storage, the mapping of names to references and the registration of events as triggers for actions. In addition, services will be defined that allow transactions, concurrency, relationships between objects and time-based properties of objects to be specified. To a large extent, such services are provided by individual languages (such as Java, C++ or Smalltalk) with their accompanying libraries and development frameworks. However, the efforts of the OMG are directed towards (the ambitious goal of) providing such services in a generic fashion, independent of a particular language or environment.

6.2.3   Persistent objects – ODMG

In a similar vein as the OMG, a number of vendors of object database management systems (including SunSoft, Object Design, Ontos, O_2 Technology, Versant, Objectivity, Hewlett Packard, POET Software, Itasca, Intellitic, Digital Equipment Corporation, Servio, Texas Instruments) have participated in the ODMG (Object Database Management systems Group) to develop a standard for the definition and manipulation of persistent objects.

The standards proposal of the ODMG encompasses an object definition language ODL, which is intended as an extension of the OMG/IDL standard, an object manipulation language, OML and an object query language, OQL, that provides SQL-like facilities for the retrieval of information.

The advantage of employing an object database system over employing a relational database system is that, in principle, the application programmer may work within a unified type system, encompassing both persistent and transient objects. See slide 6-8.

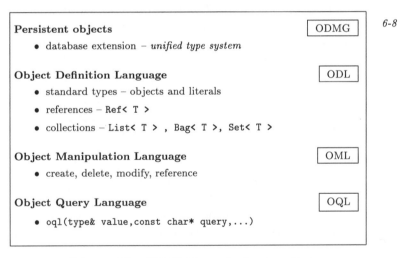

Slide 6-8: The ODMG-93 standardization efforts

The extensions to the various languages, which include C++ and Smalltalk, involve the definition of persistent objects, the creation and use of objects and facilities to pose queries concerning their attributes and relations. These extensions are proposed as language-specific bindings for respectively ODL, OML and OQL.

The object model proposed by the ODMG supports *objects* (which may have attributes and methods), *literals* (which may be considered as primitive values), *relationships between objects* (including *m-n* relations), *extents* (which contain the collection of instances of a particular type), and *named objects* (to facilitate retrieval).

To define objects and literals, the programmer may employ the standard types offered by the language, as well as a number of additional parametrized types to define references and collections. For references the ODMG-93 proposal employs a *Ref<T>* smart pointer construct. For dealing with collections a number of generic collection classes such as *List<T>*, *Bag<T>* and *Set<T>* must be provided by a standard library. (To provide a binding for Smalltalk, which does not have a type system, type annotations must be employed to define the properties of persistent objects.)

The manipulation of persistent objects conforms with the manipulation of ordinary objects as far as attribute access and method invocation are concerned. However, the language-specific OML bindings must take precautions for the creation, deletion and modification of objects. In particular, when employing a reference to a persistent object, the implementation must check whether the referenced object has been modified.

The C++ binding for the object query language OQL in the ODMG-93 proposal is quite simple. It consists merely of a function that allows the programmer to pass an extended SQL-like query as a string. The query may contain symbolic variables that are bound in a similar way as allowed by the C *printf* function.

The design principle guiding the ODMG effort has been to promote that *the programmer feels that there is one language.* However, there are a number of difficulties that arise when defining a particular language binding for the ODMG object model, as for example for C++. See slide 6-9.

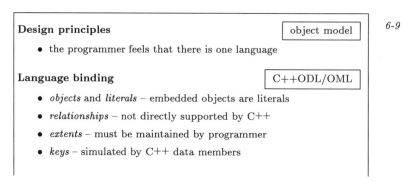

Slide 6-9: Language binding – C++ ODL/OML

Embedded objects which are defined in C++ as object data members, must be taken as literals in the ODMG object model, whereas embedded references to objects are to be taken as objects.

Relationships are not directly supported in C++. In the ODMG-93 proposal, the programmer is required to employ an explicit data structure for updating and traversing a relation.

Extents, which contain the collection of instances of a type, must explicitly be maintained by the programmer. Extents may conveniently be stored in a collection that is associated with a static data member of the class.

Keys, which are needed for efficient retrieval, must be simulated by C++ data members. Support for indexing and retrieval by key requires additional compiler support, for which no provision is made in the ODMG-93 proposal.

Other problems that arise in defining a binding to C++ involve the naming of objects, the restriction that C++ allows for only one implementation of a particular type and the duality between arrays and pointers.

Discussion Both the OMG and ODMG standardization efforts aim at the portability of software. The ODMG proposal not only entails the portability of design and source code, but also includes object code, in the form of persistent objects.

The ODMG-93 proposal is inadequate due, partially, to the self-imposed restrictions with respect to the compiler support required.

C++ODL/OML binding – *future*   *6-10*

  - no distinction between persistent and transient objects
  - better integration of the query sublanguage

Modifications to C++

  - overloading dot (access operator), r/l values, ...

Standardization efforts – *de facto market share*

  - PDES/STEP, ODA, PCTE, OSI/NMF, ISO ODP, ANSI X3

Slide 6-10: Future standardization efforts

The future C++ODL/OML binding will probably no longer distinguish between references to persistent and transient objects, and will provide a better integration of the query language OQL. To realize these goals, however, extended compiler support is needed and perhaps also modifications of C++ to allow the incorporation of code for integrity checking.

It is worth noting that there are a number of additional efforts at defining a standard object model. See slide 6-10. The ODMG proposal is explicitly meant as a superset of the object model proposed by the OMG, in order to become what they aptly phrase as a standard enforced by a *de facto market share*.

6.3   The Java platform – technology innovation

Java is the newest wave of technology. It offers a distributed object-oriented platform for the development of Web-aware applications. However, as with any wave of technology, we must ask ourselves whether it really does provide an answer to our questions. And, in the line of Lewis (1997), we may well ask ourselves what the original question was in the first place.

6-11

Perspectives

- Internet applications – *the dial-tone of the Internet*
- Software engineering – *long-term maintenance*
- Language design – *semantic compromises*
- System development – *lightweight clients, heavyweight servers*
- Computer science – *towards declarative, verifiable technology*
- IT (in) business – *standards for business objects and processes*
- Global village – *virtual world technology*

Slide 6-11: Perspectives

Whether Java does answer answer our needs for technological innovation is a matter of perspective. The question whether Java will provide an economically viable solution to corporate IT needs can not be answered at this stage. Yet, Java frameworks are being developed. See section 11.1.

In this section, we will look at the Java platform from the perspectives listed in slide 7-12. The rhetoric in these reflections must not be misunderstood as dismissing Java, but as a way to get hold of the issues that play a role in adopting the Java technology, or any of the competing technologies, for business-critical applications.

Internet applications Java was introduced in 1995 at the WWW3 Conference in Darmstadt as *'the dial-tone of the Internet'*, with applets as its killer application. The *dial-tone*, because Java is platform-neutral and network-aware. In practice, applets form only a small part of Java applications. Together with the Beans component technology and RMI, Java seems to be an ideal platform for companies that wish to employ the Internet and the Web for commercial applications. However, most developers have no idea how to adopt the Java platform without sacrificing their investment in legacy applications, such as a corporate database. The question is whether there is a migration strategy. In comparison, OMG CORBA seems to have better answers in this respect, although combinations of RMI and JNI (the Java Native Interface) have also been suggested as a technical solution.

Software engineering Lewis (1997) argues that within two decades we will have Java legacy problems similar to the legacy maintenance problems we have now. Software development with Java is not an issue. There are excellent tools, there is a large amount of good documentation, and there are loads of APIs. In general, software development with Java seems to be easier than, for example, with C++. However, long-term maintenance is a different question altogether. The answer to this question depends on standardization, and issues such as language and platform independence. We must consider that Java is a programming technology, and a good one in this respect, and not an integration technology such as CORBA, for which the specification of domain-independent and domain-specific standards, including services and facilities, is the primary issue.

Language design Java may be regarded as a second-generation third-generation programming language. Complex as this may sound, it is meant to express that Java is an object-oriented imperative language that shows the influence of many of its predecessors, the minimality of Pascal, threads, the flavor of C++. Personally, I am somewhat bothered by the semantic compromises in Java. For example, the equality operator for strings does, against all expectations, not test for string equality but for reference equality. Threads is another issue. Why only a keyword *synchronized* and not an Ada-like *select*? See, for example, PetitPierre (1998). Java has been developed in great haste. For example, assertion (like Eiffel) seem to have been omitted simply because the implementation was buggy at the time of a delivery deadline.

System development The Java virtual machine is a good idea. It can be realized on any platform, including computers of all sorts and a variety of gadgets. Java is easy to learn and there are many tools. However, a survey entitled *'Are Java Tools ready for Prime Time'* indicated that all tools still needed improvements.

Now back to the reality of software development. Many Internet applications are written in script languages. Perl for server-side scripting and Javascript on the client-side. Given the efficiency problems of Java (which are a consequence of the virtual machine approach) and the long download times for applets, Java runs the risk of being too light for heavy-duty servers and too heavy for lightweight clients.

Computer science Java has been adopted by many universities as the first programming language, and students like it. That is a good thing, although I am worried to see C++ disappear from the curriculum.

In terms of research, what Java offers is not really new. Personally, I am somewhat disappointed that the attention is focused on another third-generation language, whereas to my mind, we should have a declarative programming technology on our research agendas, a technology that supports the development of reliable and verifiable software. Nevertheless, Java appears to be an excellent platform for Web-related research.

IT (in) business Java is being adopted rapidly. It is nevertheless hard to establish to what extent this involves mission-critical applications or pilot projects. After all, at the time of writing, Java is still cutting-edge technology. And common wisdom has it not to use cutting-edge technology for strategic projects, see Cockburn (1997).

An example of a business application framework is the IBM San Francisco framework, discussed in section 11.1, which offers generic solutions for the realization of business processes, such as order management and quality control. Nevertheless, crucial issues in this area do not seem to concern technology *per se*, but rather the standardization of such notions as business objects, business processes and, of course, business logic. This is also an area of active OMG interest.

Global village On the Internet we see an increasing number of virtual communities deploying 3D technology for rendering worlds and their inhabitants. Imagine a virtual stockmarket. Decisions must be taken quickly. There is an overload of information, from a variety of sources. Stock prices, political tensions, market trends, all these must be monitored continuously. In critical situations, direct actions must be possible. A nice playground for virtual worlds technology. Is the Java platform ripe for this? It might, given the Java3D and JavaVRML97 efforts. And what about the knowledge management?

Discussion In summary, Java is a promising platform, with a wealth of APIs for the development of a variety of applications. At this stage there might be problems of efficiency and problems due to the instability and immaturity of the APIs offered. However, as indicated, there are a number of issues that surpass the reach of the Java platform since they do not depend on technical solutions only. The most important issues, I would say, concern the standardization of (domain-specific) business objects and processes, and the migration problems due to the inescapable existence of legacy applications.

6.4 An Internet-based workgroup application

The goal of the project described in this section was to develop a prototype for an Internet-based workgroup architecture using CORBA technology. CORBA provides a means for developing distributed object applications, while the Internet provides a standard and widely accessible network infrastructure. Users should not need special client software to use the system, other than a Java-enabled browser such as Netscape.

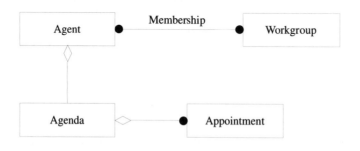

Slide 6-12: Object model

The object model guiding the implementation is depicted in slide 6-12. The most important notion in our system is that of an *agent*, which is defined as a representative of a user which can perform simple operations on the user's behalf, such as sending messages to and making appointments with other agents.

Each user participating is represented by a personal agent, which has an agenda and a message queue. Each agenda consists of several appointments. A workgroup has a membership list consisting of zero or more agents present in the system. An agent can be a member of zero or more workgroups. Possible operations on agents are sending messages to and making appointments with other agents, subscribing to a workgroup, making an appointment with a workgroup or sending a message to all workgroup members.

All interaction of the user with the system is done via Java applets, which combine a graphical user interface with Internet access and CORBA functionality. The server is implemented in C++. We used Visigenic's (formerly PostModern Computing) CORBA 2.0-compliant product ORBeline to implement the server and BlackWidow from the same vendor to implement the Java clients. The server can run on most UNIX platforms, as well as on Windows NT, while the Java applets, running on top of a Java Virtual Machine, can theoretically run on every platform that Java supports. In addition, a C++ browser/monitor was developed that can be used to interrogate agents and workgroups and to monitor message flows.

The Java client applets are first transferred to the client by the HTTP server using a web page and then contact the object server through IIOP, the Internet Inter-ORB Protocol. The client applets run in Netscape or HotJava and contain the CORBA client communications software as well as the client application code. The object server can reside on a different machine than the Web server and is running an IIOP gatekeeper, for instance on TCP port 15000, that is part of the ORB. All further communication is done through this gatekeeper.

Discussion During the development of a simple workgroup application using CORBA, we experienced a number of limitations inherent to the CORBA architecture.

The most important problem we faced was the distinction between clients and servers, where distributed objects can only reside on a server. If a client wants to make its objects available to other programs, it should be configured as a server as well, with an ORB running on the same host. This causes problems regarding overhead and licensing and is not a feasible situation for the distribution of (Java) clients over the Internet. The same architecture limitation prevents servers from notifying clients using callbacks. This feature makes it impossible for clients to pass distributed object references back to the server, forcing them to work with other identification mechanisms such as object IDs or human-readable strings.

Other minor problems we observed concern the lack of support for existing non-CORBA objects in a distributed environment. Possible solutions are converting existing classes to CORBA and making their interface available through IDL, or to write CORBA object wrappers around these objects.

Finally, not all parts of a CORBA system are compatible among ORBs at the source-code level. This problem should, however, be alleviated with the Portable Object Adapter (POA).

6.5   Crush – extending *hush* with CORBA

This section describes how the *hush* toolkit has been extended with CORBA functionality. The nickname for this effort was *crush*. The major problem that arises when extending a given toolkit or framework, such as *hush*, with CORBA IDL interfaces and classes to implement these interfaces is to provide for a seamless integration of the already existing code with the CORBA-based extensions. In *crush* we have included facilities for object creation and access, as well as client-side adaptors for the *hush* CORBA objects, to resolve the type clash between the original *hush* class hierarchy and the *hush* CORBA object classes.

Extending a framework with CORBA   *6-13*

- the legacy problem – *granularity of wrappers*
- object creation and access – *factories and tables*
- client-side adaptors – *to fit within native type system*
- events versus objects – *natural interfaces*

Slide 6-13: Extending a framework with CORBA

Extending a given framework with CORBA is not as straightforward as it may seem. First of all, one has to decide which interfaces may become public, that is may be exported as IDL interfaces. Secondly, one has to decide how object references become known to clients, and what rights clients have to create objects within a particular server. The most important problem, however, concerns the type clash between the CORBA classes implementing the IDL interfaces and the 'native' class hierarchy offered by the framework itself.

The legacy problem – integrating CORBA CORBA technology is well suited to develop distributed applications. For new projects, the restrictions imposed by CORBA can be taken into consideration from the start. For projects that carry the legacy of existing code, a decision must be made to what extent the CORBA functionality is integrated with the legacy code. On one side of the spectrum, CORBA technology can be used simply for wrapping the legacy code. For example a database may be embedded in a CORBA server, without affecting the database itself. However, for an object-oriented framework such as *hush* such a solution is not very satisfying. Instead, one would like to have the basic interfaces of *hush* available to develop distributed components of arbitrary granularity.

Object creation and access The CORBA Naming Service may be used to provide access to an object residing somewhere on a server. Alternatively, the server may export a reference to a factory object that allows the client to create objects within the server.

For giving access to objects within a particular *hush* component, we have provided *dots* (distributed object tables) for both *hush* and the *widgets* components.

Using the *dot* the client can access an object of a given type by the name it is given by the server. The object must already exist in the server.

In case clients are allowed to create objects within the server, a *factory* is provided for creating *hush* or *widget* objects.

Client-side adaptors The intermediary between clients and servers in a CORBA-based system are the CORBA IDL classes generated by the *idl* compiler from the IDL interfaces. These classes (using the C++ language binding) inherit directly from the CORBA::Object class and hence do not fit within the given class hierarchy.

To allow clients the use of CORBA IDL classes wherever one of the original *hush* classes is expected, client-side adaptors have been provided for each of the *hush* or *widgets* IDL classes. An additional advantage of client-side adaptors is that they allow for overcoming the 'weaknesses' of IDL with respect to overloading member functions, parametrized types and operator definitions.

Typically, client-side adaptors have their corresponding *hush* class as a base class and simply delegate method invocations to the CORBA object they encapsulate.

Events versus object method invocation Since GUI components are in some way typically event-driven, one may be inclined to limit the communication between such components to exchanging events. The CORBA Event Service would suffice for such communications.

Nevertheless, in our opinion events should be used in a very restricted manner. Events tend to break the 'crisp' object interfaces that are one of the benefits of an object-oriented approach to design.

For the *hush* CORBA extensions, we have chosen for retaining the original *hush* object interfaces. Note however that the IDL interfaces are somewhat more abstract than the corresponding C++ interfaces. Nevertheless, the *event* interface is part of the *hush* module. Together with the *dispatch* function of the *handler* interface incoming events resulting from user actions may be dispatched directly to remote components.

Interfaces

The IDL interfaces reflect to a large extent the functionality of the original *hush* and *widgets* interfaces. In this section a partial listing of the interfaces will be given. In comparison with the corresponding C++/Java classes, the IDL interfaces are much more abstract in the sense that many member functions required for the actual implementation of the *hush* framework may be omitted.

The *hush* module

The *hush* module contains interfaces corresponding to the basic *hush* classes, *handler*, *event*, *kit*, *widget* and *item*, as well as the auxiliary classes for iterators and containers.

```
interface handler {
      event dispatch( in event data );
      };
```

handler

The *handler* interface provides only a method for dispatching events. It may be extended in the future though. In *hush* almost every class is derived from *handler*. This is directly reflected in the *hush* IDL interfaces.

```
interface event : handler {

      attribute long type;

      attribute long x;
      attribute long y;
      };
```

event

The *event* interface offers attributes to determine the type of event and its location. Also the *event* interface will very likely be extended in the future, to allow for a greater variety of events.

```
interface kit : handler {

      void source(in string file);
      void eval(in string command);
      string result();

      widget root();
      };
```

kit

In *hush*, a *kit* provides an interface to some embedded interpreter, such as a Tcl interpreter or a logic engine. The *kit* also gives access to the underlying window environment; in particular it may be asked to provide a reference to the root window.

```
interface widget : handler {

   string path();

   void eval( in string cmd );

   void configure( in string options );
   void pack( in string options );
   };
```

widget

A widget is a user interface gadget. The *widget* interface collects the functions that all these gadgets have in common.

```
interface item : handler {                                          item

        void move( in long x, in long y );
        };
```

An *item* is obtained when creating a graphical object for a canvas. Subsequently, the item reference suffices to manipulate such objects. Also the *item* interface will very likely be extended in the future.

Iterators and lists As an alternative for CORBA arrays and sequences, the *hush* module offers interfaces for iterators and containers.

```
interface iterator {                                            iterator
        Object next();
        };
```

From a client's perspective, an *iterator* is a data generator. To deal with typed iterators, the *hush* C++ library offers template client-side adaptor classes encapsulating the untyped CORBA iterators.

```
interface container {                                          container

        long length();

        Object first();
        Object next();
        Object current();

        iterator walk();
        };
```

The *container* interface offers access to the *hush* list class. It offers functions for cursor-based list traversal as well as the *walk* function that may be used to obtain an iterator.

Factories and distributed object tables To obtain references to objects, clients may use either factory object or distributed object tables.

```
interface factory {                                             factory

            hush::kit kit(in string name);
            hush::event event(in long type);
        };
```

The *factory* interface allows only for creating a *kit* and for creating an *event*. Note that *handler* objects may not be created directly.

```
interface dot {                                                    dot

        hush::kit kit(in string name);

        hush::container container(in string name);
        hush::iterator iterator(in string name);

        hush::factory hush(in string name);
};
```

Apart from giving access to a *hush* factory, the *dot* interface allows for getting access to a *kit*, a *container* and an *iterator*. When obtaining references through a *dot* object, these objects are assumed to exist within the server.

The *widgets* module

The *widgets* module provides the actual user interface gadgets for *hush*. Below we have included only the (partial) interfaces for a *canvas* and a *message* widget.

```
module widgets {

interface canvas : hush::widget {                          canvas

        canvas create( in hush::widget anc, in string path );

        hush::item circle( in long x, in long y, in long radius, in
    string options );
        // other items ...
        };


interface message : hush::widget {                         message

        message create( in hush::widget anc, in string path );
        void text(in string txt);
        };


interface factory : hush::factory {                        factory

        widgets::canvas   canvas(in string name, in string options);
        widgets::message message(in string name, in string options);
        };

interface dot : hush::dot {                                    dot

        widgets::canvas   canvas(in string name);
        widgets::message message(in string name);
```

```
        widgets::factory widgets(in string name);
        };


    };
```

Note that each widget type has a method *create*, with which an actual widget of that type can be created. In effect this means that each widget object may act as a factory for widget objects of that type. (The server may however refuse to create such objects!) In addition to the specific gadget interfaces, the *widgets* module provides a *factory* and *dot* interface, extending the respective *hush* interfaces.

Examples

The *hush* CORBA extensions may be used in a number of ways. For example, the client does not need to be linked with *hush* when only the server side is given a graphical user interface. In the case that also the client has a graphical user interface, the client side may dispatch incoming events to the server, as illustrated in the canvas example. The communication between server and clients can be arbitrarily complex. The final example shows how to employ iterators and containers to give clients accesses to collections of information.

A remote interpreter kit

This example uses a remote kit. It shows how to get access to a message widget and a kit via a dot (which is a distributed object table). The client access the kit and the message widget by using a name (hello for the message widget and tk for the kit). The client can send Tcl/Tk interpreter commands to the kit.

<code>client</code>

```
    hush::dot*       hush;        // (distributed) object tables
    widgets::dot*    widgets;     // widgets contains hush

    hush::kit* tk;                // remote kit object
    widgets::message* banner;

    try {
        hush = widgets = widgets::dot::_bind (SERVER, argv[1]);

        tk = hush->kit("tk");
        banner = widgets->message("hello"); // must exist

    } catch (...) {
        cerr << "Unexpected exception ..." << endl;
        return -1;
    }

    while (1) {
```

```
char text = readtext(); // from stdin

banner->text( text );   // display text
tk->eval(text);
}
```

This fragment shows how a distributed object table is obtained via the *bind* function. From this table, the client obtains a kit and a message area. Queries are read in from standard input, displayed in the message area and evaluated. Queries may be arbitrary Tcl/Tk commands. In this way the client may even construct a complete user interface through Tk commands.

| server |

```
class application : public session {
public:
application(int argc, char* argv[]) : session(argc,argv,"hello") {
}
void corba();
int main() {
    tk->trace();
    kit::declare("tk",tk);

    message* m = new hello(".hello");
    m->pack();

    message::declare("hello",m);

    corba(); // make yourself available as a server

    return OK;
    }
};
```

The server is realized as a standard *hush* program, except for the call to *corba* (for which the code is given below). Note that the calls to *declare* for both the *kit* and *message* objects is needed to make these objects accessible via the *dot*.

```
void application::corba() {

widgets::dot* dw = new widgets_dot_srv(); // create dot for widgets

try {
CORBA::Orbix.registerIOCallback(it_orbix_fd_open,  FD_OPEN_CALLBACK);
CORBA::Orbix.registerIOCallback(it_orbix_fd_close, FD_CLOSE_CALLBACK);

CORBA::Orbix.impl_is_ready(SERVER,0);
CORBA::Orbix.processEvents(0);
}
```

```
catch (...) {
    cout << "apparently something went wrong" << endl;
}
```

In *application::corba()* a distributed object table is created. This object is exported as a server by a call to *Orbix.impl_is_ready(SERVER,0)*, where SERVER is a macro defining the name of the server. Calling *registerIOCallback* is needed to merge the (Orbix) CORBA server event loop with the window event loop for *hush*.

Evaluating logical queries

With a few minor changes, the client program can be adapted for accessing a logical query evaluator.

client

```
try {
    tk = hush->kit("bp");        // A kit for BinProlog
    tk->eval("consult(facts)");
    }
catch(...) {
    cout << "An exception ... " << endl;
}

while (1) {
    char* text = readtext();
    tk->eval(text);
    char* q = 0;
    while ( (q = tk->result()) )
        cout << "Result: " << q << endl;
}
```

This fragment show how to obtain a kit for BinProlog and consult a *facts* database. Since queries may produce multiple answers the client must iterate over the term resulting from the query.

A remote canvas

This example shows how a client canvas can be used to draw on a remote canvas.

draw_clt

```
class draw_clt : public canvas {
public:

void plug(widgets::canvas* x) { draw = x; }

int operator()() {
        hush::event* e = hush->event(_event->type());
```

```
        cerr << "Getting event " << e->type() << endl;
        e->x(_event->x()+10);
        e->y(_event->y()+10);
        hush::event::_duplicate(e);   // CORBA 2.0
        hush::event* res = draw->dispatch(e);
        return canvas::operator()();
        }

draw_clt(const widget* w,   char* path ) : canvas(w,path) {
        configure("-background white");
        geometry(200,100);
        self()->bind(this);
        dragging = 0;
}

draw_clt(char* path ) : canvas(path) {
        configure("-background white");
        geometry(200,100);
        self()->bind(this);
        dragging = 0;
}

void press( event& ) { dragging = 1; }

void motion( event& e) {
        if (dragging) {
                self()->circle(e.x(),e.y(),2,"-fill black");
                draw->circle(e.x(),e.y(),3,"-fill yellow");
                }
}

void release( event&  ) { dragging = 0; }

protected:
int dragging;
widgets::canvas* draw;
};
```

This fragment shows the implementation of a canvas which is simultaneously the client side of a remote canvas. The method *plug* allows for declaring the remote canvas, which is accessed via the instance variable *draw* in both the *operator* method and the *motion* method (when dragging). In the *operator* method an event is created which is dispatched to the remote canvas. Note that this is possible since a canvas is a handler. In the *motion* method, a large yellow dot is drawn on the remote canvas, whereas the local canvas draws a black dot. Combined, the actions on the remote canvas result in drawing parallel yellow and black dots.

```
    class draw_srv : public canvas {                          ┌─────────┐
    public:                                                    │ draw_srv │
                                                               └─────────┘
```

```
draw_srv( const widget* w,  char* path ) : canvas(w,path) {
        geometry(200,100);
        self()->bind(this);
        dragging = 0;
}

void press( event& ) { dragging = 1; }

void motion( event& e) {
        if (dragging) circle(e.x(),e.y(),10,"-fill black");
}

void release( event&  ) { dragging = 0; }

protected:
int dragging;
};
```

The canvas implementation on the server side straightforwardly implements a *hush* canvas. It is embedded in a CORBA server when an object reference is given to it via the distributed object table.

Moving items

This example is similar to the canvas example, but shows some additional features, such as how to manipulate a list of items.

server

```
list<hush::item>* rlist =  new list<hush::item>;
item* it = draw->circle(40,40,10,"-fill yellow");
hush::item* rit = new item_srv(it);
rlist->insert(rit);
it = draw->circle(30,30,10,"-fill red");
rit = new item_srv(it);
rlist->insert(rit);

hush::container* rx = new list_srv<hush::item>(rlist);
list<hush::item>::declare("items",rx); // store server

iter<hush::item>* riter = rlist->walk();
iter<hush::item>::declare("riter",riter);
```

The fragment above illustrates the creation of a list of items. In addition it shows how to obtain an iterator and how the iterator may be declared to make it accessible via the distributed object table.

Discussion From a design point of view, the *hush* framework proved to be sufficiently abstract to allow for recapturing its design by means of IDL interfaces. Lacking in the current realization of *crush* though, are proper exceptions to indicate possible error conditions.

This work shows how to integrate CORBA functionality with an already existing framework. In particular the need for client-side adaptors for resolving the type clash between the 'native' classes and the CORBA IDL classes has been amply demonstrated. Enriching *hush* with CORBA makes *crush* a potential competitor of Fresco, the CORBA based GUI toolkit derived from the Interviews library.

Summary

This chapter has given an overview of component technology. It discussed standards for interoperability, including (D)COM, CORBA and Java. It gave an example application using both Java and CORBA, and discussed the issues involved in extending an existing library with CORBA.

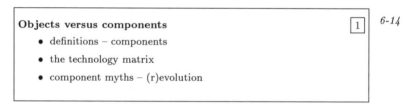

Slide 6-14: Section 6.1: Objects versus components

In section 1, we looked at some definitions of components to clarify how component technology differs from object technology. A brief overview of existing technology was given and an attempt was made to demystify component-based development.

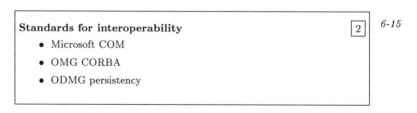

Slide 6-15: Section 6.2: Standards for interoperability

In section 2 we looked in somewhat more detail at component technologies that, each in their own way, set a standard for interoperability.

In section 3, we discussed the Java platform from a variety of perspectives, as

Slide 6-16: Section 6.3: The Java platform

listed in slide 6-16. We weighted the pros and cons of Java from each of these perspectives, and concluded that Java is a promising platform.

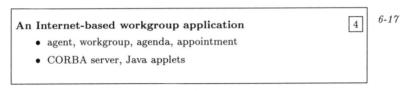

Slide 6-17: Section 6.4: An Internet-based workgroup application

In section 4, we looked at the outline of a simple workgroup application, that allows for creating appointments mediated by *agents* that act as a representative of a user. The workgroup illustrates the use of Java applets and CORBA servers.

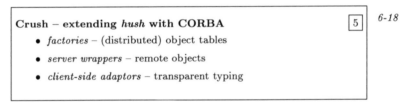

Slide 6-18: Section 6.5: Crush – extending *hush* with CORBA

Finally, in section 5, we discussed the issues involved in extending a framework such as *hush* with CORBA. Apart from the definition of interfaces and server wrappers, we defined client-side adaptors to attain a transparent integration of CORBA object handles and the types native to the framework.

Questions

1. Give a definition of the notion of *components*. How is this related to a definition of *objects*? Explain the difference between these definitions.

2. What actual component technologies can you think of? How would you compare them?

3. Describe Microsoft (D)COM, OMG CORBA, ODMG Persistent Objects. Is there any relation between these standards?

4. Discuss the Java platform. What perspectives can you think of? Discuss pros and cons.

5. Describe the architecture of an Internet-based workgroup application. What technology would you use?

6. What issues may arise in extending a given library or framework with CORBA? Can you think of any solutions?

Further reading

I recommend Szyperski (1997), both as an introduction to component-technology, and as a reference for more advanced readers. For an introduction to CORBA, you may read Siegel (1996). A readable account of the ODMG standard is given in Cattell (1994). For more information on Java, again, visit . For information on (D)COM, look at www.microsoft.com/com. Learning how to program CORBA applications is probably best learned from the manuals that come with your CORBA distribution. For an evaluation of object store management and naming schemes see Chennupati and Saiedian (1997).

7

Software architecture

To get an overall idea of the structure of a software system is intrinsically difficult. The notion of *architecture* has proven to be a powerful metaphor for describing the structure of a system, that is the components and their interrelations, in a sufficiently abstract way.

7-1

Software architecture   7

- architecture – components and boundaries
- case study – a framework for multimedia feature detection
- native objects – the language boundary
- embedded logic – the paradigm boundary
- architectural styles – distributed object technology
- cross-platform development – Unix versus Windows

Additional keywords and phrases: *components, information architecture, multimedia information retrieval, feature detection, portability*

Slide 7-1: Software architecture

In this chapter we will explore the notion of software architecture. We will first look at some definitions. As a preliminary to some technical explorations that illustrate a variety of ways to couple heterogeneous components, we will look at a case study involving a framework for multimedia feature detection, which is to be

used for the indexing and retrieval of multimedia objects on the Web. In particular
we will look at how to deploy embedded logic for managing meta-information and
knowledge, and how to define corresponding collections of objects across language
boundaries. As an example, we will discuss the Java and C++ coupling in *hush*
in some detail. Finally, we will discuss some architectural patterns and styles, as
well as some solutions for cross-platform development.

7.1   Elements of architecture

Software architecture has become an area of research in its own right. The seminal
work of Shaw and Gorlan (1996) introduced the notion of *software architecture*
as a means to describe how the various elements of a software system interact to
achieve some computational goal. For example, at a high level we can distinguish
between a pipe-lined architecture, common to many compilers, and event-driven
computation, as it occurs for example in GUI-based systems.

Elements of architecture   Perry and Wolf (1992)   *7-2*

- processing elements – transformation on data

- data elements – contain information

- connections – glue that holds elements together

Models and views   Kruchten (1995)

- logical – functional requirements

- process – performance, availability, distribution

- physical – scalability, configuration

- development – organization of software modules

- scenarios – instances of use cases

Definitions

- http://www.sei.cmu.edu/architecture/definitions.html

Slide 7-2: Elements of architecture – models and views

In the definition given in Perry and Wolf (1992), a software architecture is
described as consisting of *processing elements*, which operate on data, and *data
elements*, which somehow contain the information being processed. In addition
there are *connection elements* that glue the processing and data elements together.
Such an abstract view allows for describing a software system at a high level of
abstraction and to indicate choice points and alternatives.

A later definition, given in Kruchten (1995), makes a distinction between the
levels of abstraction, or points of view, from which a description of a system is
possible. It distinguishes between a *logical view*, which captures the functional
requirements, a *process view*, which indicates non-functional aspects such as per-

formance, availability and distribution, a *physical view*, which deals with issues such as scalability and configuration, and a *development view*, which describes the organization of the software modules. In addition, Kruchten (1995) distinguishes a *scenario view*, which may be used for formulating tests based on properly instantiated use cases. The scenario view may be regarded as orthogonal to the logical, process, physical and development models since it does not affect the structure of the system itself, but rather the way the structure is validated against proper usage tests.

An exhaustive list of definitions of the notion of *software architecture* is given at the Web site of the Software Engineering Institute (SEI), of which the url is given in slide 7-2.

At the time of writing, the most comprehensive book concerning software architectures is Bass *et al.* (1998). As a definition it proposes:

> *The software architecture of a program or computing system is the structure of the system, which comprises software components, the externally visible properties of those components, and their interrelationships.*

Note the stress on *externally visible properties* here. It is meant to express that both components and their relations must be described at a suitable level of abstraction. Also note that the phrase *relationships between components* may cover quite a lot. For example, when considering the architecture of a Web application, issues such as communication protocols and document standards must be considered as well. In addition, the technological infrastructure, elements of which are given in slide 7-3, must also be taken into account.

Technological infrastructure   Shimberg and Barnes (1997)   *7-3*

- client-platform – hardware, OS
- presentation services – windows, multimedia
- application software – code, business logic
- network – communication support
- middleware – distribution, (object) brokers
- server platform – hardware, OS
- database – data management system

Slide 7-3: Technological infrastucture

One may wonder whether the architecture metaphor, which is derived from the construction of buildings, is really appropriate for software systems. Software systems are much more dynamic than buildings, so it might perhaps be more appropriate to focus on dynamic, behavioral aspects rather than structural aspects. As a metaphor, I would prefer for example one related to an ecological system, to stress the dynamic growth that seems to be characteristic of software systems nowadays.

In the definition or rather collection of definitions, given by the IEEE Architecture Working Group, for the terms *architect, architectural description, stakeholder* and *viewpoint,* utmost care is taken to suppress the phrase *structure.* Instead, the notion of *architecting* is defined as defining, maintaining, improving and certifying proper implementation of an architecture, and an *architecture* as a collection of views relevant to the stakeholders of a system.

Distributed object architectures When considering the architecture of a system, invariably the technological infrastructure plays a role. In particular, when considering client/server or distributed object systems the choice for respectively a particular client and server platform, middleware and communication infrastructure may to a large extent determine the characteristics of the software architecture.

Explicit attention for the architecture of a system becomes increasingly relevant as the complexity of the system grows. As argued in Mowbray and Malveau (1997), an architecture is an abstraction that allows for mastering complexity and managing change.

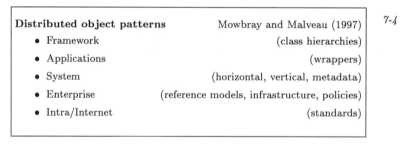

Slide 7-4: Distributed object patterns

Mowbray and Malveau (1997) present a number of patterns based on the Common Object Request Broker Architecture (CORBA). The patterns differ in scale, ranging from frameworks and systems to enterprise-level and intra/Internet-level infrastructures. According to Mowbray and Malveau (1997), software problems are due to inadequate definition and transfer of software boundaries. They criticize traditional object-oriented analysis and design methods for not paying sufficient attention to the actual interfaces that define these boundaries which may be regarded as a contract between the supplier of a service and its clients. At the higher enterprise and intra/internet levels, policies and standards are perhaps more important than interfaces *per se.* However, at the framework and system level interface definitions delineate stable boundaries between the components that constitute the system.

In business applications a distinction can be made between *horizontal components* (covering general functionality, such as GUI-aspects and document interoperability), *vertical components* (covering domain-specific functionality for one area of business, such as finance), and *meta-data*, representing the more volatile, knowledge-level aspects of a system. Mowbray and Malveau (1997) observe that each of these component types may cover one third of a system. When to consider information or a service as part of the meta-data must be determined by the extent to which that particular information or service may be considered stable. Architectural decisions must strive for an ecology of change, that is a flexible arrangement of components to promote changes in business-logic and adaptiveness to a changing environment.

7.2   Case study – multimedia feature detection

In this section, we will look at the indexing and retrieval of musical fragments. This study is primarily aimed at establishing the architectural requirements for the detection of musical features and to indicate directions for exploring the inherently difficult problem of finding proper discriminating features and similarity measures in the musical domain. In this study we have limited ourselves to the analysis of music encoded in MIDI, to avoid the technical difficulties involved in extracting basic musical properties from raw sound material. Currently we have a simple running prototype for extracting higher level features from MIDI files. In our approach to musical feature detection, we extended the basic grammar-based ACOI framework with an embedded logic component to facilitate the formulation of predicates and constraints over the musical structure obtained from the input.

The ACOI framework

The ACOI framework is intended to accomodate a broad spectrum of classification schemes, manual as well as (semi) automatic, for the indexing and retrieval of multimedia objects, Kersten *et al.* (1998).

What are stored are not the actual multimedia objects themselves, but structural descriptions of these objects (including their location) that may be used for retrieval.

The ACOI model is based on the assumption that indexing an arbitrary multimedia object is equivalent to deriving a grammatical structure that provides a namespace to reason about the object and to access its components. However, there is an important difference with ordinary parsing in that the lexical and grammatical items corresponding to the components of the multimedia object must be created dynamically by inspecting the actual object. Moreover, in general, there is not a fixed sequence of lexicals as in the case of natural or formal languages. To allow for the dynamic creation of lexical and grammatical items the ACOI framework supports both *black-box* and *white-box* (feature) detectors. Black-box detectors are algorithms, usually developed by a specialist in the media domain, that extract properties from the media object by some form of analysis. White-box detectors, on the other hand, are created by defining logical or mathematical

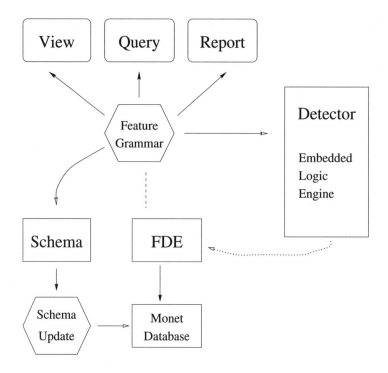

Slide 7-5: The extended ACOI architecture

expressions over the grammar itself. In this paper we will focus on black-box
detectors only.

As an example, look at the (simple) feature grammar below, specifying the
structure of a hypothetical community.

```
detector world;                              finds the name of the world
detector people;                      checks name, eliminates institutes
detector company;                  looks if there are at least two persons

atom str name;

community: world people company;

world: name;
people: person*;

person: name;
```

A *community* consists of people, and is a community only if it allows for the
people to be in each other's company.

A community has a name. The actual purpose of this grammar is to select
the persons that belong to a particular community from the input, which consists

of names of potential community members. Note that the grammar specifies three detectors. These detectors correspond to functions that are invoked when expanding the corresponding non-terminal in the grammar. An example of a detector function is the *personDetector* function partially specified below.

```
int personDetector(tree *pt, list *tks ){
...
q = query_query("kit=pl src=check.pl");

while (t = next_token(tks)) {
        sprintf(buf,"person(
sigma )",t);
        query_eval(q,buf);
        if (query_result(q,0))          // put name(person) on tokenstream
                    putAtom(tks,"name",t);
        }
...
}
```

The *personDetector* function checks for each token on the input tokenstream *tks* as to whether the token corresponds to the name of a person belonging to the community. The check is performed by an embedded logic component that contains the information needed to establish whether a person is a member of the community. Note that the query for a single token may result in adding multiple names to the token stream.

The *companyDetector* differs from the *personDetector* in that it needs to inspect the complete parse tree to see whether the (implicit) *company* predicate is satisfied.

When parsing succeeds and the *company* predicate is satisfied a given input may result in a sequence of updates of the underlying database, as illustrated below.

```
V0 := newoid();
V1 := newoid();
  community_world.insert(oid(V0),oid(V1));
     world_name.insert(oid(V1),"casa");
  community_people.insert(oid(V0),oid(V1));
V2 := newoid();
     people_person.insert(oid(V1),oid(V2));
        person_name.insert(oid(V2),"alice");
     people_person.insert(oid(V1),oid(V2));
        person_name.insert(oid(V2),"sebastiaan");
     ...
```

Evidently, the updates correspond to assigning appropriate values to the attributes of a structured object, reflecting the properties of the given community.

The overall architecture of the ACOI framework is depicted in slide 7-5. Taking a feature grammar specification, such as the simple community grammar, as a point of reference, we see that it is related to an actual feature detector (possibly containing an embedded logic component) that is invoked by the Feature Detector Engine (FDE) when an appropriate media object is presented for indexing. The feature grammar and its associated detector further result in updating respectively the data schemas and the actual information stored in the (Monet) database. The Monet database, which underlies the ACOI framework, is a customizable, high-performance, main-memory database developed at the CWI and the University of Amsterdam, see Boncz and Kersten (1995).

At the user end, a feature grammar is related to a *View*, *Query* and *Report* component, that respectively allow for inspecting a feature grammar, expressing a query, and delivering a response to a query. Some examples of these components are currently implemented as applets in Java 1.1 with Swing, as described in Kersten *et al.* (1998).

Formal specification Formally, a feature grammar G may be defined as $G = (V, T, P, S)$, where V is a collection of variables or non-terminals, T a collection of terminals, P a collection of productions of the form $V \rightarrow (V \cup T)$ and S a start symbol. A token sequence ts belongs to the language $L(G)$ if $S \xrightarrow{*} ts$. Sentential token sequences, those belonging to $L(G)$ or its sublanguages $L(G_v) = (V_v, T_v, P_v, v)$ for $v \in (T \cup V)$, correspond to a complex object C_v, which is the object corresponding to the parse tree for v, as illustrated in the community example. The parse tree defines a hierarchical structure that may be used to access and manipulate the components of the multimedia object subjected to the detector.

The anatomy of a MIDI feature detector

Automatic indexing for musical data is an inherently difficult problem. Existing systems rely on hand-crafted solutions, geared towards a particular group of users, such as for example composers of film music, see Subrahmanian (1998). In this section, we will look at a simple feature detector for MIDI-encoded musical data. It provides a skeleton for future experimentation.

The hierarchical information structure that we consider is depicted in slide 7-6. It contains only a limited number of basic properties and must be extended with information along the lines of a musical ontology including genre, mood and the like. However, the detector presented here provides a skeleton solution that accommodates an extension with arbitrary predicates over the musical structure in a transparent manner.

The grammar given below corresponds in an obvious way with the structure depicted in slide 7-6.

```
detector song;                          to get the filename
detector lyrics;                        extracts lyrics
```

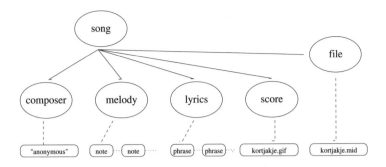

Slide 7-6: MIDI features

```
detector melody;                                              extracts melody

atom str name;
atom str text;
atom str note;

song: file lyrics melody;

file: name;
lyrics: text*;
melody: note*;
```

The start symbol is a *song*. The detector that is associated with *song* reads in a MIDI file. The musical information contained in the MIDI file is then stored a a collection of Prolog facts. This translation is very direct. In effect the MIDI file header information is stored, and events are recorded as facts, as illustrated below for a *note_on* and *note_off* event.

```
event('kortjakje',2,time=384, note_on:[chan=2,pitch=72,vol=111]).
event('kortjakje',2,time=768, note_off:[chan=2,pitch=72,vol=100]).
```

After translating the MIDI file into a Prolog format, the other detectors will be invoked, that is the *composer*, *lyrics* and *melody* detector, to extract the information related to these properties.

The actual processing is depicted in slide 7-7. The input is a MIDI file. As indicated in the top line, the MIDI file itself may be generated from a *lilypond* file. Lilypond is a LATEX-like formatting language for musical scores that also supports the generation of MIDI, described in Lilypond (1999). As indicated on the bottom line, processing a MIDI file results in a collection of features as well as in a MIDI file and lilypond file. The (result) MIDI file contains an extract of the original (input) MIDI file and the lilypond file contains a score for this extract, which may be presented to the (end) user as the result of a query. This

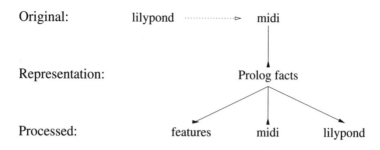

Slide 7-7: Processing MIDI file

setup allows us to verify whether our extract or abstraction of the original musical structure is effective, simply by comparing the input (midi or lilypond) musical structure with the output (midi or lilypond) extract.

To extract relevant fragments of the melody we use the melody detector, of which a partial listing is given below.

```
int melodyDetector(tree *pt, list *tks ){
char buf[1024]; char* _result;
void* q = _query;
int idq = 0;

   idq = query_eval(q,"X:melody(X)");
   while ((_result = query_result(q,idq)) ) {
          printf("note:
sigma ",_result);
          putAtom(tks,"note",_result);
          }
   return SUCCESS;
}
```

The embedded logic component is given the query X:melody(X), which results in the notes that constitute the (relevant fragment of the) melody. These notes are then added to the tokenstream. A similar detector is available for the lyrics.

Parsing a given MIDI file, for example *kortjakje.mid*, results in updating the Monet database.

The updates reflect the structure of the musical information object that corresponds to the properties defined in the grammar.

Implementation status Currently, we have a running prototype of the MIDI feature detector. It uses an adapted version of public domain MIDI processing software. The embedded logic component is part of the *hush* framework. It uses an object extension of Prolog that allows for the definition of native objects to interface with the midi processing software. The logic component allows for the definition of arbitrary predicates to extract the musical information, such as the melody and the lyrics.

Queries – the user interface

Assuming that we have an adequate solution for indexing musical data, we need to define how end users may access these data, that is search for musical objects in the information space represented by the database, for the ACOI project the World Wide Web.

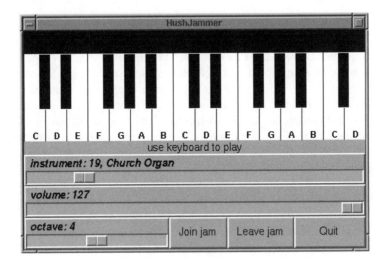

Slide 7-8: Keyboard interface

For a limited category of users, those with some musical skills, a direct interface such as a keyboard or a score editor, as provided by the *hush* framework, might provide a suitable interface for querying the musical database. Yet, for many others, a textual description, or a form-based query will be more appropriate.

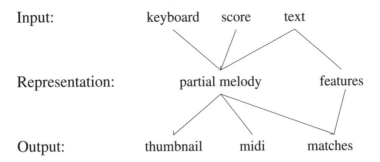

Slide 7-9: User Query Processing

In processing a query, we may in some cases derive a partial melody or rhythmic structure from the query, as well as some additional features or criteria. As explained, the output of indexing MIDI files consists of both information concerning features as well as a musical rendering of some of these features. These features can be used to match against the criteria formulated in the query. The musical renderings, which include a partial score, may be presented to the user in response to a query, to establish whether the result is acceptable.

7.3   Crossing boundaries

It is futile to hope for a single language or paradigm to solve all problems. Therefore, as our small case study concerning multimedia feature extraction indicates, components may differ in how they are realized. Some components are better implemented using knowledge-based systems technology, whereas other components require the use of a systems programming language such as C++. Even within components it may be necessary to transgress the language boundary. For example in Java applications, wrapping legacy applications or operating system-dependent code is usually done using the native language interface.

In this section we will look at some studies (executed within the *hush* framework) that exemplify a multi-paradigm and multi-lingual approach. We will first look at the issues that arise when embedding a logic (that is Prolog) interpreter. Then we will extend the embedded logic with objects that may correspond to (native) objects in the host language, that is C++. These sections may safely be skipped by readers not interested in logic programming. Finally, we will look at how to realize corresponding collections of objects in (native) C++ and Java.

7.3.1   Embedded logic – crossing the paradigm boundary

Knowledge is a substantial ingredient in many applications. By knowledge we mean information and rules operating on that information, to obtain derived information. As in any (software) engineering effort, maintenance, that is knowledge maintenance, is of crucial importance. When we do not avoid the dispersion of knowledge and information in the actual code of the system, maintenance will be difficult. Put differently, for reasons of flexibility and maintenance we need to factor out the (volatile) knowledge and information components.

Traditionally, the information components are often taken care of by a database that allows for the formulation of views to obtain (possibly aggregate) information. Logic or logic programming is a strictly more powerful mechanism to deal with information and knowledge. In our group, we have been studying the use of logic programming in knowledge-intensive software engineering applications.

> *embedded logic*

```
<query kit=pl src=local.pl cmd=X:email_address(X)>
<param format="
sigma ">
<param result="">
<param display="<h4>The query</h4>">
<param header="<h4>The adresses</h4> <ul>">
<param footer="</ul>">
```

```
email_address(E) :-
        person(X),
        property(X,name:N),
        property(X,familyname:F),
        email(X,E),
        cout(['<li>', N,' ',F,' has email adress ']),
        cout([ '<a href=mailto:', E, '>', E, '</a>',nl]).
</query>
```

As an example, consider the query above, which is expressed in an SGML/XML like syntax. The query command X:email_address(X) asks for all X for which the predicate email_address(X) holds. The predicate email_address is defined between the query begin and end tags.

The *query* tag is an element of one of the text processing filters to provide hypermedia support for software engineering described in Eliëns (1998). Processing the fragment above results in an HTML list of names and email addresses. The collection of filters itself is written in *lex*, *yacc* and C++. To process the query, an embedded logic programming interpreter is invoked. To merge the output from the query, a handler is installed for the *cout* command.

The query example was motivated by the need to maintain Web pages for the administration of a colloquium within our group. The actual knowledge base consists of a list of people and some rules to determine their affiliations and email addresses. The knowledge base is made available by consulting the file local.pl.

As concerns the implementation, the Java fragment below indicates how to access the logic programming interpreter from a (Java) program.

```
query pl = new query("kit=pl src=remote.pl");          logic.java
pl.eval("X:assistant(X)");
String res = null;
while ( (res = pl.result()) != null ) {
        System.out.println("<li> " + res);
        }
```

After creating a *query* object, the goal X:assistant(X) is invoked, which can be taken to mean, give me every X for which the predicate assistant(X) holds. The final output is obtained by iterating over the results of the evaluation of that goal. As a comment, multiple results may be obtained in Prolog by backtracking over the possible choice points.

Distributed knowledge servers

Maintaining knowledge is difficult. As a rule of thumb, avoid the replication of knowledge as much as possible. However, this means that we may need to access knowledge from remote sources. One (obvious) solution that presents itself is to allow for url-enabled consults, as illustrated in the fragment below.

```
                                                                    remote.pl
:- source('http://www.cs.vu.nl/~eliens/db/se/people.pl').
:- source('http://www.cs.vu.nl/~eliens/db/se/institute.pl').
:- source('http://www.cs.vu.nl/~eliens/db/se/property.pl').
:- source('http://www.cs.vu.nl/~eliens/db/se/query.pl').
```

This solution has (indeed) be implemented in our filters, since the url addressing scheme is straightforward and easy to implement.

However, processing the information accessed by url is still done locally. So, the next step that may be suggested is to distribute the knowledge processing itself, for example by using CORBA.

```
interface query {                                                   query.idl

        void source(in string file);
        long eval(in string cmd);
        string result(in long id);

        oneway void halt();
        };
```

Exploiting the integration of CORBA and *hush*, we have defined an interface for *query* in IDL and implemented query client and query server objects. These objects may be created by giving appropriate parameters to the *query* constructor invocation. This approach allows for embedding remote knowledge processing transparently in our collection of filters. Nevertheless, although we showed that this approach is feasible, we have not addressed the problems that may occur due to the unavailability or faults of the server.

7.3.2   Native objects – crossing the language boundary

Embedding (script) language interpreters is becoming standard practice, as testified by the existence of embeddable interpreters for Tcl, Perl, Python, Javascript, Java, and Prolog. Each of these languages also supports calling native code, that is code written in C or C++, to allow for accessing system resources or simply for reasons of efficiency.

Native bindings for these languages are available only on the level of functions. Even for Java, native methods of an object are defined as functions that receive a handle to the invoking object. Given a language with objects, possibly by adopting an object extension for the languages without objects, the problem is to find a proper correspondence between objects defined in the high-level (script) language and the native objects defined in C/C++.

In this (sub)section we will first study an extension of Prolog with objects, and then indicate a solution to establish a close correspondence between the (Prolog) objects and their native counterparts. In the next (sub)section, we will apply this approach to establish a correspondence between Java and C++ objects.

Objects in Prolog   *7-10*

- representation – *object(Handler, Class, ID, REF, Ancestors)*
- object definition – *class_method(This,...)*
- object invocation – *self(This):method(...)*
- state variables representation – *value(ID, Key, Value)*
- state variable access – *var(Key) = Value, Var = value(key)*
- native binding - *native(Handler, Method, Result)*

Slide 7-10: Objects in Prolog

In slide 7-10 our proposed object extension for Prolog (in particular SWI-Prolog, Wielemaker (1999)) is presented. Actually, there are many object extensions of Prolog around, for example the well-known Sicstus Objects. Our extension is motivated by the following considerations:

requirements

- low overhead, especially when not needed

- natural syntax for object clause definitions

- support for native objects

In our solution, objects are represented by dynamic fact clauses, containing a *Handler*, indicating how native calls are to be dealt with, a *Class*, and object identity *ID*, possibly a reference *REF* to a native C/C++ object, and a list of *Ancestors*.

Objects (or classes of objects, if you prefer) are defined by a collection of clauses with a head predicate of the form *class_method(This,...)*, specifying the *class*, *method* and object identity parameter. The actual invocation of the method takes the form *self(This):method(...)*, where the colon acts as the familiar dot object access parameter. Note that the identity parameter (*This*) does not occur among the method parameters, but is instead contained in the object specifier. Instead of the keyword *self*, we may also use a class name to enforce a cast to specific object type when invoking the method. In the actual object extension, we also support object state instance variables, which are however not relevant for our discussion here.

Object methods may be defined as native by including a goal of the form *native(Handler, Method, Result)*, where *Handler* specifies the (native) handler to be invoked, *Method* the actual request, and *Result* a variable to store the possible outcome of the request. When the *Handler* parameter is left unspecified, the handler defined for the object will be taken to effect the native call.

Let's look at some examples first, to augment this admittedly concise description.

```
midi(This):midi,                                  create midi object
Self = self(This),
Self:open('a.mid'),
Self:header(0,1,480),
Self:track(start),
Self:melody([48,50,51,53,55]),  // c d es f g, minor indeed
Self:track(end),                                         end track
```

In the fragment above we see how a *midi* object is created and how a simple melody is written to a file. Note that we use a variable *Self* for indicating the object specifier *self(This)*. Below, the actual definition of the *midi* object (class) is given.

> *midi*

```
:- use(library(midi:[midi,lily,music,process])).
:- declare(midi:object,class(midi),[handler]).

midi_midi(This) :-                                       constructor
        midi(This):handler(H),    // gets Handler from class
        declare(H,new(midi(This)),[],[],_).
```

The constructor for the *midi* object, for which the method name is equal to the class name, asks whether there is a *Handler* for *midi* objects. This handler, which is specified in the *declare* command above, is then passed to the *declare* command for the object. Since there is a handler, the constructor for the native *midi* object (defined in C++) is automatically invoked.

```
                                                      native methods
midi_read(This,F)  :- native(_,This,read(F),_).
midi_analyse(This,I,O) :- native(_,This,analyse(I,O),_).
midi_open(This,F) :- native(_,This,open(F),_).
midi_header(This,M) :- native(_,This,header(M,0,480),_).
midi_track(This,X) :- native(_,This,track(X),_).
midi_tempo(This,X) :- native(_,This,tempo(X),_).
midi_event(This,D,C,M,T,V) :- native(_,This,event(D,C,M,T,V),_).
```

All the methods listed above are implemented using the native *midi* C++ object. Note that both the *Handler* and the *Result* parameter are left unspecified. The handler is by default taken from the class declaration for the *midi* object class. There is no result when invoking these native methods.

```
midi_note(This,D,C,T,V)  :-
        Self = midi(This),                            cast to midi
        Self:event(D,C,note_on,T,V),
        Self:event(D,C,note_off,T,V).
```

```
midi_melody(This,L) :- self(This):melody(480,1,L,64).

midi_melody(_This,_,_,[],_).

midi_melody(This,D,C,[X|R],V) :-
        Self = self(This),
        Self:note(D,C,X,V),
        midi_melody(This,D,C,R,V).                        direct invocation
```

The *midi* object clauses given above augment the native methods by defining additional predicates, such as *note* and *melody*. These clauses also illustrate the liberty we have in casting the object specifier to a specific class or bypassing dynamic method invocation. Clearly, a native binding for the *midi* object is necessary, since Prolog is highly inappropriate for reading or writing midi files directly. It is however very appropriate for specifying rules for analyzing MIDI files!

C++ bindings

To redirect native method calls for our (Prolog) objects to their native C++ counterparts we need some additional machinery. First of all, we have to translate a (Prolog) method call to a format that can be passed to a C++ handler, so that the C++ handler may decide which method to invoke for what object. To get a direct correspondence between objects in Prolog and objects in C++, we store a reference to the C++ object in the *REF* variable of the Prolog object. When a native method is called, this reference is converted into an object handler or pointer in C++, to which the (native) method invocation will be addressed. We use a smart pointer to encapsulate this reference and to allow for directly invoking (native) methods for the corresponding object type.

As outlined in section 2.4.1, in the *hush* framework we use an event-based mechanism to effect foreign language bindings. This means that the information concerning the native call is stored in an event object that is passed to a handler, which invokes the *operator* function on the occurrence of an event. In the code fragment below it is shown how native method dispatching is taken care of in the *operator* function of a C++ *kit_object*, for which a corresponding object in Prolog is assumed to exist.

```
int kit_object::operator()() {
        event* e = _event;

        vm<kit> self(e);                          smart pointer
        string method = e->_method();

        if (method == "kit") {                    constructor
                kit* q = new kit(e->arg(1));
                _register(q);
                result( reference((void*)q) );
```

```
        } else if (method == "eval") {
                long res = self->eval(e->arg(1));
                result( itoa(res) );
        } else if (method == "result") {
                char* res = self->result( atoi(e->arg(1)) );
                result(res);
        } else {                              // dispatch up in the hierarchy
                return handler_object::operator()();
        }

        return 0;
        }
```

Before checking which method is invoked, which is recorded in the event, we
create a smart pointer (*self*) by instantiating a *vm* instance for the *kit* class. (The
acronym *vm* is somewhat inappropriately derived from *virtual machine*.) If the
method is a constructor, the result is a reference, that is an integer encoding of
the actual pointer. Otherwise, the method is invoked, simply by addressing the
smart pointer *self*. As a comment, the use of smart pointers is a C++ specific technique based on redefining the dereference operator, as illustrated below. When
no matching method can be found, the operator method for a handler object
higher up in the hierarchy is invoked. In our example, both the *kit_object* and
the *midi_object* are directly derived from *handler_object*. This hierarchy, which
is intended to encapsulate the native objects, parallels the original *hush* class
hierarchy in a straightforward way.

The smart pointer *vm* class, that we need for our binding of Prolog objects to
native C++ objects, is relatively straightforward.

```
        template <class T>
        class vm  {                                   ┌─────────────────────┐
        public:                                       │ smart pointer class │
                                                      └─────────────────────┘
    vm(event* e) {
            int p = 0;
            char* id = e->option("ref");
            if (id) {
                    p = atoi(id);
                    }
            _self = (T*) p;
            }


    virtual inline T* operator->() { return _self; }

    private:
    T* _self;
    };
```

In summary, the constructor converts the event argument to a reference to the parameterized object type *T*, which is used as the result of the dereference operator. This allows for invoking methods for object type *T* without further ado. As a comment, our presentation here is somewhat simplified, since we do not take into account the possibility of upcalls, that is the invocation of Prolog code from C++. We will deal with these additional details when discussing the Java/C++ binding in the next (sub)section.

7.3.3   Combining Java and C++

The designers of the Java language have created an elegant facility for incorporating native C/C++ code in Java applications, the Java Native Interface (JNI). Elegant, since native methods can be mixed freely with ordinary methods. When qualifying methods as *native*, the implementer must provide a dynamically loadable library that contains functions, of which the names and signatures must comply with the JNI standard, defining the functionality of the methods. Nevertheless, the JNI does not provide for generic means to establish a direct correspondence between an object class hierarchy in C++ that (partially) implements a corresponding object class hierarchy in Java. In this section, we will study how such a correspondence is realized in the *hush* framework, using the Java Native Interface.

The solution to establishing corresponding object class hierarchies in Java and C++ that we have adopted relies on storing a reference to the native C++ object in the Java object and the conversion of this reference to a smart pointer encapsulating access to the native C++ object. Upcalls, which occur for example when Java handlers are invoked in response to an event, require some additional machinery, as will be explained shortly.

Each Java class in *hush* is derived from the *obscure* class, which contains an instance variable *_self* that may store a C++ object reference, encoded as an integer.

```
package hush.dv.api;

class obscure {
public int _self;
...
};
```

obscure
peer object pointer

The class *obscure* has been introduced so as not to pollute the *handler* class, which is the base class for almost every *hush* class. The (Java) *handler* class is derived from *obscure*.

As an example, look at the (partial) Java class description for *kit* below.

```
package hush.dv.api;

public class kit extends handler {
```

kit

```
public kit() { _self = init(); }
protected kit(int x) { }
private native int init();

public native void source(String cmd);

public native void eval(String cmd);

public String result() {
        String _result = getresult();
        if (_result.equals("-")) return null;
        else return _result;
        }

private native String getresult();

public native void bind(String cmd, handler h);

...
};
```

Recall that the *kit* class is used to encapsulate an embedded interpreter, such as a Tcl or Prolog interpreter. When a *kit* is constructed, the instance variable *_self* is initialized with the reference obtained from the native *init* method, which will be given below. The other methods of *kit* are either native or result in invoking a native method, possibly with some additional processing.

Each native method must be implemented as a function, of which the name and signature are fixed by the JNI conventions, as illustrated below.

kit.c

```
#include <hush/hush.h>
#include <hush/java.h>
#include <native/hush_dv_api_kit.h>

#define method(X) Java_hush_dv_api_kit_# #X

JNIEXPORT jint JNICALL method(init)(JNIEnv *env, jobject obj)
{
  jint result = (jint) kit::_default; // (jint) new kit();
  if (!result) {
        kit* x = new kit("tk");
        session::_default->_register(x);
        result = (jint) x;
        }
  return result;
}
```

The *init* method, the full name of which is obtained by expanding the macro call *method(init)*, results in an integer-encoded reference to a *kit* object, which is newly created if it doesn't already exist.

```
JNIEXPORT jstring JNICALL method(getresult)(JNIEnv *env, jobject obj)
{
   java_vm<kit> vm(env,obj);
   char *s = vm->result();
   if (s) return vm.string(s);
   else return vm.string("-");
}
```

In the *getresult* method, we see how a smart pointer, instantiated for the *kit* class, is used to obtain the result from the C++ kit object. The smart pointer takes care of converting the reference stored in the Java object to an appropriate pointer.

```
JNIEXPORT void JNICALL method(bind)(JNIEnv *env, jobject obj,
               jstring s, jobject o)
{
   java_vm<kit> vm(env,obj);
   java_vm<handler>* vmp = new java_vm<handler>(env,o,"Handler");
   const char *str = vm.get(s);
   handler* h = new handler();
   session::_default->_register(h);
   h->_vmp = vmp;
   h->_register(vmp);
   vm->bind(str,h);
   vm.release(s, str);
}
```

In the *bind* method, which is used to bind a (Java) handler object to some (Tcl or Prolog) command, a new C++ handler is created. This handler is modified to contain a reference to the smart pointer, which (indeed) also gives access to the Java handler object. Notice that calling the Java handler object is an upcall, when viewed from the native implementation.

In somewhat more detail, the Java handler object is invoked through the C++ handler object created in the *bind* method of the *kit*. The C++ handler is activated when an event occurs, or a Tcl or Prolog command is given. Activating the handler amounts to calling the *dispatch* method with an appropriate event. To decide whether the activation must be passed through to the Java handler object, the *handler::dispatch* method checks for the availability of a smart pointer, as illustrated below.

handler::dispatch

```
event* handler::dispatch(event* e) {
   _event = e;
```

```
      if (_vmp) {
              return ((vm<handler>*)_vmp)->dispatch(e);
      } else {

              int result = this->operator()();

              if (result != OK) return 0;
              else return _event;
              }

      }
```

When the C++ handler contains a smart pointer, the *dispatch* method is called for that pointer.

The Java smart pointer template class for the Java/C++ binding is derived from the smart pointer template class introduced in the previous (sub)section.

```
      #include <hush/vm.h>
      #include <jni.h>

      template< class T >
      class java_vm : public vm< T > {                          java_vm
      public:

      java_vm(JNIEnv* env_, jobject obj_) {
              _env = env_;
              _obj = obj_;
              _self = self();
              }

      ...

      event* dispatch(event* e) {                          java dispatch
              call("dispatch",(int)e);
              return e;
              }

      T* operator->() { return _self; }

      T* self() {
              jfieldID fid = fieldID("_self","I");
              return (T*) _env->GetIntField( _obj, fid);
              }


      void call(const char* md, int i) { // void (*)(int)
              jmethodID mid = methodID(md,"(I)V");
              _env->CallVoidMethod(_obj, mid, i);
              }
```

```
private:
JNIEnv* _env;
jobject _obj;
T* _self;
};
```

Notice how the value of the _self_ reference field is obtained from the _self_ attribute of the Java object. Also notice that calling _dispatch_ for the Java handler is mediated by an additional _call_ function, which obtains an explicit reference to the method that must be invoked. In general, there are many possible method signatures for which such a call function could be supplied, but in our case we only need one, to invoke _dispatch_.

Discussion Interfacing Java and C++ is at first sight not very difficult, especially not when the majority of calls consists of downcalls (from Java to C++) only. The smart pointer device may then be used as a handy abbreviation. The problems occur, however, when upcalls come into play. Due to the simple design of _hush_, upcalls occur (almost) exclusively through the _dispatch_ method. This is not the result of explicit design, but in retrospect just sheer luck. When upcalls are spread over the code and may vary in signature, they will most likely bring along significant software engineering and maintenance effort.

7.4 Architectural patterns and styles

When constructing a system, how does one determine an appropriate style? There is no simple answer to this question. According to Bass _et al._ (1998), several forces play a role, for example quality requirements concerning availability and performance and technological constraints that have to do with the platform on which the system is intended to run. Also, as frankly admitted in Bass _et al._ (1998), personal experiences and preferences of the architect play a role.

Architectural choices lead to a particular decomposition into components and a characterization of the relation between components. Classifying groups of software architectures, we may speak of _architectural styles_, which may be defined, following Shaw and Gorlan (1996), as _descriptions of component types and patterns of runtime control and data transfer_.

In this section we will look at architectural styles for distributed object systems. Three styles will be introduced, and we will discuss how these styles are related to technological constraints imposed by particular component technologies. Then we will investigate how these styles work out in practice, by a simple case study in which we explore the consequences of a particular style for the solution of a specific problem, in our case the problem of dynamically changing a viewpoint or perspective in an interactive visualization system.

7.4.1   From technology to style

We distinguish between three different architectural styles:

- the distributed objects style

- the (dynamically) downloadable code style

- the mobile objects style

This distinction is arbitrary, in the sense that other distinctions are conceivable. However, the distinction above is well motivated by the technology matrix introduced in section 6.1.2, as reflected in the feature-based description given below.

	distributed objects	downloadable code	mobile objects
Component	object	object/class	agent
Connector	ORB	various	methods
Creation	server	client	any
Location	server	client	any
Client	fixed	extensible	extensible
Server	extensible	fixed	extensible

Slide 7-11: Feature classification

The *distributed objects* style comprises software architectures which consist of software components providing services to client applications. Each object is located at a single, fixed place. Objects on different machines are connected by an ORB (Object Request Broker). Example technologies supporting this architectural style are CORBA and DCOM.

The second architectural style is the *(dynamically) downloadable code* style. Classes may be downloaded, to be used on client machines for instantiating objects, which will run on the client machine. Example technologies supporting this style are Java applets, JavaBeans, and ActiveX controls.

Finally, in the *mobile objects* style, objects may migrate from host to host, carrying both functionality and data when they move. Consequently, mobile objects may communicate with the local objects of the host they currently reside on. Mobile objects are a means to implement agents which wander through a network, collecting information, negotiating with other agents, periodically reporting back results to the user who launched the agents. Technologies supporting the mobile object style are agent ORBs such as Voyager.

Features In slide 7-11, an overview is given of the characteristic features of each style. Clearly, the styles differ in what are considered as constituent parts (components and connectors), location issues (which determine where objects are created and where they are located during their lifetime), and functionality issues (that is whether either the client or server is functionally extensible).

We may regard the location issues as the prime discriminators of the architectural styles discussed. Adopting the distributed objects architectural style, new objects can be added at the server-side, where they will stay for the remainder of their lifetime. In contrast, adopting the downloadable code style, objects may be created at the client-side, from classes obtained from the server. Most flexible is the mobile objects style, which allows for objects to reside on either server or client machines.

The location properties directly affect the way that the system is extensible with new functionality. Clearly, the mobile code style offers the maximum of flexibility and functional extensibility. Nevertheless, as we will discuss shortly, there are tradeoffs involved. The maximum in flexibility and extensibility does not necessarily offer the optimal solution!

7.4.2   Case study – perspectives in visualization

To determine which architectural style to use, or which mix of styles, is to a large extent determined by practical experience. Nevertheless, at the end of this section, we will discuss some rules of thumb that may guide you in the choice of a particular style. However, first we will look at an example that illustrates the consequences of the choice of a particular style. The example comes from the distributed visualization architecture (DIVA) that is explained in more detail in section 11.4.2. DIVA is being developed in cooperation with ASZ/GAK, the largest social security provider in the Netherlands, for experimenting with business visualization to support decision making. Our case study focuses on how to support the sharing of perspectives in visualizing shared information. For example, one of the users discovers a new way to display information, uncovering aspects that would otherwise remain hidden. This new perspective must then be shared with other users to coerce them, so to speak, to this new point of view. What we will look at, here, is how the choice of a particular style affects the solution for the *sharing of perspectives* problem.

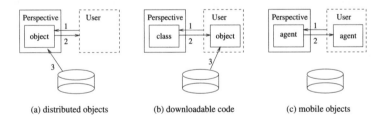

(a) distributed objects   (b) downloadable code   (c) mobile objects

Slide 7-12: Exchanging perspectives

Distributed objects style New functionality can be added by creating a new object at the server. In this case, slide 7-12(a), the user discovering a new perspective acts as the server. Then, assuming that the discovery of a new perspective is somehow announced to the other users, a user can connect to the server and request for that particular perspective (1). Then, a new visualization object is created (2), which is made accessible to the user requesting for the new perspective (3).

Downloadable code style When a new visualization perspective is discovered, a class is created that can be downloaded by the interested user, slide 7-12(b). The user connects to the server that contains the new visualization class (1), downloads the class, and instantiates a new visualization object (2). Finally, the information is retrieved from the shared information server and accordingly visualized (3).

Mobile objects style Similar as in the downloadable code style, the new visualization perspective is downloaded from a server to the client, slide 7-12(c). However, in this case, when a user requests for a new perspective (1), it is not a class, but an object, actually a clone of the object residing at the server, that is transferred to the client's machine (2). The clone, which contains all relevant information, does not have to contact the shared information server to update the user's visualization with a fresh viewpoint.

Guidelines for selecting a style

In the DIVA system, we have experimented with all these styles. In our system, we eventually made a choice of the mobile object style for sharing perspectives, since it turned out to provide the most flexible solution. It was also the most natural solution to create *display agents* for managing perspectives. See section 11.4.2.

Nevertheless, for other parts of the system we were forced to choose a different solution. For example, since we use a C++ simulation library for obtaining the information, we had to use distributed objects (read CORBA) for making the information available. And for developing control applets, agent technology seemed to be a bit of an overkill so we restricted ourselves to plain Java technology, that is the downloadable code style.

Generalizing, from our experience we can formulate the following rules of thumb, listed in slide 7-13.

Rules of thumb – *selecting an architectural style*		*7-13*
• Dedicated hardware or legacy code	distributed objects	
• Strategic or secret code	distributed objects	
• Many users	downloadable code	
• Periodic updates	downloadable code	
• Communication and negotiation	mobile objects	

Slide 7-13: Rules of thumb

Because interoperability is a key feature of distributed objects, the distributed objects style is particularly recommended for wrapping dedicated hardware or legacy software systems. Additionally, distributed objects only expose the interface and do not give away the implementation. This may be necessary for strategic or security reasons.

When a large amount of clients is running an application on a server, the server can easily become overloaded. In this case, moving the processing to the client, by deploying dynamically downloadable classes, is a natural solution. Additionally, when (parts of) an application are updated often, for example because of changing legislation, architectures based on downloadable code are much easier to keep up-to-date. Clients are then automatically using the latest version of the available software.

The latter guidelines hold for the mobile objects style as well. However, agent technology is much more complex. And there is, generally, an efficiency price to pay. So, it is reasonable to introduce agent technology only when real benefits can be expected from the migration of objects, for example when the communication and negotiation with local objects is substantial.

Concluding, we may state that the adoption of a style will often be dictated by the technological constraints a system must satisfy. Nevertheless, a word of warning is in place here. Choosing a style may well have consequences for the overall complexity of the system. Minimalism is to be strived for, in this respect. For example, adopting the mobile object style, that is the use of agents, may significantly complicate the semantics of the system, and consequently induce an increased verification and validation effort.

7.5 Cross-platform development

Platform dependencies form an important category of architectural constraints. In particular, the opportunities offered by one platform may prohibit the deployment of software on other platforms. Nowadays, there are a number of (flavors of) competing platforms, as there are the Unix flavors (of which Linux is becoming a strong contender) and the Windows family, including 3.1 (almost extinct), Windows 95, NT, 98 and (in beta release) Windows 2000. Unix (for example Sun Solaris and SGI IRIX) has by tradition a strong position in the server market. However, Windows NT is growing rapidly in importance. The Windows family, clearly, dominates the (client) desktop market.

Nevertheless, the need to support a variety of platforms will exist at least for some time, and consequently questions with regard to portability and cross-platform development may be important architectural issues.

Considering the opportunities for platform-independent or cross-platform development, we may distinguish between three approaches:

- deploying platform-independent toolkits

- porting applications from Unix to Windows

- porting applications from Windows to Unix

Cross-platform development   Unix vs NT   *7-14*
  - open toolkits and standards – OMG CORBA

Research/GNU
  - AT&T U/WIN – Posix for 95/NT
  - Cygnus – GNU-win32

Commercial
  - NuTCracker/MKS – porting Unix applications to Windows
  - Wind/U, Mainwin – porting Windows applications to Unix
  - Tributary – developing Unix applications from Windows IDE

Slide 7-14: Cross-platform development

As we have discussed previously, many of the open standards, such as OMG CORBA, and proprietary standards such as Sun Java, aim at platform independence. Also, there are numerous GUI toolkits available that offer platform-independent support. A possible disadvantage of this approach is that the platform specific technology can usually not be profited from.

When it comes to porting applications from Unix to Windows 95/98/NT, we may look at AT&T U/WIN, which provides a POSIX extension for Win32, or Cygnus GNU-win32 support, which offers many of the GNU utilities and libraries for the Windows platform. Similar functionality, as well as support for Motif/X11 GUI capabilities, is offered by the (commercial) NuTCracker environment. (A detailed discussion of the technical merits of the various offerings is beyond the scope of this book. However, the interested reader may find more information in the online version of this book.)

The Windows platform is not only popular with end-users but also with many developers, who enjoy using the Microsoft Visual Studio suite of tools and (object-oriented) frameworks such as MFC. Recently, toolkits have entered the market that allow for porting Microsoft technologies (including Visual Basic, ActiveX and MFC applications) to the Unix platform, in particular *Wind/U* from `bristol.com` and *Mainwin* from `mainsoft.com`. As a word of warning, these toolkits are still terribly expensive. Yet for more information, consult the online version of this book.

For those who wish to develop directly on the Unix platform, but using Microsoft Visual Studio, there is *Tributary*, from `bristol.com`, which offers a Unix-server and client-extensions to Visual Studio.

Discussion From an architectural perspective, it should not matter what platform is used for the actual development, nor for what target platform the software is being developed. In practice, however, given the preferences of the developers, the particularities of the platforms, and the instability of the (beta) software running on these platforms, the actual choice may make a big difference. As an admittedly weak advice, tune your strategy to your needs and experience! (And your budget.)

Summary

This chapter explored the notion of software architecture, and in particular how both problem-related issues and technological constraints determine the adoption of a particular architectural style.

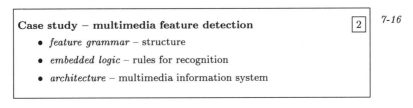

Slide 7-15: Section 7.1: Elements of architecture

In section 1, we looked at a number of definitions of the notion of *software architecture*, including the definition given in Bass *et al.* (1998). We also looked at the technological infrastructure underlying client/server architectures and discussed some selected distributed object patterns.

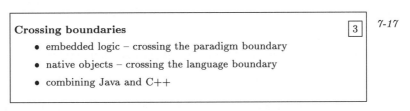

Slide 7-16: Section 7.2: Case study – multimedia feature detection

In section 2, we looked at an experimental musical feature detector, as an example architecture, that uses both a grammar to describe the structural properties of the media items involved, and (embedded) logic to express the rules governing the determination of properties and the retrieval of specified media items.

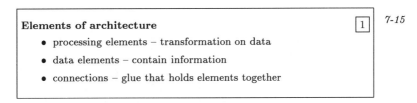

Slide 7-17: Section 7.3: Crossing boundaries

In section 3, we discussed some of the implications of the architecture sketched in section 2. We looked at *embedded logic*, as an example of crossing paradigm boundaries, and *native objects*, as an example of crossing language boundaries. In addition, some of the technical details involved in coupling (native) C++ objects to Java objects were presented.

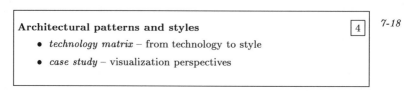

Architectural patterns and styles   4   *7-18*
  • *technology matrix* – from technology to style
  • *case study* – visualization perspectives

Slide 7-18: Section 7.4: Architectural patterns and styles

In section 4, we discussed how to decide which architectural style to adopt, based on technological constraints on the one hand and application requirements on the other hand. As an illustration, we discuss the alternatives that may arise when realizing an extension to a distributed visualization architecture.

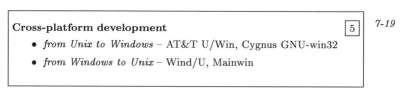

Cross-platform development   5   *7-19*
  • *from Unix to Windows* – AT&T U/Win, Cygnus GNU-win32
  • *from Windows to Unix* – Wind/U, Mainwin

Slide 7-19: Section 7.5: Cross-platform development

Finally, in section 5 we discussed some of the solutions that are available for platform-independent and cross-platform development.

Questions

1. What are the elements of a software architecture? What role does a software architecture description play in development?

2. Give a definition of software architecture. Can you think of alternative definitions?

3. What kind of patterns can you think of for distributed object architectures?

4. Give an example of a complex software architecture. Can you relate the description of the architecture to the definition given earlier?

5. Discuss the possible motivations for deploying embedded logic.

6. How would you extend a given imperative or declarative language with objects?

7. Discuss the Java Native Interface. Does it provide a solution for the problem posed in the previous question? Explain.

8. What determines the choice for an architectural style? Give an example!

Further reading

An excellent book on software architectures is Bass *et al.* (1998). You may also want to visit the SEI architecture site at www.sei.cmu.edu/architecture, which provides definitions, and a wealth of other information. As a discussion of the software engineering implications of CORBA, you may want to read Mowbray and Malveau (1997). If you are interested in multimedia information systems, read Subrahmanian (1998). For more information on ACOI, visit the ACOI website on http://www.cwi.nl/~acoi.

Part III

Foundations of Object-Oriented Modeling

8

Abstract data types

The history of programming languages may be characterized as the genesis of increasingly powerful abstractions to aid the development of reliable programs.

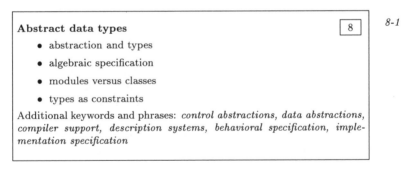

Slide 8-1: Abstract data types

In this chapter we will look at the notion of *abstract data types*, which may be regarded as an essential constituent of object-oriented modeling. In particular, we will study the notion of data abstraction from a foundational perspective, that is based on a mathematical description of types. We start this chapter by discussing the notion of *types as constraints*. Then, we look at the (first order) algebraic specification of abstract data types, and we explore the trade-offs between the traditional implementation of abstract data types by employing modules and the object-oriented approach employing classes. We conclude this chapter by exploring the distinction between classes and types, as a preparation for the treatment of (higher order) polymorphic type theories for object types and inheritance in the next chapter.

8.1   Abstraction and types

The concern for abstraction may be regarded as the driving force behind the development of programming languages (of which there are astoundingly many). In the following we will discuss the role of abstraction in programming, and especially the importance of types. We then briefly look at what mathematical means we have available to describe types from a foundational perspective and what we may (and may not) expect from types in object-oriented programming.

8.1.1   Abstraction in programming languages

In Shaw (1984), an overview is given of how increasingly powerful abstraction mechanisms have shaped the programming languages we use today. See slide 8-2.

Abstraction – *programming methodology*   8-2

  • control abstractions – *structured programming*

  • data abstraction – *information hiding*

The kind of abstraction provided by ADTs can be supported by any language with a procedure call mechanism (given that appropriate *protocols* are developed and observed by the programmer). Danforth and Tomlinson (1988)

Slide 8-2: Abstraction and programming languages

   Roughly, we may distinguish between two categories of abstractions: abstractions that aid in specifying *control* (including subroutines, procedures, *if-then-else* constructs, *while*-constructs, in short the constructs promoted by the school of *structured programming* in their battle against the *goto*); and abstractions that allow us to hide the actual representation of the data employed in a program (introduced to support the *information hiding* approach, originally advocated in Parnas (1972a)).

   Although there is clearly a pragmatic interest involved in developing and employing such abstractions, the concern with abstraction (and consequently types) is ultimately motivated by a concern with programming methodology and, as observed in Danforth and Tomlinson (1988), the need for reliable and maintainable software. However, the introduction of language features is also often motivated by programmers' desires for ease of coding and naturalness of expression.

   In the same vein, although types were originally considered as a convenient means to assist the compiler in producing efficient code, types have rapidly been recognized as a way in which to capture the meaning of a program in an implementation independent way. In particular, the notion of abstract data types (which has, so to speak, grown out of data abstraction) has become a powerful device (and guideline) to structure large software systems.

In practice, as the quotation from Danforth and Tomlinson (1988) in slide 8-2 indicates, we may employ the tools developed for structured programming to realize abstract data types in a program, but with the obvious disadvantage that we must rely on conventions with regard to the reliability of these realizations. Support for abstract data types (support in the sense as discussed in section 1.2) is offered (to some extent) by languages such as Modula-2 and Ada by means of a syntactic module or package construct, and (to a larger extent) by object-oriented languages in the form of object classes. However, both realizations are of a rather *ad hoc* and pragmatic nature, relying in the latter case on the metaphor of encapsulation and message passing. The challenge to computer science in this area is to develop a notion of types capturing the power of abstract data types in a form that is adequate both from a pragmatic point of view (in the sense of allowing efficient language support) and from a theoretical perspective (laying the foundation for a truly declarative object-oriented approach to programming).

8.1.2 A foundational perspective – types as constraints

Object-oriented programming may be regarded as a *declarative* method of programming, in the sense that it provides a computation model (expressed by the metaphor of encapsulation and message passing) that is independent of a particular implementation model. In particular, the inheritance subtype relation may be regarded as a pure description of the relations between the entities represented by the classes. Moreover, an object-oriented approach favors the development of an object model that bears close resemblance to the entities and their relations living in the application domain. However, the object-oriented programming model is rarely introduced with the mathematical precision characteristic of descriptions of the other declarative styles, for example the functional and logic programming model. Criticizing, Danforth and Tomlinson (1988) remark that *OOP is generally expressed in philosophical terms, resulting in a proliferation of opinions concerning what OOP really is.*

From a type-theoretical perspective, our interest is to identify abstract data types as elements of some *semantic* (read mathematical) domain and to characterize their properties in an unambiguous fashion. See slide 8-3.

There seems to be almost no limit to the variety and sophistication of the mathematical models proposed to characterize abstract data types and inheritance. We may make a distinction between first order approaches (based on ordinary set theory) and higher order approaches (involving typed lambda calculus and constructive logic).

The algebraic approach is a quite well-established method for the formal specification of abstract data types. A type (or sort) in an algebra corresponds to a set of elements upon which the operations of the algebra are defined. In

---

Abstract data types – *foundational perspective*   *8-3*

- unambiguous values in some *semantic* domain

Mathematical models – *types as constraints*

- algebra – *set oriented*
- second order lambda calculus – *polymorphic types*
- constructive mathematics – *formulas as types*

Slide 8-3: Mathematical models for types

the next section, we will look at how equations may be used to characterize the
behavioral aspects of an abstract data type modeled by an algebra.

Second order lambda calculus has been used to model information hiding and
the polymorphism supported by inheritance and templates. In the next chapter
we will study this approach in more detail.

In both approaches, the meaning of a type is (ultimately) a set of elements
satisfying certain restrictions. However, in a more abstract fashion, we may regard
a type as specifying a constraint. The better we specify the constraint, the
more tightly the corresponding set of elements will be defined (and hence the
smaller the set). A natural consequence of the idea of *types as constraints* is
to characterize types by means of logical formulas. This is the approach taken
by type theories based on constructive logic, in which the notion of *formulas as
types* plays an important role. Although we will not study type theories based
on constructive logic explicitly, our point of view is essentially to regard types
as constraints, ranging from purely syntactical constraints (as expressed in a
signature) to semantic constraints (as may be expressed in contracts).

From the perspective of types as constraints, a typing system may contribute
to a language framework guiding a system designer's conceptualization and supporting the verification (based on the formal properties of the types employed)
of the consistency of the descriptive information provided by the program. Such
an approach is to be preferred (both from a pragmatic and theoretical point of
view) to an *ad hoc* approach employing special annotations and support mechanisms, since these may become quite complicated and easily lead to unexpected
interactions.

Formal models There is a wide variety of formal models available in the literature. These include algebraic models (to characterize the meaning of abstract
data types), models based on the lambda-calculus and its extensions (which
are primarily used for a type theoretical analysis of object-oriented language
constructs), algebraic process calculi (which may be used to characterize the
behavior of concurrent objects), operational and denotational semantic models
(to capture structural and behavioral properties of programs), and various specification languages based on first or higher-order logics (which may be used to

specify the desired behavior of collections of objects).

We will limit ourselves to studying algebraic models capturing the properties of abstract data types and objects (section 8.2.4), type calculi based on typed extensions of the lambda calculus capturing the various flavors of polymorphism and subtyping (sections 9.3–9.6), and an operational semantic model characterizing the behavior of objects sending messages (section 10.3).

Both the algebraic and type theoretical models are primarily intended to clarify the means we have to express the desired behavior of objects and the restrictions that must be adhered to when defining objects and their relations. The operational characterization of object behavior, on the other hand, is intended to give a more precise characterization of the notion of state and state changes underlying the verification of object behavior by means of assertion logics.

Despite the numerous models introduced there are still numerous approaches not covered here. One approach worth mentioning is the work based on the *pi-calculus*. The *pi-calculus* is an extension of algebraic process calculi that allow for communication via named channels. Moreover, the *pi-calculus* allows for a notion of migration and the creation and renaming of channels. A semantics of object-based languages based on the *pi-calculus* is given in Walker (1990). However, this semantics does not cover inheritance or subtyping. A higher-order object-oriented programming language based on the *pi-calculus* is presented in Pierce at al. (1993).

Another approach of interest, also based on process calculi, is the object calculus (OC) described in Nierstrasz (1993). OC allows for modeling the operational semantics of concurrent objects. It merges the notions of agents, as used in process calculi, with the notion of functions, as present in the lambda calculus.

For alternative models the reader may look in the `comp.theory` newsgroup to which information concerning formal calculi for OOP is posted by Tom Mens of the Free University, Brussels.

8.1.3   Objectives of typed OOP

Before losing ourselves in the details of mathematical models of types, we must reflect on what we may expect from a type system and what not (at least not currently).

From a theoretical perspective our ideal is, in the words of Danforth and Tomlinson (1988), to arrive at a simple type theory that provides a consistent and flexible framework for *system descriptions* (in order to provide the programmer with sufficient descriptive power and to aid the construction of useful and understandable software, while allowing the efficient utilization of the underlying hardware).

The question now is, what support does a typing system provide in this respect. In slide 8-4, a list is given of aspects in which a typing system may be of help.

One important benefit of regarding ADTs as real types is that realizations of ADTs become so-called *first class citizens*, which means that they may be treated as any other value in the language, for instance being passed as a parameter. In

```
┌─────────────────────────────────────────────────────────────────┐
│  Objectives of typed OOP – system description          8-4        │
│     • packaging in a coherent manner                              │
│     • flexible style of associating operations with objects       │
│     • inheritance of description components – reuse, understanding │
│     • separation of specification and implementation              │
│     • explicit typing to guide binding decisions                  │
└─────────────────────────────────────────────────────────────────┘
```

Slide 8-4: Object orientation and types

contrast, syntactic solutions (such as the module of Modula-2 and the package of Ada) do not allow this.

Pragmatically, the objective of a type system is (and has been) the prevention of errors. However, if the type system lacks expressivity, adequate control for errors may result in becoming over-restrictive.

In general, the more expressive the type system the better the support that the compiler may offer. In this respect, associating constructors with types may help in relieving the programmer from dealing with simple but necessary tasks such as the initialization of complex structures. Objects, in contrast to modules or packages, allow for the automatic (compiler supported) initializations of instances of (abstract) data types, providing the programmer with relief from an error-prone routine.

Another area in which a type system may make the life of a programmer easier concerns the association of operations with objects. A polymorphic type system is needed to understand the automatic dispatching for virtual functions and the opportunity of overloading functions, which are useful mechanisms to control the complexity of a program, provided they are well understood.

Reuse and understanding are promoted by allowing inheritance and refinement of description components. (As remarked earlier, inheritance and refinement may be regarded as the essential contribution of object-oriented programming to the practice of software development.) It goes without saying that such reuse needs a firm semantical basis in order to achieve the goal of reliable and maintainable software.

Another important issue for which a powerful type system can provide support is the separation of specification and implementation. Naturally, we expect our type system to support type-safe separate compilation. But in addition, we may think of allowing multiple implementations of a single (abstract type) specification. Explicit typing may then be of help in choosing the right binding when the program is actually executed. For instance in a parallel environment, behavior may be realized in a number of ways that differ in the degree to which they affect locality of access and how they affect, for example, load balancing. With an eye to the future, these are problems that may be solved with a good type system (and accompanying compiler).

One of the desiderata for a type system for OOP, laid down in Danforth and Tomlinson (1988), is the separation of a *behavioral hierarchy* (specifying the behavior of a type in an abstract sense) and an *implementation hierarchy* (specifying the actual realization of that behavior). Separation is needed to accommodate the need for multiple realizations and to resolve the tension between subtyping and inheritance (a tension we have already noted in sections 1.1.3 and 3.3).

Remark In these chapters we cannot hope to do more than get acquainted with the material needed to understand the problems involved in developing a type system for object-oriented programming. For an alternative approach, see Palsberg and Schwartzback (1994).

8.2 Algebraic specification

Algebraic specification techniques have been developed as a means to specify the design of complex software systems in a formal way. The algebraic approach has been motivated by the notion of *information hiding* put forward in Parnas (1972a) and the ideas concerning *abstraction* expressed in Hoare (1972). Historically, the ADJ-group (see Goguen *et al.*, 1978) provided a significant impetus to the algebraic approach by showing that abstract data types may be interpreted as (many sorted) algebras. (In the context of algebraic specifications the notion of *sorts* has the same meaning as *types*. We will, however, generally speak of *types*.)

As an example of an algebraic specification, look at the module defining the data type *Bool*, as given in slide 8-5.

Algebraic specification – *ADT* | Bool | *8-5*

```
adt bool is
functions
  true : bool
  false : bool
  and, or : bool * bool -> bool
  not : bool -> bool
axioms
  [B1]  and(true,x) = x
  [B2]  and(false,x) = false
  [B3]  not(true) = false
  [B4]  not(false) = true
  [B5]  or(x,y) = not(and(not(x),not(y)))
end
```

Slide 8-5: The ADT *Bool*

In this specification two constants are introduced (the zero-ary functions *true* and *false*), three functions (respectively *and, or* and *not*). The *or* function is defined by employing *not* and *and*, according to a well-known logical law. These functions may all be considered to be (strictly) related to the type *bool*. Equations are used to specify the desired characteristics of elements of type *bool*. Obviously, this specification may mathematically be interpreted as (simply) a boolean algebra.

Mathematical models The mathematical framework of algebras allows for a direct characterization of the behavioral aspects of abstract data types by means of equations, provided the specification is consistent. Operationally, this allows for the execution of such specifications by means of term rewriting, provided that some (technical) constraints are met. The model-theoretic semantics of algebraic specifications centers around the notion of *initial algebras*, which gives us the preferred model of a specification.

To characterize the behavior of *objects* (that may modify their state) in an algebraic way, we need to extend the basic framework of initial algebra models either by allowing so-called *multiple world* semantics or by making a distinction between hidden and observable sorts (resulting in the notion of an object as an *abstract machine*). As a remark, in our treatment we obviously cannot avoid the use of some logico-mathematical formalism. If needed, the concepts introduced will be explained on the fly. Where this does not suffice, the interested reader is referred to any standard textbook on mathematical logic for further details.

8.2.1   Signatures – generators and observers

Abstract data types may be considered as modules specifying the values and functions belonging to the type. In Dahl (1992), a type T is characterized as a tuple specifying the set of elements constituting the type T and the collection of functions related to the type T. Since constants may be regarded as zero-ary functions (having no arguments), we will speak of a *signature* Σ or Σ_T defining a particular type T. Also, in accord with common parlance, we will speak of the sorts $s \in \Sigma$, which are the sorts (or types) occurring in the declaration of the functions in Σ. See slide 8-6.

A *signature* specifies the names and (function) profiles of the constants and functions of a data type. In general, the profile of a function is specified as

- $f : s_1 \times \ldots \times s_n \to s$

where $s_i (i = 1..n)$ are the sorts defining the domain (that is the types of the arguments) of the function f, and s is the sort defining the codomain (or result type) of f. In the case $n = 0$ the function f may be regarded as a constant. More generally, when $s_1, \ldots, s_n$ are all unrelated to the type T being defined, we may regard f as a relative constant. Relative constants are values that are assumed to be defined in the context where the specification is being employed.

The functions related to a data type T may be discriminated according to their role in defining T. We distinguish between *producers* $g \in P_T$, that have

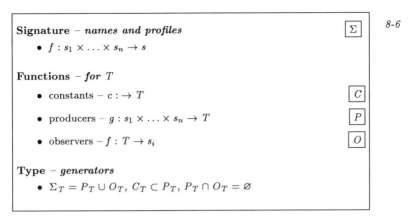

Slide 8-6: Algebraic specification

the type T under definition as their result type, and *observers* $f \in O_T$, that have T as their argument type and deliver a result of a type different from T. In other words, producer functions define how elements of T may be constructed. (In the literature one often speaks of *constructors*, but we avoid this term because it already has a precisely defined meaning in the object-oriented programming language C++.) In contrast, observer functions do not produce values of T, but give instead information on some particular aspect of T.

The signature Σ_T of a type T is uniquely defined by the union of producer functions P_T and observer functions O_T. Constants of type T are regarded as a subset of the producer functions P_T defining T. Further, we require that the collection of producers is disjoint from the collection of observers for T, that is $P_T \cap O_T = \varnothing$.

Generators The producer functions actually defining the values of a data type T are called the *generator basis* of T, or generators of T. The generators of T may be used to enumerate the elements of T, resulting in the collection of T values that is called the *generator universe* in Dahl (1992). See slide 8-7.

The generator universe of a type T consists of the closed (that is variable-free) terms that may be constructed using either constants or producer functions of T. As an example, consider the data type *Bool* with generators t and f. Obviously, the value domain of *Bool*, the generator universe GU_{Bool} consists only of the values t and f.

As another example, consider the data type *Nat* (representing the natural numbers) with generator basis $G_{Nat} = \{0, S\}$, consisting of the constant 0 and the successor function $S : Nat \to Nat$ (that delivers the successor of its argument). The terms that may be constructed by G_{Nat} is the set $GU_{Nat} = \{0, S0, SS0, \ldots\}$, which uniquely corresponds to the natural numbers $\{0, 1, 2, \ldots\}$. (More precisely, the natural numbers are isomorphic with GU_{Nat}.)

In contrast, given a type A with element a, b, ..., the generators of Set_A result

Generators – *values of* T $\boxed{T}$ *8-7*

- generator basis – $G_T = \{g \in P_T\}$
- generator universe – $GU_T = \{v_1, v_2, \ldots\}$

Examples

- $G_{Bool} = \{t, f\}, \quad GU_{Bool} = \{t, f\}$
- $G_{Nat} = \{0, S\}, \quad GU_{Nat} = \{0, S0, SS0, \ldots\}$
- $G_{Set_A} = \{\varnothing, add\}, \quad GU_{Set_A} = \{\varnothing, add(\varnothing, a), \ldots\}$

Slide 8-7: Generators – basis and universe

in a universe that contains terms such as $add(\varnothing, a)$ and $add(add(\varnothing, a), a)$ which we would like to identify, based on our conception of a set as containing only one exemplar of a particular value. To effect this we need additional equations imposing constraints expressing what we consider as the desired shape (or *normal form*) of the values contained in the universe of T. However, before we look at how to extend a signature Σ defining T with equations defining the (behavioral) properties of T we will look at another example illustrating how the choice of a generator basis may affect the structure of the value domain of a data type.

In the example presented in slide 8-8, the profiles are given of the functions that may occur in the signature specifying sequences. (The notation _ is used to indicate parameter positions.)

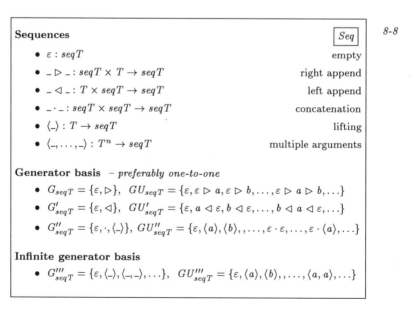

Sequences $\boxed{Seq}$ *8-8*

- $\varepsilon : seqT$ empty
- $\_ \triangleright \_ : seqT \times T \to seqT$ right append
- $\_ \triangleleft \_ : T \times seqT \to seqT$ left append
- $\_ \cdot \_ : seqT \times seqT \to seqT$ concatenation
- $\langle \_ \rangle : T \to seqT$ lifting
- $\langle \_, \ldots, \_ \rangle : T^n \to seqT$ multiple arguments

Generator basis – *preferably one-to-one*

- $G_{seqT} = \{\varepsilon, \triangleright\}, \; GU_{seqT} = \{\varepsilon, \varepsilon \triangleright a, \varepsilon \triangleright b, \ldots, \varepsilon \triangleright a \triangleright b, \ldots\}$
- $G'_{seqT} = \{\varepsilon, \triangleleft\}, \; GU'_{seqT} = \{\varepsilon, a \triangleleft \varepsilon, b \triangleleft \varepsilon, \ldots, b \triangleleft a \triangleleft \varepsilon, \ldots\}$
- $G''_{seqT} = \{\varepsilon, \cdot, \langle \_ \rangle\}, \; GU''_{seqT} = \{\varepsilon, \langle a \rangle, \langle b \rangle, \ldots, \varepsilon \cdot \varepsilon, \ldots, \varepsilon \cdot \langle a \rangle, \ldots\}$

Infinite generator basis

- $G'''_{seqT} = \{\varepsilon, \langle \_ \rangle, \langle \_, \_ \rangle, \ldots\}, \; GU'''_{seqT} = \{\varepsilon, \langle a \rangle, \langle b \rangle, \ldots, \langle a, a \rangle, \ldots\}$

Slide 8-8: The ADT *Seq*

Dependent on which producer functions are selected to generate the universe of T, the correspondence between the generated universe and the intended domain is either *one-to-one* (as for G and G') or *many-to-one* (as for G''). Since we require our specification to be first-order and finite, infinite generator bases (such as G''') must be disallowed, even if they result in a one-to-one correspondence. See Dahl (1992) for further details.

8.2.2   Equations – specifying constraints

The specification of the signature of a type (which lists the *syntactic constraints* to which a specification must comply) is in general not sufficient to characterize the properties of the values of the type. In addition, we need to impose *semantic constraints* (in the form of equations) to define the meaning of the observer functions and (very importantly) to identify the elements of the type domain that are considered equivalent (based on the intuitions one has of that particular type).

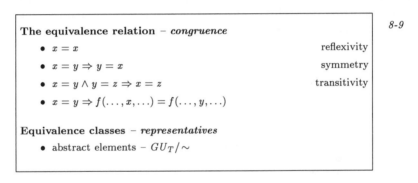

The equivalence relation – *congruence*

- $x = x$ reflexivity
- $x = y \Rightarrow y = x$ symmetry
- $x = y \wedge y = z \Rightarrow x = z$ transitivity
- $x = y \Rightarrow f(\ldots, x, \ldots) = f(\ldots, y, \ldots)$

Equivalence classes – *representatives*

- abstract elements – $GU_T / \sim$

8-9

Slide 8-9: Equivalence

Mathematically, the equality predicate may be characterized by the properties listed above, including *reflexivity* (stating that an element is equal to itself), *symmetry* (stating that the orientation of the formula is not important) and *transitivity* (stating that if one element is equal to another and that element is equal to yet another, then the first element is also equal to the latter). In addition, we have the property that, given that two elements are equal, the results of the function applied to them (separately) are also equal. (Technically, the latter property makes a *congruence* of the equality relation, lifting equality between elements to the function level.) See slide 8-9.

Given a suitable set of equations, in addition to a signature, we may identify the elements that can be proved identical by applying the equality relation. In other words, given an equational theory (of which the properties stated above must be a part), we can divide the generator universe of a type T into one or more subsets, each consisting of elements that are equal according to our theory. The subsets of $GU / \sim$, that is GU factored with respect to equivalence, may be regarded as the abstract elements constituting the type T, and from each subset we may choose a concrete element acting as a *representative* for the subset which is the equivalence class of the element.

Operationally, equations may be regarded as *rewrite rules* (oriented from left to right), that allow us to transform a term in which a term t_1 occurs as a subterm into a term in which t_1 is replaced by t_2 if $t_1 = t_2$. For this procedure to be terminating, some technical restrictions must be met, amounting (intuitively) to the requirement that the right-hand side must in some sense be simpler than the left-hand side.

Also, when defining an observer function, we must specify for each possible generator case an appropriate rewriting rule. That is, each observer must be able to give a result for each generator. The example of the natural numbers, given below, will make this clear. Identifying spurious elements by rewriting a term into a canonical form is somewhat more complex, as we will see for the example of sets.

Equational theories To illustrate the notions introduced above, we will look at specifications of some familiar types, namely the natural numbers and sets.

In slide 8-10, an algebraic specification is given of the natural numbers (as first axiomatized by Peano).

```
Natural numbers                                    Nat        8-10

    functions
    0 : Nat
    S : Nat -> Nat
    mul : Nat * Nat -> Nat
    plus : Nat * Nat -> Nat
    axioms
    [1] plus(x,0) = x
    [2] plus(x,Sy) = S(plus(x,y))
    [3] mul(x,0) = 0
    [4] mul(x,Sy) = plus(mul(x,y),x)
    end
```

Slide 8-10: The ADT *Nat*

In addition to the constant *0* and successor function *S* we also introduce a function *mul* for multiplication and a function *plus* for addition. (The notation *Sy* stands for application by juxtaposition; its meaning is simply $S(y)$.) The reader who does not immediately accept the specification in slide 8-10 as an adequate axiomatization of the natural numbers must try to unravel the computation depicted in slide 8-11.

Admittedly, not an easy way to compute with natural numbers, but fortunately term rewriting may, to a large extent, be automated (and actual calculations may be mimicked by semantics preserving primitives).

```
mul(plus(S 0,S 0),S 0) -[2]->
mul(S(plus(S 0,0)), S 0) -[1]->
mul(SS 0,S 0) -[4]->
plus(mul(SS0,0),SS0) -[3]->
plus(0,SS0) -[2*]-> SS0
```
8-11

Slide 8-11: Symbolic evaluation

Using the equational theory expressing the properties of natural numbers, we may eliminate the occurrences of the functions *mul* and *plus* to arrive (through symbolic evaluation) at something of the form $S^n 0$ (where n corresponds to the magnitude of the natural number denoted by the term).

The opportunity of symbolic evaluation by term rewriting is exactly what has made the algebraic approach so popular for the specification of software, since it allows (under some restrictions) for executable specifications.

Since they do not reappear in what may be considered the *normal forms* of terms denoting the naturals (that are obtained by applying the evaluations induced by the equality theory), the functions *plus* and *mul* may be regarded as *secondary* producers. They are not part of the generator basis of the type *Nat*.

Since we may consider *mul* and *plus* as secondary producers at best, we can easily see that when we define *mul* and *plus* for the case *0* and *Sx* for arbitrary *x*, that we have covered all possible (generator) cases. Technically, this allows us to prove properties of these functions by using structural induction on the possible generator cases. The proof obligation (in the case of the naturals) then is to prove that the property holds for the function applied to 0 and assuming that the property holds for applying the function to *x*, it also holds for *Sx*.

As our next example, consider the algebraic specification of the type *Set$_A$* in slide 8-12.

Sets | *Set* | 8-12

- $G_{Set_A} = \{\emptyset, add\}$
- $GU_{Set_A} = \{0, add(0, a), \ldots, add(add(0, a), a), \ldots\}$

Axioms

[S1] $add(add(s, x), y) = add(add(s, y), x)$ commutativity
[S2] $add(add(s, x), x) = add(s, x)$ idempotence

Slide 8-12: The ADT *Set*

In the case of sets we have the problem that we do not start with a one-to-one generator base as we had with the natural numbers. Instead, we have a many-to-one generator base, so we need equality axioms to eliminate spurious elements from the (generator) universe of sets.

```
Equivalence classes                                    GU_{Set_A}/∼        8-13

  • {∅}
  • {add(0, a), add(add(0, a), a), ...}
  • ...
  • {add(add(0, a), b), add(add(0, b), a), ...}
```

Slide 8-13: Equivalence classes for *Set*

The equivalence classes of $GU_{Set_A}/\sim$ (which is GU_{Set_A} factored by the equivalence relation), each have multiple elements (except the class representing the empty set). To select an appropriate representative from each of these classes (representing the abstract elements of the type Set_A) we need an ordering on terms, so that we can take the smaller term as its canonical representation. See slide 8-13.

8.2.3   Initial algebra semantics

In the previous section we have given a rather operational characterization of the equivalence relation induced by the equational theory and the process of term rewriting that enables us to purge the generator universe of a type, by eliminating redundant elements. However, what we actually strive for is a mathematical model that captures the meaning of an algebraic specification. Such a model is provided (or rather a class of such models) by the mathematical structures known as (not surprisingly) algebras.

A *single sorted* algebra $\mathcal{A}$ is a structure (A, Σ) where A is a set of values, and Σ specifies the signature of the functions operating on A. A *multi-sorted* algebra is a structure $\mathcal{A} = (\{A_s\}_{s \in S}, \Sigma)$ where S is a set of sort names and A_s the set of values belonging to the sort s. The set S may be ordered (in which case the ordering indicates the subtyping relationships between the sorts). We call the (multi-sorted) structure $\mathcal{A}$ a Σ-algebra.

```
Mathematical model – algebra                               8-14

  • Σ-algebra – A = ({A_s}_{s ∈ S}, Σ)
  • interpretation – eval : T_Σ → A
  • adequacy – A ⊨ t_1 = t_2 ⟺ E ⊢ t_1 = t_2
```

Slide 8-14: Interpretations and models

Having a notion of algebras, we need to have a way in which to relate an algebraic specification to such a structure. To this end we define an interpretation $eval : T_\Sigma \to \mathcal{A}$ which maps closed terms formed by following the rules given in the specification to elements of the structure $\mathcal{A}$. We may extend the interpretation $eval$ to include variables as well (which we write as $eval : T_\Sigma(X) \to \mathcal{A}$), but then we also need to assume that an assignment $\theta : X \to T_\Sigma(X)$ is given, such that when applying θ to a term t the result is free of variables, otherwise no interpretation in $\mathcal{A}$ exists. See slide 8-14.

Interpretations As an example, consider the interpretations of the specification of *Bool* and the specification of *Nat*, given in slide 8-15.

8-15

Booleans

- $\mathcal{B} = (\{tt, ff\}, \{\neg, \wedge, \vee\})$
- $eval_\mathcal{B} : T_{Bool} \to \mathcal{B} = \{or \mapsto \vee, and \mapsto \wedge, not \mapsto \neg\}$

Natural numbers

- $\mathcal{N} = (\mathbb{N}, \{++, +, \star\})$
- $eval_\mathcal{N} : T_{Nat} \to \mathcal{N} = \{S \mapsto ++, mul \mapsto \star, plus \mapsto +\}$

Slide 8-15: Interpretations of *Bool* and *Nat*

The structure $\mathcal{B}$ given above is simply a boolean algebra, with the operators $\neg$, $\wedge$ and $\vee$. The functions *not*, *and* and *or* naturally map to their semantic counterparts. In addition, we assume that the constants *true* and *false* map to the elements *tt* and *ff*.

As another example, look at the structure $\mathcal{N}$ and the interpretation $eval_\mathcal{N}$, which maps the functions *S*, *mul* and *plus* specified in *Nat* in a natural way. However, since we have also given equations for *Nat* (specifying how to eliminate the functions *mul* and *plus*) we must take precautions such that the requirement

$$\mathcal{N} \models eval_\mathcal{N}(t_1) =_\mathcal{N} eval_\mathcal{N}(t_2) \iff E_{Nat} \vdash t_1 = t_2$$

is satisfied if the structure $\mathcal{N}$ is to count as an adequate model of *Nat*. The requirement above states that whenever equality holds for two interpreted terms (in $\mathcal{N}$) then these terms must also be provably equal (by using the equations given in the specification of *Nat*), and vice versa.

As we will see illustrated later, many models may exist for a single specification, all satisfying the requirement of adequacy. The question is, do we have a means to select one of these models as (in a certain sense) the best model. The answer is yes. These are the models called *initial models*.

Initial models A model (in a mathematical sense) represents the meaning of a specification in a precise way. A model may be regarded as stating a commitment with respect to the interpretation of the specification. An initial model is intuitively the least committing model, least committing in the sense that it imposes only identifications made necessary by the equational theory of a specification. Technically, an initial model is a model from which every other model can be derived by an algebraic mapping which is a homomorphism.

Initial algebra   *8-16*

   • ΣE-algebra – $\mathcal{M} = (T_\Sigma/\sim, \Sigma/\sim)$

Properties

   • *no junk* – $\forall\, a : T_\Sigma/\sim \exists\, t \bullet eval_\mathcal{M}(t) = a$

   • *no confusion* – $\mathcal{M} \models t_1 = t_2 \iff E \vdash t_1 = t_2$

Slide 8-16: Initial models

The starting point for the construction of an initial model for a given specification with signature Σ is to construct a term algebra T_Σ with the terms that may be generated from the signature Σ as elements. The next step is then to factor the universe of generated terms into equivalence classes, such that two terms belong to the same class if they can be proven equivalent with respect to the equational theory of the specification. We will denote the representative of the equivalence class to which a term t belongs by $[t]$. Hence $t_1 = t_2$ (in the model) *iff* $[t_1] = [t_2]$.

So assume that we have constructed a structure $\mathcal{M} = (T_\Sigma/\sim, \Sigma)$ then; finally, we must define an interpretation, say $eval_\mathcal{M} : T_\Sigma \to \mathcal{M}$, that assigns closed terms to appropriate terms in the term model (namely the representatives of the equivalence class of that term). Hence, the interpretation of a function f in the structure $\mathcal{M}$ is such that

$$f_\mathcal{M}([t_1], \ldots, [t_n]) = [f(t_1, \ldots, t_n)]$$

where $f_\mathcal{M}$ is the interpretation of f in $\mathcal{M}$. In other words, the result of applying f to terms $t_1, \ldots, t_n$ belongs to the same equivalence class as the result of applying $f_\mathcal{M}$ to the representatives of the equivalence classes of $t1, \ldots, t_n$. See slide 8-16.

An initial algebra model has two important properties, known respectively as the *no junk* and *no confusion* properties. The *no junk* property states that for each element of the model there is some term for which the interpretation in $\mathcal{M}$ is equal to that element. (For the $T_\Sigma/\sim$ model this is simply a representative of the equivalence class corresponding with the element.) The *no confusion* property states that if equality of two terms can be proven in the equational theory of the specification, then the equality also holds (semantically) in the model, and vice versa. The *no confusion* property means, in other words, that sufficiently many identifications are made (namely those that may be proven to hold), but no more than that (that is, no other than those for which a proof exists). The latter property is why we may speak of an initial model as the least committing model; it simply gives no more meaning than is strictly needed.

The initial model constructed from the term algebra of a signature Σ is intuitively a very natural model since it corresponds directly with (a subset of) the generator universe of Σ. Given such a model, other models may be derived from it simply by specifying an appropriate interpretation. For example, when we construct a model for the natural numbers (as specified by *Nat*) consisting of the generator universe $\{0, S0, SS0, \ldots\}$ and the operators $\{++, +, \star\}$ (which are defined as $S^n + + = S^{n+1}$, $S^n * S^m = S^{n*m}$ and $S^n + S^m = S^{n+m}$) we may simply derive from this model the structure $(\{0, 1, 2, \ldots\}, \{++, +, \star\})$ for which the operations have their standard arithmetical meaning. Actually, this structure is also an initial model for *Nat*, since we may also make the inverse transformation.

More generally, when defining an initial model only the structural aspects (characterizing the behavior of the operators) are important, not the actual contents. Technically, this means that initial models are defined up to isomorphism, that is a mapping to equivalent models with perhaps different contents but an identical structure. Not in all cases is a structure derived from an initial model itself also an initial model, as shown in the example below.

Example Consider the specification of *Bool* as given before. For this specification we have given the structure $\mathcal{B}$ and the interpretation $eval_\mathcal{B}$ which defines an initial model for *Bool*. (Check this!)

Structure – $\mathcal{B} = (\{tt, ff\}, \{\neg, \wedge, \vee\})$ $\boxed{\mathcal{B}}$ *8-17*

- $eval_\mathcal{B} : T_{\Sigma_{Bool}} \to \mathcal{B} = \{or \mapsto \vee, not \mapsto \neg\}$
- $eval_\mathcal{B} : T_{\Sigma_{Nat}} \to \mathcal{B} = \{S \mapsto \neg, mul \mapsto \wedge, plus \mapsto xor\}$

Slide 8-17: Structure and interpretation

We may, however, also use the structure $\mathcal{B}$ to define an interpretation of *Nat*. See slide 8-17. The interpretation $eval_\mathcal{B} : T_{Nat} \to \mathcal{B}$ is such that $eval_\mathcal{B}(0) = ff$, $eval_\mathcal{B}(Sx) = \neg eval_\mathcal{B}(x)$, $eval_\mathcal{B}(mul(x, y)) = eval_\mathcal{B}(x) \wedge eval_\mathcal{B}(y)$ and $eval_\mathcal{B}(plus(x, y)) = xor(eval_\mathcal{B}(x), eval_\mathcal{B}(y))$, where $xor(p, q) = (p \vee q) \wedge (\neg(p \wedge q))$. The reader may wish to ponder on what this interpretation effects. The answer is that it interprets *Nat* as specifying the naturals modulo 2, which discriminates only between odd and even numbers. Clearly, this interpretation defines not an initial model, since it identifies all odd numbers with *ff* and all even numbers with *tt*. Even if we replace *ff* by *0* and *tt* by *1*, this is not what we generally would like to commit ourselves to when we speak about the natural numbers, simply because it assigns too much meaning.

8.2.4   Objects as algebras

The types for which we have thus far seen algebraic specifications (including *Bool*, *Seq*, *Set* and *Nat*) are all types of a mathematical kind, which (by virtue of being mathematical) define operations without side-effects. Dynamic state changes, that is side-effects, are often mentioned as determining the characteristics of objects in general. In the following we will explore how we may deal with assigning meaning to dynamic state changes in an algebraic framework.

Let us look first at the abstract data type *stack*. The type *stack* may be considered as one of the 'real life' types in the world of programming. See slide 8-18.

Abstract Data Type – *applicative* | Stack | *8-18*

    functions
        `new : stack;`
        `push : element * stack  -> stack;`
        `empty : stack -> boolean;`
        `pop : stack -> stack;`
        `top : stack -> element;`
    axioms
        `empty( new ) = ` *true*
        `empty( push(x,s) ) = ` *false*
        `top( push(x,s) ) = x`
        `pop( push(x,s) ) = s`
    preconditions
        pre: `pop( s : stack ) = ` *not* `empty(s)`
        pre: `top( s : stack ) = ` *not* `empty(s)`
    end

Slide 8-18: The ADT *Stack*

Above, a stack has been specified by giving a signature (consisting of the functions *new, push, empty, pop* and *top*). In addition to the axioms characterizing the behavior of the stack, we have included two pre-conditions to test whether the stack is empty in case *pop* or *top* is applied. The pre-conditions result in conditional axioms for the operations *pop* and *top*. Conditional axioms, however, do preserve the initial algebra semantics.

The specification given above is a maximally abstract description of the behavior of a stack. Adding more implementation detail would disrupt its nice applicative structure, without necessarily resulting in different behavior (from a sufficiently abstract perspective).

The behavior of elements of abstract data types and objects is characterized by state changes. State changes may affect the value delivered by observers or methods. Many state changes (such as the growing or shrinking of a set, sequence or stack) really are nothing but applicative transformations that may mathematically be described by the input-output behavior of an appropriate function.

An example in which the value of an object on some attribute is dependent on the history of the operations applied to the object, instead of the structure of the object itself (as in the case of a stack) is the object *account*, as specified in slide 8-19. The example is taken from Goguen and Meseguer (1986).

```
Dynamic state changes – objects                    account        8-19
        object account is
        functions
         bal : account -> money
        methods
         credit : account * money -> account
         debit : account * money -> account
        error
         overdraw : money -> money
        axioms
         bal(new(A)) = 0
         bal(credit(A,M)) = bal(A) + M
         bal(debit(A,M)) = bal(A) - M if bal(A) >= M
        error-axioms
         bal(debit(A,M)) = overdraw(M) if bal(A) < M
        end
```

Slide 8-19: The algebraic specification of an account

An *account* object has one attribute function (called *bal*) that delivers the amount of money that is (still) in the account. In addition, there are two method functions, *credit* and *debit* that may respectively be used to add or withdraw money from the account. Finally, there is one special error function, *overdraw*, that is used to define the result of *balance* when there is not enough money left to grant a *debit* request. Error axioms are needed whenever the proper axioms are stated conditionally, that is contain an *if* expression. The conditional parts of the axioms, including the error axioms, must cover all possible cases.

Now, first look at the form of the axioms. The axioms are specified as

$$fn(method(Object, Args)) = expr$$

where *fn* specifies an attribute function (*bal* in the case of account) and *method* a method (either *new*, which is used to create new accounts, *credit* or *debit*). By convention, we assume that $method(Object, ...) = Object$, that is that a method function returns its first argument. Applying a method thus results in redefining the value of the function *fn*. For example, invoking the method $credit(acc, 10)$ for the account *acc* results in modifying the function *bal* to deliver the value $bal(acc) + 10$ instead of simply $bal(acc)$. In the example above, the axioms define the meaning of the function *bal* with respect to the possible method applications. It is not difficult to see that these operations are of a non-applicative nature, non-applicative in the sense that each time a method is invoked the actual definition of *bal* is changed. The change is necessary because, in contrast to, for example, the functions employed in a boolean algebra, the actual value of the account may change in time in a completely arbitrary way. A first order framework of (multi sorted) algebras is not sufficiently strong to define the meaning of such changes. What we need may be characterized as a *multiple world semantics*, where each world corresponds to a possible state of the account. As an alternative semantics we will also discuss the interpretation of an object as an *abstract machine*, which resembles an (initial) algebra with hidden sorts.

Multiple world semantics From a semantic perspective, an object that changes its state may be regarded as moving from one world to another, when we see a world as representing a particular state of affairs. Take for example an arbitrary (say John's) account, which has a balance of *500*. We may express this as *balance(accountJohn)* = 500. Now, when we invoke the method *credit*, as in *credit(accountJohn, 200)*, then we expect the balance of the account to be raised to *700*. In the language of the specification, this is expressed as

$$bal(credit(accountJohn, 200)) = bal(accountJohn) + 200$$

Semantically, the result is a state of affairs in which $bal(accountJohn) = 700$.

In Goguen and Meseguer (1986) an operational interpretation is given of a multiple world semantics by introducing a database D (that stores the values of the attribute functions of objects as first order terms) which is transformed as the result of invoking a method, into a new database D' (that has an updated value for the attribute function modified by the method). The meaning of each database (or world) may be characterized by an algebra and an interpretation as before.

The rules according to which transformations on a database take place may be formulated as in slide 8-20.

Multiple world semantics – *inference rules*   *8-20*

- $\langle f(t_1, \ldots, t_n), D \rangle \rightarrow \langle v, D \rangle$ attribute
- $\langle m(t_1, \ldots, t_n), D \rangle \rightarrow \langle t_1, D' \rangle$ method
- $\langle t, D \rangle \rightarrow \langle t', D' \rangle \Rightarrow \langle e(\ldots, t, \ldots), D \rangle \rightarrow \langle e(\ldots, t', \ldots), D' \rangle$

Slide 8-20: The interpretation of change

The first rule (*attribute*) describes how attribute functions are evaluated. Whenever a function f with arguments $t_1, \ldots, t_n$ evaluates to a value (or expression) v, then the term $f(t_1, \ldots, t_n)$ may be replaced by v without affecting the database D. (We have simplified the treatment by omitting all aspects having to do with matching and substitutions, since such details are not needed to understand the process of symbolic evaluation in a multiple world context.) The next rule (*method*) describes the result of evaluating a method. We assume that invoking the method changes the database D into D'. Recall that, by convention, a method returns its first argument. Finally, the last rule (*composition*) describes how we may glue all this together.

No doubt, the reader needs an example to get a picture of how this machinery actually works.

Example - a counter object   *8-21*

```
object ctr is                                    ctr
function n : ctr -> nat
method incr : ctr -> ctr
axioms
    n(new(C)) = 0
    n(incr(C)) = n(C) + 1
end
```

Slide 8-21: The object *ctr*

In slide 8-21, we have specified a simple object *ctr* with an attribute function *value* (delivering the value of the counter) and a method function *incr* (that may be used to increment the value of the counter).

Abstract evaluation   *8-22*

```
<n(incr(incr(new(C)))),{ C }> -[new]->
<n(incr(incr(C))),{ C[n:=0] }> -[incr]->
<n(incr(C)),{ C[n:=1] }> -[incr]->
<n(C), { C[n:=2] }> -[n]->
<2, { C[n:=2] }>
```

Slide 8-22: An example of abstract evaluation

The end result of the evaluation depicted in slide 8-22 is the value *2* and a context (or database) in which the value of the counter *C* is (also) *2*. The database is modified in each step in which the method *incr* is applied. When the attribute function *value* is evaluated the database remains unchanged, since it is merely consulted.

Objects as abstract machines Multiple world semantics provide a very powerful framework in which to define the meaning of object specifications. Yet, as illustrated above, the reasoning involved has a very operational flavor and lacks the appealing simplicity of the initial algebra semantics given for abstract data types. As an alternative, Goguen and Meseguer (1986) propose an interpretation of objects (with dynamic state changes) as *abstract machines*.

Recall that an initial algebra semantics defines a model in which the elements are equivalence classes representing the abstract values of the data type. In effect, initial models are defined only up to isomorphism (that is, structural equivalence with similar models). In essence, the framework of initial algebra semantics allows us to abstract from the particular representation of a data type, when assigning meaning to a specification. From this perspective it does not matter, for example, whether integers are represented in binary or decimal notation.

The notion of *abstract machines* generalizes the notion of initial algebras in that it loosens the requirement of (structural) isomorphism, to allow for what we may call *behavioral equivalence*. The idea underlying the notion of behavioral equivalence is to make a distinction between *visible* sorts and *hidden* sorts and to look only at the visible sorts to determine whether two algebras A and B are behaviorally equivalent. According to Goguen and Meseguer (1986), two algebras A and B are behaviorally equivalent if and only if the result of evaluating any expression of a visible sort in A is the same as the result of evaluating that expression in B.

Now, an *abstract machine* (in the sense of Goguen and Meseguer, 1986) is simply the equivalence class of behaviorally equivalent algebras, or in other words the maximally abstract characterization of the visible behavior of an abstract data type with (hidden) states.

The notion of abstract machines is of particular relevance as a formal framework to characterize the (implementation) refinement relation between objects. For example, it is easy to determine that the behavior of a stack implemented as a list is equivalent to the behavior of a stack implemented by a pointer array, whereas these objects are clearly not equivalent from a structural point of view. Moreover, the behavior of both conform (in an abstract sense) with the behavior specified in an algebraic way. Together, the notions of abstract machine and behavioral equivalence provide a formalization of the notion of *information hiding* in an algebraic setting. In the chapters that follow we will look at alternative formalisms to explain information hiding, polymorphism and behavioral refinement.

8.3 Decomposition – modules versus objects

Abstract data types allow the programmer to define a complex data structure and an associated collection of functions, operating on that structure, in a consistent way. Historically, the idea of data abstraction was originally not type-oriented but arose from a more pragmatic concern with information hiding and representation abstraction, see Parnas (1972b). The first realization of the idea of data abstraction was in the form of modules grouping a collection of functions and allowing the actual representation of the data structures underlying the values of the (abstract) type domain to be hidden, see also Parnas (1972a).

In Cook (1990), a comparison is made between the way in which abstract data types are realized traditionally (as modules) and the way abstract data types may be realized using object-oriented programming techniques. According to Cook (1990), these approaches must be regarded as being orthogonal to one another and, being to some extent complementary, deserve to be integrated in a common framework.

After presenting an example highlighting the differences between the two approaches, we will further explore these differences and study the trade-offs with respect to possible extensions and reuse of code.

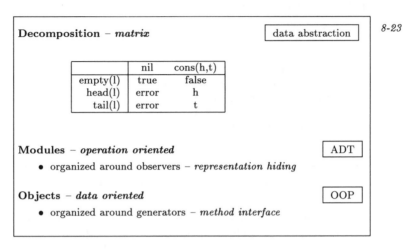

Slide 8-23: Decomposition and data abstraction

Recall that abstract data types may be completely characterized by a finite collection of generators and a number of observer functions that are defined with respect to each possible generator. Following this idea, we may approach the specification of a data abstraction by constructing a *matrix* listing the generators column-wise and the observers row-wise, which for each *observer/generator* pair specifies the value of the observer for that particular generator. Incidentally, the definition of such a matrix allows us to check in an easy way whether we have given a complete characterization of the data type. Above, an example is given of the specification of a *list*, with generators *nil* and *cons*, and observers *empty*, *head* and *tail*. (Note that we group the secondary producer *tail* with the observers.)

Now, the traditional way of realizing abstract data types as modules may be characterized as *operation oriented*, in the sense that the module realization of the type is organized around the observers, resulting in a horizontal decomposition of the matrix.

On the other hand, an object-oriented approach may be characterized as *data oriented*, since the object realization of a type is based on specifying a method interface for each possible generator (sub)type, resulting in a vertical decomposition of the matrix. See slide 8-23.

Note, however, that in practice, different generators need not necessarily correspond to different (sub)classes. Behavior may be subsumed in variables, as an object cannot change its class/type.

8.3.1   Abstract interfaces

When choosing for the module realization of the data abstraction *list* in C style, we are likely to have an abstract functional interface as specified in slide 8-24.

Modules – *a functional interface* | ADT | *8-24*

```
typedef int element;
struct list;

extern list* nil();
extern list* cons(element e, list* l);
extern element head(list* l);
extern list* tail(list* l);
extern bool equal(list* l, list* m);
```

Slide 8-24: Modules – a functional interface

For convenience, the *list* has been restricted to contain integer elements only. However, at the expense of additional notation, we could also easily define a generic list by employing template functions as provided by C++. This is left as an exercise for the reader.

The interface of the abstract class *list* given in slide 8-25 has been defined generically by employing templates.

Objects – *a method interface* | OOP | *8-25*

```
template< class E >
class list {
public:
list() { }
virtual ~list() { }
virtual bool empty() = 0;
virtual E head()   = 0;
virtual list<E>* tail() = 0;
virtual bool operator==(list<E>* m) = 0;
};
```

Slide 8-25: Objects – a method interface

Note that the *equal* function in the ADT interface takes two arguments, whereas the *operator==* function in the OOP interface takes only one, since the other is implicitly provided by the object itself.

8.3.2 Representation and implementation

The realization of abstract data types as modules with functions requires additional means to hide the representation of the *list* type. In contrast, with an object-oriented approach, data hiding is effected by employing the encapsulation facilities of classes.

Modules – representation hiding Modules provide a syntactic means to group related pieces of code and to hide particular aspects of that code. In slide 8-26 an example is given of the representation and the generator functions for a list of integers.

Modules – *representation hiding* |ADT| *8-26*

```
typedef int element;

enum { NIL, CONS };

struct list {
int tag;
element e;
list* next;
};
```

Generators

```
list* nil() {                              nil
list* l = new list; l->tag = NIL; return l;
}

list* cons( element e, list* l) {          cons
list* x = new list;
x->tag = CONS; x->e = e; x->next = l;
return x;
}
```

Slide 8-26: Data abstraction and modules

For implementing the *list* as a collection of functions (ADT style), we employ a *struct* with an explicit tag field, indicating whether the list corresponds to *nil* or a *cons*.

The functions corresponding with the generators create a new structure and initialize the tag field. In addition, the *cons* operator sets the *element* and *next* field of the structure to the arguments of *cons*.

The implementation of the *observers* is given in slide 8-27.

```
Modules – observers                                    ADT      8-27

    int empty(list* lst) { return !lst || lst->tag
       == NIL; }

    element head(list* l) {                         head
    require( ! empty(l) );
    return l->e;
    }

    list* tail(list* l) {                            tail
    require( ! empty(l) );
    return l->next;
    }

    bool equal(list* l, list* m) {                  equal
    switch( l->tag) {
      case NIL: return empty(m);
      case CONS: return !empty(m) &&
                    head(l) == head(m) &&
                    tail(l) == tail(m);

      }
    }
```

Slide 8-27: Modules – observers

To determine whether the list is *empty* it suffices to check whether the tag of
the list is equal to *NIL*. For both *head* and *tail* the pre-condition is that the list
given as an argument is not empty. If the pre-condition holds, the appropriate
field of the *list* structure is returned.

The equality operator, finally, performs an explicit switch on the tag field,
stating for each case under what conditions the lists are equal.

Below, a program fragment is given that illustrates the use of the list.

```
list* r = cons(1,cons(2,nil()));
while (!empty(r)) {
        cout << head(r) << endl;
        r = tail(r);
        }
```

Note that both the generator functions *nil* and *cons* take care of creating a new
list structure. Writing a function to destroy a list is left as an exercise for the
reader.

Objects – method interface The idea underlying an object-oriented decomposition of the specification matrix of an abstract type is to make a distinction

between the (syntactic) subtypes of the data type (corresponding with its generators) and to specify for each subtype the value of all possible observer functions. (We speak of *syntactic* subtypes, following Dahl (1992), since these subtypes correspond to the generators defining the value domain of the data type. See Dahl (1992) for a more extensive treatment.)

```
Method interface – list                              OOP      8-28

    template< class E >
    class nil : public list< E > {           nil
    public:
    nil() {}
    bool empty() { return 1; }
    E head() { require( false ); return E(); }
    list< E >* tail() { require( 0 ); return 0; }
    bool operator==(list<E>* m) { return
       m->empty(); }
    };


    template< class E >
    class cons : public list< E > {          cons
    public:
    cons(E e, list<E>* l) : _e(e), next(l) {}
    ~cons() { delete next; }
    bool empty() { return 0; }
    E head() { return _e; }
    list<E>* tail() { return next; }
    bool operator==(list<E>* m);
    protected:
    E _e;
    list<E>* next;
    };
```

Slide 8-28: Data abstraction and objects

In the object realization in slide 8-28, each subtype element is defined as a class inheriting from the *list* class. For both generator types *nil* and *cons* the observer functions are defined in a straightforward way. Note that, in contrast to the ADT realization, the distinction between the various cases is implicit in the member function definitions of the generator classes.

As an example of using the *list* classes consider the program fragment below.

```
list<int>* r = new cons<int>(1, new cons<int>(2, new nil<int>));
while (! r->empty()) {
        cout << r->head() << endl;
        r = r->tail();
        }
```

```
delete r;
```

For deleting a list we may employ the (virtual) destructor of *list*, which recursively destroys the tail of a list.

8.3.3   Adding new generators

Abstract data types were developed with correctness and security in mind, and not so much from a concern with extensibility and reuse. Nevertheless, it is interesting to compare the traditional approach of realizing abstract data types (employing modules) and the object-oriented approach (employing objects as generator subtypes) with regard to the ease with which a specification may be extended, either by adding new generators or by adding new observers.

Adding new generators – *representation*   [ADT]   *8-29*

```
typedef int element;

enum { NIL, CONS, INTERVAL };

struct list {
int tag;
element e;
union { element z; list* next; };
};
```

Generator
```
list* interval( element x, element y ) {
        list* l = new list;
        if ( x <= y ) {
                l->tag = INTERVAL;
                l->e = x; l->z = y;
                }
        else l->tag = NIL;
        return l;
        }
```

Slide 8-29: Modules and generators

Let us first look at what happens when we add a new generator to a data type, such as an interval list subtype, containing the integers in the interval between two given integers.

For the module realization of the list, adding an *interval*(x, y) generator will result in an extension of the (hidden) representation types with an additional representation tag type *INTERVAL* and the definition of a suitable generator function.

To represent the *interval* list type, we employ a union to select between the *next* field, which is used by the *cons* generator, and the *z* field, which indicates the end of the interval.

Modifying the observers | ADT | *8-30*

```
    element head(list* l) {                        | head |
      require( ! empty(l) );
      return l->e;          for both CONS and INTERVAL
    }

    list* tail(list* l) {                           | tail |
      require( ! empty(l) );
      switch( l->tag ) {
        case CONS: return l->next;
        case INTERVAL:
            return interval((l->e)+1,l->z);
          }
    }
```

Slide 8-30: Modifying the observers

Also, we need to modify the observer functions by adding an appropriate case for the new interval representation type, as pictured in slide 8-30.

Clearly, unless special constructs are provided, the addition of a new generator case requires disrupting the code implementing the given data type manually, to extend the definition of the observers with the new case.

In contrast, not surprisingly, when we wish to add a new generator case to the object realization of the list, we do not need to disrupt the given code, but we may simply add the definition of the generator subtype as given in slide 8-31.

Adding a new generator subtype corresponds to defining the realization for an abstract interface class, which gives a method interface that its subclasses must respect.

Observe, however, that we cannot exploit the fact that a list is defined by an interval when testing equality, since we cannot inspect the type of the list as for the ADT implementation.

8.3.4   Adding new observers

Now, for the complementary case, what happens when we add new observers to the specification of a data type? Somewhat surprisingly, the object-oriented approach now seems to be at a disadvantage.

```
Adding new generators                          OOP        8-31

    class interval : public list<int> {      interval
    public:
    interval(int x, int y) : _x(x), _y(y) { require(
      x <= y ); }
    bool empty() { return 0; }
    int head() { return _x; }
    list< int >* tail() {
      return (_x+1 <= _y)?
             new interval(_x+1,_y):
             new nil<int>;
    }
    bool operator==(list@lt;int>* m) {
      return !m->empty() &&
      _x == m->head() && tail() == m->tail();
    }
    protected:
    int _x; int _y;
    };
```

Slide 8-31: Objects and generators

Since in a module realization of an abstract data type the code is organized around observers, adding a new observer function amounts simply to adding a new operation with a case for each of the possible generator types, as shown in slide 8-32.

```
Adding new observers                           ADT        8-32

    int length( list* l ) {                  length
        switch( l->tag ) {
        case NIL: return 0;
        case CONS: return 1 + length(l->next);
        case INTERVAL: return l->z - l->e + 1;
        };
    }
```

Slide 8-32: Modules and observers

When we look at how we may extend a given object realization of an abstract data type with a new observer we are facing a problem.

The obvious solution is to modify the source code and add the *length* function to the *list* interface class and each of the generator classes. This is, however, against the spirit of object orientation and may not always be feasible.

Another, rather awkward solution, is to extend the collection of possible generator subtypes with a number of new generator subtypes that explicitly incorporate the new observer function. However, this also means redefining the *tail* function since it must deliver an instance of a *list with length* class.

As a workaround, one may define a function *length* and an extended version of the *list* template class supporting only the *length* (observer) member function as depicted in slide 8-33.

Adding new observers | OOP | *8-33*

```
template< class E >
int length(list< E >* l) {                          length
   return l->empty() ? 0 : 1 + length(
   l->tail() );
}


template< class E >
class listWL : public list<E> {                     list WL
public:
int length() { return ::length( this ); }
};
```

Slide 8-33: Objects and observers

A program fragment illustrating the use of the *listWL* class is given below.

```
list<int>* r = new cons<int>(1,new cons<int>(2,new interval(3,7)));
while (! r->empty()) {
        cout << ((listWL< int >*)r)->length() << endl;
        r = r->tail();
        }
delete r;
```

Evidently, we need to employ a cast whenever we wish to apply the *length* observer function. Hence, this seems not to be the right solution.

Alternatively, we may use the function *length* directly. However, we are then forced to mix method syntax of the form $ref \rightarrow op(args)$ with function syntax of the form $fun(ref, args)$, which may easily lead to confusion.

Discussion We may wonder why an object-oriented approach, that is supposed to support extensibility, is at a disadvantage here when compared to a more traditional module-based approach.

As observed in Cook (1990), the problem lies in the fact that neither of the two approaches reflect the full potential and flexibility of the matrix specification of an abstract data type. Each of the approaches represents a particular choice with respect to the decomposition of the matrix, into either an *operations-oriented* (horizontal) decomposition or a *data-oriented* (vertical) decomposition.

The apparent misbehavior of an object realization with respect to extending the specification with observer functions explains why in some cases we prefer the use of overloaded functions rather than methods, since overloaded functions allow for implicit dispatching to take place on multiple arguments, whereas method dispatching behavior is determined only by the type of the object.

However, it must be noted that the dispatching behavior of overloaded functions in C++ is of a purely syntactic nature. This means that we cannot exploit the information specific for a class type as we can when using virtual functions. Hence, to employ this information we would be required to write as many variants of overloaded functions as there are combinations of argument types.

Dynamic dispatching on multiple arguments is supported by *multi-methods* in CLOS, see Paepcke (1993). According to Cook (1990), the need for such methods might be taken as a hint that objects only partially realize the true potential of *data abstraction*.

8.4   Types versus classes

Types are primarily an aid in arriving at a consistent system description. Most (typed) object-oriented programming languages offer support for types by employing classes as a device to define the functionality of objects. Classes, however, have originated from a far more pragmatic concern, namely as a construct to enable the definition and creation of objects. Concluding this chapter, we will reflect on the distinction between types and classes, and discuss the role types and classes play in reusing software through derivation by inheritance. This discussion is meant to prepare the ground for a more formal treatment to be given in the next chapter. It closely follows the exposition given in Wegner and Zdonik (1988).

Types must primarily be understood as predicates to guide the process of type checking, whereas classes have come into being originally as templates for object creation.

It is interesting to note how (and how easily) this distinction may be obscured. In practice, when compiling a program in Java or C++, the compiler will notify the user of an error when a member function is called that is not listed in the public interface of the objects class. As another example, the runtime system of Smalltalk will raise an exception, notifying the user of a dynamic type error, when a method is invoked that is not defined in the object's class or any of its superclasses. Both kinds of errors have the flavor of a typing error, yet they rely on different notions of typing and are based on a radically different interpretation of classes as types.

To put types into perspective, we must ask ourselves what means we have to indicate the type of an expression, including expressions that somehow reference a class description.

In Wegner and Zdonik (1988), three attitudes towards typing are distinguished:

(1) typing may be regarded as an administrative aid to check for simple typos and other administrative errors, (2) typing may be regarded as the ultimate solution to defining the behavior of a system, or (3) typing may (pragmatically) be regarded as a consequence of defining the behavior of an object. See slide 8-34. Before continuing, the reader is invited to sort the various programming languages discussed into the three slots mentioned.

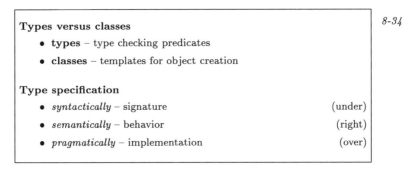

Types versus classes   *8-34*

- **types** – type checking predicates
- **classes** – templates for object creation

Type specification

- *syntactically* – signature   (under)
- *semantically* – behavior   (right)
- *pragmatically* – implementation   (over)

Slide 8-34: Types and classes

Typing as an administrative aid is typically a task for which we rely on a compiler to check for possible errors. Evidently, the notion of typing that a compiler employs is of a rather syntactic nature. Provided we have specified a signature correctly, we may trust a compiler with the routine of checking for errors. As languages that supports signature type checking we may (obviously) mention Java and C++.

Evidently, we cannot trust the compiler to detect conceptual errors, that is incomplete or ill-conceived definitions of the functionality of an object or collections of objects. Yet, ultimately we want to be able to specify the behavior of an object in a formal way and to check mechanically for the adequacy of this definition. This ideal of *semantic types* underlies the design of Eiffel, not so much the Eiffel type system as supported by the Eiffel compiler, but the integration of assertions in the Eiffel language and the notion of *contracts* as a design principle. Pragmatically, we need to rely on runtime (consistency) checks to detect erroneous behavior, since there are (theoretically rather severe) limits on the extent to which we may verify behavioral properties in advance. (Nevertheless, see section 10.4 for some attempts in this direction.)

Finally, we can take a far more pragmatic view towards typing, by regarding the actual specification of a class as an implicit characterization of the type of the instances of the class. Actually, this is the way (not surprisingly, I would say) types are dealt with in Smalltalk. Each object in Smalltalk is typed, by virtue of being an instance of a class. Yet, a typing error may only be detected dynamically, as the result of not responding to a message.

A distinction between perspectives on types (respectively syntactic, behavioral and pragmatic) may seem rather academic at first sight. However, the differences

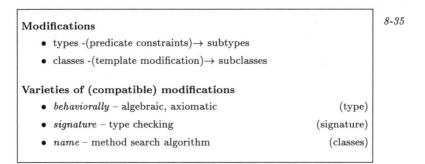

Slide 8-35: Type modifications

are, so to speak, amplified when studied in the context of type modifications, as for example effected by inheritance.

Wegner and Zdonik (1988) make a distinction between three notions of *compatible modifications*, corresponding to the three perspectives on types, respectively *signature compatible modifications* (which require the preservation of the static signature), *behaviorally compatible modification* (which rely on a mathematical notion of definability for a type) and *name compatible modifications* (that rely on an operationally defined method search algorithm). See slide 8-35.

Signature compatible modifications The assumption underlying the notion of *types as signatures* is that behavior is approximated by a (static) signature. Now the question is: to what extent can we define semantics preserving extensions to a given class or object?

```
Signature compatible modifications                         8-36

    • behavior is approximated by signature

Semantics preserving extensions

    • horizontal – Person = Citizen +  age :  0..120
    • vertical – Retiree = Person +  age :  65..120

Principle of substitutability

    • an instance of a subtype can always be used in any context in which
      an instance of a supertype can be used

Retiree ≮subtype Person            subsets are not subtypes

Read-only substitutability

    • subset subtypes, isomorphically embedded subtypes
```

Slide 8-36: The principle of substitutability

When we conceive of an object as a record consisting of (data and method) fields, we may think of two possible kinds of modifications. We may think of a *horizontal* modification when adding a new field, and similarly we may think of a modification as being *vertical* when redefining or constraining a particular field. For example, when we define *Citizen* as an entity with a name, we may define (at the risk of being somewhat awkward) a *Person* as a *Citizen* with an age and a *Retiree* as a *Person* with an age that is restricted to the range 65..120.

The principle by which we may judge these extensions valid (or not) may be characterized as the *principle of substitutability*, which may be phrased as: *an instance of a subtype can always be used in any context in which an instance of a supertype can be used.*

Unfortunately, for the extension given here we have an easy counterexample, showing that syntactic signature compatibility is not sufficient. Clearly, a *Person* is a supertype of *Retiree* (we will demonstrate this more precisely in section 9.2). Assume that we have a function

```
set_age : Person * Integer -> Void
```

that is defined as `set_age(p,n)` `p.age = n; .` Now consider the following fragment of code:

```
Person* p = r;                                  r refers to some Retiree
p->set_age(40);
```

where we employ object reference notation when calling *set_age*. Since we have assigned r (which is referring to a *Retiree*) to p, we know that p now points to a *Retiree*, and since a *Retiree* is a person we may apply the function *set_age*. However, *set_age* sets the *age* of the *Retiree* to *40*, which gives (by common standards) a semantic error. The lesson that we may draw from this is that being a subset is no guarantee for being a subtype as defined by the principle of substitutability. However, we may characterize the relation between a *Retiree* and a *Person* as being of a weaker kind, namely *read-only substitutability*, expressing that the (value of) the subtype may be used safely everywhere an instance of the supertype is expected, as long as it is not modified. Read-only substitutability holds for a type that stands in a subset relation to another type or is embeddable (as a subset) into that type. See slide 8-36.

Behaviorally compatible modifications If the subset relation is not a sufficient condition for being in a subtype relation, what is? To establish whether the (stronger) substitutability relation holds we must take the possible functions associated with the types into consideration as well. First, let us consider what relations may exist between types. Recall that semantically a type corresponds to a set together with a collection of operations that are defined for the set and that the subtype relation corresponds to the subset relation in the sense that (taking a type as a constraint) the definition of a subtype involves adding a constraint and, consequently, a narrowing of the set of elements corresponding to the supertype.

Complete compatibility is what we achieve when the principle of substitutability holds. Theoretically, complete compatibility may be assured when the behavior of the subtype fully complies with the behavior of the supertype. Behavioral compatibility, however, is a quite demanding notion. We will deal with it more extensively in chapter 10, when discussing *behavioral refinement*. Unfortunately, in practice we must often rely on the theoretically much weaker notion of *name compatibility*.

Name compatible modifications   *8-37*

- operational semantics – no extra compile/run-time checks

```
procedure search(name, module)
if name = action then do action
elsif inherited = nil
            then undefined
else search(name, inherited)
```

Slide 8-37: The inheritance search algorithm

Name compatible modifications Name compatible modifications approximate behaviorally compatible modifications in the sense that substitutability is guaranteed, albeit not in a semantically verifiable way.

Operationally, substitutability can be enforced by requiring that each subclass (that we may characterize as a pragmatic subtype) provides at least the operations of its superclasses (while giving a sensible result on all argument types allowed by its superclasses). Actually, name compatibility is an immediate consequence of the overriding semantics of derivation by inheritance, as reflected in the search algorithm underlying method lookup. See slide 8-37. Although name compatible modifications are by far the most flexible, from a theoretical point of view they are the least satisfying since they do not allow for any theory formation concerning the (desired) behavior of (the components of) the system under development.

Summary

This chapter has presented an introduction to the theoretical foundations of abstract data types. In particular, a characterization was given of *types as constraints*.

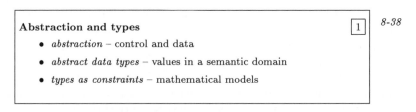

Slide 8-38: Section 8.1: Abstraction and types

In section 1, we discussed the notion of abstraction in programming languages and distinguished between control and data abstractions. Abstract data types were characterized as values in some domain, and we looked at the various ways in which to define mathematical models for types.

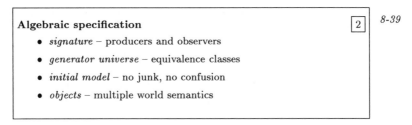

Slide 8-39: Section 8.2: Algebraic specification

In section 2, we studied the algebraic specification of abstract data types by means of a signature characterizing producers and observers. We discussed the notions of equivalence classes and initial models, which consist of precisely the equivalence classes that are needed. ,p¿ Also, we looked at the interpretation of objects as algebras, and we discussed a multiple world semantics allowing for dynamic state changes.

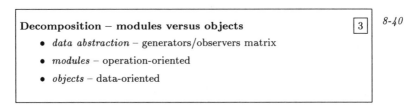

Slide 8-40: Section 8.3: Decomposition – modules versus objects

In section 3, we looked at the various ways we may realize data abstractions and we distinguished between a modular approach, defining a collection of operations, and a data-oriented approach, employing objects.

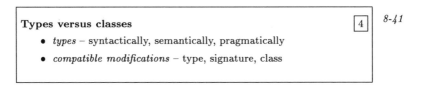

Slide 8-41: Section 8.4: Types versus classes

Finally, in section 4, we discussed the differences between a syntactic, semantic and operational interpretation of types, and how these viewpoints affect our notion of refinement or compatible modification.

Questions

1. Characterize the differences between control abstractions and data abstractions. Explain how these two kinds of abstractions may be embodied in programming language constructs.

2. How can you model the meaning of abstract data types in a mathematical way? Do you know any alternative ways?

3. Explain how types may affect object-oriented programming.

4. Explain how you may characterize an abstract data type by means of a matrix with generator columns and observer rows. What benefits does such an organization have?

5. How would you characterize the differences between the realization of abstract data types by modules and by objects? Discuss the trade-offs involved.

6. How would you characterize the distinction between types and classes? Mention three ways of specifying types. How are these kinds related to each other?

7. How would you characterize behavior compatible modifications? What alternatives can you think of?

Further reading

There is a vast amount of literature on the algebraic specification of abstract data types. You may consult, for example, Dahl (1992).

9

Polymorphism

From a theoretical perspective, object orientation may be characterized as combining *abstract data types* and *polymorphism*. These notions may be considered as the theoretical counterparts of the more operational notions of *encapsulation* and *inheritance*.

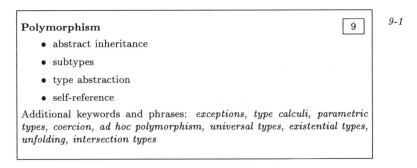

Slide 9-1: Polymorphism

In this chapter we will study the notion of polymorphism. We start our exploration by looking at the role of inheritance in knowledge representation. Then we will formally characterize the (signature) subtype relation and explain the *contravariance* rule for function subtypes. To better understand polymorphism and its relation to inheritance, we will develop a type calculus, allowing us to define abstract types using universally and existentially quantified type expressions. In a similar way, we will look at polymorphism due to overloading and generic type definitions. Finally, we will look at the role of self-reference in typing object descriptions derived by inheritance. Together with developing the calculi, examples will be given that illustrate the properties of the C++ and Eiffel type systems.

9.1   Abstract inheritance

Inheritance hierarchies play a role both in knowledge representation systems and object-oriented programming languages, see Lenzerini *et al.* (1990). In effect, historically, the notions of *frames* and *is-a hierarchies* (that play a role in knowledge representation) and the notions of *classes* and *inheritance* (that have primarily been developed in a programming language context) have mutually influenced each other.

In object-oriented programming languages, classes and inheritance are strongly related to types and polymorphism, and directed towards the construction of reliable programming artifacts. In contrast, the goal of knowledge representation is to develop a semantically consistent description of some real world domain, which allows us to reason about the properties of the elements in that domain.

Abstract inheritance   *9-2*

  • *declarative relation among entities*

Inheritance networks

  • *isa-trees* – partial ordering

  • *isa/is-not* – bipolar, is-not inference

Non-monotonic reasoning

```
        Nixon is-a Quaker
        Nixon is-a Republican
        Quakers are Pacifists
        Republicans are not Pacifists
```

Incremental system evolution is in practice non-monotonic!

Slide 9-2: Knowledge representation and inheritance

One of the first formal analyses of the declarative aspects of inheritance systems was given in Touretzky (1986). The theoretical framework developed in Touretzky (1986) covers the inheritance formalisms found in frame systems such as FRL, KRL, KLONE and NETL, but also to some extent the inheritance mechanisms of Simula, Smalltalk, Flavors and Loops. The focus of Touretzky (1986), however, is to develop a formal theory of inheritance networks including defaults and exceptions. The values of attributes play a far more important role in such networks than in a programming context. In particular, to determine whether the relationships expressed in an inheritance graph are consistent, we must be able to reason about the values of these attributes. In contrast, the use of inheritance in programming languages is primarily focused on sharing instance variables and overriding (virtual) member functions, and is not so much concerned with the actual values of instance variables.

Inheritance networks in knowledge representation systems are often *non mono-tonic* as a result of having *is-not* relations in addition to *is-a* relations and also because properties (for example *can-fly*) can be deleted.

Monotonicity is basically the requirement that all properties are preserved, which is the case for strict inheritance satisfying the substitution principle. It is a requirement that should be adhered to at the risk of jeopardizing the integrity of the system. Nevertheless, strict inheritance may be regarded as too inflexible to express real world properties in a knowledge representation system.

The meaning of *is-a* and *is-not* relations in a knowledge representation inheritance graph may equivalently be expressed as predicate logic statements. For example, the statements

- $\forall x.Quaker(x) \rightarrow Human(x)$

- $\forall x.Republican(x) \rightarrow Human(x)$

express the relation between, respectively, the predicates *Quaker* and *Republican* to the predicate *Human* in the graph above. In addition, the statements

- $\forall x.Quaker(x) \rightarrow Pacifist(x)$

- $\forall x.Republican(x) \rightarrow \neg Pacifist(x)$

introduce the predicate *Pacifist* that leads to an inconsistency when considering the statement that *Nixon is a Quaker and a Republican*.

Some other examples of statements expressing relations between entities in a taxonomic structure are given in slide 9-3.

9-3

Taxonomic structure
- $\forall x.Elephant(x) \rightarrow Mammal(x)$
- $\forall x.Elephant(x) \rightarrow color(x) = gray$
- $\forall x.Penguin(x) \rightarrow Bird(x) \land \neg CanFly(x)$

Slide 9-3: Taxonomies and predicate logic

The latter is often used as an example of non-monotonicity that may occur when using defaults (in this case the assumption that *all birds can fly*).

The mathematical semantics for declarative taxonomic hierarchies, as given in Touretzky (1986), are based on the notion of constructible lattices of predicates, expressing a partial order between the predicates involved in a taxonomy (such as, for example, *Quaker* and *Human*). A substantial part of the analysis presented in Touretzky (1986), however, is concerned with employing the graph representation of inheritance structures to improve on the efficiency of reasoning about the entities populating the graph. In the presence of multiple inheritance and non-monotonicity due to exceptions and defaults, care must be taken to follow the right path through the inheritance graph when searching for the value of a particular attribute. Operationally, the solution presented by Touretzky (1986) involves an ordering of inference paths (working upwards) according to the number of intermediate nodes. Intuitively, this corresponds to the distance between the node using an attribute and the node defining the value of the attribute. In strictly monotonic situations such a measure plays no role, however!

9.2   The subtype relation

In this section, we will study the subtype relation in a more formal manner. First we investigate the notion of subtypes in relation to the interpretation of *types as sets*, and then we characterize the subtype relation for a number of constructs occurring in programming languages (such as ranges, functions and records). Finally, we will characterize objects as records and correspondingly define the subtype relation for simple record (object) types. These characterizations may be regarded as a preliminary to the type calculi to be developed in subsequent sections.

9.2.1   Types as sets

A type, basically, denotes a set of elements. A type may be defined either extensionally, by listing all the elements constituting the type, or descriptively, as a constraint that must be satisfied by an individual to be classified as an element of the type.

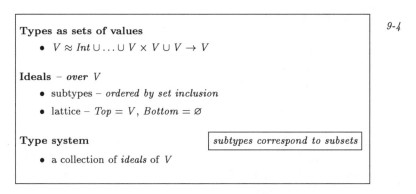

Slide 9-4: The interpretation of types as sets

Formally, we may define the value set of a type with subtypes as an isomorphism of the form

$$V \approx Int \cup \ldots \cup V \times V \cup V \to V$$

which expresses that the collection of values V consists of (the union of) basic types (such as Int) and compound types (of which V itself may be a component) such as record types (denoted by the product $V \times V$) and function types (being part of the function space $V \to V$).

Within this value space V, subtypes correspond to subsets that are ordered by set inclusion. Technically, the subsets corresponding to the subtypes must be *ideals*, which comes down to the requirement that any two types have a maximal type containing both (in the set inclusion sense).

Intuitively, the subtype relation may be characterized as a refinement relation, constraining the set of individuals belonging to a type. The subtype refinement relation may best be understood in terms of improving our knowledge with respect to (the elements of) the type. For a similar view, see Ghelli and Orsini (1990). In case we have no knowledge of a particular element we simply (must) assume that it belongs to the value set V. Having no knowledge is represented by the maximal element of the lattice *Top*, which denotes the complete set V. Whenever we improve our knowledge, we may be more specific about the type of the element, since fewer elements will satisfy the constraints implied by our information. The bottom element *Bottom* of our type lattice denotes the type with no elements, and may be taken to consist of the elements for which we have contradictory information. See slide 9-4.

Mathematically, a type system is nothing but a collection with ideals within some lattice V. In our subsequent treatment, however, we will primarily look at the refinement relation between two elements, rather than the set inclusion relation between their corresponding types.

9.2.2 The subtype refinement relation

In determining whether a given type is a subtype of another type, we must make a distinction between simple (or basic) types built into the language and compound (or user-defined) types explicitly declared by the programmer. Compound types, such as *integer subranges, functions, records* and *variant records*, themselves make use of other (basic or compound) types. Basic types are (in principle) only a subtype of themselves, although many languages allow for an implicit subtyping relation between for example integers and reals. The rules given in slide 9-5 characterize the subtyping relation for the compound types mentioned.

We use the relation symbol $\leqslant$ to denote the subtype relation. Types (both basic and compound) are denoted by σ and τ. For subranges, a given (integer) subrange σ is a subtype of another subrange τ if σ is (strictly) included in τ as a subset. In other words, if $\sigma = n'..m'$ and $\tau = n..m$ then the subtyping condition is $n \leqslant n'$ and $m' \leqslant m$. We may also write $n'..m' \subseteq n..m$ in this case.

For functions we have a somewhat similar rule, a function $f' : \sigma' \to \tau'$ (with domain σ' and range or codomain τ') is a subtype of a function $f : \sigma \to \tau$

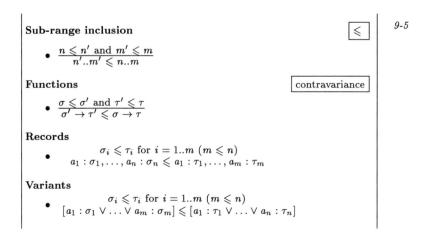

Slide 9-5: The subtype refinement relation

(with domain σ and codomain τ) if the subtype condition $\sigma \leqslant \sigma'$ and $\tau' \leqslant \tau$ is satisfied. Note that the relation between the domains is contravariant, whereas the relation between the ranges is covariant. We will discuss this phenomenon of contravariance below.

Records may be regarded as a collection of labels (the record fields) that may have values of a particular type. The subtyping rule for records expresses that a given record (type) may be extended to a (record) subtype by adding new labels, provided that the types for labels which occur in both records are refined in the subtype. The intuition underlying this rule is that by extending a record we add, so to speak, more information concerning the individuals described by such a record, and hence we constrain the set of possible elements belonging to that (sub)type.

Variants are (a kind of) record that leave the choice between a (finite) number of possible values, each represented by a label. The subtyping rules for variants states that we may create a subtype of a given variant record if we reduce the choice by eliminating one or more possibilities. This is in accord with our notion of refinement as improving our knowledge, since by reducing the choice we constrain the set of possible individuals described by the variant record.

The subtyping rules given above specify what checks to perform in order to determine whether a given (compound) type is a subtype of another type. In the following we will look in more detail at the justification underlying these rules, and also hint at some of the restrictions and problems implied. However, let us first look at some examples. See slide 9-6.

As a first example, when we define a function $f' : 8..12 \to 3..5$ and a function $f : 9..11 \to 2..6$ then, according to our rules, we have $f' \leqslant f$. Recall that we required subtypes to be compatible with their supertypes, compatible in the sense that an instance of the subtype may be used at all places where an instance of the supertype may be used. With regard to its signature, obviously, f' may be used

> **Examples**   subtyping   *9-6*
>
> - $8..12 \rightarrow 3..5 \leqslant 9..11 \rightarrow 2..6$
> - $\{age : int, speed : int, fuel : int\} \leqslant \{age : int, speed : int\}$
> - $[yellow \lor blue] < [yellow \lor blue \lor green]$

Slide 9-6: Examples of subtyping

everywhere where f may be used, since f' will deliver a result that falls within the range of the results expected from f and, further, any valid argument for f will also be accepted by f' (since the domain of f' is larger, due contravariance, than the domain of f).

As another example, look at the relation between the record types $\{age : int, speed : int, fuel : int\}$ and $\{age : int, speed : int\}$. Since the former has an additional field *fuel* it delimits so to speak the possible entities falling under its description and hence may be regarded as a subtype of the latter.

Finally, look at the relation between the variant records $[yellow : color \lor blue : color]$ and $[yellow : color \lor blue : color \lor green : color]$. The former leaves us the choice between the colors *yellow* and *blue*, whereas the latter also allows for *green* objects and, hence, encompasses the set associated with $[yellow : color \lor blue : color]$.

Contravariance rule The subtyping rules given above are all rather intuitive, except possibly for the *function* subtyping rule. Actually, the *contravariance* expressed in the function subtyping rule is somewhat of an embarrassment since it reduces the opportunities for specializing functions to particular types. See slide 9-7.

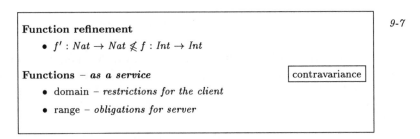

> **Function refinement**   *9-7*
>
> - $f' : Nat \rightarrow Nat \not\leqslant f : Int \rightarrow Int$
>
> **Functions – *as a service***   contravariance
> - domain – *restrictions for the client*
> - range – *obligations for server*

Slide 9-7: The function subtype relation

Consider, for example, that we have a function $f : Int \rightarrow Int$, then it seems quite natural to specialize this function into a function $f' : Nat \rightarrow Nat$ (which may make use of the fact that *Nat* only contains the positive elements of *Int*). However, according to our subtyping rule $f' \not\leqslant f$, since the domain of f' is smaller than the domain of f.

For an intuitive understanding of the function subtyping rule, it may be helpful to regard a function as a *service*. The domain of the function may then be interpreted as characterizing the restrictions imposed on the client of the service (the caller of the function) and the codomain of the function as somehow expressing the benefits for the client and the obligations for the (implementor of the) function. Now, as we have already indicated, to refine or improve on a service means to relax the restrictions imposed on the client and to strengthen the obligations of the server. This, albeit in a syntactic way, is precisely what is expressed by the contravariance rule for function subtyping.

9.2.3   Objects as records

Our interest in the subtype relation is primarily directed towards objects. However, since real objects involve self-reference and possibly recursively defined methods, we will first study the subtyping relation for objects as (simple) records. Our notion of *objects as records* is based on the views expressed in Cardelli (1984).

Objects may be regarded as records (where a record is understood as a finite association of values to labels), provided we allow functions to occur as the value of a record field.

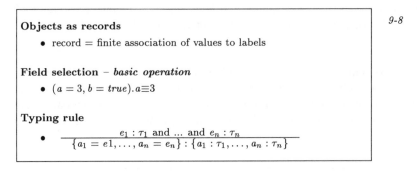

Slide 9-8: The object subtype relation

The basic operation with records is *field selection* which, when the value of the field accessed is a function, may be applied for method invocation. The typing rule for records follows the construction of the record: the type of a record is simply the record type composed of the types of the record's components. See slide 9-8.

In the previous section we have already characterized the subtyping relation between records. This characterization is repeated in slide 9-9. The following is meant to justify this characterization.

Let us first look at a number of examples that illustrate how the subtype relation fits into the mechanism of derivation by inheritance.

Suppose we define the type *any* as the record type having no fields. In our view of *types as constraints*, the empty record may be regarded as imposing no constraints. This is in agreement with our formal characterization of subtyping,

---

Subtyping – *examples*   *9-9*

```
type any = { }
type entity = { age : int }
type vehicle = { age : int, speed : int }
type machine = { age : int, fuel : string }
type car = { age : int, speed : int, fuel :
    string }
```

Subtyping rules

- $\tau \leqslant \tau$

- $$\frac{\sigma_1 \leqslant \tau_1, \ldots, \sigma_n \leqslant \tau_n}{\{a_1 : \sigma_1, \ldots, a_{n+m} : \sigma_{n+m}\} \leqslant \{a_1 : \tau_1, \ldots, a_n : \tau_n\}}$$

Slide 9-9: Examples of object subtyping

since according to the record subtyping rule the record type *any* is a supertype of any other record type.

Subtyping in the sense of refinement means adding constraints, that is information that constrains the set of possible elements associated with the type. The record type *entity*, which assumes a field *age*, is a subtype of *any*, adding the information that *age* is a relevant property for an entity. Following the same line of reasoning, we may regard the types *vehicle* and *machine* as subtypes of the type *entity*.

Clearly, we may have derived the respective types by applying inheritance. For example, we may derive *vehicle* from *entity* by adding the field *speed*, and *machine* from *entity* by adding the field *fuel*. Similarly, we may apply multiple inheritance to derive the type *car* from *vehicle* and *machine*, where we assume that the common field *age* (ultimately inherited from *entity*) only occurs once. Obviously, the type *car* is a subtype of both *vehicle* and *machine*.

Each of the successive types listed above adds information that constrains the possible applicability of the type as a descriptive device. The other way around, however, we may regard each object of a particular (sub)type to be an instance of its supertype simply by ignoring the information that specifically belongs to the subtype. Mathematically, we may explain this as a projection onto the fields of the supertype. Put differently, a subtype allows us to make finer distinctions. For example, from the perspective of the supertype two entities are the same whenever they have identical ages but they may be different when regarded as vehicles (by allowing different speeds).

Conformance The importance of subtyping for practical software development comes from the *conformance* requirement (or substitutability property) stating that any instance of a subtype may be used when an instance of a supertype is expected. This property allows the programmer to express the functionality of a program in a maximally abstract way, while simultaneously allowing for the refinement of these abstract types needed to arrive at an acceptable implementation.

For objects as records, the refinement relation concerns both attributes and functions (as members of the object record). For attributes, refinement means providing more information. Syntactically, with respect to the (signature) type of the attribute, this means a restriction of its range. In other words, the possible values an attribute may take may only be restricted. Alternatively, the refinement relation may be characterized as restricting the non-determinism contained in the specification of the supertype, by making a more specific choice. For example, if we specify the speed range of a *vehicle* initially as 0..300.000 then we may restrict the speed range of a *car* safely to 0..300. However, to stay within the regime of subtyping we may not subsequently enlarge this range by defining a subtype *racing car* with a speed range of 0..400. Intuitively, subtyping means enforcing determinism, the restriction of possible choices.

Our (syntactic) characterization of the subtyping relation between object types does not yet allow for data hiding, generics or self-reference. These issues will be treated in sections 9.5 and 9.6. However, before that, let us look at the characterization of the subtyping relation between object types as defined (for example) for the language Emerald. The characterization given in slide 9-10 is taken from Danforth and Tomlinson (1988).

Subtyping in Emerald – *S conforms to T*   *9-10*

- S provides at least the operations of T

- for each operation in T, the corresponding operation in S has the same number of arguments

- the type of the result of operations of S conform to those of the operations of T

- the types of arguments of operations of T conform to those of the operations of S

Slide 9-10: The subtype relation in Emerald

The object subtyping relation in Emerald is characterized in terms of *conformance*. The rules given above specify when an object type S conforms to an object (super) type T. These rules are in agreement with the subtyping rules given previously, including the contravariance required for the argument types of operations. Taken as a guideline, the rules specify what restrictions to obey (minimally) when specifying a subtype by inheritance. However, as we will discuss in the next section, polymorphism and subtyping is not restricted to object types only. Nor are the restrictions mentioned a sufficient criterion for a semantically safe use of inheritance.

9.3   Flavors of polymorphism

Polymorphism is not a feature exclusive to object-oriented languages. For example the ML language is a prime example of a non object-oriented language supporting a polymorphic type system (see Milner *et al.*, 1990). Also, most languages, including Fortran and Pascal, support implicit conversion between integers and floats, and backwards from floats to integers, and (in Pascal) from integer subranges to integers. Polymorphism (including such conversions) is a means to relieve the programmer from the rigidity imposed by typing. Put differently, it's a way in which to increase the expressivity of the type system.

Typing *– protection against errors*   *9-11*

- *static* – type checking at compile time

- *strong* – all expressions are type consistent

Untyped *– flexibility*

- bitstrings, sets, λ-calculus

Exceptions to monomorphic typing:

- *overloading, coercion, subranging, value-sharing (nil)*

Slide 9-11: The nature of types

Typing, as we have argued before, is important as a means to protect against errors. We must distinguish between *static typing* (which means that type checking takes place at compile time) and *strong typing* (which means that each expression must be type consistent). In other words, strong typing allows illegal operations to be recognized and rejected. Object-oriented languages (such as Eiffel, and to a certain extent C++) provide strong typing which is a mixture of static typing and runtime checks to effect the dynamic binding of method invocations. See slide 9-11.

Typed languages impose rather severe constraints on the programmer. It may require considerable effort to arrive at a consistently typed system and to deal with the additional notational complexity of defining the appropriate types. In practice, many programmers and mathematicians seem to have a preference for working in an untyped formalism, like bitstrings, (untyped) sets or (untyped) lambda calculus. We may further note that languages such as Lisp, Prolog and Smalltalk are popular precisely because of the flexibility due to the absence of static type checking.

For reliable software development, working in an untyped setting is often considered as not satisfactory. However, to make typing practical, we need to relieve the typing regime by supporting well-understood exceptions to monomorphic typing, such as overloaded functions, coercion between data types and value sharing between types (as provided by a generic nil value). More importantly,

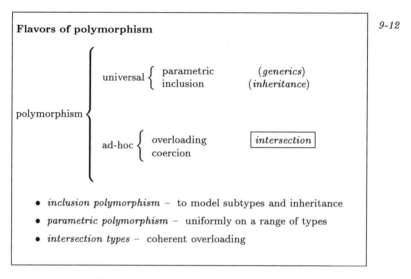

Slide 9-12: Flavors of polymorphism

however, we must provide for controlled forms of polymorphism.

In Cardelli and Wegner (1985), a distinction is made between *ad hoc* polymorphism (which characterizes the mechanisms mentioned as common exceptions to monomorphic typing) and *universal* polymorphism (which allows for theoretically well-founded means of polymorphism). Universal polymorphism may take the form of *inclusion polymorphism* (which is a consequence of derivation by inheritance) or *parametric polymorphism* (which supports generic types, as the template mechanism offered by C++). See slide 9-12. The term *inclusion polymorphism* may be understood by regarding inheritance as a means to define the properties of a (sub)type incrementally, and thus (by adding information) delimiting a subset of the elements corresponding to the supertype. When overloading is done in a systematic fashion we may speak of *intersection* types, which allows for polymorphism based on a finite enumeration of types. See section 9.4.1.

Inheritance as incremental modification

The notion of inheritance as incremental modification was originally introduced in Wegner and Zdonik (1988). Abstractly, we may characterize derivation by inheritance in a formula as $R = P + M$, where R is the result obtained by modifying the parent P by (modifier) M. See slide 9-13.

For example, we may define the record consisting of attributes $a_1 \ldots a_n$ by adding $\{a_2, a_3\}$ to the parent $\{a_1, a_2\}$. Clearly, we must make a distinction between *independent* attributes (that occur in either P or M) and *overlapping* attributes (that occur in both P and M and are taken to be overruled by the definition given in M).

An important property of objects, not taken into account in our interpretation

---

Inheritance – *incremental modification*

   • **Result** = **Parent** + **Modifier**

Example: $R = \{a1, a2\} + \{a2, a3\} = \{a1, a2, a3\}$
Independent attributes: M disjoint from P
Overlapping attributes: M overrules P

Dynamic binding

   • $R = \ldots, P_i : self!A, \ldots + \{\ldots, M_j : self!B, \ldots\}$

9-13

Slide 9-13: Inheritance as incremental modification

of *object as records* given before, is that objects (as supported by object-oriented languages) may be referring to themselves. For example, both in the parent and the modifier methods may be defined that refer to a variable *this* or *self* (denoting the object itself). It is important to note that the variable *self* is dynamically bound to the object and not (statically) to the textual module in which the variable *self* occurs. Wegner and Zdonik (1988) make a distinction between attributes that are redefined in *M*, *virtual* attributes (that need to be defined in *M*) and *recursive* attributes (that are defined in *P*). Each of these attributes may represent methods which (implicitly) reference *self*. (In many object-oriented languages, the variable *self* or *this* is implicitly assumed whenever a method defined within the scope of the object is invoked.) Self-reference (implicit or explicit) underlies dynamic binding and hence is where the power of inheritance comes from. Without self-reference method calls would reduce to statically bound function invocation.

Generic abstract data types

Our goal is to arrive at a type theory with sufficient power to define generic (polymorphic) abstract data types. In the following section, we will develop a number of type calculi (following Pierce, 1993) that enable us to define polymorphic types by employing *type abstraction*.

Type abstraction may be used to define generic types, data hiding and (inheritance) subtypes. The idea is that we may characterize generic types by quantifying over a type variable. For example, we may define the identity function *id* generically as $\forall\, T.id(x : T) = x$, stating that for arbitrary type T and element x of type T, the result of applying *id* to x is x. Evidently this holds for any T.

In a similar way, we may employ type parameters to define generic abstract data types. Further, we may improve on our notion of *objects as records* by defining a packaging construct that allows for data hiding by requiring merely that there exists a particular type implementing the hidden component.

Also, we may characterize the (inheritance) subtyping relation in terms of bounded quantification, that is quantification over a restricted collection of types (restricted by imposing constraints with respect to the syntactic structure of the type instantiating the type parameter).

9.4   Type abstraction

In this section we will study type calculi that allow us to express the various forms of polymorphism, including *inclusion polymorphism* (due to inheritance), *parametric polymorphism* (due to generics) and *intersection types* (due to over-loading), in a syntactic way, by means of appropriate *type expressions*.

The type calculi are based on the typed lambda calculus originally introduced in Cardelli (1984) to study the semantics of multiple inheritance. We will first study some simple extensions to the typed lambda calculus and then discuss examples involving universal quantification (defining parametric types), existen-tial quantification (hiding implementation details) and bounded quantification (modeling subtypes derived by inheritance). For those not familiar with the lambda calculus, a very elementary introduction is given below. For each calculus, examples will be given to relate the insights developed to properties of the C++ type system.

The lambda calculus The lambda calculus provides a very concise, yet powerful formalism to reason about computational abstraction. The introduction given here has been taken from Barendrecht (1984), which is a standard reference on this subject.

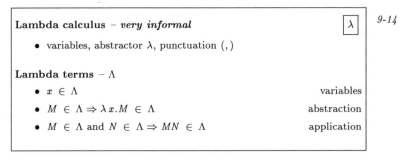

Slide 9-14: The lambda calculus – terms

Syntactically, lambda terms are built from a very simple syntax, figuring variables, the abstractor λ (that is used to bind variables in an expression), and punctuation symbols. Abstractors may be used to abstract a lambda term M into a function $\lambda x.M$ with parameter x. The expression $\lambda x.M$ must be read as denoting the function with body M and formal parameter x. The variable x is called the bound variable, since it is bound by the abstractor λ. In addition to function abstraction, we also have (function) application, which is written as the juxtaposition of two lambda terms. See slide 9-14.

Behaviorally, lambda terms have a number of properties, as expressed in the laws given in slide 9-15.

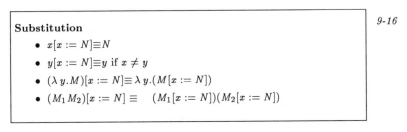

Slide 9-15: The lambda calculus – laws

The most important rule is the *beta conversion* rule, which describes in a manner of speaking how parameter passing is handled. In other words function call, that is the application $(\lambda x.M)N$, results in the function body M in which N is substituted for x. Two other laws are the so-called extensionality axioms, which express how equality of lambda terms is propagated into application and function abstraction. These laws impose constraints upon the models characterizing the meaning of lambda terms.

Substitution   *9-16*

- $x[x := N] \equiv N$
- $y[x := N] \equiv y$ if $x \neq y$
- $(\lambda y.M)[x := N] \equiv \lambda y.(M[x := N])$
- $(M_1 M_2)[x := N] \equiv \quad (M_1[x := N])(M_2[x := N])$

Slide 9-16: The lambda calculus – substitution

Substitution is defined by induction on the structure of lambda terms. A variable y is replaced by N (for a substitution $[x := N]$) if y is x and remains y otherwise. A substitution $[x := N]$ performed on an abstraction $\lambda y.M$ results in substituting N for x in M if x is not y. If x is identical to y, then y must first be replaced by a fresh variable (not occurring in M). A substitution performed on an application simply results in applying the substitution to both components of the application. See slide 9-16.

Some examples of *beta conversion* are given in slide 9-17. In the examples, for simplicity we employ ordinary arithmetical values and operators. This does not perturb the underlying λ-theory, since both values and operations may be expressed as proper λ-terms.

Note that the result of a substitution may still contain free variables (as in the third example) that may be bound in the surrounding environment (as in the fourth example).

Lambda calculus may be used to state properties of functions (and other programming constructs) in a general way.

9-17

Examples

$(\lambda x.x)1 = x[x := 1] = 1$

$(\lambda x.x + 1)2 = (x + 1)[x := 2] = 2 + 1$

$(\lambda x.x + y + 1)3 = (x + y + 1)[x := 3] = 3 + y + 1$

$(\lambda y.(\lambda x.x + y + 1)3)4) =$

$\qquad\qquad ((\lambda x.x + y + 1)3)[y := 4] = 3 + 4 + 1$

Slide 9-17: Beta conversion – examples

9-18

Properties

- $\forall M (\lambda x.x) M = M$ \hfill identity
- $\forall F \exists X.FX = X$ \hfill fixed point

Proof: take $W = \lambda x.F(xx)$ and $X = WW$, then

$$X = WW = (\lambda x.F(xx)) W = F(WW) = FX$$

Slide 9-18: The lambda calculus – properties

Consider, for example, the statement that the identity function works for each lambda term as expected. The quantification with respect to M indicates that in each possible model for the lambda calculus (that respects the extensionality axioms given above) the identity $(\lambda x.x)M = M$ holds. See slide 9-18.

As another example, consider the statement that each function F has a fixed point, that is a value X for which $FX = X$. The proof given above, however, does not give us any information concerning the actual contents of the fixed point, but merely proves its existence. In the following (see section 9.6) we will write $\mathbf{Y}\ (F)$ for the fixed point of a function F.

In Barendrecht (1984), an extensive account is given of how to construct mathematical models for the lambda calculus. A semantics of our type calculus may be given in terms of such models; however we will not pursue this any further here.

9.4.1   A simple type calculus

In our first version of a type calculus we will restrict ourselves to a given set of basic types (indicated by the letter ρ) and function types (written $\sigma \to \tau$, where σ stands for the domain and τ for the range or codomain). This version of the typed lambda calculus (with subtyping) is called $\lambda_{\leqslant}$ in Pierce (1993) from which most of the material is taken. The $\lambda_{\leqslant}$ calculus is a first order calculus, since it does not involve quantification over types. See slide 9-19.

The structure of type expressions is given by the definition

$$\tau ::= \rho \mid \tau_1 \to \tau_2$$

where we use τ as a type identifier and ρ as a meta variable for basic types. The expressions of our language, that we indicate with the letter e, are similar to lambda terms, except for the typing of the abstraction variable in $\lambda x : \tau.e$.

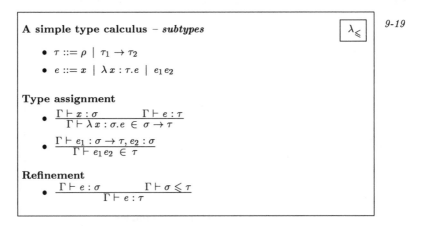

A simple type calculus – subtypes $\lambda_{\leqslant}$ 9-19

- $\tau ::= \rho \mid \tau_1 \to \tau_2$
- $e ::= x \mid \lambda x : \tau.e \mid e_1 e_2$

Type assignment

- $$\frac{\Gamma \vdash x : \sigma \qquad \Gamma \vdash e : \tau}{\Gamma \vdash \lambda x : \sigma.e \in \sigma \to \tau}$$

- $$\frac{\Gamma \vdash e_1 : \sigma \to \tau, e_2 : \sigma}{\Gamma \vdash e_1 e_2 \in \tau}$$

Refinement

- $$\frac{\Gamma \vdash e : \sigma \qquad \Gamma \vdash \sigma \leqslant \tau}{\Gamma \vdash e : \tau}$$

Slide 9-19: The subtype calculus

To determine whether an expression e is correctly typed (with some type expression τ) we need type assignment rules, as given above. Typing is usually based on a collection of assumptions Γ, that contains the typing of expressions occurring in the expression for which we are determining the type. In the type assignment rules and the (subtyping) refinement rules, the phrase $\Gamma \vdash e : \tau$ means that the expression e has type τ, under the assumption that the type assignments in Γ are valid. When Γ is empty, as in $\vdash e : \tau$, the type assignment holds unconditionally. Occasionally, we write $\Gamma \vdash e \in \tau$ instead of $\Gamma \vdash e : \tau$ for readability. These two expressions have identical meaning.

The premises of a type assignment rule are given above the line. The type assignment given below the line states the assignment that may be made on the basis of these premises.

For example, the first type assignment rule states that, assuming $\Gamma \vdash x : \sigma$ (x has type σ) and $\Gamma \vdash e : \tau$ (e has type τ) then $\Gamma \vdash \lambda x : \sigma.e \in \sigma \to \tau$, in other words the abstraction $\lambda x : \sigma.e$ may be validly typed as $\sigma \to \tau$.

Similarly, the second type assignment rule states that applying a function $e_1 : \sigma \to \tau$ to an expression e_2 of type σ results in an (application) expression $e_1 e_2$ of type τ.

We may assume the basic types denoted by ρ to include (integer) subranges, records and variants. As a consequence, we may employ the subtyping rules given in section 9.2 to determine the subtyping relation between these types. The (subtyping) refinement rule repeated here expresses the substitutability property of subtypes, which allows us to consider an expression e of type σ, with $\sigma \leqslant \tau$, as being of type τ.

In slide 9-20, some examples are given illustrating the assignment of types to expressions. Type assignment may to a certain extent be done automatically, by type inference, as for example in ML, see Milner *et al.* (1990). However, in general, typing is not decidable when we include the more powerful type expressions treated later. In those cases the programmer is required to provide sufficient type information to enable the type checker to determine the types.

Examples   *9-20*

- $S = \lambda x : Int.x + 1$
  $S : Int \to Int$

- $twice = \lambda f : Int \to Int. \lambda y : Int.f(f(y))$
  $twice : (Int \to Int) \to Int \to Int$

Application

- $S0 = 1 \in Int$

- $twice(S) = \lambda x.SSx \in Int \to Int$

Slide 9-20: Subtypes – examples

When we define the successor function S as $\lambda x : Int.x + 1$ then we may type S straightforwardly as being of type $Int \to Int$. Similarly, we may type the (higher order) function *twice* as being of type $(Int \to Int) \to Int \to Int$. Note that the first argument to *twice* must be a function. Applying *twice* to a function argument only results in a function. When applied to S it results in a function of type $Int \to Int$ that results in applying S twice to its (integer) argument. The subtyping rules (partly imported from section 9.2) work as expected. We may define, for example, a function $+ : Real \times Real \to Int$ as a subtype of $+ : Int \times Int \to Int$ (according to the contra-variant subtyping rule for functions).

Subtyping in C++ Subtyping is supported in C++ only to a very limited extent. Function subtypes are completely absent. However, class subtypes due to derivation by inheritance may be employed. Also, built-in conversions are provided, some of which are in accordance with the subtyping requirements, and some of which, unfortunately, violate the subtyping requirements. Built-in conversions exist, for example, between *double* and *int*, in both ways. However, whereas the conversion from *int* to *double* is safe, the other way around may cause loss of information by truncation.

The type system sketched in slide 9-19 is quite easily mapped to a C++ context. For example, we may mimic the functions S and *twice* as given in slide 9-20 in C++ as:

```
int S(int x) { return x+1; }
int twice(int f(int), int y) { return f(f(y)); }
```

```
int twice_S(int y) { return twice(S,y); }
```

Nevertheless, the type system of C++ imposes some severe restrictions. For example, functions may not be returned as a value from functions. (Although we may provide a workaround, when we employ the *operator*() function for objects.)

The absence of function subtyping becomes clear when, for example, we call the function *twice* with the function *SD*, which is defined as:

```
int SD(double x) { return x+1; }
```

According to the subtyping rules and in accordance with the substitutability requirement, we employ *SD* whenever we may employ *S*. But not so in C++.

We run into similar limitations when we try to refine an object class descriptions following the object subtype refinement rules.

```
class P {                                          P        9-21
public:
P() { _self = 0; }
virtual P* self() {
        return _self?_self->self():this;
        }
virtual void attach(C* p) {
        _self = p;
        }
private:
P* _self;
};

class C : public P {                            C ⩽ P
public:
C() : P(this) { }
C* self() {                                    ANSI/ISO
        return _self?_self->self():this;
        }
void attach(P* p) {                            rejected
        p->attach(self());
        }
void redirect(C* c) { _self = c; }
private:
C* _self;
};
```

Slide 9-21: Subtyping in C++

Suppose we have a parent class *P* which offers the member functions *self* and *attach*, as in slide 9-21. The meaning of the function *self* is that it de-references the *_self* variable if it is non-zero and delivers *this* otherwise. (See section 4.1 for an example of its use.) The function *attach* may be used to connect an instance of *C* to the *_self* variable.

The class *C* in its turn inherits from *P* and redefines *self* and *attach*. Syntactically, both refinements are allowed, due to the function subtype refinements rules. The function *self* is redefined to deliver a more tightly specified result, and the *attach* function is allowed to take a wider range of arguments.

In a number of compilers for C++, both redefinitions are considered illegal. However, in the ANSI/ISO standard of C++, redefining a member function to deliver a subtype (that is, derived class) pointer will be allowed. Redefining *attach*, as has been done for *C* is probably not a wise thing to do, since it changes the semantics of *attach* as defined for the parent class *P*. In effect, it allows us to write $c \rightarrow attach(p)$ instead of $p \rightarrow attach(c \rightarrow self())$, for $P * p$ and $C * c$. Nevertheless, from a type theoretical perspective, there seem to be no grounds for forbidding it.

9.4.2 Intersection types

We define our second version of the typed lambda calculus $(\lambda_\wedge)$ as an extension of the first version $(\lambda_\leqslant)$, an extension which provides facilities for (*ad hoc*) overloading polymorphism. Our extension consists of adding a type expression $\bigwedge[\tau_1, \ldots, \tau_n]$ which denotes a finite conjunction of types. Such a conjunction of types, that we will also write as $\tau_1 \wedge \ldots \wedge \tau_n$ is called an intersection type. The idea is that an expression e of type $\bigwedge[\tau_1, \ldots, \tau_n]$ is correctly typed if $e : \tau_i$ for some i in $1..n$. This is expressed in the type assignment rule given in slide 9-22.

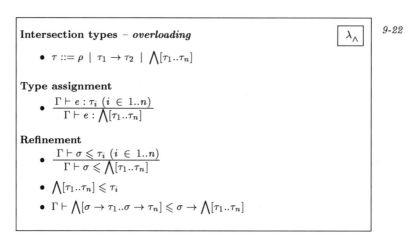

Slide 9-22: The intersection type calculus

The subtyping rule for intersection types states that any subtype of a type occurring in the intersection type $\bigwedge[\tau_1, \ldots, \tau_n]$ is itself a subtype of the intersection type.

In addition we have two subtyping rules without premises, the first of which says that the intersection type itself may be regarded as a subtype of any of its components. In other words, from a typing perspective an intersection type is equal (hence may be replaced by) any of its component types.

Also, we may refine a function, with domain σ, which has an intersection type $\bigwedge[\tau_1, \ldots, \tau_n]$ as its range into an intersection type consisting of functions $\sigma \to \tau_i$ for $i = 1..n$.

Intersection types allow us to express a limited form of overloading, by enumerating a finite collection of possible types. Since the collection of types comprising an intersection type is finite, we do not need a higher order calculus here, although we might have used type abstraction to characterize intersection types.

Examples   *9-23*

- $+ : \bigwedge[Int \times Int \to Int, Real \times Real \to Real]$

- $Int \to Int \leqslant \bigwedge[Int \to Int, Real \to Real]$

- $Msg \to Obj1 \wedge Msg \to Obj2 \leqslant Msg \to \bigwedge[Obj1, Obj2]$

Slide 9-23: Intersection types – examples

A typical example of an intersection type is presented by the addition operator, overloaded for integers and reals, which we may define as

$$+ : \bigwedge[Int \times Int \to Int, Real \times Real \to Real]$$

According to our refinement rule, we may specialize an intersection type into any of its components. For example, when we have an intersection type defining a mapping for integers and a mapping for reals, we may choose the one that fits our purposes best. This example illustrates that intersection types may be an important tool for realizing optimizations that depend upon (dynamic) typing.

Similarly, we may refine a generic function working on objects into a collection of (specialized) functions by dividing out the range type. See slide 9-23. The resulting intersection type itself may subsequently be specialized into one of the component functions. In Castagna *et al.* (1993), a similar kind of type is used to model the overloading of methods in objects, that may but need not necessarily be related by inheritance. The idea is to regard message passing to objects as calling a polymorphic function that dispatches on its first argument. When the type of the first argument is compatible with multiple functions (which may happen for methods that are refined in the inheritance hierarchy) the most specific function component is chosen, that is the method with the minimal object type. A similar idea is encountered in CLOS, which allows for the definition of *multi-methods* for which dynamic dispatching takes place for all arguments. (A problem that occurs in modeling methods as overloaded functions is that the subtyping relation between methods no longer holds, due to the domain contravariance requirement. See Castagna *et al.* (1993) for a possible solution.)

Overloading in C++ Although C++ does not provide support for subtyping, it does provide extensive support for function overloading. Given a collection of functions (overloading a particular function name) C++ employs a *system of matches* to select the function that is most appropriate for a particular call.

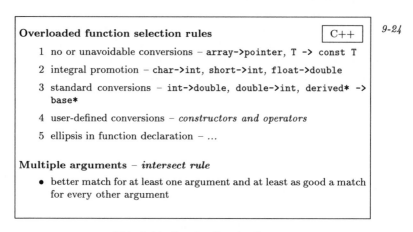

9-24

Slide 9-24: Overloading in C++

Matches may involve built-in or user-defined conversions. The general rule underlying the application of conversions is that *conversions that are considered less error-prone and surprising are to be preferred over the others*. This rule is reflected in the ordering of the C++ overloading selection rules depicted in slide 9-24.

According to the rules, the absence of conversions is to be preferred. For compatibility, with C, *array* to *pointer* conversions are applied automatically, and also *T* to `const` T conversions are considered as unproblematic. Next, we have the integral promotion rules, allowing for the conversion of *char* to *int* and *short* to *int*, for example. These conversions are also directly inherited from C, and are safe in the sense that no information loss occurs. Further, we have the standard conversions such as *int* to *double* and `derived*` to `base*`, user-defined conversions (as determined by the definition of one-argument constructors and conversion operators), and the ... ellipsis notation, which allows us to avoid type-checking in an arbitrary manner.

For selecting the proper function from a collection of overloaded functions with multiple arguments, the so-called *intersect* rule is used, which states that the function is selected with a better match for at least one argument and at least as good a match for every other argument. In the case that no *winner* can be found because there are multiple candidate functions with an equally good match, the compiler issues an error, as in the example below:

```
void f(int, double);
void f(double, int);
```

```
f(1,2.0);                                                      f(int, double);
f(2.0,1);                                                      f(double,int);
f(1,1);                                                        error: ambiguous
```

The reason that C++ employs a system of matches based on declarations and actual parameters of functions is that the graph of built-in conversions (as inherited from C) contains cycles. For example, implicit conversions exist from *int* to *double* and *double* to *int* (although in the latter case the C++ compiler gives a warning). Theoretically, however, the selection of the best function according to the subtype relation would be preferable. However, the notion of *best* is not unproblematic in itself. For example, consider the definition of the overloaded function *f* and the classes *P* and *C* in slide 9-25.

9-25

```
class P;
class C;

void f(P* p) { cout << "f(P*)"; }              (1)
void f(C* c) { cout << "f(C*)"; }              (2)

class P {
public:
virtual void f() { cout << "P::f"; }           (3)
};

class C : public P {
public:
virtual void f() { cout << "C::f"; }           (4)
};
```

Slide 9-25: Static versus dynamic selection

What must be considered the best function *f*, given a choice between (1), (2), (3) and (4)?

```
P* p = new P;                                  static and dynamic P*
C* c = new C;                                  static and dynamic C*
P* pc = new C;                                 static P*, dynamic C*

f(p);                                          f(P*)
f(c);                                          f(C*)
f(pc);                                         f(P*)

p->f();                                        P::f
c->f();                                        C::f
pc->f();                                       C::f
```

In the example given above, we see that for the functions f (corresponding to
(1) and (2)) the choice is determined by the static type of the argument, whereas
for the member functions f (corresponding to (3) and (4)) the choice is determined
by the dynamic type.

We have a dilemma. When we base the choice of functions on the dynamic
type of the argument, the function subtype refinement rule is violated. On the
other hand, adhering to the domain contravariance property seems to lead to
ignoring the potentially useful information captured by the dynamic type of the
argument.

9.4.3   Bounded polymorphism

Our next extension, which we call $F_\leqslant$, involves (bounded) universal quantification.
For technical reasons we need to introduce a primitive type Top, which may be
considered as the supertype of all types (including itself). Also we need type
abstraction variables, that we will write as α and β. Our notation for a universally
quantified (bounded) type is $\forall \alpha \leqslant \sigma.\tau$, which denotes the type τ with the type
variable α replaced by any subtype σ' of σ. In a number of cases, we will simply
write $\forall \alpha.\tau$, which must be read as $\forall \alpha \leqslant Top.\tau$. Recall that any type is a subtype
of Top. Observe that, in contrast to $\lambda_\leqslant$ and $\lambda_\wedge$, the calculus $F_\leqslant$ is second order
(due to the quantification over types).

In addition to the (value) expressions found in the two previous calculi, $F_\leqslant$
introduces a *type abstraction* expression of the form $\Lambda \alpha \leqslant \tau.e$ and a *type instantiation* expression of the form $e[\tau]$. The type abstraction expression $\Lambda \alpha \leqslant \tau.e$ is used
in a similar way as the function abstraction expression, although the abstraction
involves types and not values. Similar to the corresponding type expression,
we write $\Lambda \alpha.e$ as an abbreviation for $\Lambda \alpha \leqslant Top.e$. The (complementary) type
instantiation statement is written as $e[\tau]$, which denotes the expression e in which
the type identifier τ is substituted for the type variable bound by the first type
abstractor.

The type assignment rule for type abstraction states that, when we may type
an expression e as being of type τ (under the assumption that $\alpha \leqslant \sigma$), then we
may type $\Lambda \alpha \leqslant \sigma.e$ as being of type $\forall \alpha \leqslant \sigma.\tau$.

The type assignment rule for type instantiation characterizes the relation
between type instantiation and substitution (which is notationally very similar).
When we have an expression e of type $\forall \alpha \leqslant \sigma.\tau$ and we have that $\sigma' \leqslant \sigma$, then
$e[\sigma']$ is of type $\tau[\alpha := \sigma']$, which is τ with σ' substituted for α. See slide 9-26.

The refinement rule for bounded types states the subtyping relation between
two bounded types. We have that $\forall \alpha \leqslant \sigma'.\tau'$ is a subtype of $\forall \alpha \leqslant \sigma.\tau$ whenever
$\sigma \leqslant \sigma'$ and $\tau' \leqslant \tau$. Notice that the relation is contravariant with respect to the
types bounding the abstraction, similar as for the domains of function subtypes
in the function subtyping rule.

In contrast to the polymorphism due to object type extensions and overloading, bounded polymorphism (employing type quantifiers) is an example of what
we have called parametric polymorphism. In effect, this means that we must

---

Bounded polymorphism – *abstraction* $\boxed{F_\leqslant}$ *9-26*

- $\tau ::= Top \mid \alpha \mid \rho \mid \tau_1 \to \tau_2 \mid \forall \alpha \leqslant \tau_1.\tau_2$
- $e ::= x \mid \lambda x : \tau.e \mid e_1 e_2 \mid \Lambda \alpha \leqslant \tau.e \mid e[\tau]$

Type assignment

- $$\frac{\Gamma, \alpha \leqslant \sigma \vdash e : \tau}{\Gamma \vdash \Lambda \alpha \leqslant \sigma.e \in \forall \alpha \leqslant \sigma.\tau}$$

- $$\frac{\Gamma, e : \forall \alpha \leqslant \sigma.\tau \qquad \Gamma \vdash \sigma' \leqslant \sigma}{\Gamma \vdash e[\sigma'] \in \tau[\alpha := \sigma']}$$

Refinement

- $$\frac{\Gamma \vdash \sigma \leqslant \sigma' \qquad \Gamma \vdash \tau' \leqslant \tau}{\Gamma \vdash \forall \alpha \leqslant \sigma'.\tau' \leqslant \forall \alpha \leqslant \sigma.\tau}$$

Slide 9-26: The bounded type calculus

explicitly give a type parameter to instantiate an object or function of a bounded (parametric) type, similar to when we use a template in C++.

The examples given in slide 9-27 illustrate how we may define and subsequently type parametric functions. In these examples, we employ the convention that in the absence of a bounding type we assume *Top* as an upper limit. The examples are taken from Cardelli and Wegner (1985).

Examples   *9-27*

- $id = \Lambda \alpha. \lambda x : \alpha.x$
  $id : \forall \alpha.\alpha \to \alpha$
- $twice1 = \Lambda \alpha. \lambda f : \Lambda \beta.\beta \to \beta. \lambda x : \alpha.f[\alpha](f[\alpha](x))$
  $twice1 : \forall \alpha. \forall \beta.(\beta \to \beta) \to \alpha \to \beta$
- $twice2 = \Lambda \alpha. \lambda f : \alpha \to \alpha. \lambda x : \alpha.f(f(x))$
  $twice2 : \forall \alpha.(\alpha \to \alpha) \to \alpha \to \alpha$

Applications

- $id[Int](3) = 3$
- $twice1[Int](id)(3) = 3$
- $twice1[Int](S) = illegal$
- $twice2[Int](S)(3) = 5$

Slide 9-27: Parametrized types – examples

The (generic) identity function *id* is defined as $\Lambda \alpha. \lambda x : \alpha.x$, which states that when we supply a particular type, say *Int*, then we obtain the function $\lambda x : Int.x$. Since the actual type used to instantiate *id* is not important, we may type *id* as being of type $\forall \alpha.\alpha \to \alpha$. In a similar way, we may define and type the two (generic) variants of the function *twice*. Notice the difference between the two definitions of *twice*. The first variant requires the function argument itself to be of a generic type, and fails (is incorrectly typed) for the successor function S which is (non generic) of type $Int \to Int$. In contrast, the second variant accepts S, and we may rely on the automatic conversion of $id : \forall \alpha.\alpha \to \alpha$ to $id[Int] : Int \to Int$ (based on the second type assignment rule) to accept *id* as well.

The interplay between *parametric* and *inclusion* polymorphism is illustrated in the examples presented in slide 9-28. Recall that inclusion polymorphism is based on the subtyping relation between records (which states that refinement of a record type involves the addition of components and/or refinement of components that already belong to the super type).

Bounded quantification 9-28

- $g = \Lambda \alpha \leqslant \{one : Int\}. \lambda x : \alpha.(x.one)$
  $g : \forall \alpha \leqslant \{one : int\}.\alpha \to Int$

- $g' = \Lambda \beta.\Lambda \alpha \leqslant \{one : \beta\}. \lambda x : \alpha.(x.one)$
  $g' : \forall \beta.\forall \alpha \leqslant \{one : \beta\}.\alpha \to \beta$

- $move = \Lambda \alpha \leqslant Point. \lambda p : \alpha. \lambda d : Int.(p.x := p.x + d); p$
  $move : \forall \alpha \leqslant Point. \alpha \to Int \to \alpha$

Application

- $g'[Int][\{one : Int, two : Bool\}](\{one = 3, two = true\}) = 3$
- $move[\{x : Int, y : Int\}](\{x = 0, y = 0\})(1) = \{x = 1, y = 0\}$

Slide 9-28: Bounded quantification – examples

The first example defines a function g that works on a record with at least one component *one* and delivers as a result the value of the component *one* of the argument record. The function g' is a generalized version of g that abstracts from the particular type of the *one* component. Notice that both g and g' may be applied to any record that conforms to the requirement stated in the bound, such as the record $\{one = 3, two = true\}$.

As another example of employing bounds to impose requirements, look at the function *move* that is defined for subtypes of *Point* (which we assume to be a record containing x and y coordinates). It expects a record (that is similar to or extends *Point*) and an (integer) distance, and as a result delivers the modified record.

Discussion Parametric polymorphism is an important means to incorporate subtyping in a coherent fashion. Apart from Pierce (1993), from which we have taken most of the material presented here, we may mention Plotkin and Abadi (1993) as a reference for further study. In Pierce (1993) a calculus $F_\wedge$ is also introduced in which intersection polymorphism is expressed by means of an explicit type variable. The resulting type may be written as $\forall \alpha \in \{...\}$, where

{...} denotes a finite collection of types. As already mentioned, intersection types may also be used to model inclusion polymorphism (see Castagna *et al.*, 1993).

It is an interesting research issue to explore the relation between parametric polymorphism and inclusion polymorphism further along this line. However, we will not pursue this line here. Instead, in the next section we will look at another application of parametric polymorphism, namely existential types that allow us to abstract from hidden component types. This treatment is based on Cardelli and Wegner (1985). In the last section of this chapter, we will look in more detail at the role of self-reference in defining (recursive) object types, following Cook *et al.* (1990). We will conclude this chapter with some observations concerning the relevance of such type theories for actual programming languages. In particular, we will show that Eiffel is not type consistent.

Type abstraction in C++ Type abstraction in C++ may occur in various guises. One important means of type abstraction is to employ what we have called polymorphic base class hierarchies. For example, the function *move*, which was somewhat loosely characterized in slide 9-28, may be defined in C++ as follows:

```
Point* move(Point* p, int d);                require int Point::x
Point* move(Point* p, int d) { p.x += d; return p; }
```

In effect, the function *move* accepts a pointer to an instance of *Point*, or any class derived from *Point*, satisfying the requirement that it has a public integer data member *x*.

Similar restrictions generally hold when instantiating a template class, but in contrast to base class subtyping requirements, these restrictions will only be verified at link time.

9-29

```
template< class T >              requires T::value()
class P {
public:
P(T& r) : t(r) {}
int operator==( P<T>& p) {
        return t.value() == p.t.value();
        }
private:
T& t;
};
```

Slide 9-29: Type abstraction in C++

Consider the template class definition given in slide 9-29. Evidently, for the comparison function to operate properly, each instantiation type substituted for the type parameter *T* must satisfy the requirement that it has a public member function *value*.

```
template< class T >
class A {                                          A<T>
public:
virtual T value() = 0;
};

class Int : public A<int> {          Int ≤ A<int>
public:
Int(int n = 0) : _n(n) {}
int value() { return _n; }
private:
int _n;
};
```

9-30

Slide 9-30: Type instantiation

Such a requirement may also be expressed by defining an abstract class A defining a pure virtual member function *value*. See slide 9-30. The restrictions on instantiating P may then be stated informally as the requirement that each instantiation type T must be a subtype of $A<X>$ for arbitrary type X. The class *Int* is an example of a type complying with the implicit requirements imposed by the definition of P. An example of using P is given below

```
Int i1, i2;
P<Int> p1(i1), p2(i2);
if ( p1 == p2 ) cout << "OK" << endl;                        OK
```

Note, however, that the derivation of $A<int>$ is by no means necessary or in any way enforced by C++.

9.5   Existential types – hiding

Existential types were introduced in Cardelli and Wegner (1985) to model aspects of data abstraction and hiding. The language introduced in Cardelli and Wegner (1985) is essentially a variant of the typed lambda calculi we have looked at previously.

Our new calculus, that we call $F_\exists$, is an extension of $F_\leq$ with type expressions of the form $\exists \alpha \leq \sigma.\tau$ (to denote existential types) and expressions of the form $pack[\alpha = \sigma \ in \ \tau]$ (to denote values with hidden types). Intuitively, the meaning of the expression $pack[\alpha = \sigma \ in \ \tau]$ is that we represent the abstract type α occurring in the type expression τ by the actual type σ (in order to realize the value e). Following the type assignment rule, we may actually provide an instance of a subtype of the bounding type as the realization of a hidden type. See slide 9-31.

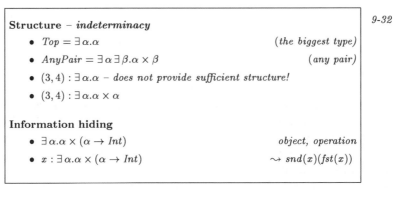

Slide 9-31: The existential type calculus

The subtyping refinement rule is similar to the refinement rule for universally quantified types. Notice also here the contravariance relation between the bounding types.

More interesting is what bounding types allow us to express. (As before, we will write $\exists\alpha.\tau$ to denote $\exists\alpha \leqslant Top.\tau$.) First, existential types allow us to indicate that the realization of a particular type exists, even if we do not indicate how. The declaration $e : \exists\alpha.\tau$ tells us that there must be some type σ such that e of type τ can be realized. Apart from claiming that a particular type exists, we may also provide information concerning its structure, while leaving its actual type undetermined.

Structure – *indeterminacy*   *9-32*

- $Top = \exists\alpha.\alpha$ *(the biggest type)*
- $AnyPair = \exists\alpha\,\exists\beta.\alpha \times \beta$ *(any pair)*
- $(3,4) : \exists\alpha.\alpha$ – *does not provide sufficient structure!*
- $(3,4) : \exists\alpha.\alpha \times \alpha$

Information hiding

- $\exists\alpha.\alpha \times (\alpha \to Int)$ *object, operation*
- $x : \exists\alpha.\alpha \times (\alpha \to Int)$ $\leadsto snd(x)(fst(x))$

Slide 9-32: Existential types – examples

For example, the type $\exists\alpha.\alpha$ (which may clearly be realized by any type) carries no information whatsoever, hence it may be considered to be equal to the type *Top*. More information, for example, is provided by the type $\exists\alpha\,\exists\beta.\alpha \times \beta$ which defines the product type consisting of two (possibly distinct) types. (A product may be regarded as an unlabeled record.) The type $\exists\alpha.\alpha \times \alpha$ gives even more information concerning the structure of a product type, namely that the two components are of the same type. Hence, for the actual product $(3,4)$ the latter is the best choice. See slide 9-32.

Existential types may be used to impose structure on the contents of a value, while hiding its actual representation. For example, when we have a variable x of which we know that it has type $\exists \alpha.\alpha \times (\alpha \rightarrow Int)$ then we may use the second component of x to produce an integer value from its first component, by $snd(x)(fst(x))$, where fst extracts the first and snd the second component of a product. Clearly, we do not need to know the actual representation type for α.

A similar idea may be employed for (labeled) records. For example, when we have a record x of type $\exists \alpha.\{val : \alpha, op : \alpha \rightarrow Int\}$ then we may use the expression $x.op(x.val)$ to apply the operation op to the value val. Again, no knowledge of the type of val is required in this case. However, to be able to use an element of an existential type we must provide an actual representation type, by instantiating the type parameter in a *pack* statement.

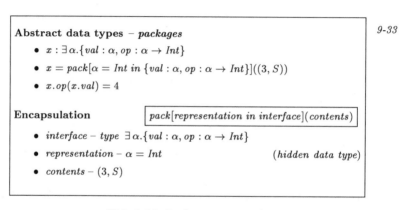

Abstract data types – *packages*   *9-33*

- $x : \exists \alpha.\{val : \alpha, op : \alpha \rightarrow Int\}$
- $x = pack[\alpha = Int\ in\ \{val : \alpha, op : \alpha \rightarrow Int\}]((3, S))$
- $x.op(x.val) = 4$

Encapsulation $\boxed{pack[representation\ in\ interface](contents)}$

- *interface* – *type* $\exists \alpha.\{val : \alpha, op : \alpha \rightarrow Int\}$
- *representation* – $\alpha = Int$ (*hidden data type*)
- *contents* – $(3, S)$

Slide 9-33: Packages – examples

The *pack* statement may be regarded as an encapsulation construct, allowing us to protect the inner parts of an abstract data type. When we look more closely at the *pack* statement, we can see three components. First, we have an *interface* specification corresponding to the existential type associated with the *pack* expression. Secondly, we need to provide an actual representation of the hidden type, *Int* in the example above. And finally, we need to provide the actual contents of the structure. See slide 9-33.

In combination with the notion of *objects as records*, existential types provide us with a model of abstract data types. Real objects, however, require a notion of *self-reference* that we have not captured yet. In the next section we will conclude our exploration of type theories by discussing the F_μ calculus that supports recursive (object) types and inheritance.

Hiding in C++ Naturally, the classical way of data hiding in C++ is to employ *private* or *protected* access protection. Nevertheless, an equally important means is to employ an abstract interface class in combination with forwarding.

```
class event {                                    event          9-34
protected:
event(event* x) : ev(x) {}
public:
int type() { return ev->type(); }
void* rawevent() { return ev; }
private:
event* ev;
};

class xevent : public event {                      X
public:
int type() { return X->type(); }
private:
struct XEvent* X;
};
```

Slide 9-34: Hiding in C++

For example, as depicted in slide 9-34, we may offer the user a class *event* which records information concerning events occurring in a window environment, while hiding completely the underlying implementation. The actual *xevent* class realizing the type *event* may itself need access to other structures, as for example those provided by the X window environment. Yet, the *xevent* class itself may remain entirely hidden from the user, since events are not something created directly (note the protected constructor) but only indirectly, generally by the system in response to some action by the user.

9.6 Self-reference

Recursive types are compound types in which the type itself occurs as the type of one of its components. Self-reference in objects clearly involves recursive types since the expression *self* denotes the object itself, and hence has the type of the object. In F_μ, our extension of $F_\leqslant$ taken from Cook *et al.* (1990), recursive types are written as $\mu\alpha.\tau[\alpha]$, where μ is the recursion abstractor and α a type variable. The dependence of τ on α is made explicit by writing $\tau[\alpha]$. We will use the type expressions $\mu\alpha.\tau[\alpha]$ to type object specifications of the form $\lambda(self).\{a_1 = e_1, \ldots, a_n = e_n\}$ as indicated by the type assignment rule below. Object specifications may be regarded as class descriptions in C++ or Eiffel.

The subtype refinement rule for recursive types states that $\mu\alpha.\sigma[\alpha] \leqslant \mu\beta.\tau[\beta]$ if we can prove that $\sigma \leqslant \tau$ assuming that $\alpha \leqslant \beta$.

Self-reference – *recursive types* $\boxed{F_\mu}$ 9-35

- $\tau ::= \ldots \mid \mu\alpha.\tau[\alpha]$
- $e ::= \ldots \mid \lambda(self).\{a1 = e_1, \ldots, a_n = e_n\}$

Type assignment

$$\bullet \quad \frac{\Gamma \vdash e_i : \tau_i \qquad (i = 1..n)}{\Gamma \vdash \lambda(self).\{a1 = \tau_1, .., a_n = \tau_n\} \in \mu\alpha.\{a1 : \tau_1, .., a_n : \tau_n\}[\alpha]}$$

Refinement

$$\bullet \quad \frac{\Gamma, \alpha \leqslant \beta \vdash \sigma \leqslant \tau}{\Gamma \vdash \mu\alpha.\sigma[\alpha] \leqslant \mu\beta.\tau[\beta]}$$

Slide 9-35: A calculus for recursive types

An object specification $\lambda(self).\{\ldots\}$ is a function with the type of the actual object as its domain and (naturally) also as its range. For convenience we will write an object specification as $\lambda(self).F$, where F denotes the object record, and the type of an object specification as $\mu\alpha.F[\alpha]$, where $F[\alpha]$ denotes the (abstract) type of the record F.

To obtain from an object specification $\lambda(self).F$ the object that it specifies, we need to find some type σ that types the record specification F as being of type σ precisely when we assign the expression $self$ in F the type σ. Technically, this means that the object of type σ is a fixed point of the object specification $\lambda(self).F(self)$ which is of type $\sigma \to \sigma$. We write this as $\mathbf{Y}\ (\lambda(self).F(self)) : \sigma$, which says that the object corresponding to the object specification is of type σ. See slide 9-35.

Object semantics – *fixed point $\sigma = F[\sigma]$*   9-36

- $\mathbf{Y}\ (\lambda(self).F(self)) : \sigma$

Unrolling – *unraveling a type*

- $\mu\alpha.F[\alpha] = F[\mu\alpha.F[\alpha]]$

Example

$$T = \mu\alpha.\{a : int, c : \alpha, b : \alpha \to \alpha\}$$
$$T_1 = \{a : int, c : T, b : T \to T, d : bool\}$$
$$T_2 = \mu\alpha.\{a : int, c : \alpha, b : T \to T, d : bool\}$$
$$T_3 = \mu\alpha.\{a : int, c : \alpha, b : \alpha \to \alpha, d : bool\}$$

$T_1, T_2 \leqslant T, T_3 \nleqslant T$ (contravariance)

Slide 9-36: Recursive types – examples

Finding the fixed point of a specification involves technically a procedure known as *unrolling*, which allows us to rewrite the type $\mu\alpha.F[\alpha]$ as $F[\mu\alpha.F[\alpha]]$. Notice that unrolling is valid, precisely because of the fixed point property. Namely, the object type σ is equal to $\mu\alpha.F[\alpha]$, due to the type assignment rule, and we have that $\sigma = F[\sigma]$. See slide 9-36.

Unrolling allows us to reason on the level of types and to determine the subtyping relation between recursive subtypes. Consider, for example, the type declarations T and T_i ($i = 1..3$) above. Based on the refinement rules for object records, functions and recursive types, we may establish that $T_1 \leqslant T$, $T_2 \leqslant T$ but $T_3 \not\leqslant T$. To see that $T_1 \leqslant T$, it suffices to substitute T for α in F, where $F = \{a : Int, c : \alpha, b : \alpha \to \alpha\}$. Since $F[T] = \{a : Int, c : T, b : T \to T\}$ we immediately see that T_1 only extends T with the field $d : Bool$, hence $T_1 \leqslant T$. A similar line of reasoning is involved to determine that $T_2 \leqslant T$, only we need to unroll T_2 as well. We must then establish that $c : T_2 \leqslant c : T$, which follows from an application of the refinement rule.

To show that $T_3 \not\leqslant T$, let $G[\beta] = \{a : Int, c : \beta, b : \beta \to \beta, d : Bool\}$ and $T_3 = \mu\beta.G[\beta]$. Then, by unrolling, $T_3 = G[T_3] = \{a : Int, c : T_3, b : T_3 \to T_3, d : Bool\}$. Now, suppose that $T_3 \leqslant T$, then $G[T_3] \leqslant F[T_3]$ and consequently $b : T_3 \to T_3$ must refine $b : T \to T$. But from the latter requirement it follows that $T_3 \leqslant T$ and that $T \leqslant T_3$ (by the contravariance rule for function subtyping). However, this leads to a contradiction since T is clearly not equal to T_3 because T_3 contains a field $d : Bool$ that does not occur in T.

Although analyses of this kind are to some extent satisfactory in themselves, the reader may wonder where this all leads to. In the following we will apply these techniques to show the necessity of dynamic binding and to illustrate that inheritance may easily violate the subtyping requirements.

Inheritance In section 9.3 we have characterized inheritance as an incremental modification mechanism, which involves a dynamic interpretation of the expression *self*. In the recursive type calculus F_μ we may characterize this more precisely, by regarding a derived object specification C as the result of applying the modifier M to the object specification P. We employ the notation $C = \lambda(self).P(self)$ with $\{a'_1 = e'_1, \ldots, a'_k = e'_k\}$ to characterize derivation by inheritance, and we assume the modifier M corresponding with $\{a'_1 = e'_1, \ldots, a'_k = e'_k\}$ to extend the record associated with P in the usual sense. See slide 9-37.

The meaning of an object specification C is again a fixed point $\mathbf{Y}(C)$, that is $\mathbf{Y}(\lambda(self).M(self)(P(self)))$. Now when we assume that the object specification is of type $\tau \to \tau$ (and hence $\mathbf{Y}(P)$ of type τ), and that C is of type $\sigma \to \sigma$ (and hence $\mathbf{Y}(C)$ of type σ), then we must require that $\sigma \leqslant \tau$ to obtain a properly typed derivation. We write $C \leqslant P$ whenever $\sigma \leqslant \tau$.

A first question that arises when we characterize inheritance as incremental modification is how we obtain the meaning of the composition of two object specifications.

Let (parent) P and (child) C be defined as above. Now, if we know that the type of $\mathbf{Y}(P)$ is τ then we may simply characterize $\mathbf{Y}(C)$ as being of type $\sigma = \{i : Bool, id : \tau, b : Bool\}$. However, when we delay the typing of the P

9-37

Inheritance – $C = P + M$

- $P = \lambda(self).\{a1 = e1, \ldots, a_n = e_n\}$
- $C = \lambda(self).P(self)$ **with** $\{a1' = e1', \ldots, a_k' = e_k'\}$

Semantics – $\mathbf{Y}\ (C) = \mathbf{Y}\ (\lambda(self).M(self)(P(self)))$

- $P : \sigma \to \sigma \Rightarrow \mathbf{Y}\ (P) : \sigma$
- $C = \lambda(s).M(s)(P(s)) : \tau \to \tau \Rightarrow \mathbf{Y}\ (C) : \tau$

Slide 9-37: Inheritance semantics – self-reference

9-38

Object inheritance – *dynamic binding*
$P = \lambda(self).\{i = 5, id = self\}$
$C = \lambda(self).P(self)$ **with** $\{b = true\}$
$\mathbf{Y}\ (P) : \tau$ where $\tau = \mu\,\alpha.\{i : int, id : \alpha\}$ and $P : \tau \to \tau$
Simple typing – $\mathbf{Y}\ (C) : \sigma = \{i : int, id : \tau, b : bool\}$
Delayed – $\mathbf{Y}\ (C) : \sigma' = \mu\,\alpha.\{i : int, id : \alpha, b : bool\}$
We have $\sigma' \leqslant \sigma$ (more information)

Slide 9-38: Object inheritance – dynamic binding

component (by first composing the record specifications before abstracting from *self*) then we may obtain $\sigma' = \mu\,\alpha.\{i : Int, id : \alpha, b : Bool\}$ as the type of $\mathbf{Y}\ (C)$. By employing the refinement rule and unrolling we can show that $\sigma' \leqslant \sigma$. Hence, delayed typing clearly provides more information and must be considered as the best choice. Note, however, that both $\sigma' \leqslant \tau$ and $\sigma \leqslant \tau$ hold. See slide 9-38.

A second, important question that emerges with respect to inheritance is how self-reference affects the subtyping relation between object specifications related by inheritance.

Consider the object specifications P and C given in slide 9-39. In the (derived) specification C, the method eq is redefined to include an equality test for the b component. However, when we determine the object types corresponding to the specifications P and C we observe that $C \not\leqslant P$.

The reasoning is as follows. For $\mathbf{Y}\ (P) : \tau$ and $\mathbf{Y}\ (C) : \sigma$, we have that $\sigma = \mu\,\beta.\{i : Int, id : \beta \to Bool, b : Bool\}$ which is (by unrolling) equal to $\{i : Int, id : \sigma \to Bool, b : Bool\}$. Now suppose that $\sigma \leqslant \tau$, then we have that $\{i : Int, eq : \sigma \to Bool, b : Bool\}$ is a subtype of $\{i : Int, eq : \tau \to Bool\}$ which is true when $eq : \sigma \to Bool \leqslant eq : \tau \to Bool$ and hence (by contravariance) when $\sigma \leqslant \tau$. Clearly, this is impossible. Hence $\sigma \not\leqslant \tau$.

We have a problem here, since the fact that $C \not\leqslant P$ means that the type checker will not be able to accept the derivation of C from P, although C is clearly dependent on P. The solution to our problem lies in making the type dependency involved in deriving C from P explicit. Notice, in this respect, that

Contravariance

- $P = \lambda(self).\{i = 5, eq = \lambda(o).(o.i = self.i)\}$

  $C = \lambda(self).P(self)$ **with** $\{b = true,$
  $\qquad eq = \lambda(o).(o.i = self.i$ *and*
  $\qquad o.b = self.b)$
  $\}$

Y $(P) : \tau$ where $\tau = \mu\alpha.\{i : int, eq : \alpha \to bool\}$
Y $(C) : \sigma$ where $\sigma = \mu\alpha.\{i : int, id : \alpha \to bool, b : bool\}$
However $\sigma \not\leqslant \tau$ **(subtyping error)**

Slide 9-39: Object inheritance – contravariance

in the example above we have omitted the type of the abstraction variable in the definition of *eq*, which would have to be written as $\lambda x : \mathbf{Y}\ (P).x.i = self.i$ (and in a similar way for C) to do it properly.

Type dependency The expression *self* is essentially of a polymorphic nature. To make the dependency of object specification on *self* explicit, we will employ an explicit type variable similar as in $F_{\leqslant}$.

Let $F[\alpha]$ stand for $\{a_1 : \tau_1, \ldots, a_n : \tau\}$ as before. We may regard $F[\alpha]$ as a type function, in the sense that for some type τ the expression $F[\tau]$ results in a type. To determine the type of an object specification we must find a type σ that satisfies both $\sigma \leqslant F[\sigma]$ and $F[\sigma] \leqslant \sigma$.

Type dependency – *is polymorphic*

- Let $F[\alpha] = \{m_1 : \sigma_1, \ldots, m_j : \sigma_j\}$ (type function)

- $P : \forall\alpha \leqslant F[\alpha].t \to F[\alpha]$

- $P = \Lambda\alpha \leqslant F[\alpha].\lambda(self : \alpha).\{m_1 : e1, \ldots, m_j : e_j\}$

F-bounded constraint $\alpha \leqslant F[\alpha]$
Object instantiation: **Y** $(P[\sigma])$ for $\sigma = \mu t.F[t]$
We have $P[\sigma] : \sigma \to F[\sigma]$ because $F[\sigma] = \sigma$

Slide 9-40: Bounded type constraints

We may write an object specification as $\Lambda\alpha \leqslant F[\alpha].\lambda(self : \alpha).\{a_1 = e_1, \ldots, a_n = e_n\}$, which is typed as $\forall\alpha \leqslant F[\alpha].\alpha \to F[\alpha]$. The constraint that $\alpha \leqslant F[\alpha]$, which is called an *F-bounded constraint*, requires that the subtype substituted for α is a (structural) refinement of the record type $F[\alpha]$. As before, we have that $\mathbf{Y}\ (P[\sigma]) = \sigma$ with $\sigma = \mu\alpha.F[\alpha]$, which differs from our previous definition only by making the type dependency in P explicit. See slide 9-40.

Now, when applying this extended notion of object specification to the characterization of inheritance, we may relax our requirement that $\mathbf{Y}$ (C) must be a subtype of $\mathbf{Y}$ (P) into the requirement that $G[\alpha] \leqslant F[\alpha]$ for any α, where F is the record specification of P and G the record specification of C.

Inheritance   *9-41*

$$P = \Lambda\alpha \leqslant F[\alpha].\lambda(self : \alpha).\{\ldots\}$$
$$C = \Lambda\alpha \leqslant G[\alpha].\lambda(self : \alpha).P[\alpha](self) \text{ with } \{\ldots\}$$

with recursive types
$F[\alpha] = \{i : int, id : \alpha \to bool\}$
$G[\alpha] = \{i : int, id : \alpha \to bool, b : bool\}$
Valid, because $G[\alpha] \leqslant F[\alpha]$
However $\mathbf{Y}$ $(C[\sigma]) \nleqslant_{subtype} \mathbf{Y}$ $(P[\tau])$

Slide 9-41: Inheritance and constraints

For example, when we declare $F[\alpha]$ and $G[\alpha]$ as in slide 9-41, we have that $G[\alpha] \leqslant F[\alpha]$ for every value for α. However, when we find types σ and τ such that $\mathbf{Y}$ $(C[\sigma])$: σ and $\mathbf{Y}$ $(P[\tau])$: τ we (still) have that $\sigma \nleqslant \tau$. Conclusion, inheritance allows more than subtyping. In other words, our type checker may guard the structural application of inheritance, yet will not guarantee that the resulting object types behaviorally satisfy the subtype relation.

Discussion – Eiffel is not type consistent We have limited our exploration of the recursive structure of objects to (polymorphic) object variables. Self-reference, however, may also occur to *class variables*. The interested reader is referred to Cook *et al.* (1990). The question that interests us more at this particular point is what benefits we may have from the techniques employed here and what lessons we may draw from applying them.

One lesson, which should not come as a surprise, is that a language may allow us to write programs that are accepted by the compiler yet are behaviorally incorrect. However, if we can determine syntactically that the subtyping relations between classes is violated we may at least expect a warning from the compiler. So one benefit, possibly, is that we may improve our compilers on the basis of the type theory presented in this chapter. Another potential benefit is that we may better understand the trade-offs between the particular forms of polymorphism offered by our language of choice.

The analysis given in Cook *et al.* (1990) indeed leads to a rather surprising result. Contrary to the claims made by its developer, Cook *et al.* (1990) demonstrate that Eiffel is *not* type consistent. The argument runs as follows. Suppose we define a class C with a method *eq* that takes an argument of a type similar to the type of the object itself (which may be written in Eiffel as *like Current*). We further assume that the class P is defined in a similar way, but with an integer field i and a method *eq* that tests only on i. See slide 9-42.

We may then declare variables v and p of type P. Now suppose that we have

```
Inheritance != subtyping                              Eiffel     9-42

    class C inherit P redefine eq
    feature
      b : Boolean is true;
      eq( other : like Current ) : Boolean is
      begin
           Result := (other.i = Current.i) and
                        (other.b = Current.b)
      end
    end C
```

Slide 9-42: Inheritance and subtyping in Eiffel

an object c of type C, then we may assign c to v and invoke the method eq for v, asking whether p is equal to v, as in

```
p,v:P, c:C
```

```
v:=c;
v.eq(p);                                              error p has no b
```

Since v is associated with an instance of C, but syntactically declared as being of type P, the compiler accepts the call. Nevertheless, when p is associated with an instance of P trouble will arise, since (due to dynamic binding) the method eq defined for C will be invoked while p not necessarily has a field b.

When we compare the definition of C in Eiffel with how we may define C in C++, then we are immediately confronted with the restriction that we do not have such a dynamic typing mechanism as *like Current* in C++. Instead, we may use overloading, as shown in slide 9-43.

```
                                                           9-43
    class C : public P {                      C++
    int b;
    public:
    C() { ... }
    bool eq(C& other) { return other.i == i &&
        other.b == b; }
    bool eq(P& other) { return other.i == i; }
    };
```

Slide 9-43: Inheritance and subtyping in C++

When we would have omitted the P variant of eq, the compiler complains about hiding a virtual function. However, the same problem arises when we define eq

to be virtual in P, unless we take care to explicitly cast p into either a C or P reference. (Overloading is also used in Liskov and Wing (1993) to solve a similar problem.) In the case we choose for a non-virtual definition of *eq*, it is determined statically which variant is chosen and (obviously) no problem occurs.

Considering that determining equality between two objects is somehow orthogonal to the functionality of the object proper, we may perhaps better employ externally defined overloaded functions to express relations between objects. This observation could be an argument to have overloaded functions apart from objects, not as a means to support a hybrid approach but as a means to characterize relations between objects in a type consistent (polymorphic) fashion.

Summary

This chapter has treated polymorphism from a foundational perspective.

In section 1, we looked at abstract inheritance as employed in knowledge representation.

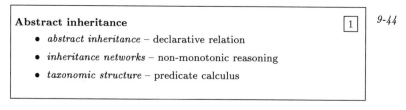

Slide 9-44: Section 9.1: Abstract inheritance

We discussed the non-monotonic aspects of inheritance networks and looked at a first order logic interpretation of taxonomic structures.

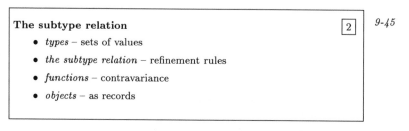

Slide 9-45: Section 9.2: The subtype relation

In section 2, a characterization of types as sets of values was given. We looked at a formal definition of the subtype relation and discussed the refinement rules for functions and objects.

In section 3, we discussed types as a means to prevent errors, and distinguished between various flavors of polymorphism, including parametric polymorphism,

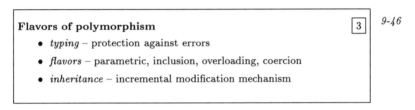

Slide 9-46: Section 9.3: Flavors of polymorphism

inclusion polymorphism, overloading and coercion. Inheritance was characterized as an incremental modification mechanism, resulting in inclusion polymorphism.

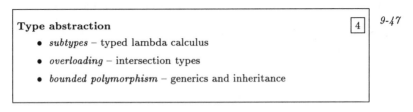

Slide 9-47: Section 9.4: Type abstraction

In section 4, some formal type calculi were presented, based on the typed lambda calculus. These included a calculus for simple subtyping, a calculus for overloading, employing intersection types, and a calculus for bounded polymorphism, employing type abstraction. Examples were discussed illustrating the (lack of) features of the C++ type system.

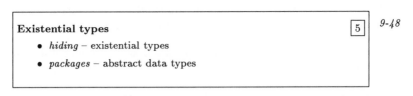

Slide 9-48: Section 9.5: Existential types

In section 5, we looked at a calculus employing existential types, modeling abstract data types and hiding by means of packages and type abstraction.

Finally, in section 6, we discussed self-reference and looked at a calculus employing recursive types. It was shown how object semantics may be determined by unrolling, and we studied the semantic interpretation of dynamic binding. Concluding this chapter, an example was given showing an inconsistency in the Eiffel type system.

6 | 9-49

Self-reference

- *self-reference* – recursive types
- *object semantics* – unrolling
- *inheritance* – dynamic binding
- *subtyping* – inconsistencies

Slide 9-49: Section 9.6: Self-reference

Questions

1. How would you characterize inheritance as applied in knowledge representation? Discuss the problems that arise due to non-monotony.

2. How would you render the meaning of an inheritance lattice? Give some examples.

3. What is the meaning of a type? How would you characterize the relation between a type and its subtypes?

4. Characterize the subtyping rules for ranges, functions, records and variant records. Give some examples.

5. What is the intuition underlying the function subtyping rule?

6. What is understood by the notion of *objects as records*? Explain the subtyping rule for objects.

7. Discuss the relative merits of typed formalisms and untyped formalisms.

8. What flavors of polymorphism can you think of? Explain how the various flavors are related to programming language constructs.

9. Discuss how inheritance may be understood as an incremental modification mechanism.

10. Characterize the simple type calculus $\lambda_{\leqslant}$, that is the syntax, type assignment and refinement rules. Do the same for $F_{\wedge}$ and $F_{\leqslant}$.

11. Type the following expressions: (a) $\{a = 1, f = \lambda x : Int.x + 1\}$, (b) $\lambda x : Int.x * x$, and (c) $\lambda x : \{b : Bool, f : \{a : Bool\}\} \rightarrow Int.x.f(x)$.

12. Verify whether: (a) $f' : 2..5 \rightarrow Int \leqslant f : 1..4 \rightarrow Int$, (b) $\{a : Bool, f : Bool \rightarrow Int\} \leqslant \{a : Int, f : Int \rightarrow Int\}$, and (c) $\lambda x : \{a : Bool\} \rightarrow Int \leqslant \lambda x : \{a : Bool, f : Bool \rightarrow Int\} \rightarrow Int$.

13. Explain how you may model abstract data types as existential types.

14. What realizations of the type $\exists \alpha.\{a : \alpha, f : \alpha \to Bool\}$ can you think of? Give at least two examples.

15. Prove that $\mu \alpha.\{c : \alpha, b : \alpha \to \alpha\} \not\leqslant \mu \alpha.\{b : \alpha \to \alpha\}$.

16. Prove that $\mu \alpha.\{c : \alpha, b : \tau \to \alpha\} \leqslant \tau$, for $\tau = \mu \alpha.\{b : \alpha \to \alpha\}$.

Further reading

As further reading I recommend Cardelli and Wegner (1985) and Pierce (1993). As another source of material and exercises consult Palsberg and Schwartzback (1994). Bezem en Grootte (1993) contains a number of relevant papers. An exhaustive overview of the semantics of object systems, in both first order and second order calculi, is further given in Abadi and Cardelli (1996).

10

Behavioral refinement

Ultimately, types are meant to specify behavior in an abstract way. To capture behavioral properties, we will generalize our notion of *types as constraints* to include behavioral descriptions in the form of logical assertions.

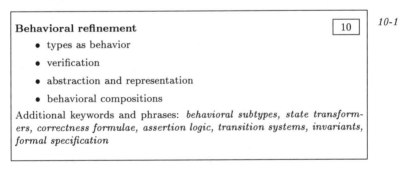

Slide 10-1: Behavioral refinement

In this chapter we will explore the notion of behavioral (sub)types. First we characterize the trade-offs between statically imposed (typing) constraints and dynamic constraints resulting from the specification of behavioral properties. We will provide a brief introduction to the assertion logic underlying the verification of behavioral constraints. Also, we look at how we may characterize the behavior of object-based systems in a mathematical way. Then we will describe the duality between abstraction and representation in defining behavioral subtypes that define concrete realizations of abstract specifications. In particular, we specify the correspondence requirements for behavioral subtypes. We will conclude this chapter by discussing the problems involved in specifying behavioral compositions, and explore what specification techniques are available to model the behavior of object-based systems.

10.1   Types as behavior

In the previous chapter we have developed a formal definition of types and the subtyping relation. However, we have restricted ourselves to (syntactic) signatures only, omitting (semantic) behavioral properties associated with function and object types.

Subtype requirements – *signature and behavior*   *10-2*

  • preservation of behavioral properties

Safety properties – *nothing bad*

  • invariant properties – *true of all states*

  • history properties – *true of all execution sequences*

Slide 10-2: Subtyping and behavior

From a behavioral perspective, the subtype requirements (implied by the substitutability property) may be stated abstractly as *the preservation of behavioral properties*. According to Liskov and Wing (1993), behavioral properties encompass *safety properties* (which express that nothing bad will happen) and *liveness properties* (which express that eventually something good will happen). For safety properties we may further make a distinction between *invariant properties* (which must be satisfied in all possible states) and *history properties* (which hold for all possible execution sequences). See slide 10-2.

Behavioral properties (which are generally not captured by the signature only) may be important for the correct execution of a program. For example, when we replace a *stack* by a *queue* (which both have the same signature if we rename *push* and *insert* into *put*, and *pop* and *retrieve* into *get*) then we will get incorrect results when our program depends upon the *LIFO* (*last-in first-out*) behavior of the stack.

As another example, consider the relation between a type *FatSet* (which supports the methods *insert*, *select* and *size*) and a type *IntSet* (which supports the methods *insert*, *delete*, *select* and *size*). See slide 10-3.

With respect to its signature, *IntSet* merely extends *FatSet* with a *delete* method and hence could be regarded as a subtype of *FatSet*. However, consider the history property stated above, which says that for any (*FatSet*) s, when an integer x is an element of s in state ϕ then x will also be an element of s in any

---

Example – *IntSet ⊄ FatSet*   *10-3*

- *FatSet – insert, select, size*
- *IntSet – insert, delete, select, size*

History property – *not satisfied by IntSet*

- $\forall s : FatSet.\, \forall \phi, \psi : State.\phi{<}\psi \wedge s \in dom(\psi).$
$$\forall x : Int.x \in s_\phi \Rightarrow x \in s_\psi$$

Slide 10-3: History properties – example

state ψ that comes after ϕ. This property holds since instances of *FatSet* do not have a method *delete* by which elements can be removed. Now if we take this property into account, *IntSet* may not be regarded as a subtype of *FatSet*, since instances of *IntSet* may grow and shrink and hence do not respect the *FatSet* history property.

This observation raises two questions. Firstly, how can we characterize the behavior of an object or function and, more importantly, how can we extend our notion of types to include a behavioral description? And secondly, assuming that we have the means to characterize the behavior of a function or object type, how can we verify that a subtype respects the behavioral constraints imposed by the supertype?

The answer to the first question is suggested by the observation that we may also express the constraints imposed by the signature by means of logical formulae that state the constraints as assertions which must be satisfied.

Types as behavior – *constraints*   *10-4*

- $x : 9..11 \Longleftrightarrow x : Int \wedge 9 \leqslant x \leqslant 11$

Behavioral constraints – *signature versus assertions*

- $f(x : 9..11) : 3..5\{\ldots\}$

```
int f(int x) {
    require( 9 <= x  && x <= 11 );
    ...
    promise( 3 <= result && result <= 5);
    return result;
    }
```

Slide 10-4: Types and behavioral constraints

For example, we may express the requirement imposed by typing a variable as an element of an integer subrange also by stating that the variable is an integer variable that respects the bounds of the subrange. Similarly, we can express the typing constraints on the domain and range of a function by means of pre- and post-conditions asserting these constraints. See slide 10-4.

More generally, we may characterize the behavior of a function type by means of pre- and post-conditions and the behavior of an object type by means of pre- and post-conditions for its methods and an invariant clause expressing the invariant properties of its state and behavior. Recall that this is precisely what is captured in our notion of *contract*, as discussed in section 3.3.

With regard to the second question, to verify behavioral properties (expressed as assertions) we need an assertion logic in the style of Hoare. Such a logic will be discussed in the next section. In addition, we need a way in which to verify that (an instance of) a subtype respects the behavioral properties of its supertype. In section 10.4.2 we will give precise guidelines for a programmer to check the behavioral correspondence between two types.

10.2 Verifying behavioral properties

The concern with program correctness stems from a period when projects were haunted by what was called the *software crisis*. Projects delivered software that contained numerous bugs and large programs seemed to become unmanageable, that is never error-free. One of the most radical ideas proposed to counteract the software crisis was to require that programs should formally be proven correct before acceptance. The charm of the idea, I find personally, is that programming in a way becomes imbued with the flavor of mathematics, which may in itself be one of the reasons that the method never became very popular.

10.2.1 State transformers

Proving the correctness of (imperative) programs is based on the notion of *states* and the interpretation of programs as *state transformers*. A *state*, in a mathematical sense, is simply a function that records a value for each variable in the program. For example, having a program S in which the (integer) variable i occurs, and a state ϕ, we may have $\phi(i) = 3$. States may be modified by actions that result from executing the program, such as by an assignment of a value to a variable. We employ *substitutions* to modify a state. As before, substitutions may be defined by an equation, as given in slide 10-5.

Substitutions   *10-5*

$$\phi[x := v](y) = \begin{cases} v & \text{if } x = y \\ \phi(y) & \text{otherwise} \end{cases}$$

Slide 10-5: Substitution

A substitution $\phi[x := v](y)$ states that modifying ϕ by assigning the value v to the variable x then, for a variable y, the state ϕ will deliver v whenever y is identical to x and $\phi(y)$ otherwise.

When we have, for example, an assignment $i = 5$ then we have as the corresponding transition $\phi - i = 5 \rightarrow \phi'$ where $\phi' = \phi[i := 5]$, that is ϕ' is like ϕ except for the variable i for which the value 5 will now be delivered.

Whenever we have a sequence of actions $a_1, \ldots, a_n$ then, starting from a state ϕ_0 we have corresponding state transformations resulting in states $\phi_1, \ldots, \phi_{n-1}$ as intermediary states and ϕ_n as the final state. Often the states ϕ_0 and ϕ_n are referred to as respectively the *input* and *output* state and the program that results in the actions $a_1, \ldots, a_n$ as the *state transformer* modifying ϕ_0 into ϕ_n.

10-6

Program state $- \phi$

- $\phi \in \Sigma : Var \rightarrow Value$

State transformations $-$ *operations $a_1, a_2, \ldots, a_n$*

- $\phi_0 - a_1 \rightarrow \phi_1 \ldots - a_n \rightarrow \phi_n$

Correctness formulae $-$ *Hoare logic*

- $\{P\}S\{Q\}$

Verification

- $\phi_i \xrightarrow{a} \phi_j \wedge \phi_i \models P \Rightarrow \phi_j \models Q$

Slide 10-6: The verification of state transformations

To characterize the actions that result from executing a program, we need an operational semantics that relates the programming constructs to the dynamic behavior of a program. We will study such a semantics in section 10.3.

The requirements a program (fragment) has to meet may be expressed by using predicates characterizing certain properties of a program state. Then, all we need to do is check whether the final state of a computation satisfies these requirements.

Predicates characterizing the properties of a state before and after executing a program (fragment) may be conveniently stated by correctness formulae of the form $\{P\}S\{Q\}$ where S denotes a program (fragment) and P and Q respectively the pre-condition and post-condition associated with S.

A formula of the form $\{P\}S\{Q\}$ is true if, for every initial state ϕ that satisfies P and for which the computation characterized by S terminates, the final state ϕ' satisfies Q. This interpretation of $\{P\}S\{Q\}$ characterizes *partial correctness*, partial since the truth of the formula is dependent on the termination of S (which may, for example, for a *while statement*, not always be guaranteed). When termination can be guaranteed, then we may use the stronger notion of *total correctness*, which makes the truth of $\{P\}S\{Q\}$ no longer dependent on the termination of S.

Pre- and post-conditions may also be used to check invariance properties. As an example, consider the following correctness formula: $\{s = i * (i + 1)/2\}i = i + 1; \ s = s + i; \ \{s = i * (i + 1)/2\}$ It states that the begin and end state of the computation characterized by $i = i + 1; \ s = s + i$ is invariant with respect to the condition $s = i * (i + 1)/2$. As an exercise, try to establish the correctness of this formula!

To verify whether for a particular program fragment S and (initial) state ϕ_i satisfying P the correctness formula $\{P\}S\{Q\}$ holds, we need to compute the (final) state ϕ_j and check that Q is true for ϕ_j. In general, for example in the case of non-deterministic programs, there may be multiple (final) states resulting from the execution of S. For each of these states we have to establish that it satisfies (the post-condition) Q. We call the collection of possible computation sequences of a program fragment S the *traces* of S. Traces characterize the (operational) behavior of a program.

10.2.2 Assertion logic

Reasoning about program states based on the traces of a program may be quite cumbersome. Moreover, a disadvantage is that it relies to a great extent on our operational intuition of the effect of a program on a state. Instead, Hoare (1969) has proposed using an axiomatic characterization of the correctness properties of programming constructs. An axiomatic definition allows us to prove the correctness of a program with respect to the conditions stating its requirements by applying the appropriate inference rules.

Axioms   *10-7*

- assignment – $\{Q[x := e]\}x = e\{Q\}$
- composition – $\{P\}S1\{R\} \wedge \{R\}S2\{Q\} \Rightarrow \{P\}S1; \ S2\{Q\}$
- conditional – $\{P \wedge b\}S\{Q\} \Rightarrow \{P\}if(b)S\{Q\}$
- iteration – $\{I \wedge b\}S\{I\} \Rightarrow \{I\}while(b)S\{I \wedge \neg b\}$

Consequence rules

- $P \rightarrow R \wedge \{R\}S\{Q\} \Rightarrow \{P\}S\{Q\}$
- $R \rightarrow Q \wedge \{P\}S\{R\} \Rightarrow \{P\}S\{Q\}$

Procedural abstraction

- $m(x) \mapsto S(x) \wedge \{P\}S(e)\{Q\} \Rightarrow \{P\}m(e)\{Q\}$

Slide 10-7: The correctness calculus

In slide 10-7 correctness axioms have been given for *assignment, sequential composition, conditional statements* and *iteration*. These axioms rely on the side-effect free nature of expressions in the programming language. Also, they assume convertibility between programming language expressions and the expressions used in the assertion language.

The *assignment* axiom states that for any post-condition Q we can derive the (weakest) pre-condition by substituting the value e assigned to the variable x for x in Q. This axiom is related to the weakest pre-condition calculus introduced by Dijkstra (1976). It is perhaps the most basic axiom in the correctness calculus for imperative programs. As an example, consider the assignment $x = 3$ and the requirement $\{P\}\, x = 3\, \{y = x\}$. Applying the assignment axiom we have $\{y = 3\}\, x = 3\, \{y = x\}$. Consequently, when we are able to prove that P implies $y = 3$, we have, by virtue of the first *consequence* rule, proved that $\{P\}\, x = 3\, \{x = y\}$.

The next rule, for *sequential composition*, allows us to break a program (fragment) into parts. For convenience, the correctness formulae for multiple program fragments that are composed in sequential order are often organized as a so-called proof outline of the form $\{P\}\, S1\, \{R\}\, S2\, \{Q\}$. When sufficiently detailed, proof outlines may be regarded as a proof. For example, the proof outline $\{s = i * (i + 1)/2\}\, i = i + 1;\ \{s + i = i * (i + 1)/2\}\, s = s + i;\ \{s = i * (i + 1)/2\}$ constitutes a proof for the invariance property discussed earlier. Clearly, the correctness formula for the two individual components can be proved by applying the assignment axiom. Using the sequential composition rule, these components can now be easily glued together.

As a third rule, we have a rule for conditional statements of the form $if(b)\, S$. As an example, consider the correctness formula $\{true\}\, if(x>y)\, z = x;\ \{z>y\}$. All we need to prove, by virtue of the inference rule for conditional statements, is that $\{x>y\}\, z = x\, \{z>y\}$ which (again) immediately follows from the assignment axiom.

As the last rule for proving correctness, we present here the inference rule for iterative (*while*) statements. The rule states that whenever we can prove that a certain invariant I is maintained when executing the body of the *while* statement (provided that the condition b is satisfied) then, when terminating the loop, we know that both I and $\neg b$ hold. As an example, the formula $\{true\}$ `while` $(i>0)$ `i--;` $\{i \leqslant 0\}$ trivially follows from the *while* rule by taking I to be *true*.

Actually, the *while* rule plays a crucial role in constructing verifiable algorithms in a structured way. The central idea, advocated among others by Gries (1981), is to develop the algorithm around a well-chosen invariant. Several heuristics may be applied to find the proper invariant starting from the requirements expressed in the (output) predicate stating the post-condition.

In addition to the assignment axiom and the basic inference rules related to the major constructs of imperative programming languages, we may use so-called *structural* rules to facilitate the actual proof of a correctness formula. The first structural (*consequence*) rule states that we may replace a particular pre-condition for which we can prove a correctness formula (pertaining to a program fragment S) by any pre-condition of which the original pre-condition is a consequence, in other words which is stronger than the original pre-condition. Similarly, we may replace a post-condition for which we know a correctness formula to hold by any post-condition that is weaker than the original post-condition. As an example, suppose that we have proved the formula $\{x \geqslant 0\}\, S\, \{x<0\}$ then we may, by simultaneously applying the two consequence rules, derive the formula $\{x>0\}\, S\, \{x \leqslant 0\}$ which amounts to strengthening the pre-condition and weakening the post-condition. The intuition justifying this derivation is that we can safely *promise less and require more*, as it were.

Finally, the rule most important to us in the present context is the inference rule characterizing correctness under *procedural abstraction*. Assuming that we have a function m with formal parameter x (for convenience we assume we have only one parameter, but this can easily be generalized to multiple parameters), of which the (function) body consists of $S(x)$. Now, moreover, assume that we can prove for an arbitrary expression e the correctness formula $\{P\}\, S(e)\, \{Q\}$, with e substituted for the formal parameter x in both the conditions and the function body, then we also have that $\{P\}\, m(e)\, \{Q\}$, provided that P and Q do not contain references to local variables of the function m.

In other words, we may abstract from a complex program fragment by defining a function or procedure and use the original (local) correctness proof by properly substituting actual parameters for formal parameters. The *procedural abstraction* rule, which allows us to employ functions to perform correct operations, may be regarded as the basic construct needed to verify that an object embodies a (client/server) *contract*.

10.3   On the notion of behavior

The assertion logic presented in the previous section allows us to reason about the behavior of a system without explicitly generating the possible sequences of states resulting from the execution of the program. However, underlying the inference rules of our assertion logic we need a mathematical model for the operational behavior of a system.

An operational model is needed to prove the soundness of the inference rules. Further, an operational model may aid in understanding the meaning of particular language constructs and their associated correctness rules. In the following we will sketch the construction of a *transition system* modeling the behavior of an object-based program. Studying the formal semantics is relevant to understanding object orientation only in so far as it provides a means with which to characterize the desired behavior of object creation and message passing in an unambiguous manner.

Transition system A transition system for a program is a collection of rules that collectively describe the effect of executing the statements of the program. A labeled transition system is one that enables us to label the transition from one state to another by some label indicating the observable behavior of a program step.

In the transition system defined below, we will employ states ϕ, which may be decorated by object identifiers α, as in ϕ^α. Object identifiers are created when creating a new instance of an object type τ. We assume newly created object identifiers to be unique.

We assume that each object type τ has a constructor (which is a, possibly empty, statement that we write as S_τ) and an arbitrary number of methods m. Each method m is assumed to be defined by some statement, which we write as $S_m(e)$, for method calls of the form $m(e)$. Also we allow an object α of type τ to have attributes or instance variables v that may be accessed (read-only) as $\alpha.v$ for an object identifier α or $x.v$ for an object variable x (which must have α as its value).

To determine the visible behavior of a program, we will employ labels of the form α (to denote the creation of an object α) and m_α (to indicate the invocation of a method m for object α). We allow transitions to be labeled by sequences of labels that we write as λ and which are concatenated in the usual way.

We will define a transition system for a simple language of which the syntax is defined in slide 10-8.

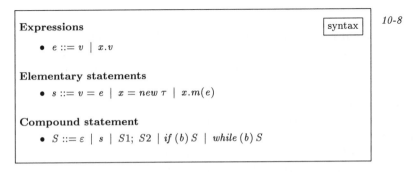

Slide 10-8: The syntax of a simple OO language

Expressions are either local variables v or object instance variables that we write as $x.v$, where x is an object variable. As elementary statements we have $v = e$ (indicating the assignment of (the value of) an expression e to a local variable v), $x = new\ \tau$ (which stands for the creation of a new object of type τ), and $x.m(e)$ (which calls a method m with arguments e for object x). The object variable x is associated with an object identifier α by the state ϕ in which the statement in which x occurs is executed. As compound statements we have an empty statement ε (which is needed for technical reasons), an elementary statement s (as defined above), a sequential composition statement, a conditional statement and an iteration statement, similar to that in the previous section. The transition rules for elementary statements are given in slide 10-9.

The *assignment* rule states that the assignment of (the value of) an expression e to a (local) variable v in state ϕ decorated by an object identifier α results in the empty statement and the state ϕ modified by assigning the value of e in ϕ (which is written as e_ϕ) to the instance variable v of object α. Hence, decorations allow us to work in the local environment of the object indicated by the decoration.

The *object creation* rule states that if we assume a transition $\langle S_\tau, \phi^\alpha \rangle \xrightarrow{\lambda} \langle \varepsilon, \phi' \rangle$ (which states that the constructor for type τ executed in state ϕ decorated by α results in the state ϕ' with behavior λ) then we may interpret the creation

Assignment $\boxed{\text{rules}}$ *10-9*

- $\langle v = e, \phi^\alpha \rangle \to \langle \varepsilon, \phi[\alpha.v := e_\phi] \rangle$

Object creation

- $$\frac{\langle S_\tau, \phi^\alpha \rangle \xrightarrow{\lambda} \langle \varepsilon, \phi' \rangle}{\langle x = new\ \tau, \phi \rangle \xrightarrow{\alpha \cdot \lambda} \langle \varepsilon, \phi'[x := \alpha] \rangle}$$

Method call

- $$\frac{\langle S_m(e), \phi^\alpha \rangle \xrightarrow{\lambda} \langle \varepsilon, \phi' \rangle}{\langle x.m(e), \phi \rangle \xrightarrow{m_\alpha \cdot \lambda} \langle \varepsilon, \phi' \rangle}$$

Slide 10-9: Transition system – rules

of a new τ object to result in behavior $\alpha \cdot \lambda$ (where α is the newly created object identifier) and state ϕ' in which the object variable x has the value α.

Finally, in a similar way, the *method call* rule states that if we assume a transition $\langle S_m(e), \phi^\alpha \rangle \xrightarrow{\lambda} \langle \varepsilon, \phi' \rangle$ (which states that executing the statement $S_m(e)$, that is the code associated with method m and arguments e, for object α in state ϕ, results in behavior λ and state ϕ') then we may interpret the method call $x.m(e)$ in ϕ as a transition to state ϕ' displaying behavior $m_\alpha \cdot \lambda$.

The rules for object creation and method call already indicate that transition rules may be used to construct a complex transition from elementary steps. In other words, a transition system defines a collection of proof rules that allow us to derive (state) transitions and to characterize the behavior that may be observed. To obtain a full derivation, we need in addition to the rules for elementary statements the rules for compound statements listed in slide 10-10.

The *composition* rule states that if a statement S_1 transforms ϕ into ϕ' with behavior λ_1 and S_2 transforms ϕ' into ϕ'' with behavior λ_2 then the compound statement $S_1; S_2$ transforms ϕ into ϕ'' with behavior $\lambda_1 \cdot \lambda_2$.

The *conditional* rules state that, dependent on the value of the boolean b, the statement *if* (b) S has either no effect or results in a state ϕ' assuming that S transforms ϕ into ϕ' with behavior λ.

The *iteration* rules state that dependent on the value of the boolean b the statement *while* (b) S has either no effect or results in a state ϕ' assuming that S transforms ϕ into ϕ' with behavior λ. In contrast to the conditional, an iteration statement is repeated when b is true, in accordance with our operational understanding of iteration.

Example In our rules we have made a distinction between unadorned states ϕ and states ϕ^α decorated with an object identifier α. This reflects the distinction between the execution of a program fragment in a global context and a local context, within the confines of a particular object α.

Assume, for example, that we have defined a counter type *ctr* with a method

---

Composition   [compound]   *10-10*

$$\bullet \quad \frac{\langle S_1, \phi \rangle \xrightarrow{\lambda_1} \langle \varepsilon, \phi' \rangle \qquad \langle S_2, \phi' \rangle \xrightarrow{\lambda_2} \langle \varepsilon, \phi'' \rangle}{\langle S_1; \ S_2, \phi \rangle \xrightarrow{\lambda_1 \cdot \lambda_2} \langle \varepsilon, \phi'' \rangle}$$

Conditional

- $\langle if(b) \ S, \phi \rangle \to \langle \varepsilon, \phi \rangle$ if $\phi(b) \equiv false$

$$\bullet \quad \frac{\langle S, \phi \rangle \xrightarrow{\lambda} \langle \varepsilon, \phi' \rangle}{\langle if(b) \ S, \phi \rangle \xrightarrow{\lambda} \langle \varepsilon, \phi' \rangle} \quad \text{if } \phi(b) \equiv true$$

Iteration

- $\langle while \ (b) \ S, \phi \rangle \to \langle \varepsilon, \phi \rangle$ if $\phi(b) \equiv false$

$$\bullet \quad \frac{\langle S, \phi \rangle \xrightarrow{\lambda} \langle \varepsilon, \phi' \rangle}{\langle while \ (b) \ S, \phi \rangle \xrightarrow{\lambda} \langle while \ (b) \ S, \phi' \rangle} \quad \text{if } \phi(b) \equiv true$$

Slide 10-10: Transition system – compound statement

inc that adds one to an instance variable n. In slide 10-11, a derivation is given of the behavior resulting from a program fragment consisting of the creation of an instance of *ctr*, a method call to *inc* and the assignment of the value of the attribute n of the counter to a variable v.

Program   *10-11*

- $x = new \ ctr; \ x.inc(); \ v = x.n$

Transitions

- $\langle x = new \ ctr, \phi_1 \rangle \xrightarrow{ctr_1} \langle \varepsilon, \phi_1[x := ctr_1] \rangle$ [1]
- $\langle n = n + 1, \phi_2^\alpha \rangle \to \langle \varepsilon, \phi_2[\alpha.n = \alpha.n + 1] \rangle$ [2]
- $\langle x.inc(), \phi_2 \rangle \xrightarrow{inc_\alpha} \langle \varepsilon, \phi_2[\phi_2(x).n := \phi_2(x).n] \rangle$ [2']
- $\langle v = x.n, \phi_3 \rangle \to \langle \varepsilon, \phi_3[v := \phi_3(x).n] \rangle$ [3]

Trace

- $\phi \xrightarrow{\lambda} \phi'$ with $\phi = \phi_1$, $\phi' = \phi_3$ and $\lambda = ctr_1 \cdot inc_\alpha$

Slide 10-11: Transitions – example

To derive the transition $\phi \xrightarrow{\lambda} \phi'$ corresponding with the program fragment $x = new \ ctr; \ x.inc(); \ v = x.n$ we must dissect the fragment and construct transitions for each of its (elementary) statements as shown in [1], [2] and [3]. The second statement, the method call $x.inc()$, needs two transitions [2] and [2'], of which the first represents the execution of the body of *inc* in the local context of the object created in [1] and the second represents the effect of the method call from a global perspective. For the first statement, we have assumed that the constructor for *ctr* is empty and may hence be omitted. Notice that the object identifier α (introduced in [1]) is assumed in [2] to effect the appropriate local changes to n.

After constructing the transitions for the individual statements we may compose these transitions by applying the composition rule and, in this case, identifying ϕ_2 with $\phi_1[x := \alpha]$ and ϕ_3 with $\phi_2[\alpha.n := \alpha.n + 1]$. As observable behavior we obtain $ctr_1 \cdot inc_\alpha$ (where $ctr_1 = \alpha$), which represents the creation of a counter and its subsequent modification by *inc*.

Discussion Transition systems, such as the one given above, were originally introduced as a means to model the behavior of CSP. They have been extensively used to model the operational semantics of programming languages, including concurrent and object-oriented languages. See, for example, America *et al.* (1989) and Eliëns (1992).

In Apt and Olderog (1991), transition systems have been used as a model to prove the soundness and completeness of correctness rules for concurrent programming constructs. Also in America and de Boer (1993), transition systems are used to demonstrate the validity of a proof system for a parallel object-oriented programming language. The interested reader is invited to explore the sources mentioned for further study.

10.4   Objects as behavioral types

A syntax-directed correctness calculus as presented in section 10.2 provides, in principle, excellent support for a problem-oriented approach to program development, provided that the requirements a program has to meet can be made explicit in a mathematical, logical framework.

When specifying requirements, we are primarily interested in the abstract properties of a program, as may be expressed in some mathematical domain. However, when actually implementing the program (and verifying its correctness) we mostly need to take recourse to details we do not wish to bother with when reasoning on an abstract level. In this section we will discuss how we may verify that an abstract type is correctly implemented by a behavioral (implementation) subtype, following America (1990). Also, we will define precise guidelines for determining whether two (behavioral) types satisfy the (behavioral) subtype relation, following Liskov and Wing (1993).

10.4.1   Abstraction and representation

In America (1990) a proposal is sketched to define the functionality of objects by means of *behavioral types*. Behavioral types characterize the behavioral properties of objects in terms of (possible) modifications of an abstract state. So as to be able to ignore the details of an implementation when reasoning about the properties of a particular program, we may employ a *representation abstraction function* which maps the concrete data structures and operations to their counterparts in the abstract domain.

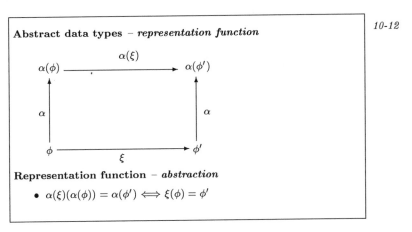

Slide 10-12: Abstraction and representation

The diagram in slide 10-12 pictures the reasoning involved in proving that a particular implementation is correct with respect to a specification in some abstract mathematical domain. Assume that we have, in the concrete domain, an action a that corresponds with a state transformation function ξ. Now assume that we have a similar operation in the abstract domain, that we will write as $\alpha(a)$, with a corresponding state transformation function $\alpha(\xi)$. To prove that the concrete operation a correctly implements the abstract operation $\alpha(a)$, we must prove that the concrete state modification ξ resulting from a corresponds with the modification that occurs in the abstract domain. Technically speaking, we must prove that the diagram above commutes, that is, that $\xi(\phi) = \phi' \iff \alpha(\xi)(\alpha(\phi)) = \alpha(\phi')$ whenever we have that $\phi \xrightarrow{a} \phi'$.

To prove that a particular implementation a respects the abstract operation $\alpha(a)$, for which we assume that it has abstract pre- and post-conditions $\alpha(P)$ and $\alpha(Q)$, we must find a representation invariant I and (concrete) pre- and post-conditions P and Q for which we can prove that $\alpha(P) \wedge I \Rightarrow P$ and that $\alpha(Q) \wedge I \Rightarrow Q$. Furthermore, the representation invariant I must hold before and after the concrete operation a.

The proof strategy outlined above is of particular relevance for object-oriented program development, since the behavior of objects may, as we have already seen, be adequately captured by *contracts*. As an additional advantage, however, the method outlined enables us to specify the behavior of an object in a more abstract way than allowed by contracts as supported by Eiffel.

Realization As an example, consider the specification of a generic *stack* as given in slide 10-13. The specification of the stack is based on the (mathematically) well-known notion of *sequences*. We distinguish between empty sequences, that we write as $\langle\rangle$, and non-empty (finite) sequences, that we write as $\langle x1, \ldots, x_n \rangle$. Further, we assume to have a concatenation operator for which we define $s \cdot \langle\rangle = \langle\rangle \cdot s = s$ and $\langle x1, \ldots, x_n \rangle \cdot \langle y1, \ldots, y_m \rangle = \langle x1, \ldots, x_n, y_1, \ldots, y_m \rangle$. A sequence is employed to represent the state of the stack.

Sequences – *abstract domain*   *10-13*

- empty sequence – $\langle\rangle$

- concatenation – $\langle x1, .., x_n \rangle \cdot \langle y1, .., y_m \rangle = \langle x1, .., x_n, y1, .., y_m \rangle$

Specification

```
type stack T {
s : seq T;
axioms:
{true}push(t : T){s' = s · ⟨t⟩}
{s ≠ ⟨⟩}pop(){s = s' · ⟨result⟩}
};
```

Slide 10-13: The specification of a stack

The operations *push* and *pop* may conveniently be defined with reference to the sequence representing the (abstract) state of the stack. We use s and s' to represent the state respectively before and after the operation. The operations themselves are completely specified by their respective pre- and post-conditions. Pushing an element e results in concatenating the one-element sequence $\langle e \rangle$ to the stacks state. For the operation *pop* we require that the state of the stack must be non-empty. The post-condition specifies that the resulting state s' is a prefix of the original state, that is the original state with the last element (which is returned as a result) removed.

To prove that a particular implementation of the *stack* is conformant with the type definition given above we must prove that $\{I \wedge pre(\alpha(m(e)))\}m(e)\{I' \wedge post(\alpha(m(e)))\}$ for both methods *push* and *pop*. These proofs involve both an abstraction function α and a representation invariant I, relating the abstract state of the stack to the concrete state of the implementation.

Now consider an implementation of the generic stack in C++, as given in slide 10-14.

To prove that this implementation may be regarded as an element of the (abstract) type *stack*, we must find a representation (abstraction) function to map the concrete implementation to the abstract domain, and further we must specify a *representation invariant* that allows us to relate the abstract properties to the properties of the implementation.

For the implementation in slide 10-14, the abstraction function α simply cre-

```
template<class T >                    implementation          10-14

class as {
int t;
T a[MAX];
public:
as() { t = 0; }
void push(T e) {
        require(t<MAX-1); a[t++] = e;
        }
T pop() { require(t>0); return a[--t]; }

invariant:
        0 <= t && t < MAX;
};
```

Slide 10-14: The realization of a stack

ates the sequence of length t, with elements $a[0], \ldots, a[t-1]$. The representation invariant, moreover, gives an explicit definition of this relation. See slide 10-15.

10-15

Abstraction function

- $\alpha(a, t) = <a[0], \ldots, a[t]>$

Representation invariant

- $I(a, t, s) \equiv t = length(s) \wedge t \geqslant 0 \wedge s = \alpha(a, t)$

Slide 10-15: Abstraction function and representation invariant

In order to verify that our implementation of the abstract data type *stack* is correct (that is as long as the bound MAX is not exceeded), we must show, given that the representation invariant holds, that the pre-conditions of the concrete operations imply the pre-conditions of the corresponding abstract operations, and, similarly, that the post-conditions of the abstract operations imply the post-conditions of the concrete operations.

First, we show that for the operation *push* the post-condition of the abstract type specification is indeed stronger than the (implicit) post-condition of the implementation. This is expressed by the following formula.

$$s' = s \cdot <e> \wedge I(a', t', s') \Rightarrow t' = t + 1 \wedge a'[t'] = e$$

Since we know that $I(a', t', s')$, we may derive that $t' = t + 1$ and $a'[t'] = e$.

To establish the correctness of the operation *pop*, we must prove that the pre-condition specified for the abstract operation is indeed stronger than the pre-condition specified for the concrete operation, as expressed by the formula

$$I(a, t, s) \land s \neq <> \Rightarrow t > 0$$

It is easy to see that $t>0$ immediately follows from the requirement that the sequence is non-empty.

Finally, to prove that the operator *pop* leaves the stack in a correct state, we must prove that $s = s' \cdot <result> \land I(a', t', s') \Rightarrow result = a'[t] \land t' = t - 1$ which is done in a similar manner as for *push*.

10.4.2   The correspondence relation

Behavioral refinement is not restricted to the realization of abstract specifications. We will now look at a definition of behavioral refinement, following Liskov and Wing (1993), that may serve as a guideline for programmers to define behavioral subtypes, both abstract and concrete, including subtypes extending the behavioral repertoire of their supertypes.

In Liskov and Wing (1993) the relation between behavioral types is explained by means of a so-called *correspondence mapping*, that relates a subtype to its (abstract) supertype.

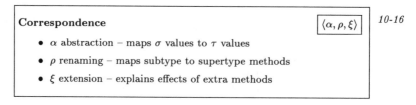

Slide 10-16: The subtype correspondence mapping

A *correspondence mapping* is a triple consisting of an *abstraction* function α (that projects the values of the subtype on the value domain of the supertype), a *renaming* ρ (that defines the relation between methods defined in both types) and an *extension* map ξ (that defines the meaning of additional methods). See slide 10-16. Technically, the function α must be *onto*, that is each value of the supertype domain must be representable by one or more values of the subtype domain. Generally, when applying the abstraction function, we loose information (which is irrelevant from the perspective of the supertype), for example the specific ordering of items in a container.

To determine whether a type σ is a (behavioral) subtype of a type τ, one has to define a correspondence mapping $\langle \alpha, \rho, \xi \rangle$ and check the issues listed in slide 10-17. First, syntactically, we must check that the signature of σ and τ satisfy the (signature) subtyping relation defined in the previous chapter. In other words, for each method m associated with the object type τ (which we call m_τ), and corresponding method m_σ (which is determined by applying the

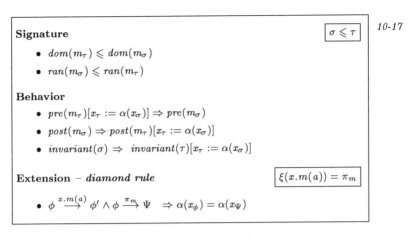

Slide 10-17: Behavioral subtyping constraints

renaming ρ) we must check the (contravariant) function subtyping rule, that is $dom(m_\tau) \leqslant dom(m_\sigma)$ and $ran(m_\sigma) \leqslant ran(m_\tau)$, where ran is the range or result type of m.

Secondly, we must check that the behavioral properties of σ respect those of τ. In other words, for each method m occurring in τ we must check that $pre(m_\tau)[x_\tau := \alpha(x_\sigma)] \Rightarrow pre(m_\sigma)$ and that $post(m_\sigma) \Rightarrow post(m_\tau)[x_\tau := \alpha(x_\sigma)]$. Moreover, the invariant characterizing σ must respect the invariant characterizing τ, that is $invariant(\sigma) \Rightarrow invariant(\tau)[x_\tau := \alpha(x_\sigma)]$. The substitutions $[x_\tau := \alpha(x_\sigma)]$ occurring in the behavioral rules are meant to indicate that each variable of type τ must be replaced by a corresponding variable of type σ to which the abstraction function is applied (in order to obtain a value in the (abstract) domain of τ).

And thirdly, in the final place, it must be shown that the extension map ξ is well-defined. The extension map must be defined in such a way that each method call for an object x of type σ, which we write as $x.m(a)$ where a represents the arguments to the call, is mapped to a program π_m in which only calls appear to methods shared by σ and τ (modulo renaming) or external function or method calls. In addition the *diamond rule* must be satisfied, which means that the states ϕ' and ψ resulting from applying respectively $x.m(a)$ and π_m in state ϕ must deliver identical values for x from the perspective of τ, that is after applying the abstraction function. In other words, extension maps allow us to understand the effect of adding new methods and to establish whether they endanger behavioral compatibility.

In Liskov and Wing (1993) a distinction is made between *constructors* (by which objects are created), *mutators* (that modify the state or value of an object) and *observers* (that leave the state of an object unaffected). Extension maps are only needed for mutator methods. Clearly, for *observer* methods the result of ξ is empty, and *constructors* are taken care of by the abstraction function.

Behavioral subtypes The behavioral subtyping rules defined above are applicable to arbitrary (sub)types, and not only to (sub)types defined by inheritance. As an example, we will sketch (still following Liskov and Wing (1993)) that a *stack* may be defined as a behavioral subtype of the type *bag*. Recall that a *bag* is a *set* allowing duplicates. See slide 10-18.

Behavioral subtypes $\boxed{stack \leqslant bag}$ *10-18*

- *bag* – *put, get*
- *stack* – *push, pop, settop*

Representation

- *bag* – $\langle elems, bound \rangle$ multiset
- *stack* – $\langle items, limit \rangle$ sequence

Behavior – *put/push*

$put(i)$:
   require $size(b.elems) < b.bound$
   promise $b' = \langle b.elems \uplus \{i\}, b.bound \rangle$

$push(i)$:
   require $length(s.items) < s.limit$
   promise $s' = \langle s.items \cdot i, s.limit \rangle$

Slide 10-18: Behavioral subtypes – example

Let the type *bag* support the methods $put(i : Int)$ and $get() : Int$ and assume that the type *stack* supports the methods $push(i : Int)$, $pop() : Int$ and in addition a method $settop(i : Int)$ that replaces the top element of the stack with its argument. Now, assume that a *bag* is represented by a pair $\langle elems, bound \rangle$, where *elems* is a multiset (which is a set which may contain multiple elements of the same value) and *bound* is an integer indicating the maximal number of elements that may be in the *bag*. Further, we assume that a *stack* is represented as a pair $\langle items, limit \rangle$, where *items* is a sequence and *limit* is the maximal length of the sequence. For example $\langle \{1, 2, 7, 1\}, 12 \rangle$ is a legal value of *bag* and $\langle 1 \cdot 2 \cdot 7 \cdot 1, 12 \rangle$ is a legal value of *stack*.

The behavioral constraints for respectively the method *put* for *bag* and *push* for *stack* are given as pre- and post-conditions in slide 10-18. To apply *put*, we require that the size of the multiset is strictly smaller than the bound and we ensure that the element i is inserted when that pre-condition is satisfied. The multi-set union operator $\uplus$ is employed to add the new element to the bag. Similarly, for *push* we require the length of the sequence to be smaller than the limit of the stack and we then ensure that the element is appended to the sequence. As before, we use the primed variables b' and s' to denote the value of respectively the bag b and the stack s after applying the operations, respectively *put* and *push*.

Proceeding from the characterization of *bag* and *stack* we may define the correspondence mapping $\langle \alpha, \rho, \xi \rangle$ as in slide 10-19.

Correspondence | $stack \rightarrow bag$ | *10-19*

- $\alpha(\langle items, limit \rangle) = \langle mk\_set(items), limit \rangle$
  where

  $$mk\_set(\varepsilon) = \varnothing$$
  $$mk\_set(e \cdot s) = mk\_set(s) \uplus \{e\}$$

- $\rho(push) = put,\ \rho(pop) = get$
- $\xi(s.settop(i)) = s.pop();\ s.push(i);$

Slide 10-19: Behavioral subtypes – correspondence

To map the representation of a stack to the bag representation we use the function *mk_set* (which is inductively defined to map the empty sequence to the empty set and to transform a non-empty sequence into the union of the one-element multiset of its first element and the result of applying *mk_set* to the remaining part). The stack *limit* is left unchanged, since it directly corresponds with the bound of the bag.

The renaming function ρ maps *push* to *put* and *pop* to *get*, straightforwardly. And, the extension map describes the result of *settop(i)* as the application of (subsequently) *pop()* and *push(i)*.

                                                                                    10-20

Proof obligations – *push/put*

- $size(\alpha(s).elems) < \alpha(s).bound$
  $\Rightarrow$
  $length(s.items) < s.limit$
- $s' = \langle s.items \cdot i, s.limit \rangle$
  $\Rightarrow$
  $\alpha(s') = \quad \langle \alpha(s).elems \uplus \{i\}, \alpha(s).bound \rangle$

Slide 10-20: Behavioral subtypes – proof obligations

With respect to the behavioral definitions given for *push* and *put* we have to verify that $pre(put(i))[b := \alpha(s)] \Rightarrow pre(push(i))$ and that $post(push(i)) \Rightarrow post(put(i))[b := \alpha(s)]$. These conditions, written out fully in slide 10-20, are easy to verify.

Generally, a formal proof is not really necessary to check that two types satisfy the behavioral subtype relation. As argued in Liskov and Wing (1993), the definition of the appropriate behavioral constraints and the formulation of a correspondence mapping is already a significant step towards verifying that the types have the desired behavioral properties.

10.5   Specifying behavioral compositions

The notion of *behavioral types* may be regarded as the formal underpinning of the notion of *contracts* specifying the interaction between a client and server (object); cf. Meyer (1993). Due to the limited power of the (boolean) assertion language, contracts as supported by Eiffel are more limited in what may be specified than (a general notion of) behavioral types. However, some of the limitations are due, not to limitations on the assertion language, but to the local nature of specifying object behavior by means of contracts. See also Meyer (1993).

To conclude this chapter, we will look at an example illustrating the need to specify global invariants. Further we will briefly look at alternative formalisms for specifying the behavior of collections of objects, and in particular we will explore the interpretation of *contracts* as behavioral compositions.

Global invariants Invariants specify the constraints on the state of a system that must be met for the system to be consistent. Clearly, as elementary logic teaches us, an inconsistent system is totally unreliable.

Some inconsistencies cannot be detected locally, within the scope of an object, since they may be caused by actions that do not involve the object directly. An example of a situation in which an externally caused inconsistent object state may occur is given in slide 10-21. (The example is taken from Meyer (1993), but rephrased in C++.)

When creating an instance of *A*, the *forward* pointer to an instance of *B* is still empty. Hence, after creation, the invariant of the object is satisfied. Similarly when, after creating an instance of *B*, this instance is attached to the *forward* pointer, and as a consequence the object itself is attached to the *backward* pointer of the instance of *B*. After this, the invariant is still satisfied. However, when a second instance of *A* is created, for which the same instance of *B* is attached to the *forward* pointer, the invariant for this object will hold, but as a result the invariance for the first instance of *A* will become violated. See below.

```
A a1, a2; B b;
a1.attach(b);
a2.attach(b);                              // violates invariant a1
```

This violation cannot be detected by the object itself, since it is not involved in any activity. Of course, it is possible to check externally for the objects not directly involved whether their invariants are still satisfied. However, the cost of exhaustive checking will in general be prohibitive. Selective checking is feasible only when guided by an adequate specification of the possible interferences between object states.

Problem – *dynamic aliasing*

```
class A {
public:
A() { forward = 0; }
attach(B* b) { forward = b; b->attach(this); }
bool invariant() {
    return !forward || forward->backward ==
    this;
    }
private:
B* forward;
};

class B {
public:
B() { backward = 0; }
attach(A* a) { backward = a; }
bool invariant() {
    return !backward || backward->forward ==
    this;
    }
private:
A* backward;
};
```

Slide 10-21: Establishing global invariants

Specifying interaction Elementary logic and set-theory provide a powerful vehicle for specifying the behavior of a system, including the interaction between its components. However, taking into account that many software developers prefer a more operational mode of thinking when dealing with the intricacies of complex interactions, we will briefly look at formalisms that allow a more explicit specification of the operational aspects of interaction and communication, yet support to some extent to reason about such specifications. See slide 10-22.

In Helm *et al.* (1990), a notion of *behavioral contracts* is introduced that allows for characterizing the behavior of compositions of objects. Behavioral contracts fit quite naturally in the object oriented paradigm, since they allow both refinement and (type) conformance declarations. See below. Somewhat unclear, yet, is what specification language the *behavioral contracts* formalism is intended to support. On the other hand, from an implementation perspective the interactions captured by behavioral contracts seem to be expressible also within the confines of a class system supporting generic classes and inheritance.

A similar criticism seems to be applicable to the formalism of (role) *scripts* as proposed in Francez *et al.* (1989). Role scripts allow the developer to specify the behavior of a system as a set of roles and the interaction between objects as

```
┌─────────────────────────────────────────────────────┐      10-22
│ Contracts – behavioral compositions    │interaction│ │
│   • specification, refinement, conformance declarations│
│                                                        │
│ Scripts – cooperation by enrollment                    │
│   • roles, initialization/termination protocols, critical role set│
│                                                        │
│ Multiparty interactions – communication primitive      │
│   • frozen state, fault-tolerance, weakening synchrony  │
│                                                        │
│ Joint action systems – action-oriented                 │
│   • state charts, refinement, superposition             │
└─────────────────────────────────────────────────────┘
```

Slide 10-22: Specifying interactions

subscribing to a role. In contrast to behavioral contracts, the script formalism may also be applied to describe the behavior of concurrently active objects. In particular, the script formalism allows for the specification of predefined initialization and termination policies and for the designation of a so-called *critical role set*, specifying the number and kind of participants minimally required for a successful computation.

Also directed towards the specification of concurrent systems is the *multi-party interactions* formalism proposed in Evangelist *et al.* (1989), which is centered around a (synchronous) communication primitive allowing multiple objects to interact simultaneously. The notion of *frozen state* (which may be understood as an invariance requirement that holds during the interaction) may be useful in particular for the specification of fault-tolerant systems. An interesting research issue in this respect is to what extent the assumption of synchrony may be weakened in favor of efficiency.

A rather different orientation towards specifying the interaction between collections of concurrently active objects is embodied by the *joint action systems* approach described in Kurki-Suonio and Jarvinen (1989). Instead of relying on the direct communication between objects, *joint action systems* proceed from the assumption that there exists some global decision procedure that decides which actions (and interactions) are appropriate.

```
┌─────────────────────────────────────────────────────┐      10-23
│ Joint action systems                                   │
│                                                        │
│     action service() by client c; server s is          │
│     when c.requesting && s.free do                     │
│             <body>                                      │
└─────────────────────────────────────────────────────┘
```

Slide 10-23: Specifying actions – example

An example of an *action* specification is given in slide 10-23. Whether the *service* is performed depends upon the state of both the client and the server object selected by the action manager. Kurki-Suonio and Jarvinen (1989) characterize their approach as *action-oriented* to stress the importance of specifying actions in an independent manner (as entities separate from classes and objects). An interesting feature of the *joint action systems* approach is that the behavior of individual objects is specified by means of *state charts*, a visual specification formalism based on Harel (1987). The specification formalism adopted gives rise to interesting variants on the object-oriented repertoire, such as inheritance and refinement by superposition. From a pragmatic viewpoint, the assumption of a global manager seems to impose high demands on system resources. Yet, as a specification technique, the concept of *actions* may turn out to be surprisingly powerful.

In summary, this brief survey of specification formalisms demonstrates that there is a wide variety of potentially useful constructs that all bear some relevance to object-oriented modeling, and as such may enrich the repertoire of (object-oriented) system developers.

Contracts as protocols of interaction Contracts as supported by Eiffel and Annotated C++ are a very powerful means of characterizing the interaction between a server object and a client object. However, with software becoming increasingly complex, what we need is a mechanism to characterize the behavior of collections or compositions of objects as embodied in the notion of *behavioral contracts* as introduced in Helm *et al.* (1990).

A *contract* (in the extended sense) lists the objects that participate in the task and characterizes the dependencies and constraints imposed on their mutual interaction. For example, the contract *model-view*, shown below (in a slightly different notation than the original presentation in Helm *et al.* (1990)), introduces the object *model* and a collection of *view* objects. Also, it characterizes the minimal assumptions with respect to the functionality these objects must support and it gives an abstract characterization of the effect of each of the supported operations.

To indicate the type of variables, the notation $v : type$ is used expressing that variable v is typed as *type*. The object *subject* of type *model* has an instance variable *state* of type V that represents (in an abstract fashion) the value of the *model* object. Methods are defined using the notation

- method $\mapsto$ action

Actions may consist either of other method calls or conditions that are considered to be satisfied after calling the method. Quantification as for example in

- $\forall$ v ϵ views • v.update()

is used to express that the method *update()* is to be called for all elements in *views*.

The *model-view* contract specifies in more formal terms the MV part of the MVC paradigm discussed in section **??**. Recall, that the idea of a *model-view*

```
                                                                    10-24
  contract model-view< V > {              ┌──────────┐
                                          │  MV(C)   │
  subject : model supports [              └──────────┘
    state : V;
    value( val : V ) ↦ [state = val]; notify();
    notify() ↦ ∀v ∈ views • v.update();
    attach( v : view ) ↦ v ∈ views;
    detach( v : view ) ↦ v ∉ views;
  ]
  views : set<view> where view supports [
    update() ↦ [view reflects state];
    subject( m : model ) ↦ subject = m;
  ]
  invariant:
    ∀ v ∈ views • [v reflects subject.state]
  instantiation:
    ∀ v ∈ views • subject.attach(v) &
      v.subject(subject);
    subject.notify();
  }
```

Slide 10-24: The Model-View contract

pair is to distinguish between the actual information (which is contained in the *model* object) and the presentation of that information, which is taken care of by possibly multiple *view* objects.

The actual protocol of interaction between a *model* and its *view* objects is quite straightforward. Each *view* object may be considered as a handler that must minimally have a method to install a model and a method *update* which is invoked, as the result of the *model* object calling *notify*, whenever the information contained in the model changes. The effect of calling *notify()* is abstractly characterized as a universal quantification over the collection of *view* object. Calling *notify()* for *subject* results in calling *update()* for each *view*. The meaning of *update()* is abstractly represented as

- update() ↦ [view *reflects* state];

which tells us that the *state* of the *subject* is adequately reflected by the *view* object.

The invariant clause of the *model-view* contract states that every change of the (state of the) *model* will be reflected by each *view*. The instantiation clause describes, in a rather operational way, how to initialize each object participating in the contract.

In order to instantiate such a contract, we need to define appropriate classes realizing the abstract entities participating in the contract, and further we need to define how these classes are related to their abstract counterparts in the contract by means of what we may call, following Helm *et al.* (1990), *conformance declarations.* Conformance declarations specify, in other words, how concrete classes embody an abstract role, in the same sense as in in the realization of a partial type by means of inheritance.

Summary

This chapter extended the notion of subtyping to include behavioral properties.

In section 1, we discussed the interpretation of types as behavior and we looked at the issues involved in preserving invariance and history properties.

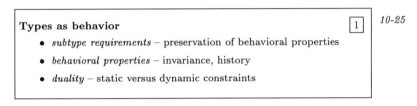

Slide 10-25: Section 10.1: Types as behavior

Also, we discussed the duality between static and dynamic type constraints.

In section 2, a brief characterization of an assertion logic for verifying behavioral properties was given.

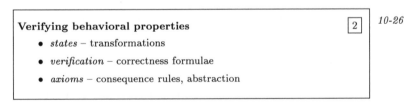

Slide 10-26: Section 10.2: Verifying behavioral properties

We looked at a formal characterization of states and state transitions and correctness formulae were introduced as a means to verify the correctness of transitions. We also looked at an axiomatic characterization of the correctness properties of programming language constructs.

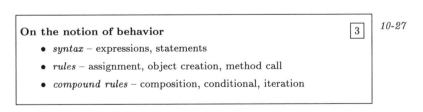

Slide 10-27: Section 10.3: On the notion of behavior

In section 3, we looked at how the behavior of an object may be defined in a formal way by means of a transition system. A transition system for an object-based language specifies the rules for assignment, object creation and method call, as well as the computation steps resulting from the evaluation of compound statements.

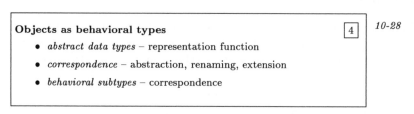

Slide 10-28: Section 10.4: Objects as behavioral types

In section 4, it was shown how actual objects may be related to abstract types by means of a representation abstraction function. Further, we discussed explicit guidelines for defining a subtype correspondence relation between behavioral types.

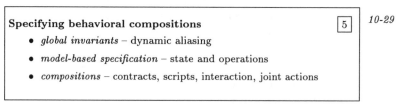

Slide 10-29: Section 10.5: Specifying behavioral compositions

Finally, in section 5, we looked at the problems involved in determining global invariants and we discussed what formal means we have available to specify behavioral properties of a collection of objects.

Questions

1. How would you characterize the conformance requirements for subtyping? Explain what properties are involved.

2. Give an example of signature-compatible types not satisfying the history property.

3. Explain the duality between imposing constraints statically and dynamically.

4. How would you formally characterize program states and state transformations?

5. Explain how you may verify the behavior of a program by means of correctness formulae.

6. Characterize how the behavior of objects may be modeled by means of a transition system and specify a transition system for a simple object-oriented language.

7. How would you characterize the relation between an abstract data type and its realizations?

8. Give an example of an abstract specification of a *stack*. Define a realization and show that the realization is correct with respect to its abstract specification.

9. Explain the notion of correspondence for behavioral subtypes.

10. Show that a *stack* is a behavioral subtype of a *bag* by defining an appropriate correspondence relation. What proof obligations must be met?

11. Discuss the problems involved in satisfying global invariance properties.

12. What formal methods do you know that deal with specifying the behavior of collections of objects?

Further reading

As further reading with respect to the verification of programs, I recommend Apt and Olderog (1991) and Dahl (1992). An assertion logic for a parallel object-oriented language is presented in America and de Boer (1993).

Part IV

Object-Oriented Application Frameworks

11

Business process redesign

Adopting an object-oriented approach is ultimately motivated by the need to develop applications. In this chapter we will look at business applications.

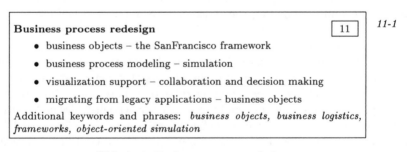

11-1

Business process redesign | 11 |

- business objects – the SanFrancisco framework
- business process modeling – simulation
- visualization support – collaboration and decision making
- migrating from legacy applications – business objects

Additional keywords and phrases: *business objects, business logistics, frameworks, object-oriented simulation*

Slide 11-1: Business process redesign

We will start by discussing the San Franscisco framework, which offers template business objects and business processes for developing (business) applications. Since IT is becoming the spine around which business is organized, we will explore methods for modeling and simulating business processes. We will then briefly describe an object-oriented simulation toolkit, and discuss support for the visualization of business processes and its potential role in collaborative decision making. Finally, we will reflect on the need to migrate from legacy applications.

11.1   Business objects – SanFrancisco framework

What are business objects? From the perspective of typical business end-users, that is accountants, engineers, managers, business objects provide access to corporate information. Traditionally, corporate information resides in legacy databases, and access means looking at tables and pasting these into documents.

Business objects   *11-2*
  • access to (relational) data

Designer – define data model
  • universes, classes, objects – shield from tables

Business user – deploy views
  • select, order, summarize, aggregate, tabulate

Slide 11-2: Business objects

Even within this kind of limited usage, it makes sense to speak of *business objects*, as a way to shield the user from the actual structure of the underlying (relational) database and the use of query languages such as SQL to obtain the actual data, see Jackson (1998). Business objects, as a metaphor for bringing information to the desktop, allow for accessing corporate databases in a transparent manner, and for building the tools that allow business end-users to extract information from the database in a flexible way, and to use this information for further analysis and manipulation. In Jackson (1998), a distinction is made between three types of end-users involved in the construction and use of business objects. The *designer*, who creates the objects that act as an interface to the database, the actual *end user*, who uses these objects to obtain information (and thus implicitly creates queries), and the *supervisor*, who provides users with access to the various regions or universes defined for the database. The actual *business objects* toolset, described in Jackson (1998), provides a GUI-based drawing tool to create queries by composing objects and creating relations between objects.

Business objects, then, are a means to access corporate data. This is a first, but nonetheless important, step. An immediate advantage, obviously, is that business objects may be defined according to actual business needs, instead of being dictated by (relational) technology. More generally, business objects may be regarded as abstractions underlying the definition of business processes. In the following we will explore whether we can generically define business processes and whether there is a collection of abstractions that we may denote as *business objects*.

The SanFrancisco framework

The SanFrancisco framework (IBM) is an example of a framework meant to develop business applications. A business application, as we understand it here, is an application that deploys business objects to (partially) automate business processes, such as order or warehouse management.

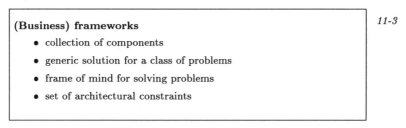

11-3

(Business) frameworks

- collection of components
- generic solution for a class of problems
- frame of mind for solving problems
- set of architectural constraints

Slide 11-3: Business frameworks

A framework is a collection of components, but may also be considered as a generic solution for a class of problems. It sets a frame of mind for solving problems and provides the means to realize solutions in software. In practice, adopting a framework means accepting a set of architectural constraints.

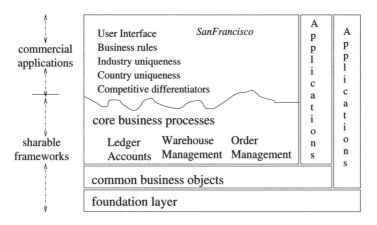

Slide 11-4: The SanFrancisco framework

As a framework, SanFrancisco aims at providing both a software solution for implementing business applications, as well as a collection of concepts or strategies to develop effective business applications.

In the white paper accompanying the introduction of the SanFrancisco framework, we read that the project was started when several software vendors asked IBM to help in modernizing their application products. These vendors asked for help because there were several barriers that prevented them from modernizing their applications themselves. Barriers such as (1) the risk in moving to new technologies (such as client/server and the Web), (2) the need to retrain their development staff to effectively use an object-oriented approach, (3) the cost of change. As the white paper states, as software developers they needed some basic infrastructure, and most companies could not afford to develop this infrastructure themselves.

The SanFrancisco framework provides such an infrastucture, and moreover, the white paper claims, an object-oriented infrastructure that provides a consistent application programming model, with many well-tested services and a collection of *core business process components* and *common business objects*.

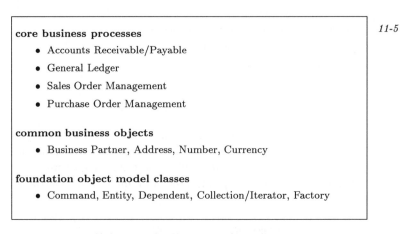

core business processes   *11-5*
- Accounts Receivable/Payable
- General Ledger
- Sales Order Management
- Purchase Order Management

common business objects
- Business Partner, Address, Number, Currency

foundation object model classes
- Command, Entity, Dependent, Collection/Iterator, Factory

Slide 11-5: SanFrancisco object layers

The SanFrancisco framework offers three layers of functionality, business processes, business objects, and foundation classes, each of which may be used and extended by developers to build their applications. The *process* layer itself may be regarded as a collection of frameworks, as indicated in slide 11-5, which build upon the business objects and foundation layers. Note that the foundation layer contains realizations of the by now familiar patterns, see chapter 2.

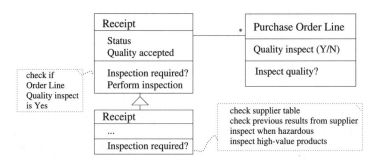

Slide 11-6: Refining quality control

The SanFrancisco framework is an object-oriented framework. It allows for the classical way of extending the framework, by inheritance. As an example, think of a *Receipt* object which may contain an arbitrary number of *Purchase Order Line* instances, see slide 11-6. *Purchase Order Line* has an attribute *Quality inspect* which is read by *Receipt* to determine whether quality control is needed. This reflects the default (business) logic for processing orders as defined by the framework.

To enhance this logic, that is to be able to execute more strict quality control, one may derive a new *Receipt* class from the old *Receipt* class and override the method by which to determine whether quality inspection is required, for example by including a check on the supplier, previous outcomes of quality control, or whether it concerns hazardous materials or high-value products.

As a remark, note that this approach assumes that the business logic is to a large extent hardwired in the (structure of the) classes of the framework, whereas a decoupling of the logic and the actual processing might be preferable.

Discussion The SanFrancisco framework is based on Java technology. Its introduction marks the transition towards client/server and Web technology, and clearly addresses the need for many companies to migrate to the new technology. Apart from technological considerations, however, the major issue in adopting a framework such as the SanFrancisco framework is whether it sufficiently reflects emerging consensus and standards concerning the definition and utilization of business objects and processes. Related efforts of business object standardization are undertaken by the OMG. On the technology side, it is difficult to establish who will win the component war, Java, OMG CORBA, or Microsoft (D)COM and ActiveX.

11.2   Business process modeling

Having looked at business objects, we may well ask ourselves what *business processes* are, and what role IT plays in business processes. Following Davenport and Short (1995) we define a business process as *'a set of logically related tasks performed to achieve some well-defined business outcome'*. Following Davenport and Short (1995) we may observe that IT plays a dual role. On the one hand, IT is an enabler of new process structures, since it allows for automating (parts of) business processes. And on the other hand, IT provides support for the (re)design of business processes, as a means to model and simulate various aspects of business processes. In this section we will look at an approach to modeling business processes supporting the simulation and evaluation of logistic aspects of business processes. Simulation may help in determining the effectiveness of business process (re)designs.

11.2.1   Logistics-based modeling

Improvements in business performance and productivity may be achieved by critically examining some of the rules that govern a business process. Business process redesign (BPR) is the generic label for many emerging methodologies aimed at producing these improvements. Re-design implies that the current state of affairs is no longer acceptable and can no longer be refined or evolved.

Despite the importance of qualitative assessments in BPR, as noted in Hammer (1990), for modeling we favor a more quantitative approach for which we provide support by means of a simulation library (BPSIM) based on the logistics-based business modeling method (LBM) presented in Gerrits (1995).

Logistics-based modeling – criteria for redesign   *11-7*

- the time spent in executing a business process.

Product lead time – time between order and delivery
- *processing time* – actual working time
- *queue time* – waiting for a resource
- *setup time* – for the job to get started
- *wait time* – waiting for a job to complete
- *transport time* – between resources or operations

Slide 11-7: Logistics-based business models

Logistics-based modeling allows for analysing the time spent in executing a business process. The *product lead time* is defined as the time that passes between the moment a customer orders a product and the moment a product is delivered. In more detail, we can distinguish between *processing time* (the time actually worked on a job or operation), *queue time* (the time a jobs waits for a resource to become available), *setup time* (the time that passes between the moment a resource becomes available and the moment work on the job is started), *wait time* (the time that is spent waiting for another job to complete), and *transport time* (the time that is needed to move a job from a resource at a certain location to a resource at another location).

For a particular model, measurements may be obtained by running a series of simulations. Based on an analysis of the simulation results, alternative models may be proposed. For example, when the setup time for a job is relatively large, combining jobs into a single task for an employee may be more efficient.

The LBM method offers a number of primitives, with associated graphic icons, from which a business process model may be constructed as a network of resources connected by transport arcs.

The primitive entities offered by LBM are listed in slide 11-8. Operations are atomic in the sense that wait time, queue time and transport time may not be part of an operation. Only setup time and process time are part of an operation. Tasks are introduced to allow for a series of jobs or operations to be processed, for example by one employee, in order to reduce the setup time needed. Transport entities represent the time it takes for information to flow from one resource (that is operation or task) to another. Transport implicitly defines the sequential

---

Logistics-based modeling primitives   *11-8*

- *operation* – processing component
- *task* – a series of consecutive operations
- *transport* – transport of information
- *choice* – affects flow of information
- *organizational units* – to represent departmental boundaries
- *external agents* – opaque entities
- *archives* – paper-based storage facilities

Slide 11-8: Logistics-based modeling primitives

structure of a process. However, duplications of information, and consequently parallel operations, are allowed. In addition to the primitives mentioned above, LBM allows us to characterize *organizational units* to represent departmental boundaries, *external agents* to represent opaque information producing or consuming entities, and *archives* to represent paper-based storage facilities. Also, employees may need additional *means* to engage in an operation or task.

11.2.2   Business process simulation

The classes provided by the business process simulation library BPSIM reflect the entities provided by the logistics-based business modeling method LBM. The BPSIM library is an extension of the simulation library SIM, described in Bolier and Eliëns (1994). SIM is a C++ library, which is part of the *hush* framework, offering classes supporting discrete event simulation, based on standard simulation techniques, developed in Watkins (1993). It will be described in the next section.

On a somewhat more abstract level, one may regard a business process simulation as consisting of *data*, flowing through the process, and handlers – *datahandlers* – performing some action on the data, such as transportation or specific operations.

Accordingly, BPSIM provides two base classes underlying the classes corresponding to LBM entities:

- *data* – which represents the product or case, i.e. the information, that flows through the process.

- *datahandler* – which is the basis for all classes that handle information.

As an aside, LBM contains no symbol for data as it only depicts the objects that handle the information.

The classes depicted in slide 11-9 are derived from the *datahandler* class. They realize the corresponding entities in LBM.

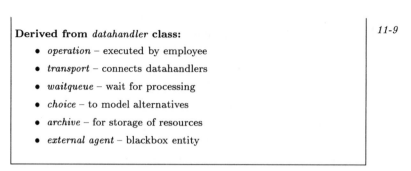

<mark>Slide 11-9: Classes derived from *datahandler*</mark>

An *operation* takes time, and is executed by an employee. Sometimes an operation results in more than one outgoing dataflow, for instance when it issues a request for additional information from a different department.

A *waitqueue* functions as a regular queue if it has one incoming dataflow, i.e. transport. When there are more incoming flows, it functions as a synchronized queue. Data from one flow is not passed on to the next datahandler until the data from the other flow has arrived. This happens for instance when work on a case cannot continue until additional information has arrived.

An external *agent* can either generate data according to some random number distribution, or take data, process it and pass it on to the next datahandler. In the latter case the agent functions as a black box: we only care how long the processing takes, not how it is exactly performed.

In addition, BPSIM offers the classes *means* (which can be used to model resources that are necessary to perform certain operations), and *employee* (which models the different people that perform the operations).

As one can see, the entities *task* and *organization unit* from LBM have no specific counterpart in BPSIM. The reason for this is that having no other *datahandler* between two operations already implies that those operations belong to the same task. Consequently they are executed with no time in between and by the same employee. Also, the fact that tasks are executed in different *organization units* does not add any information that changes the behaviour of the simulation. If it takes time to transport information between different units, then that time can be represented by the object of class *transport* between those units.

For the gathering and analyzing of results, the SIM classes *histogram* and *analysis* are used. The class *agent*, for example, can be given a histogram to track the lead time of data it has generated.

A script interface for BPSIM Employing the facilities of the *hush* library a script interface has been defined for BPSIM that allows the user, that is the designer of business models, to construct and run business simulation models with a short turnaround time. Each class in the BPSIM library corresponds to a command in the script language. As illustrated in the next section, script

commands allow for a graphic representation of the model, which may be displayed
in a Web page as an applet.

11.2.3   Example – requests for loans

Now let us take a look at an example business process model based on the objects
made available in BPSIM. The example will detail possible situations before and
after business process redesign has taken place.

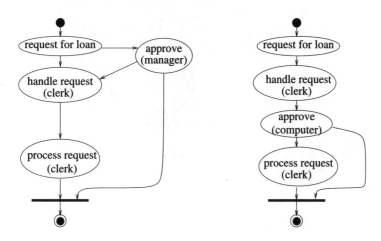

Slide 11-10: Processing alternatives

Current situation: Our first model, slide 11-10 (left), which represents the
current situation, consists of a client producing, for example, requests for a
loan at a bank. The requests are initially handled by a clerk whose task is
to send requests for amounts greater than $10,000 to the boss. The boss,
whose task is to approve or deny the loan, sends the result back to the clerk
for processing. If the amount is less than $10,000, the clerk has authority
to process the request himself.

Redesign alternative: In our second model, slide 11-10(right), which is the
result of a redesign effort, requests are handled by a clerk who enters the data
into a computer. The computer now makes the decision as to whether the
loan is improved – for loans of value less than and greater than 10,000. The
clerk then passes the results on to another clerk for the task of dispatching
loans.

In slide 11-11 the visual representation of the model resulting from the redesign
effort is shown, embedded in a Web page. In addition to the model, the page
contains some results obtained by running a simulation. For example, the text
indicates that an employee is busy handling incoming requests only 33% of the
time. The histogram depicts the distribution of the lead times of incoming loan

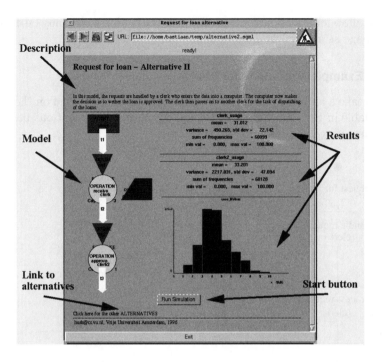

Slide 11-11: Presenting a redesign alternative

requests, that is the time that passes between receiving a request and giving an answer. The Web page further contains a button to start a simulation run, a description of the model and links to alternative models.

The script In the fragment below, a histogram for recording leadtimes is created as well as an agent generating requests and a transport to a clerk handling the requests.

```
histogram leadtimes
agent client generate leadtimes
client -duration 60 poisson
transport t1
t1 -duration 20
employee clerk
operation receive clerk
receive -duration 20.0 5.0 normal
```

The duration of the agent is specified using a poisson distribution with $\lambda = 60$. The clerk is declared to perform a receive operation, the duration of which takes values from a normal distribution with *means* = 20 and *standard deviation* = 5.0.

After defining the components of the model and their connection a simulation may be started by pressing the start button. If desired, users may change the parameters concerning for example setup and wait time, to explore the various scenarios a model has to satisfy.

Discussion As observed in Wastell *et al.* (1994), organizational change is a 'highly threatening and stressful experience for many participants and ... high levels of stress can have a pernicious effect on individuals, group processes and organizational learning'. Hence, directly involving the users in the modeling phase of the BPR project may be an important step towards capturing the human aspects that are necessary for the production of an optimal model. It may also help to lessen the anxiety of employees.

On a technological level, we advocate the use of business process simulation. Nevertheless, to accomodate the social aspects, it is important to support the visualization of such models and their integration in an arbitrarily complex information context, such as the World Wide Web. Developing visualisation and animation support for simulation models is a topic of ongoing research. See section 11.4.2.

11.3   Object-oriented simulation

Historically, there is a close connection between simulation and object-orientation. The first object-oriented language, SIMULA, was a programming language meant for discrete event simulation, see Dahl and Nygaard (1966).

In Hill (1996), an overview is given of what is required for complex system modeling, and more in particular how object-oriented analysis and design may aid in defining models that lend themselves to performance evaluation by means of simulation studies. Performance evaluation belongs traditionally to the field of statistics and operations research. However, according to Hill (1996), for a clear understanding of the behavior of complex systems and the interpretation of measurement results, we need to derive our action models, which are used to perform the simulations, from domain and system object models, describing the structure of the system and its relation to reality. In other words, an object-oriented approach may help us in arriving at better models, provided that we have the stochastic support needed to perform reliable performance studies.

In this section, we will briefly discuss the SIM library, as an example of object-oriented support for discrete event simulation. See Hill (1996) for a great many alternatives.

The SIM library

SIM is a C++ library offering classes supporting discrete event simulation, based on standard simulation techniques described in Watkins (1993). In discrete event simulation, the components of the model consists of events, which are activated at certain points in time and in this way affect the overall state of the system. The simulation library consists of the classes as listed in slide 11-12.

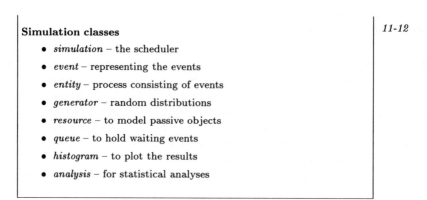

Simulation classes   *11-12*

- *simulation* – the scheduler
- *event* – representing the events
- *entity* – process consisting of events
- *generator* – random distributions
- *resource* – to model passive objects
- *queue* – to hold waiting events
- *histogram* – to plot the results
- *analysis* – for statistical analyses

Slide 11-12: Simulation classes

The SIM library is integrated with the *hush* library, which may be used for defining a script interface to the simulation package, for developing a graphical user interface and for visualizing simulation models.

The event scheduling strategy In its most simple form, a simulation runs until there are no events left. Events are user-defined objects that represent the functionality of the system to be modeled. At the time an event is due to be activated, it is extracted from the scheduler and the main simulation routine executes the code from the *operator()* method of that event.

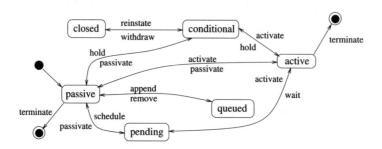

Slide 11-13: State diagram for event

The scheduling algorithm extracts all events with the same activation time. It activates the events in priority order with the highest scheduling priority first. Before executing the events, the simulation clock is updated to the activation time of the current events. Furthermore, a FIFO conditional list (containing events that occur when some condition is met) is traversed in priority order with highest scheduling priority first. Events that can run now are executed. Events that are not used anymore should be terminated to prevent the system from overflow.

In slide 11-13 a state-diagram is given, which depicts the states (see slide 11-14) an event object can be in. The state of an event can be affected both

Event states

- *passive* - currently not available for any processing
- *active* - this is the event currently being processed
- *queued* - the event is in a queue
- *pending* - the event is in the scheduler
- *conditional* - the event is on the conditional list
- *closed* - on the conditional list but unavailable

Slide 11-14: Event states

by the scheduler as well as from within the user-defined methods of the event. The labels on the arrows indicate the methods that result in a state transition. (As a convention, the methods above the arrows indicate a transition from left to right, the methods below the arrow a transition from right to left, in case of a bi-directional relation between states.)

Example – dining philosophers

Consider the following (classical) problem. Five philosophers sit around a table with five chopsticks in between. They think, and if they are hungry and if two chopsticks are available, they eat. If a philosopher gets hungry and s/he cannot acquire a chopstick, the philosopher waits until s/he can. The philosopher does not think, if s/he is waiting or eating. We are interested in the fraction of the time, that a philosopher actually thinks.

In slide 11-15 a graphical rendering is given of a simulation at work. The applet displayed in the *hush* browser is written with the Tcl/Tk command binding to the SIM library.

We will now look at two methods to define the actual simulation mode, an *event-based* method and a *process-based* method.

The event-based approach With the event-based approach of writing a simulation program we first identify the events in the model. The behavior of an event is implemented by deriving it from the class event and overriding the function operator of this class.

We develop this program in the following steps. First, the library is included as sim.h. The declarations of the global variables and constants follow after that. The time unit in this simulation is an hour, so a philosopher has a mean eating time of two hours and a mean thinking time of five hours. The duration of the simulation is a year. After that, we define the various events.

```
#include <sim/sim.h>

const double duration = 52*7*24.0;                          // a year
```

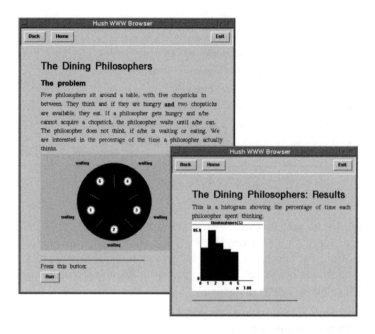

Slide 11-15: Dining philosophers

```
const int number = 5;                          // philosophers
const int eatingtime = 2;                       // 2 hours
const int thinkingtime = 5;                     // 5 hours
simulation* sim;
generator* g;
resource* chopstick[number];
histogram* thinking;
```

After defining the global variables, we define the actual event classes. To model this problem, three events can be identified, eat, think and await. The corresponding classes are derived from the class event. Furthermore we need a chopstick for every philosopher. These are represented as a resource. The thinking times are gathered in an instance of the class histogram and the generator takes care of the variations in the time needed to think and eat.

```
class eat : public event
{
public :
  eat(int i);                               // constructor, taking identity
  virtual int operator()();                 // function operator
private :
  int id;                                   // identity of the philosopher
};
```

```
class think : public event
{
public :
   think(int i);                          // constructor, taking identity
   virtual int operator()();              // function operator
private :
   int id;                                // identity of the philosopher
};

class await : public event
{
public :
   await(int i);                          // constructor, taking identity
   virtual int operator()();              // function operator
private :
   int id;                                // identity of the philosopher
};
```

Next, we implement the various events. An event is given its functionality by deriving it from the class event and overriding its function operator.

The logic of the eat event is that the philosopher eats for a random time, exponentially distributed with a mean eating time. So, we first determine the actual eating time and schedule a think event to be activated after this eating time. The eat event can be terminated.

```
eat::eat(int i) : event()
{
   id = i;                                // set identity
}

int eat::operator()()
{
   double t = g -> exponential(eatingtime);       // eating time
   think* th = new think(id);                      // create a thinking event
   sim -> schedule(th,t);                          // schedule thinking
   sim -> terminate(this);                         // terminate this eat event
   return OK;
}
```

If a philosopher starts to think, the philosopher first releases both chopsticks. The thinking time is determined and a sample is made of the percentage of this thinking time towards the total time. An await event is scheduled and the think event is terminated.

```
think::think(int i) : event()
{
   id = i;                                // set identity
}
```

```
int think::operator()()
{
   chopstick[id] -> release();                    // release left chopstick
   chopstick[(id+1) % number] -> release();           // release right
   double t = g -> exponential(thinkingtime);        // thinking time
   thinking -> sample(id,t/duration*100);          // add a sample (%)
   await* aw = new await(id);                      // create await event
   sim -> schedule(aw,t);                          // schedule waiting
   sim -> terminate(this);                         // terminate thinking
   return OK;
}
```

The await event acquires the left and right chopstick and schedules an eat event immediately, if both chopsticks are available. The await event is passivated as it could be on the conditional list. If no chopsticks are available, the await event stays on the conditional list or, if it was not conditional as is the case the first time it is activated, it is added to the conditional list.

```
await::await(int i) : event()
{
   id = i;                                          // set identity
}
```

```
int await::operator()()
{
   if ( (chopstick[id] -> available()) &&            // available ?
        (chopstick[(id+1) % number] -> available()) )
   {
      chopstick[id] -> acquire();                       // acquire left
      chopstick[(id+1) % number] -> acquire();        // acquire right
      eat* e = new eat(id);
      sim -> passivate(this);              // extract from conditional list
      sim -> schedule(e,0);           // schedule eat event immediately
      sim -> terminate(this);               // terminate await event
   }
   else if (!conditional())                  // not on conditional list
      sim -> hold(this);                     // add to conditional list
   return OK;
}
```

The following step is the definition and implementation of an application, which is derived from session. The application::main function first creates the simulation object. Furthermore, a frequency histogram and five resources that represent the chopsticks are created. The histogram is created with its widget path and with its (default) options. Afterwards it is packed to the display. The simulation starts with all philosophers waiting and runs for a year (52*7*24 hours). After running the simulation, the resulting histogram is printed.

```
int application::main()              // tk is an instance variable of session
{
   sim = new simulation();
   g = new generator(80,20,19);                       // gets three seeds
   thinking = new histogram(".h","-columns 5 -title thinkingtime");
   tk -> pack(thinking);                              // add to display;
   tk -> update();                                    // update display;
   for (int i=0;i<number;i++)
   {
      chopstick[i] = new resource(1);                 // create chopsticks
      await* aw = new await(i);                       // schedule each
      sim -> schedule(aw,0);                      // philosopher waiting
   }
   sim -> run(duration);                            // run for duration
   cout << (*thinking) << endl;          // print resulting histogram
   delete thinking;
   delete sim;
   return 0;                                  // successful termination
}
```

The process-oriented approach With the process-oriented approach the components of the model consist of entities, which represent the existence of some object in the system such as a philosopher. An entity receives a user-defined phase that determines the behavior of the entity.

The *entity* class is derived from the *event* class. It may be regarded as a compound event, that is it maintains an additional phase variable to record the actual phase it is in.

We first identify the entities (or the types) in the model. The events are represented as methods of an entity. The function operator calls these events based on the phase the entity is in, as illustrated in the definition of a *philosopher*.

```
enum {EATING,THINKING,WAITING};              // phases of a philosopher

class philosopher : public entity
{
public :
   philosopher(int ph,int i);        // constructor, taking phase and id
   virtual int operator()();                       // function operator
   int eat();                                             // eat event
   int think();                                         // think event
   int await();                                         // await event
private :
   int id;
   generator* g;
};

philosopher::philosopher(int ph,int i) : entity(ph)
```

```
{
  id = i;                                  // set phase and identity
  g = new generator(20,10,999);
}

int philosopher::operator()()
{
  switch (phase())                         // what phase is the philosopher in?
  {
  case EATING :
    return eat();                          // the philosopher eats
  case THINKING :
    return think();                        // the philosopher thinks
  case WAITING :
    return await();                        // the philosopher waits
  }
  return FALSE;
}

int philosopher::eat()
{
  double t = g -> exponential(eatingtime);    // determine eating
    time
  sim -> wait(t);                          // schedule this philosopher thinking
  phase(THINKING);                         // set phase to thinking
  return OK;
}

int philosopher::think()
{
  chopstick[id] -> release();              // release left chopstick
  chopstick[(id+1) % number] -> release();    // release right
  double t = g -> exponential(thinkingtime);    // determine
    thinking time
  thinking -> sample(id,t/duration*100);      // sample (%)
  sim -> wait(t);                          // schedule this philosopher waiting
  phase(WAITING);                          // set phase on waiting
  return OK;
}

int philosopher::await()
{
  if ( (chopstick[id] -> available()) &&      // available?
     (chopstick[(id+1) % number] -> available()) )
  {
    chopstick[id] -> acquire();            // acquire left chopstick
    chopstick[(id+1) % number] -> acquire();    // acquire right
    sim -> passivate(this);                // make passive
    sim -> activate(this);                 // activate as eating
    phase(EATING);                         // set phase on eating
```

```
    }
    else if (!conditional())
        sim -> hold(this);                        // add to conditional
    return OK;
}
```

Dependent on the phase the philosopher is in, the appropriate action on the simulation environment is taken. These actions closely resemble the events, described in the event-based approach of this problem. The main difference is in the use of phase. If, for example, a philosopher finishes eating, his/her phase is set to THINKING and he/she is scheduled after t time units, whereas in the event-based approach a think event is scheduled and the eat event is explicitly terminated. So, in the process-oriented solution a philosopher exists for the entire simulation. In the application::main function the simulation is set up by scheduling the five philosophers, initially waiting, instead of scheduling five await events.

11.4   Visualization support

Visualization is one of the oldest forms of communication. As expressed in the programmers manual of In3D from Visible Decisions (1997), visualization may be used to convey information and to help us manage, analyze, control and comprehend vast amounts of information.

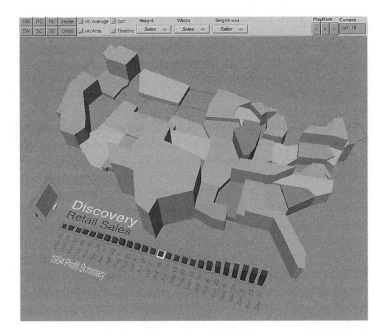

Slide 11-16: Retail USA ©1995–1999 Visible Decisions Inc.

The visualization in slide 11-16, which is one of the examples that comes with In3D, depicts sales figures in the USA, embedded in an obvious geographical metaphor. The image, which may be animated to display the time-dependent changes in sales figures, contains a wealth of information that would be much more difficult to comprehend if presented numerically or even in (plain) 2D graphs.

In this section will discuss how visualization may be used to give access to information and what role visualization can play in decision making. We will also look at the design rationale underlying a generic distributed architecture for information visualization, which is based on Java and VRML technology.

11.4.1   So many users, so many perspectives

The title of this section is from an article, Schönhage *et al.* (1998). It is meant to express that visualization must be flexible in order to accommodate the individual user's information needs. Originally, visualization was primarily used for the analysis of scientific data, resulting from measurements or some physical model. Nowadays, visualization is increasingly applied to non-scientific data, for better understanding of the contents and the relations between the data. In business data visualization there is not necessarily a physical model underlying the data. Nevertheless, it is worthwhile to visualize the data in order to explore structural patterns and temporal relations.

extension layer	Charting				
core layer	Observer Models	Mapper	Compound Views Single/Multi Views	Sensors Controllers	Viewers Frames
foundation layer	Commands		Expressions	OpenGL/VRML Rendering	

Slide 11-17: In3D architecture

The In3D toolkit, Visible Decisions (1997), provides an object-oriented framework for the visualization of business data. It is based on the *Model–View–Control* paradigm, and provides the functionality to define data models or containers, observers for these models, mappings to transform the data to be displayed, a variety of views to display the data, sensors and controllers to create interactive applications, and frames and viewers for displaying visualizations on the screen. The In3D toolkit is built on OpenGL and allows for VRML import and export. An overview of the In3D architecture is given in slide 11-17.

Creating an effective visualization may be quite demanding. First of all, one has to make the choice for an appropriate metaphor. Basically, the choice is between a *literal* metaphor, such as the geographical metaphor used in slide 11-16, or an abstract metaphor, such as a data cube or an abstract topology. Next, it is important to organize the data, and to find suitable visual primitives to display the data content and the inherent relationships of the data. Finally, user interaction capabilities must be added, to allow for explorative behavior and drill down. See slide 11-18.

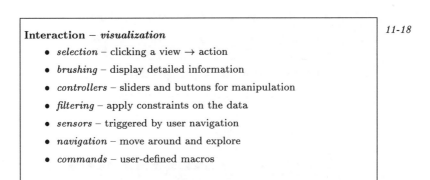

Slide 11-18: User interaction

Available systems The In3D toolkit (http://www.vdi.com) was one of the first around for business data visualization. Recently, a number of VRML-based visualization kits have been introduced (for example http://www.em7.com and http://www.platinum.com).

11.4.2 DIVA – distributed visualization architecture

The DIVA project aims at creating a flexible architecture and framework for dynamic information visualization, in particular business process visualization, that is the visualization of the outcomes and implications of business process simulations.

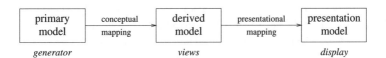

Slide 11-19: Conceptual architecture (DIVA)

DIVA is based on three requirements

- to allow for multiple views or perspectives, according to the users' information needs;

- to provide adaptive visualizations, allowing for experimentation; and

- to support a networked, Web-based infrastructure.

Conceptually, a visualization may be regarded as a transition of data through a sequence of models, as depicted in slide 11-19.

In the case of business process visualization, the primary model, or generator component, is a simulation of a business process. The derived model collects these data, filters some out, and computes aggregate data, as for example the average waiting time for a queue. The presentation model defines how the data

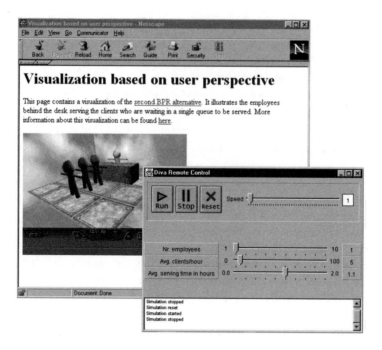

Slide 11-20: Screenshot

is presented, that is what visual gadgets are used to display the outcome and the dynamics of the simulation.

As an example, look at the visualization displayed in slide 11-20. It presents a waiting queue, which is the result of a business process simulation, as described in Schönhage *et al.* (1998), and a dialog that allows to restart the simulation.

Collaborative visualization The conceptual architecture in slide 11-19 allows for having multiple perspectives on the same data. For example, instead of the queue length, we might also display the actual throughput or the product lead time. In Schönhage *et al.* (1998), we have investigated how to extend the DIVA architecture to support collaborative visualization and decision making, for example in a process re-engineering or redesign effort.

Obviously, the original DIVA architecture needs to be extended with sessions, defining a (virtual) meeting and corresponding roles, such as a chair, listeners, talkers, and interactors. Restarting the simulation is an example of the action of an interactor. Clearly, such interactions disrupt the actual course of events and must be limited to privileged participants.

To deploy visualizations effectively in actual argumentation, it must be possible, literally, to share one's point of view with other participants, or to enforce one's perspective. In practice this means that a particular visualization, that is presentation of a perspective, is displayed to the other users. So, instead of the length of the queue, the average waiting times may be displayed, for example to

> **Collaborative visualization** *11-21*
>
> - sessions – meetings/roles
> - roles – chair, listener, talker, interactor
> - interactor – disruptive or non-disruptive
> - perspectives – sharing and enforcing
> - communication – telepointers, chatting, ...

Slide 11-21: Collaborative visualization

illustrate that customer satisfaction will not be affected. Technically, our solution for sharing or exporting views is based on mobile object technology, as will be discussed shortly.

Finally, we need additional means to communicate with the other participants, such as a telepointer and a chatting facility.

Display agents To allow for sharing or enforcing perspectives, we introduced so-called *display agents*, mobile Java objects that may be used by a Java applet to create a VRML world using the external authoring interface (EAI). See Schönhage and Eliëns (1999).

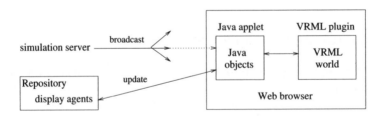

Slide 11-22: Architecture DIVA – display agents

As sketched in slide 11-22, the simulation server sends events to the visualization, embedded in a Web browser. A visualization consists of a VRML world and Java objects that intercept the visualization events (using the CORBA Event Service) and react to possible user actions. The content of VRML worlds are stored as display agents, which reflect the contents of the secondary model or concept space. Display agents are mobile objects that may be activated on demand, to display the simulation scene, or to update the other participants' view.

Implementation details DIVA is designed as a distributed object-oriented system. The DIVA components are written in C++ and Java, and can run on different platforms. We use the Common Object Request Broker Architecture (CORBA) to let our distributed objects communicate with each other. By using the interface definition language (IDL) to describe the interfaces between components and by making use of the object request broker (ORB), distributed components are able to communicate.

Voyager, described in ObjectSpace (1997), is an agent ORB written purely in Java, which supports CORBA. Voyager allows us to use mobile objects, a feature which CORBA does not have. We use Voyager to construct the mobile controller components. These components are able to 'dock' at a user environment and can subsequently show their user interface on the screen to let the user interact with it.

We use VRML, see ISO (1997), as the main visualization tool. The users are able to navigate through the VRML worlds by using a VRML-browser. The External Authoring Interface (EAI) makes it possible to control the VRML worlds dynamically via the Java and Javascript languages.

The visualization gadgets in the presentation component are represented by mobile display agents. These agents are constructed using Voyager. Display agents can also 'dock' in a user environment and, in addition, get access to the local VRML world. They collect the needed information from shared concept spaces to build and maintain the 3D visualization.

The combination of CORBA and the Web enables access to information resources by means of HTML, Java and VRML. For example, the simulation and shared concept space, that is the derived model, can be hosted on a Unix server while the presentation components are executed in a Web-browser on Windows client machines.

11.5   Migrating from legacy applications

With IT becoming the spine of business processes, many companies are urged to move away from their legacy applications and jump right into the new technologies, to take advantage of the rich GUI capabilities of current desktops, client/server computing and the Web. However, most companies are still tied to their (mainframe) legacy systems, and the cost of (re)development is in general too high.

As phrased by Noffsinger *et al.* (1998), what they need is an unobtrusive method of integrating terminal-based (legacy) software with newer technologies, to provide the existing information and services with some new (GUI and Web-based) clothing.

In slide 11-23, it is depicted how such an integration might be achieved with a three-tier architecture employing a terminal emulation or screen-scraping API for encapsulating the legacy objects, and a HTTP server to deliver the functionality to a (thin) Web client. (Information about the Legacy Object Framework can be found at http://www.yrrid.com.)

The advantage of a three-tier solution is the decoupling of the legacy application from both GUI functionality and (middleware) business logic. The legacy object modeling, which reflects the business logic, is taken care of in a middleware layer, to allow for thin or ignorant clients. In Noffsinger *et al.* (1998), alternative

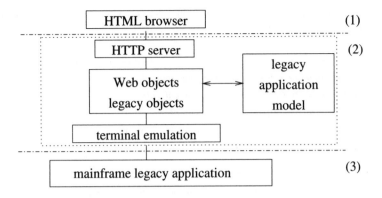

Slide 11-23: Three-tier architecture

solutions are discussed as well, including CORBA-based three-tier solutions as well as a variety of two-tier architectures with fat clients that carry all the knowledge about the business logic underlying the legacy application themselves. In comparison, three-tier solutions are to be preferred, since they allow for better maintenance. Nevertheless, according to Noffsinger *et al.* (1998), the development effort is significantly higher.

Discussion At ASZ/GAK, the IT section of a large social security organiza-tion in the Netherlands, students of the Vrije Universiteit have been involved in projects aimed at developing a new information infrastructure. There we studied intensively the three tiers and in particular the boundaries between these tiers, notably the *GUI/Business Objects* boundary and the *Business Objects/Database* boundary, using Java, CORBA, (D)COM and proprietary middleware. General-izing, our conclusions thus far are that decoupling is much harder to achieve than we expected. For example, defining transactions using business objects seems to require more knowledge of the database backend than is desirable. Also, it seemed necessary to replicate much of the business logic inherent in the database. And, defining user interaction with business objects in a purely abstract fashion, that is independent of an actual interface technology, proved to be difficult as well.

For an organization such as ASZ/GAK, migration is necessary, simply because the risk of an abrupt transition is too high. This may also explain why the IT staff of ASZ/GAK who were responsible for maintaining the system were at first not too eager to experiment with the new technologies. Our experiments, however, convinced them that there is hope for the future.

Summary

This chapter has dealt with business objects, business applications and the issues involved in business process redesign. Since business process redesign may be motivated by changes in technology, we also discuss the migration from legacy applications.

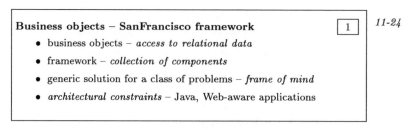

Slide 11-24: Section 11.1: Business objects – SanFrancisco framework

In section 1, we discussed the need for business objects and looked at the San Francisco framework, which aims to provide a generic solution to creating business applications.

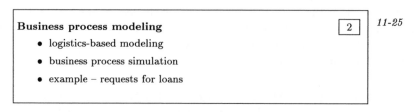

Slide 11-25: Section 11.2: Business process modeling

In section 2, we looked at the issues involved in business process modeling, which we consider as a prerequisite for business process redesign. We dealt with the simulation of the logistic aspects of business processes and concluded with a small example.

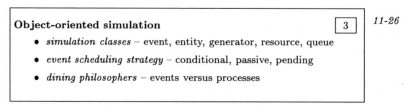

Slide 11-26: Section 11.3: Object-oriented simulation

In section 3, we treated object-oriented simulation in somewhat more detail. An overview was given of useful simulation classes. We discussed event scheduling strategies, and looked at the classic *dining philosophers* example, both from an event-based simulation perspective and a process-based simulation perspective.

In section 4, we looked at interactive information visualization as a means to support business process redesign and decision making. An overview was given of

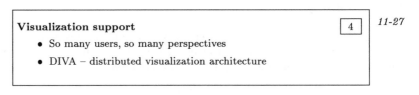

Slide 11-27: Section 11.4: Visualization support

the DIVA software architecture, which allows for distribution, user perspectives and collaboration.

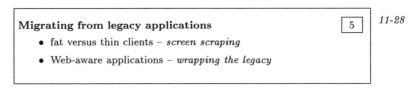

Slide 11-28: Section 11.5: Migrating from legacy applications

We concluded, in section 5, with a discussion of the opportunities to migrate from legacy applications to a modern, object-oriented, Web-aware architecture.

Questions

1. Why would you need business objects? Discuss this from the perspective of the end-user as well as from the perspective of management.

2. What are the motivations underlying the San Francisco framework?

3. Give an overview of the component layers constituting the San Francisco framework.

4. Explain the goals of logistics-based business modeling. Discuss possible means to support business modeling.

5. Give an example of business process simulation.

6. What classes can you think of for a library supporting object-oriented simulation?

7. What are the requirements for visualization support? Can you think of actual classes?

8. Discuss the issues that may arise in migrating from legacy applications. What possible solutions can you think of?

Further reading

For more information on business process redesign, consult Davenport and Short (1995), Hammer (1990) and Wastell *et al.* (1994). For an in-depth treatment of simulation, you may read, for example, Watkins (1993).

12

Web applications

The explosive growth of the Web is perhaps the single most important event in the history of computing technology. What started as an information infrastructure is now turning into an infrastructure encompassing both information and applications, and is becoming the backbone for the commercial deployment of the Internet.

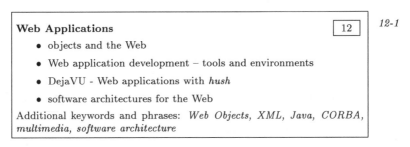

12-1

Slide 12-1: Web applications

In this chapter, we will explore how the Web affects (object-oriented) software development. First of all, we will discuss whether object orientation has any relevance for the Web and for the development of Web applications. We will look at some of the current trends and technologies, discuss the possible occurrence of the Object Web, and look at an example deploying Web technology to provide an infrastructure for distributed object computing. We will reflect on the computation model underlying the Web, to explore how to program the Web to suit our needs. We will also look at the phenomenon of intelligent agents on the Web, which may aid the user in retrieving the right information and perform his/her tasks in a more convenient way. We then present some of our early research on extending the Web with multimedia fuctionality, carried out in the DejaVU project at the Vrije Universiteit. Concluding this chapter, and the book, we will discuss the forces that play a role in defining a suitable software architecture for (object-oriented) Web applications.

12.1   Objects and the Web

The Web originated from an initiative at CERN, nicknamed the World Wide Web (WWW), to provide an infrastructure for the exchange of information between scientists. Undoubtedly, the initiative succeeded beyond expectation. As described by Bass *et al.* (1998), at the time there were other such initiatives. Nevertheless, the effort at CERN contained two novel ideas: the use of hypertext, to allow for easy navigation between documents, and the deployment of a client/server architecture, to separate presentation from the delivery of documents.

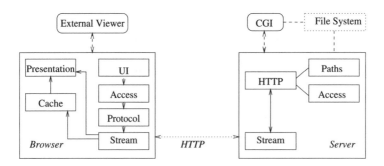

Slide 12-2: Client/server pair

Among the original requirements of the WWW was *extensibility*. As slide 12-2 indicates, which is an adapted rendering from a chapter about the Web in Bass *et al.* (1998), both the browser (client) and the (HTTP) server may be extended with, respectively, additional viewers on the client side and arbitrary programs through the Common Gateway Interface (CGI) on the server side. Together with these extensions the original infrastructure, which consists of HTML (Hypertext Markup Language) as the document format and HTTP (Hypertext Transfer Protocol) for the transport of documents, proved to be sufficient for the Web to be widely adopted. In retrospect, one may wonder why the Web was not based on, for example, distributed object technology or remote procedure calls. Accepting the Web as it is, we may still ask ourselves what role objects may play in developing Web applications.

12.1.1 Trends and technologies

The Web came as a surprise, both to the hypertext community and to the distributed systems community. As a surprise because, despite its simplicity, or probably because of its simplicity, the adoption of the Web is unsurpassed, in absolute volume and growth rate. Its simplicity lies both in terms of the underlying TCP/IP-based HTTP transport protocol, and the (conceptual) functionality of the HTML hypertext format, which more or less defines the services offered by the Web.

Transport and Services   *12-3*

	Web	Corba
Services	HTML	IDL
Transport	HTTP	ORB/IIOP

Alternatives

- ANSAWeb – CORBA-based Web infrastructure
- WebBroker – HTTP as a transport protocol for ORBs
- orblets – Java applets with ORB

Slide 12-3: Transport and services

It is probably not an exaggeration to say that the entire academic community was shocked to see the sudden mass-scale adoption of a technology that was only a shallow reflection of the original conceptions of globally distributed systems and hypermedia. Not surprisingly, however, academia and other research and development institutes reacted to the Web by redirecting their research programs, in order to jump on the wagon.

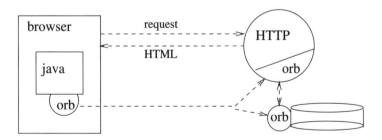

Slide 12-4: Java applet with ORB

As an example, in the August/September 1996 issue of the Object Expert (Europe) the question was posed *'How to survive the Internet revolution?'*. In answer to that question, the Web was first criticized for offering a monolithic HTML/HTTP-based structure that gave rise to many proprietary extensions.

Then, as a solution, CORBA was praised as an infrastructure that allows for the creation of well-behaved extensions through the use of IDL. The most radical alternative, indeed, would be to base the Web entirely on CORBA, of which the ANSAWeb proposal is an example. A rather different route is to adopt HTTP as the transport protocol for object request brokers and turn the Web into a global infrastructure for distributed object computing, as for example suggested in the WebBroker proposal that will be discussed later.

A more modest, and realistic, approach is to enhance Java applets with the capability to connect with CORBA servers, as indicated in slide 12-4 and slide 12-5.

In slide 12-4, we see a browser with an HTML page that contains a Java applet, which may connect through an ORB directly to, for example, a database server. Alternatively, a request may pass through a CGI process to an ORB attached to the HTTP server.

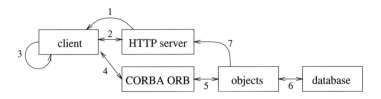

Slide 12-5: Processing steps

In more detail, when we look at the processing steps, as depicted in slide 12-5, we may distinguish between

1. get the HTML page,

2. load the applet,

3. start the applet,

4. connect to a CORBA server from the applet,

5. get access to the remote objects,

6. connect optionally to a database, and

7. send output either in HTML format or directly to the applet.

Based on this setup, we may think of several alternatives and refinements, as for example the use of Java RMI or an extension of the Java ORB with full server functionality, to allow for callbacks from the objects (server) to the client (applet).

The WebBroker proposal In the scenario sketched above, Java and CORBA were used to extend the basic functionality of the Web. In a similar vein, Microsoft DCOM, as an alternative distributed object technology, might have been used to incorporate objects in the Web. The WebBroker proposal, as explained in the technical note submitted to the W3C, 11 May 1998, attempts to unify distributed object technology and the Web publishing infrastructure by providing a common *Web computing* standard based on HTTP and XML. (XML, the eXtendable Markup Language, may be considered as a lightweight version of SGML, suitable for the description of the structure and content of arbitrary documents.)

The objective of the *WebBroker* is, as stated in the proposal, to have a system which is less complicated than the OMG CORBA and Microsoft COM+ distributed computing systems and which is more powerful than HTML forms and CGI. The principal advantage of the WebBroker approach is that it is Web-native. However, with the universal adoption of IIOP, which is now also the transport protocol of Java RMI, the advantage of a more efficient protocol gains more weight.

12.1.2   The Object Web – CORBA/Java versus Microsoft

No doubt, the Object Web is coming, as testified by the appearance of the *Object Web Survival Guide*, see Orfali *et al.* (1999).

Slide 12-6: Client-Server/CGI

To state the argument for the Object Web once more, as depicted in slide 12-6 what we have, basically, is a client/server architecture of which the server-side may be arbitrarily extended with CGI-processes. However, CGI extensions are slow, they do not scale and, most important, they do not allow for state unless unreliable programming tricks such as cookies are used. Now, according to (the ads for) Orfali *et al.* (1999), there are two camps: *Microsoft* and *Everyone Else*. We will start with the latter, which we will refer to as the *Java/CORBA Web*.

The Netscape way – Java/CORBA Web

When we consider the browser market, there are at the time of writing two major players, Netscape and Microsoft. Although Netscape is certainly not the only company selling Web servers, we will nevertheless take Netscape as representing *everyone else* to see how the Java/CORBA Web may take shape.

First of all, it must be noted that Netscape made a serious commitment to CORBA and IIOP. For example, all Java CORBA support classes are shipped with their browser. Secondly, as indicated in slide 12-7, we may observe that the functionality of Web servers has been significantly enhanced since the beginning days of the Web. Facilities for publishing, (intelligent) agents, search and management are now more or less standard commodities provided on top of a programmable content store, running on a variety of operating systems.

In slide 12-8, an architectural overview is given of one of the earlier versions of the Netscape Enterprise Server. When going from the top to the bottom, we

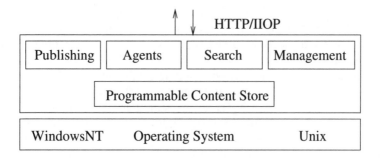

Slide 12-7: Content store

see that content may be delivered in a variety of formats, including Java applets, Javascript, plain HTML, some legacy plugin format or any combination thereof. See section 12.4 for a discussion of plugins. More to the bottom, Netscape offers LiveConnect technology to allow (client) components to interact. For example, a Java applet or a plugin may be addressed from Javascript code. In addition, there is IIOP to connect to CORBA-enabled servers.

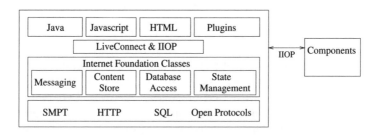

Slide 12-8: Netscape Enterprise Server

For programming server facilities, Netscape offered the Internet Foundation Classes as part of the Open Network Environment (ONE), which is based on standards such as SMPT, HTTP and SQL. However, the Internet Foundation Classes for Java have become part of the Java Foundation Classes that are delivered with Java 1.2. Server facilities include messaging, content store, database access and state management. Additional components may be provided either as server extensions through the NSAPI, or through CORBA IIOP.

For the actual creation of content and the deployment of all that technology, there is a large variety of tools from Netscape and other vendors, and plenty of documentation that may be obtained from Netscape's Web site.

The Microsoft way – DNA

It is interesting to note that Microsoft's commitment to the Web came relatively late. Nevertheless, there is no doubt that Microsoft recognizes the importance of the Internet and the Web as the infrastructure of what it calls the *Digital Nervous System* of corporations.

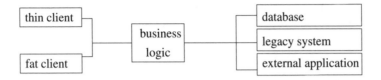

Slide 12-9: Business logic

In February 1999, I had the pleasure of hearing Bill Gates speak about the *Digital Nervous System*, as a unifying concept for corporations to execute and record transactions electronically, and as a means to create corporate awareness of the actual state of business and current business goals. I found this view quite appealing, although the complexity involved in the actual archiving, search, retrieval and presentation of such material is quite immense.

Ideally, as depicted in slide 12-9, central to any corporate information structure must be the business logic that governs the policies and information needs of the organization. At the backend of the system we may have a database, legacy systems, or external applications delivering information. For end-users, depending on the particular architecture chosen, there may be thin or fat clients giving access to the information and communication facilities.

Tools		
Presentation	*Business Logic*	*Data*
(D)HTML Scripting Components Win32	COM+ MSMQ IIS	ADO OLE-DB XML
System Services		

Slide 12-10: Microsoft DNA

To turn to actual technology, Microsoft's proposal to realize their vision is the Microsoft Dynamic Networking Architecture (DNA), of which the basic components are given in slide 12-10. In the column on the left, we have the *presentation facilities*, ranging from (dynamic) HTML to Win32 applications, going from thin to fat, indeed. In the *business logic* column, we have COM+ (which is the followup on (D)COM), the Microsoft Message Queue Server (MSMQ), and the Internet Information Server, which is a powerful server that allows for server-side scripting, Active Server Pages (ASP), and COM-based objects. For handling data, Microsoft offers the ActiveX Data Objects format (ADO), OLE-DB to connect to databases, and XML. It must be noted here that Microsoft is actively engaged in promoting XML as a data interchange standard, in cooperation with the W3C.

In summary, Microsoft DNA offers Presentation Services, Application Services, Data Services and System Services. In addition, Microsoft offers an appealing suite of tools collected in the Visual Studio, including Visual C++, Visual Basic and Visual Interdev, for creating dynamic data-driven Web applications. Although I do not intend to make this sound like an ad, it cannot be denied that Microsoft is a serious player!

12.2   Programming the Web – a search for APIs

Leaving the Object Web for what it is, in construction obviously, we may raise the question as to what support should be provided for developing Web applications that are more finely tuned to the needs of end-users. To answer this question, or more appropriately, to gain insight into the requirements and state-of-the-art technology that was available, I organized a series of two workshops, one for the WWW5 Conference, entitled *'Programming the Web – a search for APIs'*, and one for the WWW6 Conference, entitled *'Logic Programming and the Web'*.

In this section we will discuss some of the issues treated in these workshops. In particular, we will reflect on the computation model underlying the Web, taking the views of Luca Cardelli presented at the WWW5 workshop as a starting point, to establish general requirements for APIs for programming the Web. Then we will look at another interesting phenomenon, intelligent agents on the Web, and discuss what would constitute a suitable framework for agent technology.

12.2.1   Models of computation

The *Programming the Web* workshop was intended to focus on concepts and requirements for high-level APIs suitable for developing Web-aware applications. The papers that were submitted, which are available on the CDROM accompanying this book, covered a wide range of interests, including computation models, applications and user requirements, software architectures and libraries, as well as heuristics and guidelines for API developers.

The kickoff for the workshop was given by Luca Cardelli, who raised the question 'What is the Web's model of computation?'. This question appeared to be of critical importance for understanding the requirements for APIs and for evaluating possible solutions. In summary, we may observe that there is some notion of global computation for the Web, but that computation on the Web is fraught with many obstacles, such as the lack of referential integrity (e.g. dead links), unreliable services (both in availability and quality), failures (due to servers or network congestion). What we need, in conclusion, is some (formal) model of computation that captures these properties. In addition, we need to be able to deal with such properties in our Web programs, for example we may wish to anticipate on the possible unavailability of a Web server, and provide an alternative in that case.

In slide 12-11, an overview is given of the complaints about the functionality of the Web, observations concerning its 'nature', general requirements for open sys-

```
Complaints                                                          12-11
    • lack of referential integrity

    • undetected failures

    • no control over quality of service
Observations
    • dynamic quality of services

    • complex interaction
Requirements
    • uniformity, openness, flexibility, orthogonality, layered
Behavior
    • reliable, configurable, monitoring, notification, thread-safe
Answers
    • object-oriented, components, virtual APIs, callbacks, plug-ins
```

Slide 12-11: Requirements for APIs

tems development, a wish-list of desired behavioral characteristics and potential (technological) answers.

```
Actions                                                            12-12
    • define a distributed model of computation that suits the Web.

    • define canonical (language-independent?)   object models for ...
      resources, application domains ...
Perspectives
    • servers - extensions

    • browsers - clients, viewers, configuration

    • agents - e.g. payment
Interests
    • distributed objects

    • plugin components

    • formalization of requirements and solutions
```

Slide 12-12: Dimensions of APIs

Not surprisingly, there did not seem to be a canonical approach to the definition and development of APIs and Web applications, perhaps not in the last place because the demarcation between computation models, languages and APIs is not clear-cut.

Nevertheless, as summarized in slide 12-12, it seemed clear that we need to define a suitable computation model as well as (abstract) object models that capture the requirements for resources and application domains (such as for example e-commerce). In addition we must distinguish between client and server perspectives, with autonomous (intelligent) agents as a possible third perspective. And, naturally, our own (technological) interests play a role as well, to the extent that it may determine possible solutions.

Considering the basic needs for the development of Web-aware applications, as expressed by the workshop's participants, which ranged over resolving URLs, billing and payment facilities, and quality of service constraints, we may observe that facilities for Web programming are nowadays as a standard provided (as extensions) by languages such as Tcl, Perl, Python and Java. More domain-specific facilities are being developed in a CORBA context, or for frameworks such as San Francisco.

Document Object Model

Client-side scripting has been popularized by Dynamic HTML (DHTML) as originally introduced by Netscape and Microsoft. Nevertheless, scripting facilities are not standard accross the various browsers. To remedy this situation, the W3C has developed a recommendation for a *Document Object Model* (DOM), that provides a standard application programmer interface to access the structure and content of HTML and XML Web pages. The DOM allows XML and HTML pages to be treated in an object-oriented way, providing facilities for access, navigation and manipulation.

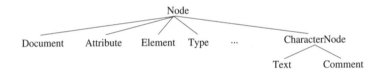

Slide 12-13: Hierarchical structure of DOM

Since XML is increasingly being used for other applications, such as Electronic Data Interchange (EDI), the DOM may in effect provide a foundation for developing Web applications.

The W3C DOM Recommendation provides interfaces, described in a language and platform-independent way in IDL, for the structural components that may be used in XML and HTML documents, as indicated in slide 12-13. These interfaces have been refined independently for both XML and HTML, to allow programmers to access XML and HTML-specific features. In addition to the IDL interfaces, a language-binding is specified for ECMAscript, which may serve as an example for similar bindings for Javascript and other languages, such as Java.

12.2.2   Intelligent agents

In Negroponte (1995), *intelligent agents* are characterized as autonomous, intelligent processes aiding the user in complex tasks, such as answering email, gathering information and planning activities. In practice, agents on the Internet may help in monitoring changes in Web pages, collecting information on topics of interest, or searching based on personal preferences. See Caglayan and Harrison (1997), Cheong (1996). Other types of agents, such as the *shopping agents* described in Kiniry and Zimmerman (1997) or even *virtual players* as those described in Watson (1996), might become possible in the future. However, despite the range of possible examples, the notion of *intelligent agent* is not very clear.

In Wooldridge and Jennings (1995), two definitions of *agent* are given, a soft definition, characterizing agents as autonomous processes that show some intelligence, and a hard definition attributing agents with mentalistic properties such as belief, desire and intentions. At this stage, the hard definition is clearly no more than a metaphor, since there is no technology that actually supports it. Taking the soft definition, one could argue that it is (partly) realized by modern object technology, as embodied in Java and CORBA, omitting the intelligence that is.

Whether or not adopting the agent metaphor, there is definitely a challenge of making applications more intelligent, and perhaps even more human. Cf. Petrie (1997) and Maes (1997). To my mind, one fundamental problem that we must solve to realize this goal is to define the technology, or the combination of technologies, needed to support the anthropomorphic metaphor of agents.

Given the merits of logic programming in a variety of application areas, encompassing areas such as diagnostic expert systems, natural language processing, and control systems, it seemed natural to organize a workshop called *Logic Programming and the Web* to investigate how logic programming technology might be deployed to make the Web more intelligent. Nevertheless, although the presentations at the workshop indicated that logic programming could fruitfully be applied in for example the creation of virtual worlds, e-commerce applications, and intelligent rental advisors, it did not shed any light on how to bridge the gap between the (mentalistic) agent metaphor and its software realization.

In the remainder of this section we will discuss the *Web Agent Support Program* research project to delineate the requirements for a framework providing agent technology support for Web applications.

Web Agent Support Program

The WASP project, of which an outline is given in Eliëns *et al.* (1997a), concerns the development of Web Agent Support to enable average users to keep track of relevant information on the Web.

The project was envisaged to result in a framework providing support for:

- intelligent navigation and information retrieval,

- information and document maintenance,

- user interfaces for Web-aware applications,

- dynamic documents with user-defined applets,

- declarative descriptions of agent behavior based on user preferences,

- declarative modeling of coordinated and cooperative behavior of software agents, and

- programming single and multi-agent systems.

As an target product for the WASP project, we envisaged developing *Pamela* (Personal Assistant for Maintaining Electronic Archives), an application combining the functional and architectural features mentioned above.

In summary, our project aims at providing insight in and solutions for

- modeling the behavior of cooperating agents,

- generic means for realizing actual agents in a Web-aware context,

- architectural support for programming agent-based systems.

The aspects of our research as indicated above address the problems involved in defining and realizing the potential of the *agent* metaphor as a human–computer interface in the distributed information system domain, in particular the Web.

The architectural requirements for realizing agents in a Web-aware context consist of (a) high-level support for distribution to allow for notification and the communication between agents, (b) access to the Web both in terms of server-side and client-side computation, and (c) support for information retrieval and data management.

Framework components | Web-aware agents | *12-14*

- a *methodology* for developing agent-based applications, as well as
- a *logical foundation* for modeling agent behavior; and in addition
- *guidelines* for realizing actual agent applications, and
- *software components* that can be used as building blocks, including
- a *language* for programming agent behavior.

Slide 12-14: Framework components

The WASP project is aimed to result in a framework (in its extended meaning) for the development of agent-based Web-aware applications. The components provided by such a framework are listed in slide 12-14. In addition to the proper software components, the framework includes a methodology, as well as a logical foundation. Further we wish to develop guidelines for realizing actual agent applications, and our hope is to develop a language for programming agent applications, based on the language DLP, described in appendix E.

12.3   The DejaVU experience – jamming (on) the Web

The *hush* library was originally developed to have an easy-to-use and flexible GUI library for the Software Engineering practicum at the Vrije Universiteit.

New components and extensions were created by students and research assistants, including components for (Csound-based) music, video, (OpenGL-based) VRML and MIDI. Since the Web was then in its early stages, we also built a Web browser and created a number of experimental extensions to enhance the functionality of the Web with new media and communication facilities. See slide 12-15.

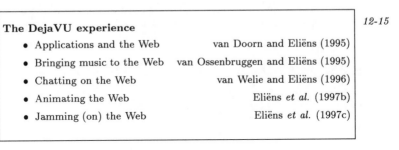

Slide 12-15: The DejaVU experience

Our approach was simple but effective. First we created the components that provided the desired functionality, then we provided a script interface for these components, and finally we provided new (HTML-like) tags for the syntactic description of the new functionality. We used stylesheets to separate the syntactical description from its operational realization. These stylesheets were written in Tcl. As the Web was maturing, we did not pursue this line of research. Nevertheless, since this work still represents a valid approach, we will discuss one of my favorite extensions, an extension that allows for jamming (on) the Web.

Jamming (on) the Web

Compared to textual and graphical material, the capabilities of the Web for musical information are rather poor. The embedding of music, or sound in general, rarely goes beyond links to raw audio and MIDI files or to streamed audio connections. To display a musical work, HTML authors have to use images containing the score. All of these solutions are very low level as they basically regard music as being just sound (or a picture in the case of a score).

True score files are usually a few orders of magnitude smaller, and the audio signal can be synthesized at the client side at any appropriate sample rate. Additionally, a high-level description of music provides the browser with far more information when compared to the raw samples. In previous work we proposed to transmit musical scores (instead of the raw samples) across the Internet and to add sound synthesis functionality to Web browsers, see van Ossenbruggen and Eliëns (1995), and the use of generic SGML to encode structured documents, see Eliëns et al. (1997b).

In this section, we describe an experimental framework that offers many of the ingredients for true networked music support including facilities for editing, displaying and playing musical scores as well as facilities for high-level exchange of musical material and real-time collaborative work involving music and sound. Our approach is based on traditional music notation and on MIDI for playing facilities. The framework builds upon the work done in the DejaVU project at the Software Engineering section of the Vrije Universiteit, which resulted in a suite of components for developing distributed Web-aware hypermedia applications.

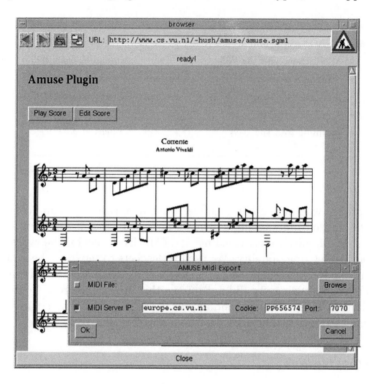

Slide 12-16: The score in a plugin

Scores on the Web The most ambitious markup language for the dissemination of music on the Web is probably the Standard Music Description Language, described in ISO (1996). SMDL expresses a musical work in terms of four basic domains. The *logical domain* – the primary focus of SMDL – is, according to the standard, describable as 'the composer's intentions with respect to pitches, rhythms, harmonies, dynamics, tempi, articulations, accents, etc.'. The central element of the logical domain, the *cantus* element, is an abstract, one-dimensional finite coordinate space onto which musical and non-musical events can be scheduled. This allows for the inclusion of any dependent time sequences (such as automated lighting information) in a musical work. The standard uses HyTime, ISO (1992), hyperlinking to specify the relations with information from the other three domains: the *gestural domain* – describing any number of particular performances (e.g. MIDI files or digital audio) of the work, the *visual domain* – describing any number of scores (a printable/displayable version) of the work, and the *analytical* *domain* – comprising any number of theoretical analyses or commentaries about the information in the three other domains. The addressing power of HyTime makes it possible to link directly into information expressed in other formats, including MIDI files, digital audio recordings or specific score notations, without modification. Our approach is more modest and we deploy a much simpler SGML representation, primarily geared to encode printable/displayable versions of the score (i.e. SMDL's visual domain). However, the format used is sufficiently rich to be able to generate a playable MIDI representation as well. Information which is usually added by performers (in SMDL this is represented in the gestural domain), such as explicit interpretations of tempi, articulations and accents, are not supported in the current version.

```
<SCORE>
  <TITLE>Corrente</TITLE>
  <COMPOSER>Antonio Vivaldi</COMPOSER>
  <STAFF>
    <MEASURE Sig="3,4" Key=F Clef=Gclef>
      <NOTE Pos="1,3" Stem=down>d6 4 0
      <REST Pos="3,6">C6 8 0
      <NOTE Pos="4,6" Stem=up>a5 8 0
      <NOTETUPLE Stem=down>
        <NOTE Pos="5,6">f5 8 0</NOTE>
        <NOTE Pos="6,6">a5 8 0</NOTE>
      </NOTETUPLE>
    </MEASURE>
    ...
  </STAFF>
</SCORE>
```

To support display and editing of SGML scores on the Web, we developed the Amuse score editor as a plugin for our Web browser (see slide 12-16). The editor has a graphical user interface and does not require any SGML knowledge from the user. Above is a fragment of an example score file, for which the associated style sheet with a CSS1-like syntax is shown below. Both documents can be edited by the graphical score editor plugin. Changes in the style sheet are dynamically reflected in the display of the score. A significant enlargement of the page-width parameter, for example, will allow for more measures on a single staff, and will result in a redraw of the complete score.

```
SCORE {
  margin-left : 30;
  margin-right : 30;
  margin-top : 80;
  margin-bottom : 20;
  page-height : 1000;
  page-width : 920;
}
TITLE {
```

```
    title-align : Center;
    title-font : -*-Times-Bold-R-Normal--*-240-*;
}
COMPOSER {
  composer-align : Center;
  composer-font : -*-Times-*-R-Normal--*-180-*;
}
```

Playing on the Web The playback facilities of our framework are centered around the *MIDI server*. After registering as a MIDI client, the score editor is able to send the generated MIDI version of the score to the separate MIDI server. The MIDI server builds upon a socket-level client/server library and a class library that provides the basic functionality for MIDI devices, MIDI clients and the MIDI server. Note that the audio device is usually an exclusive resource, and by connecting to a single MIDI server, several client applications can have simultaneous access to a single MIDI output device. The functionality of the MIDI server comprises:

- registering and unregistering MIDI devices,

- routing MIDI data between clients and MIDI devices, and

- administration and security checks.

When a MIDI device is registered, a *cookie* is given out that may be used by a client to request the server to set up a virtual connection with that device. The cookie also prohibits unauthorized clients from accessing a MIDI output device.

Collective improvisation We developed the keyboard applet, depicted in slide 7-8, as an alternative input device to be able to send 'live' MIDI data to our server. Since multiple applications can have access to the MIDI server, a user can have a score edit session running, and simultaneously be playing a keyboard applet.

To engage in a jam session, the keyboard applet connects to the *JamServer* instead of the MIDI server. The JamServer acts as the central point of a jam session, keeping track of all clients engaged in the session.

To start a jam session, all jam clients connect to a single JamServer and send it their MIDI data. The JamServer is connected to one or more MIDI servers, as depicted in slide 12-17. By having the JamServer separate from the MIDI server itself, the latter is relieved from the burden of jam session management. Every connected MIDI device will receive all the MIDI data submitted by the jam clients. This data is relayed to these devices by the MIDI server(s), through the virtual MIDI data stream that is created when registering as a jam client.

In slide 12-17 we see three jam clients connected to a single JamServer (on machine B). The MIDI server is running on the same machine as the JamServer. Both the clients on machine A and C have registered a MIDI-out device (a software

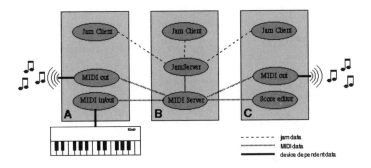

Slide 12-17: The jam server

sound synthesis MIDI program developed for Solaris) with the MIDI server on B. The user on A has additionally registered a MIDI-in device (the keyboard). Using the keyboard, the user on A can contribute to the jamming. The score editor on C is directly connected to the MIDI server and is not engaged in the jam session. The MIDI server will redirect MIDI requests from the score editor only to the MIDI device on C.

Measurements To give an indication of the speed and response times of our system, we have used a special jam client, *jamping*, that measures the average delay between sending a MIDI message to the JamServer and receiving the same message on a connected MIDI device. For a 486DX2-66 PC with Linux with one client and both servers local, this resulted in a round-trip-delay time of 5.5 milliseconds. A similar setup on a Sparc-5 with Solaris resulted in 2.6 milliseconds. A similar configuration with the JamServer on a LAN gave 3.5 milliseconds average round-trip-delay time. Nevertheless, with a server in Amsterdam and a client in Sweden, we obtained an average round-trip-delay time of 87 milliseconds, with a peak of 1.6 seconds. Clearly, the length and variability of round-trip-delay times may be a prohibiting factor for jamming on a global scale.

Architecture of the Web components The software described so far was developed for our SGML-based Web browser as an extension to the *hush* class library, Eliëns *et al.* (1997b).

In slide 12-18 an overview is given of the basic Web-related components of the hush library. The browser provides the top-level user interface for all Web components, including a viewer, a scrollbar, navigation buttons (back, forward, home, reload) and an entry box to enter URLs. The netclient, web and MIMEviewer components form the conceptual base of our approach of connecting to the Web:

- *viewer* – a widget for the inline display of several MIME types, such as HTML, VRML and Amuse score formats.

- *web* – an extension of the *MIMEviewer* with history and caching.

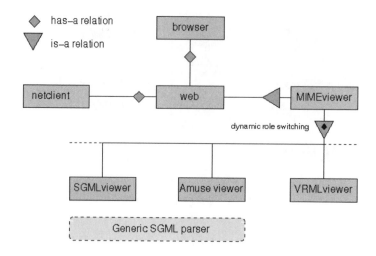

Slide 12-18: Web components

- *netclient* – the interface to the Internet, supporting several protocols.

The MIMEviewer component provides an abstract interface to viewers for several MIME types. The web widget only knows about the (abstract) MIMEviewer class while the actual functionality is implemented in several concrete viewer classes, one per MIME type. Specific viewers for new MIME types can be plugged dynamically into the MIMEviewer object.

When the MIMEviewer gets the instruction to display a document of a certain MIME type, it changes its role and becomes a viewer for that particular MIME type. This dynamic role-switching idiom is discussed in more detail in chapter 2. As a result, the addition of new viewers can be done without changing the web widget.

The netclient component builds the bridge between the local web widget and the World Wide Web by providing an abstract and uniform interface to network (file) access and transport protocols. In the realization of the netclient components we have employed the dynamic role-switching idiom in the same way as in the implementation of the MIMEviewer components.

The web object creates a MIMEviewer object and tells which role it should play (e.g. SGML, Amuse or VRMLviewer). This role can be changed during the lifetime of a single MIMEviewer object by calling a method to change its role. A browser typically uses only one single MIMEviewer object that changes its role according to the type of data that should be displayed. The SGMLviewer is the default viewer, it displays generic SGML documents by using style sheets for each document type. By default, a style sheet for HTML is used. Since our generic SGMLviewer is better suited to textual documents and does not offer editing support, we developed a separate viewer/editor to process our Amuse/SGML score files.

Since the MIMEviewer provides no network functionality at all, it generates
events whenever it needs to retrieve data pointed to by a URL. Such events
are generated as a response to user interaction (e.g. clicking an anchor) or to
fetch inline data during the parsing process. These events are typically handled
by the web component which plays a central role in our approach because it
combines the functionality of the MIMEviewer and the netclient components.
Additionally, the web component adds a history and caching mechanism to the
MIMEviewer. The web component's behavior is similar to the standard widgets
of the *hush* framework, and can be conveniently used as a part of an application's
GUI. Because the web widget has both a C++ class interface and a script interface,
it is easy to create, or extend, applications with Web functionality.

12.4   Software architectures revisited

The Web is, at the time of writing, still in flux. Yet it is becoming more and more
the standard infrastructure on which applications are built. A recurring question
is, *'how do we build Web applications?'*. There is no definite answer to this
question. There is no body of solutions that may serve to indicate proven practice.
But there is, definitely, a convergence towards *objectifying*, or *object-orienting* as
it is called in Wiggins (1999), the Web and its applications. Anyway, the following
quote, taken from Bass *et al.* (1998), p. 10, says it all.

> *It is a brave architect who, in today's environment, does not develop,
> or at least consider, an object-oriented design.*

Clearly, the architecture of the technological infrastructure of the Web, as well
as the architecture of Web applications, may benefit from an object-oriented
approach. Nevertheless, knowing this, we still do not know how to build actual
Web applications.

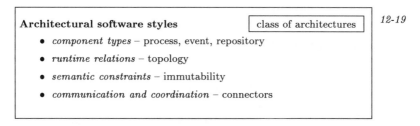

Slide 12-19: Architectural software styles

From the perspective of software architectures, we may ask ourselves what
architectural style, or for that matter which mix of architectural styles, we may
deploy for building such applications. As a reminder, an architectural style, which
characterizes a class of software architectures, consists of a description of the
types of components used (processes, events, repositories), the (runtime) relations

between these components (for example the network topology), possible semantic constraints (such as the immutability of particular components) and properties concerning communication and cooperation (such as the connectors or protocols used).

Themes and variations   technological constraints   *12-20*

- OO – simple call and return
- CORBA – independent components
- WWW – data centered
- events – independent components
- logic – virtual machine architecture

Slide 12-20: Themes and variations

A rather simple-minded categorization of architectural styles, reflecting obvious technological constraints, is given in slide 12-20. Each of the styles is characterized by a single phrase capturing a central feature of the style. For example, an OO approach may be characterized by the fact that it embodies a simple call and return mechanism, which, by the way, gets its power from the fact that it concerns methods or, in C++ jargon, virtual functions. Events have proven to be an excellent means to obtain a high degree of independence between components. And logic, as has been argued in section 7.3.1, may be used to promote a clear separation between knowledge-level and system-level aspects of a system, by embedding a (virtual) logic machine.

The categorization is, however, simple-minded because, as we may observe in retrospect, most of the applications discussed contain elements of at least a couple of the styles mentioned. So, instead of discussing one style, we need to consider a mix of styles, and determine what mix of styles may be effectively used to create the applications we have in mind.

The architecture of the Web

To return to the Web, why is the notion of software architecture important? As indicated in slide 12-21, for one, the Web is still growing at a rapid rate, and it is becoming increasingly important economically. So, we are faced with the problem of managing this growth, and, much sooner than we could have expected, with the problem of maintaining the applications that populate the Web.

Secondly, the Web is continuously enhanced with new functionality, including, for example, *synchronized multimedia* as proposed in the SMIL standard, see SMIL (1999). Consequently, with respect to the technological infrastructure, we need to be able to accommodate new requirements, such as *quality of service*, needed for the timely delivery of multimedia material.

And thirdly, many attempts are being undertaken to improve the quality of

```
┌─────────────────────────────────────────────────────────┐
│ Architectural issues                          12-21      │
│                                                          │
│   • managing growth, maintaining installed base          │
│   • enhanced functionality – synchronized multimedia     │
│   • improved technological infrastructure – HTTP-NG      │
│                                                          │
└─────────────────────────────────────────────────────────┘
```

Slide 12-21: Architectural issues

the infrastructure itself, as exemplified by the HTTP-NG effort, which aims at higher speeds and a state-full communication protocol, see Janssen (1999).

As clearly stated by the Web's principal architect, Tim Berners-Lee, graceful extensibility has always been one of the primary goals in developing the architecture for the Web. In this respect, the Web differs significantly from other distributed technologies, such as CORBA, which does not allow for non-compliant extensions. In contrast, the Web does to a great degree allow for non-compliant extensions simply by ignoring them, until they become a standard. The challenge, then, from an architectural point of view, is to come up with better standards and better technologies without sacrificing the extensibility allowed by non-strict technologies such as HTML and HTTP.

Plugin architectures

To conclude this chapter, I would like to discuss briefly an extension mechanism that has proved to be invaluable for developing Web applications, the *plugin architecture*. Plugin architectures are becoming more and more popular, for 'ordinary' tools such as Adobe Photoshop and Macromedia Director. In a Web context, the most notable examples are Netscape Navigator and Microsoft Internet Explorer, which both provide a facility to extend the browser with new functionality that is available in a dynamically loadable library.

Client NPP/Callbacks	Browser NPN/Calls
Instantiation and Destruction	Version Info
Stream Notification	Stream Creation and Destruction
Reading and Writing Streams	StreamAsFile
LiveConnect	

Plugin architectures are realized by using callbacks, in the same way as in object-oriented frameworks. Above, an overview is given of the callback functions required by the Netscape plugin architecture. These functions must be implemented by the (plugin) client, so that the browser can recognize and activate the plugin. Such callbacks encompass instantiation and destruction functions, notification when a stream is ready, functions for reading and writing streams, and the *Live Connect* functions, which enable the (plugin) client to communicate with Javascript functions and Java applets that are currently active. The browser, in return, provides convenience functions to obtain version information, to create or destroy streams or to store the contents of a stream in a temporary file.

It should be noted that the actual API for the creation of (Netscape) plugins is not object-oriented, although a partial class library is available to create plugins in an object-oriented manner.

Nevertheless, ignoring details, plugin architectures indicate what may become the dominant paradigm of the future, framework-like environments that are extensible by components following a clearly defined pattern or protocol; that is to say, components created according to the principles of object-oriented software development.

Summary

This chapter discussed the relevance of object-oriented technology to the development of Web-applications.

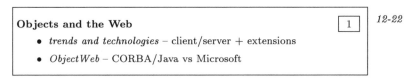

Slide 12-22: Section 12.1: Objects and the Web

In section 1, we looked at trends and technologies, in particular the ongoing creation of the *ObjectWeb*, which is essentially an ongoing war between Microsoft and the rest of the world.

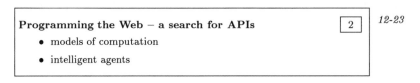

Slide 12-23: Section 12.2: Programming the Web – a search for APIs

In section 2, we discussed the model of computation underlying the Web. We looked at the requirements we may have for APIs, and we explored the notion of intelligent agents on the Web,

In section 3, some of the research efforts carried out in the DejaVU project were presented. In particular, we looked at an SGML-based approach to extend the Web with new media and communication facilities.

Finally, in section 4, we discussed some remaining architectural issues. We concluded that many of the applications discussed in this book draw from a mixture of technologies and architectural styles.

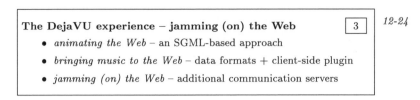

Slide 12-24: Section 12.3: The DejaVU experience – jamming (on) the Web

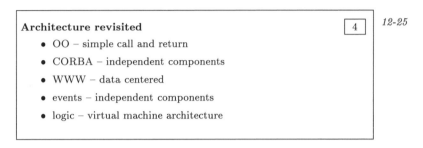

Slide 12-25: Section 12.4: Architecture revisited

Questions

1. Describe the architecture of the Web. Explain the relevance of objects for the Web.

2. Sketch the Microsoft approach to the ObjectWeb. Discuss its pros and cons.

3. In what ways can Java and CORBA be deployed in Web applications?

4. Indicate how the computation model underlying the Web deviates from the computation models underlying, respectively, object systems and client-server systems.

5. What requirements can you think of for libraries or frameworks for developing Web applications?

6. Discuss the Document Object Model.

7. What are the requirements for a framework supporting intelligent agents?

8. Explain the issues that arise in extending the Web with additional media functionality. What solutions can you think of? Can you give an example?

Further reading

For information concerning the Web, have a look at http://www.w3c.org which give a detailed account on the history of the Web and many other issues. For

an exposition of the issues and technologies that play a role in the battle for
the ObjectWeb, consult Orfali *et al.* (1999). A good introduction to agents
and its associated technology is given in Wooldridge and Jennings (1995). For
architectural issues, again, I recommend Bass *et al.* (1998).

Appendices

A

The language Smalltalk

Smalltalk has been, without doubt, the most influential of all object-oriented programming languages. Originally meant as an *easy-to-use* programming language for the *Dynabook* (a laptop *avant-la-lettre* developed in 1972 at Xerox Parc), it has developed into a powerful general purpose programming language (which has stabilized in Smalltalk-80) that runs on many platforms. From the start, an interactive programming environment has been an integral part of the language implementation. Later implementations also include support for the interactive construction of user interfaces.

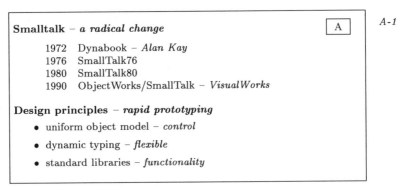

Slide A-1: The language Smalltalk

Influenced by the ideas of objects and classes embodied in Simula, the design philosophy underlying Smalltalk clearly reflects the desire to effect nothing less than a radical change in programming practice. Characteristic for the design of Smalltalk is a *uniform object model* (which is even used to support common control constructs), *dynamic typing* (which accounts for much of the flexibility of Smalltalk) and a sizeable collection of *standard library classes* (providing the functionality necessary to build complex applications). Smalltalk has successfully been used, in particular, for rapid prototyping.

Terminology The introduction of Smalltalk came along with an, at the time, astounding terminology. See slide A-2.

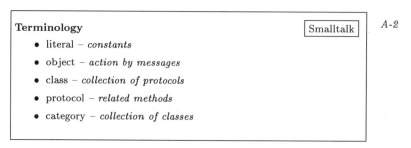

Slide A-2: Smalltalk – terminology

Most important is the notion of *object*, which is something that acts in response to messages (by executing a *method* procedure). In Smalltalk, everything is an object. Moreover, every object is an instance of a class. A *class* is the description of a collection of objects which share the same structure and applicable methods. The methods of both objects and classes (considered as an object) are grouped in so-called *protocols*. Related collections of classes may be grouped in so-called *categories*. Both *protocols* and *categories* are merely syntactic add-ons, meant to facilitate programming.

Expressions The syntax of Smalltalk needs some time to get used to. Since everything is an object, expressions may be regarded as being composed of constants, variables and method expressions.

There is a large variety of literal constants (including numbers, characters, strings, symbols, byte arrays and literal arrays), as depicted in slide A-3.

```
Literal constants                                              A-3

   • number – 1, 34.6, 8r24

   • character – $a, $b, ...

   • string – "this is a string"

   • symbol – #Float

   • byte array – # [0 255 2 7]

   • array of literals – # (12.1 # ($a $b))
```

Slide A-3: Smalltalk – expressions (1)

Expressions may be assigned to variables. Usually, variables are given a name that betrays their expected type, as for example *anInteger*. (In Smalltalk, class names start with an upper case and variables with a lower case letter.)

```
                                                                    A-4
  Assignment
      • aVar := 1.

  Variables
      • temporary, instance, class, pool, global

  Block expressions
      •  [ :arg | expression ]
```

Slide A-4: Smalltalk – expressions (2)

We distinguish between *temporary variables* (having a method scope), *instance variables* (having an object scope), *class variables* (having as their scope the collection of instances of the class), *pool variables* (that have a category as their scope) and *global variables* (that are visible everywhere). See slide A-4.

A special kind of expression is the *block expression* that consists of a program fragment, possibly parametrized with an argument. Block expressions are used to define control structures employing message expressions. Block expressions correspond to function literals (lambda-expressions) in languages such as Lisp and Smalltalk.

Message expressions may be characterized as either *unary, binary* or *keyword* messages. See slide A-5.

```
                                                                    A-5
  Message expressions
      • unary, binary, keyword

  Unary
      •  1.0 sin ,  Random new

  Binary
      • arithmetic – ctr + 1
      • comparison –  aVar >= 200
      • combination –  100 @ 200
      • association –   # Two -> 2
```

Slide A-5: Smalltalk – expressions (3)

Unary messages consist of a single method name addressed at an expression denoting an object, for example a constant or a class.

As binary method expressions, we have the familiar arithmetic and comparison expressions as well as the less familiar combination expression (used for graphics

coordinates) and association expression (used to define associative maps). All
binary (infix) message selectors have the same precedence and bind to the left.
Despite their common appearance, these are all true message expressions (which
may lead to surprises, for example in the case of a non-commutative definition of
the arithmetic operations). Examples of keyword message selectors are given in
slide A-6.

Control Smalltalk has no control structures except message passing. However,
familiar control structures are defined as methods on *booleans* and *integers*. See
slide A-6.

Keyword methods   *A-6*

```
        (i <= 7)
                ifTrue: [ m:= "oke" ]
                ifFalse: [ ... ]
```

Control structures

- conditional – ifTrue: ifFalse:
- iteration – whileTrue:
- looping – to: by: do: [:i | ...]

Slide A-6: Smalltalk – control

For example, an *if-statement* may be obtained by defining the method *ifTrue:
ifFalse:* on booleans. (Despite the use of keywords, parameter passing in Smalltalk
is positional. Each sequence of keywords may be regarded as a different method.)

In a similar vein, we may define iteration and looping. For looping, we may
employ the parameter mechanism of blocks, as indicated above.

Objects Everything in Smalltalk is an object. An *object* may be regarded as
consisting of instance variables and a collection of methods.

Object – *behavior*   *A-7*

- instance variables, methods

Class – *description*

- class variables, class methods

Self – *self reference*

- *super* for ancestors

Slide A-7: Smalltalk – objects (1)

A *class* is the description of a collection of objects, its instances. Considered as an object, a class may be said to have class variables and class methods.

For self-reference the special expression *self* may be used. To invoke methods from the parent class the expression *super* may be used.

An example of an object class description is given in slide A-8. The class *Ctr* is defined as a subclass of the class *behavior*. It supports an *initialization* protocol (containing the method *initialize*), a protocol for modification (containing the method *add*), and an *inspection* protocol (containing the method *value*).

Example – *class*   *A-8*

```
Behavior subclass: #Ctr
instanceVariableNames: 'value'
Ctr methodsFor: 'initialization'
   initialize
         value := 0.
Ctr methodsFor: 'modifications'
   add: aValue
         value := value + aValue.
Ctr methodsFor: 'inspection'
   value
         ^value
```

Slide A-8: Smalltalk – objects (2)

Note that *value* occurs both as an instance variable and as a method. Only the method is accessible by the user.

In addition, we need a class description defining the object functionality of Ctr, which consists of an *instance creation* protocol defining the class method *new*. See slide A-9. This class description is (implicitly) an instance of a meta class generated by the Smalltalk system. See section 5.5.

Class description – *meta class*   *A-9*

```
Ctr class
instanceVariableNames: ''
Ctr class methodsFor: 'instance creation'
      new
            ^super new initialize
```

Slide A-9: Smalltalk – objects (3)

Inheritance Each class in the Smalltalk library is (ultimately) a subclass of the class *Object*. See slide A-10.

```
┌─────────────────────────────────────────────────────────┐
│ Inheritance                                    A-10      │
│                                                          │
│         Object                                           │
│            Magnitude                                     │
│               ArithmeticValue                            │
│                  Number                                  │
│                     Integer                              │
│                                                          │
│                                                          │
└─────────────────────────────────────────────────────────┘
```

Slide A-10: Smalltalk – inheritance

Smalltalk supports only single inheritance. Above, the ancestor classes of the class *Integer* are depicted as a branch of the inheritance tree.

Technology Inheritance, in combination with message passing, allows for powerful programming techniques. As an example, an illustration is given of the cooperation between two objects employing the *Model/View* paradigm. The *model* class *Ctr*, depicted in slide A-11, may be regarded as embodying the proper functionality of the application.

```
┌──────────────────────────────────────────────────────────┐
│                                                 A-11     │
│   Model subclass: #Ctr                  ┌─────────┐      │
│                                         │  Model  │      │
│     ...                                 └─────────┘      │
│     initialize                                           │
│       value := 0.                                        │
│       TV open: self.                                     │
│     ...                                                  │
│     add: anInt                                           │
│       value := value + anInt.                            │
│       self changed: #value.                              │
│                                                          │
└──────────────────────────────────────────────────────────┘
```

Slide A-11: Smalltalk – technology (1)

A *view* class defines an object that may be used to monitor the behavior of the *model* instance in a non-intrusive way. To support monitoring, the model class *Ctr* needs to install one or more view objects during initialization, and further, it must notify its view object(s) whenever its contents have been modified, as in *add*. See slide A-12.

The view class *TV* defines a class method *open* to create a new view object for an instance of the *Ctr* class. It must further define a method *update* (that will automatically be invoked when the *Ctr* instance signals a change) to display some message, for example the value of the *Ctr* object monitored.

The programming environment forms an integral part of the Smalltalk system.

```
                                                                      A-12
     View subclass: #TV                          View
     instanceVariableNames: ''
     TV methodsFor: 'updating'
     update: aValue
          Transcript show: 'ok'; cr .
     TV class
     instanceVariableNames: ''
     TV class methodsFor: 'instance creation'
          open: aCtr
             self new model: aCtr
```

Slide A-12: Smalltalk – technology (2)

The code depicted above (which clearly reflects the object nature of classes) is usually not the result of text editing, but is generated by the system. The Smalltalk programming system, in particular the standard library, however, will take some time to get familiar with.

Summary This section presented a brief introduction to the programming language Smalltalk.

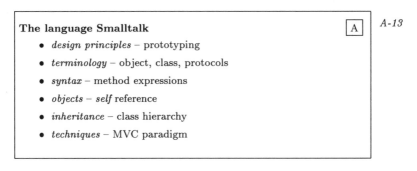

Slide A-13: Smalltalk – summary

It discussed the design principles underlying Smalltalk and the terminology originally associated with Smalltalk. It further covered the basic syntactic constructs and characterized object behavior and inheritance using examples. Also, an illustration was given of the use of the MVC paradigm.

B

The language Eiffel

The language Eiffel has been designed with a clear concern for correctness and validation. It supports a bottom-up development approach, centered around the design of robust classes. Along with the language, Meyer (1988) introduces the notion of *contracts* as a means to specify the mutual obligations between the user of an object and the object in terms of a *client/server* relation.

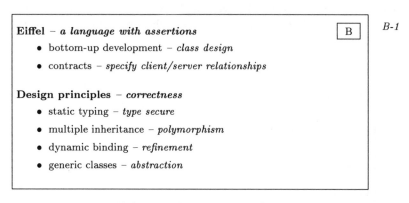

Slide B-1: The language Eiffel

Eiffel is a (type secure) *statically typed* language, providing *multiple inheritance* and generic classes. Recently, Eiffel-3 has been introduced, supporting a number of features (such as overloading) inspired by C++. See Meyer (1992a).

Terminology The design of Eiffel also reflects a concern with the software engineering issues involved in the development and maintenance of class libraries. The language is built around a number of keywords, which accounts for an easy to read, albeit somewhat verbose, layout of programs.

The keyword *class* precedes a class definition, which, according to Meyer (1988), may be considered as a model for a collection of objects. The keyword *feature* precedes the attributes, functions and procedures defined by a class. The

411

The language Eiffel – *keywords* *B-2*

- *class* – a model for a set of objects
- *feature* – attribute, function, procedure
- *export* – interface declaration
- *inherit* – class inclusion and subtyping (!)
- *redefine, rename* – to change inherited features
- *deferred* – to postpone the implementation
- *require, ensure, invariant* – assertions

Slide B-2: Eiffel – terminology

keyword *export* precedes the list of visible features, in other words the interface declaration of the class. The keyword *inherit* precedes the list of inherited classes, specifying class inclusion and the subtyping relationships. The keywords *rename* and *redefine* are used to change inherited features. The keyword *deferred* may be used to indicate that a feature will be implemented (in the future) in an inherited class, and the keyword *obsolete* may be used to indicate that a feature will not be supported in a future release. Finally, the keywords *require, ensure* and *invariant* indicate assertions that specify respectively the pre- and post-conditions for a (method) feature and the class invariant.

Type expressions – *conformance* *B-3*

- basic types – *Boolean, Integer*
- formal parameter types – *Array[T], List[T]*
- class types – *user-defined*
- anchored types – **like** *current*

Value expressions

- arithmetic, comparison, method evaluation – *o.m(...)*

Assignment

- *var := expression*

Slide B-3: Eiffel – type expressions

Expressions Eiffel is a strongly typed language. In Eiffel, variables must be explicitly typed by means of a declaration involving type expressions. Type expressions range over *basic types* (such as *Boolean* and *Integer*), *formal type parameters* of generic types (as the T in *Array[T]*, which stands for the type of the elements of the array), *class types* (that are defined by the user) and *anchored types*, for instance *like current* (which results in the type of the *current* object, or *self* in Smalltalk terminology). Anchored types present some problems for the type safety of Eiffel programs. See section 9.6 for a discussion.

In Meyer (1988) *conformance* rules are specified which are used to determine whether a given type is a subtype of another type. See section 9.2 for an extensive discussion of the subtyping relationship.

Value expressions in Eiffel comprise the familiar arithmetical and comparison operations, as well as the message expressions of the form $o.m(\ldots)$ that result in the evaluation of the method m by the object o. Parameter passing in Eiffel is positional. See slide B-3.

Control structures Control in Eiffel is meant to be effected primarily by defining (and redefining) the appropriate classes. However, control constructs both for branching and iteration are provided. See slide B-4.

Control – *method refinement*   *B-4*

- branching – *if ... then ... elsif ... else ... end*
- iterations – *from ... until ... loop ... end*

Slide B-4: Eiffel – control

The *if-statement* has a classical form, as in Pascal. The *iteration-statement* may be used in a variety of ways, as a *for-loop* and as a *while-statement* (by omitting the *from*) part).

Objects Objects in Eiffel are defined by classes. A typical class definition is given in slide B-5.

The class *counter* exports the features *inc* and *val*. The feature *count* is hence private to an instance of *counter*, since it does not appear in the interface defined by the *export* part.

The *create* feature is automatically exported, and is used to create an instance of *counter* by the statement *x.create* for a variable *x* of type *counter*. The reserved word *Result* is used to return a value from a function feature. The method feature *inc* specifies both a pre-condition and a post-condition. The reserved word *old* is used to access the value of the instance variable *count* before evaluating *inc*. Finally, the invariance states the constraint that a *counter* instance never has a value below zero.

Inheritance Eiffel supports multiple inheritance. As an example, look at the class *FixedList* in slide B-6, which is implemented as a combination (by inheritance) of a generic *List* and a generic *Array*.

Using (multiple) inheritance implies that a *FixedList* may be regarded as a

```
       class counter export inc val feature
       count : Integer
       create is do count := 0 end
       inc( n : Integer ) is
                require n > 0 do
                count := count + n
                ensure count = old count + n
                end
       val : Integer is do Result := count end
       invariant count >= 0
       end -- class counter
```

B-5

Slide B-5: Eiffel – objects

```
Multiple inheritance

       class Fixed_List [T] export ...
       inherit
                List [T]
                Array [T]
       feature
        ...
       end
```

B-6

Slide B-6: Eiffel – inheritance

subtype of both *Array* and *List*. However, the *export* list in the end determines what interface is provided and hence what type the class embodies.

Technology Developing programs in Eiffel is meant to be primarily a matter of modeling, that is designing classes and the (inheritance) relations between classes. An essential ingredient of class development is the design of appropriate interfaces.

```
Rename and/or redefine

       class C export ... inherit
       A rename m as m1 redefine p
       B rename m as m2 redefine q
       feature
        ...
       end
```

B-7

Slide B-7: Eiffel – techniques

To define a class as (derived from) a combination of classes, Eiffel allows both the renaming and redefinition of inherited features. See slide B-7. In Meyer (1988), many practical hints are given and numerous examples employing these mechanisms.

Summary This section has given an introduction to the Eiffel language. It discussed the design principles underlying Eiffel, which may be characterized as being focused on static typing and support for the development of reliable programs.

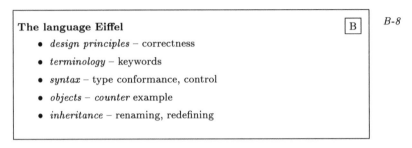

Slide B-8: Eiffel – summary

Further, it presented an overview of the keywords related to the constructs offered, and discussed type expressions, value expressions and control statements. An example was given to illustrate the features offered. Finally, we looked at the mechanisms of renaming and redefining, which are needed to avoid name clashes when using multiple inheritance.

C

The language C++

C++ is often disparaged because of its C heritage. Nevertheless, not only is C++ in many respects better than C, it also offers much more. From its conception, C++ has reflected a strong concern with static typing. As such it has influenced the ANSI C standard accepted in 1985.

Ellis and Stroustrup (1990) describe most of what has become the ANSI/ISO C++ standard, which is implemented by, among others, the GNU and Cygnus C++ compilers, and Microsoft Visual C++.

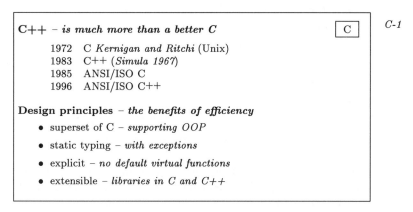

Slide C-1: The language C++

The leading design principle underlying C++ is to support object-oriented programming, yet allow the programmer and user the benefits of (runtime) efficiency. It has been designed as (almost) a superset of C, to allow the integration of C code in a seamless way. It provides strong static typing, yet allows the programmer to escape the rigidity of typing if absolutely necessary. C++ is designed to be extensible. This means that no assumptions are made with regard to a programming environment or standard library classes.

The C language was originally introduced as a (Unix) systems programming language, and is gradually being replaced by C++ for this purpose. However, C++ lends itself to many other applications, including mathematical programming and business applications.

Terminology The C++ language is without doubt a large and complex language. Fortunately, an increasing number of textbooks have become available which provide an appropriate introduction to C++ and its use for the realization of abstract data types, including Headington and Riley (1994) and Weiss (1993).

Among the additional keywords introduced in C++ (extending C) we have the keyword *const* (which may be used to define constants), the keyword *inline* (which may be used to define inline expanded functions, that for C have to be defined using macros), the keyword *new* (to dynamically create objects on the heap), the keyword *delete* (to destroy dynamically created objects) and, finally, the keywords *private*, *public* and *protected* (to indicate access restrictions for the instances of an object class). See slide C-2.

Keywords: | C++ overview | *C-2*

  • **inline, new, delete, private, protected, public**

Language features:

  • constructors – *to create and initialize*
  • destructors – *to reclaim resources*
  • virtual functions – *dynamic binding*
  • (multiple) inheritance – *for refinement*
  • type conversions – *to express relations between types*
  • private, protected, public – *for access protection*
  • friends – *to allow for efficient access*

Slide C-2: C++ – terminology (1)

The language features offered by C++ supporting object-oriented programming include *constructors* (which are defined for each class to create and initialize instances), *destructors* (which may be used to reclaim resources), *virtual functions* (which must be used to effect dynamic binding), *multiple inheritance* (to specify behavioral refinement), *type conversions* (which allow the user to define coercion relations between, both system-defined and user-defined, data types), and *friend declarations* (which may be used to grant efficient access to selected functions or classes).

The annotated reference manual (ARM) is not a book to be used to learn the language, but provides an excellent source of detailed technical explanations and the motivations underlying particular design decisions.

To get an idea of the full set of features offered by C++, look at the meaning of a name in C++ (as described in the ARM). See slide C-3. A *name* can either

---

Some basic terminology   *C-3*

name – *denotes an object, a function, set of functions, enumerator, type, class member, template, a value or a label*

- introduced by a *declaration*,
- used within a *scope*, and
- has a *type* which determines its use.

object – *region of storage*

- a named object has a *storage class* that determines its *lifetime*, and
- the *meaning* of the values found in an object is determined by the *type* of the expression used to *access* it

---

Slide C-3: C++ – terminology (2)

denote an object, a function, a set of functions, an enumerator, a type (including classes, structs and unions), a class member, a template (class or function), a value or a label. A name is typically introduced by a declaration, and is used within a scope. Moreover, each name has a type which determines its use. An *object* in C++ is nothing but a *region of storage*, with a lifetime determined by its storage class (that is, whether it is created on the stack or on the heap). Meaning is given to an object by the type used to access it, which is determined during compile time. The only information needed at runtime in C++ is concerned with virtual functions (which require a virtual function dispatch table for dynamic binding).

Expressions Again due to its C heritage, C++ supports many *basic types* (including *int*, *char* and *float*) and *compound types* (including arrays, functions, pointer types, reference types, and user-defined class, union or struct types). See slide C-4.

Type expressions   *C-4*

- basic types – *int, char, float, ...*
- array – *int* ar[SIZE]
- function – *void* f(int)
- pointer – int* , char*, void (*f)(int)
- reference – int&, char*&
- class, union, struct – *user-defined*

Slide C-4: C++ – expressions (1)

Pointer types encompass pointers to basic types and pointers to user-defined types, such as functions and classes. The difference between *object*, *reference* and *pointer types* may be succinctly characterized as the difference between the actual thing, an alias (that looks like the actual thing but isn't) and an address of the actual thing (where you have to go to get it).

Expressions
C-5

- operators – + , - ,.., < , <= ,.., == , != ,.., && , ||
- indexing – o[e]
- application – o(...)
- access – o.m(...)
- dereference – p->m(...)
- in/decrement – o++, o--
- conditional – b?e1:e2

Assignment

- var = expression
- modifying – +=. -=, ...

Slide C-5: C++ – expressions (2)

Value expressions may be created using arithmetic and comparison operators (including **==** for equality and **!=** for inequality). As logical operators, C++ includes conjunction (**&&**) and disjunction (**||**), as well as a number of bitwise logical operators. Also, we have an *indexing* operator (which may be defined for arbitrary types), an *application* operator (which may also be defined for arbitrary types), an *access* operator (which is as a standard used for member function invocation or method calls), a *dereference* operator (which is used to invoke member functions through a pointer to an object) and *in-* and *decrement* operations (that, again, may be defined for arbitrary types). Needless to say, user-defined operators must be applied with care. Also, we have a conditional expression of the form $b?e_1:e_2$ testing the condition b to deliver e_1 when it evaluates to true and e_2 otherwise. Also, C++ allows for sequencing within expressions of the form $(e_1, \ldots, e_n)$, which evaluates $e_1, \ldots, e_n$ in that order and delivers e_n as its value.

Assignments in C++, it is important to note, are written as *var = expression* with a single = symbol. This convention is known to cause mistakes by programmers raised with languages such as Pascal or Modula-2. In addition, C++ offers modifying assignments, which may be used as, for example, in *n += 1*, which is identical in meaning to $n = n + 1$.

Control C++ provides a number of elementary control structures, directly inherited from C. See slide C-6.

These include a *conditional* statement (of which the else part may be omitted), a *selection* statement (that allows for a default branch), an *iteration* statement (which is also offered in a reversed form to allow a repeat), a *loop* statement (consisting of an initialization part, a part to test for termination, and a repetition

---

Control *C-6*

- conditional – *if (b) S1; else S2;*
- selection – *switch(n){case n1 : S1; break; ... default : ...}*
- iteration – *while (b) S*
- looping – *for(int i = 1; i ⩽ MAX; i + +) S*
- jumps – *return, break, continue, goto*

Slide C-6: C++ – control

part to increase the loop variable) and, finally, *jumps* (including the so much despised *goto*).

Objects Despite the (at first sight) overwhelming possibilities of defining values and control, the essence of programming in C++ must be the development of the abstract data types. To illustrate the difference between C and C++, let us first look at the realization of abstract data type in a procedural way in a C style (employing references), and then at the realization in C++ employing the class construct. Note that in plain C, pointers must be used instead of references.

ADT in C style *C-7*

```
struct ctr { int n; }

void ctr_init(ctr& c) { c.n = 0; }
void ctr_add(ctr& c, int i) { c.n = c.n + i; }
int ctr_val(ctr& c) { return c.n; }
```

Usage

```
ctr c; ctr_init(c); ctr_add(c,1);
ctr* p = new ctr; ctr_init(*p); ctr_add(*p);
```

Slide C-7: C++ – objects (1)

The *ctr* type defined in slide C-7 may be regarded as a standard realization of abstract data types in a procedural language. It defines a data structure *ctr*, an initialization function *ctr_init*, a function *ctr_add* to modify the value or state of an element of the (abstract) type and an observation function *ctr_val* that informs us about its value. We may either declare a *ctr* object or a pointer to a *ctr* instance and invoke the functions as indicated.

In contrast, to define (the realization of) an abstract data type in C++, we employ the class construct and define member functions (or methods) that operate on the data encapsulated by instances of the class. See slide C-8.

ADT in C++

```
class ctr {
public:
    ctr() { n = 0; }                        constructor
    ~ctr() { cout << "bye"; };              destructor
    void add( int i = 1) { n = n + i; }
    int val( ) { return n; }
private:
    int n;
};
```

Usage

```
ctr c; c.add(1); cout << c.val();
ctr* p = new ctr(); c->add(1);  ...
```

Slide C-8: C++ – objects (2)

Inheritance Not only is C++ an efficient language, but it also offers features lacking in Smalltalk and Eiffel. In particular, it allows us to make a distinction between (private) members of a class that are inaccessible to everybody (including descendants), (protected) members that are inaccessible to ordinary clients (but not to descendants), and (public) members that are accessible to everybody.

Inheritance

```
class A {                              ancestor
public:
A() { n = 0; }
void add( int i ) { n = n + i; }
virtual int val() { return n; }
protected:            private would deny access to D
int n;
};

class D : public A {                   descendant
public:
D() : A() { }
int val() { return n % 2; }
};
```

Slide C-9: C++ – inheritance

In the example in slide C-9, using *private* instead of protected would deny access to the instance variable n of A. The example also illustrates the use of virtual functions (to refine the observation *val* to deliver the value of the object modulo two) and the invocation of constructors of ancestor classes (which need not be explicitly specified by the user).

Allowing descendants full access to the instance variables defined by ancestors, however, increases the dependency on the actual implementation of these ancestors, with the risk of a total collapse when the implementation of an ancestor changes.

Technology In addition to the elements introduced thus far, C++ offers a number of other features that may profitably be used in the development of libraries and programs. See slide C-10.

Techniques   *C-10*

- templates – `template<class T> class C { ... }`
- overloading – *void read(int); void read(float)*
- friends – *to bypass protection*
- type conversions – *by class constructors or type operators*
- type coercion – *by explicit casts* (is dangerous)
- smart pointers – *by overloading de-reference*

Slide C-10: C++ – techniques (1)

For instance, C++ offers *templates* (to define generic classes and functions), *overloading* (to define a single function for multiple types), *friends* (to bypass protection), *type conversion* (which may be defined by class constructors or type operators), *type coercions* (or casts, which may be used to resolve ambiguity or to escape a too rigid typing regime), and *smart pointers* (obtained by overloading the dereference operator). An integral part of standard C++ is the Standard Template Library, offering a generic collection of containers, of which a brief description is given in section 2.1.2.

To get some of the flavor of using C++, look at the definition of the *ctr* class in slide C-11 employing multiple constructors, operators, default arguments and type conversion.

The *ctr* provides a constructor, with an integer argument (which is by default set to zero, if omitted) and a string argument (that expects a name for the counter). The increment operator is used to define the function *add* (which by default increments by one), and the application operator is used instead of *val*. Also, a type conversion operator is defined to deliver the value of the *ctr* instance anywhere where an integer is expected. In addition, a *char*∗ type conversion operator is used to return the name of the *ctr*.

Again, the difference is most clearly reflected in how an instance of *ctr* is used. This example illustrates that C++ offers many of the features that allow us to

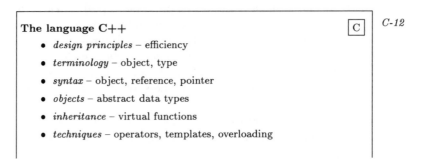

```
class ctr {                                      C++
public:
ctr(int i = 0, char* x = "ctr") {
        n = i; strcpy(s,x);
        }
ctr& operator++(int) { n++; return *this; }
int operator()() { return n; }
operator int()   { return n; }
operator char*() { return s; }
private:
int n; char s[64];
};
```

Usage

```
ctr c; cout << (char*) c++ << "=" << c();
```

C-11

Slide C-11: C++ - techniques (2)

define objects which may be used in a (more or less) natural way. In the end, this
is what software development is about, to please the user, within reason.

Summary This section has presented an overview of C++. It gave an outline of
its history, and discussed the design principles underlying C++ and its heritage
from C.

C-12

The language C++   C

- *design principles* – efficiency
- *terminology* – object, type
- *syntax* – object, reference, pointer
- *objects* – abstract data types
- *inheritance* – virtual functions
- *techniques* – operators, templates, overloading

Slide C-12: C++ – summary

It listed the keywords that C++ introduces in addition to the keywords employed in C and characterized the object-oriented constructs supported by C++.
An example was given to illustrate the difference between realizing an abstract
data type in C and realizing the same abstract data type in C++. Further, it
illustrated the use of virtual functions when deriving classes by inheritance, and
discussed a number of additional features supported by C++.

D

The language Java

Java has a direct heritage from C++. Started as an interpreted C++ like language under the name Oak, it became a hype due to its introduction as *the dial-tone of the Internet* in 1995.

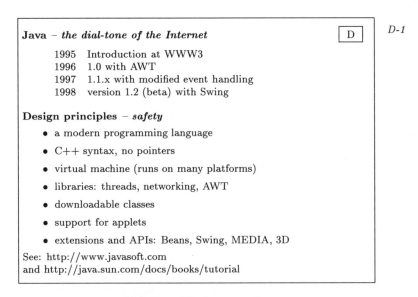

Slide D-1: The language Java

The impact of Java has been enormous, not only in terms of its adoption in the software industry, but also in terms of the number of books written and sold. Java has also become the language of choice for introductory programming courses.

The original design purpose stated for Java was to provide a safe environment for executing so-called applets, written in a general purpose programming language, in a Web-browser. For that reason Java programs are executed by a virtual machine, in which the programs can be executed as in a *sandbox* protecting the environment from possibly malicious programs. In addition, the virtual machine gives a high degree of platform independence. The slogan that has accompanied the introduction of Java, *write once, run everywhere* does nevertheless not completely hold true when it concerns user interfaces, since the particularities of the various platforms have proved to be hard to master.

Whatever one may think of Java as a language, a lot of effort is put into coming to an agreement about the numerous APIs that are part of the Java platform. These include the Swing GUI framework, the component Beans, the reflection API, the native code interface, the multimedia framework, not forgetting the Java3D and VRML classes. This makes the Java platform indeed a very powerful and productive environment.

Java is very well documented. Apart from the many books about Java, there is also an excellent tutorial online, for free. See the URLs in slide D-1.

Terminology In comparison with C++, Java is almost as rich in keywords. Notably lacking, however, is the keyword *virtual*. This is not needed, since in Java every method is by definition subject to dynamic dispatching. Also, since Java doesn't allow multiple inheritance, there is no need to use it for avoiding multiple copies of inherited base classes.

D-2

Keywords: | Java overview |

- **new, finalize, extends, implements, synchronized**

Language features:

- no pointers – *references only simplify life*
- garbage collection – *no programmers' intervention*
- constructors – *to create and initialize*
- single inheritance – *for refinement*
- interfaces – *abstract classes*
- synchronized – *to prevent concurrent invocation*
- private, protected, public – *for access protection*

Slide D-2: Java – terminology (1)

New is the keyword *interface* in Java. Defining an *interface* is equivalent to defining an abstract class in C++. One merely lists the methods provided by the (abstract) claas, without providing an implementation. A concrete class may then indicate that it *implements* the interface. In this way multiple (interface) inheritance is supported in a nice and clean way.

Also new is the keyword *synchronized*, reflecting the built-in support for concurrency in Java. A *synchronized* method excludes multiple invocations of that method, which might otherwise occur in a multi-threaded program.

The keyword *final* may be used to indicate that a particular value may not be changed. In this sense it is similar to the C++ keyword *const*. It must be noted that Java is even more elaborate in the use of the keywords *private, protected* and *public* than C++. They are used to indicate access restrictions for the methods of an object for objects inside and outside the package in which the objects' class is defined.

The language features offered by Java resemble those of C++. However, in many respects Java is much simpler than C++. Most notably, the absence of pointers, a sure source of errors, makes programmers' lives easier. In particular since Java offers automatic garbage collection, programmers need not to worry about disposing objects created dynamically. Resource management, however, may be done by defining a method *finalize*. The counterpart, however, of that is that all objects in Java come into existence by explicit dynamic creation.

The availability of *interfaces* compensates for the restriction to single inheritance, which must be indicated by the keyword *extends* instead of the colon. It has often been argued that multiple inheritance is not really necessary. This holds true, however, only for implementation inheritance. Multiple (interface) inheritance is a powerful feature that has interesting applications once one has discovered how to use it.

Expressions Java supports *basic types* (including *int, char* and *float*) and *compound types* similar to C++. It does not offer pointer or reference types. However, it offers *Array* and *String* types. No need to say that it also allows for user-definable classes.

Type expressions   *D-3*

- basic types -- int, char, float, ...
- Array – *int* ar[SIZE]
- String – String[] args
- class – *user-defined*

Slide D-3: Java – expressions (1)

It will be no surprise that the expressions also are similar to those of C++. However, Java does *not* allow for operator overloading. That means that the operators, as listed below, may only be used for the built-in types.

The operators defined for the built-in types do sometimes behave in an unexpected way. For example, whereas the + operator defined for *String* concatenates two strings (as expected), the comparison operator == does not compare the values of the two strings, but instead the (opaque) references. One must use s1.equals(s2) to compare the values of the strings *s1* and *s2*.

Value expressions may be created using arithmetic and comparison operators (including == for equality and != for inequality).

As logical operators Java includes, as C++, conjunction (&&) and disjunction (||), as well as a number of bitwise logical operators. Also, we have an *indexing*

Expressions   *D-4*

- operators – + , - ,.., < , <= ,.., == , ! = ,.., && , ||
- indexing – o[e]
- access – o.m(...)
- in/decrement – o++, o--
- conditional – b?e1:e2

Assignment

- var = expression
- modifying – +=. -=, ...

Slide D-4: Java – expressions (2)

operator which, unlike for C++, may be not defined for arbitrary types. Access
to both static and dynamic methods involves the use of the *dot* operator.

The *increment* and *decrement* are defined only for the scalar types. Also, we
have a conditional expression of the form $b?e_1:e_2$ testing the condition b to deliver
e_1 when it evaluates to true and e_2 otherwise.

Assignments in Java, like in C++, are written as *var = expression* with a single
= symbol. As remarked previously, this convention is known to cause mistakes
by programmers raised with languages such as Pascal or Modula-2.

In addition, Java offers, like C++, modifying assignments, which may be used
as, for example, in *n += 1*, which is identical in meaning to *n = n + 1*.

Control Java provides roughly the same elementary control structures as C++.

Control   *D-5*

- conditional – if (b) S1; else S2;
- selection   –   switch(n) { case n1: S1; break; ... default:
  ... }
- iteration – while (b) S
- looping – for(int i = 1; i <= MAX; i++) S
- jumps – *return, break, continue*

Slide D-5: Java – control

These include a *conditional* statement (of which the else part may be omitted),
a *selection* statement (that allows for a default branch), an *iteration* statement
(which is also offered in a reversed form to allow a repeat), a *loop* statement
(consisting of an initialization part, a part to test for termination, and a repetition
part to increase the loop variable) and, finally, *jumps*.

Objects An object is an instance of a class. In Java, a program is executed by calling the static *main* method a class. Look for example at the *HelloWorld* class in slide D-6.

Hello World – Java (1)   *D-6*

```
    public class HelloWorld {
    public static void main(String[] args) {
            System.out.println("Hello World");
            }
    };
```

Slide D-6: Java – objects (1)

The *HelloWorld* example is taken from a collection of *hello world* programs located at http://www.latech.edu/~acm/HelloWorld.shtml.

To illustrate the use of *interface* definitions, slide D-7 presents a slightly modified version. The actual *HelloWorld* class announces that it *implements* the *World* interface.

Hello World - interface   *D-7*

```
    public interface World {
    public void hello();
    };
```

Hello World - class

```
    public class HelloWorld implements World {
    public void hello() {
            System.out.println("Hello World");
            }
    };
```

Slide D-7: Java – objects (2)

Both classes make use of the standard out stream defined in the class *System* to emit their message to the world.

Inheritance In Java, all classes are derived from the class *Object*, defined in the package java.lang. As an advantage, every object class defined in Java is known to support a number of basic methods, such as *clone, equals, finalize, hashCode, toString*. Of course, the programmer of the class is responsible for redefining these methods if appropriate. For example, when the method *clone* is invoked, the object throws an exception unless the method clone has been defined.

The following members of *Object*, however, cannot be overridden: *getClass*, *notify*, *notifyAll*, *wait*. The latter three reflect Java's support for threads; they should not be used when the object is not a thread.

D-8

Hello World – Java (2)

```
import java.awt.Graphics;
public class HelloWorld extends
  java.applet.Applet {

public void init() { resize(150,50); }

public void paint(Graphics g) {
      g.drawString("Hello, World!", 50, 25);
      }
};
```

Slide D-8: Java – inheritance

A simple example of a class that inherits from the Java *Applet* class is given in slide D-8. It redefines the *init* and the *paint* method, which says *'Hello World'*.

Technology The Java platform, that is the Java language enriched with the numerous libraries, frameworks and extensions, offers the software developer a rich environment for developing (distributed) Internet-aware applications.

Perhaps the most well-known feature of Java is its support for so-called *applets*, light weight applications that may enrich your Web-browser with graphics, multimedia and additional communication facilities. Browsers such as Netscape and Microsoft Internet Explorer have an embedded Java Virtual Machine that enables them to execute Java applets. Applets may also be executed by the Java plugin that has been provided by Sun Microsystems as an alternative to the browsers' built-in virtual machines.

Server-side extensions are made possible by *servlets*. The server must then be written in Java, or provide for a virtual machine.

Java offers a number of facilities for networking, including support for retrieving resources by URL, sockets, and remote method invocation. Remote method invocation (RMI) may be considered a light weight alternative for CORBA distributed programming.

In contrast with CORBA (version 2.0), Java allows for sending objects over the network due to its powerful *Reflection API* that gives runtime access to the properties of objects, including class types and methods.

The *Beans* framework offers component technology, that allows developers to exchange (beans) objects and inspect their properties in a uniform manner. For

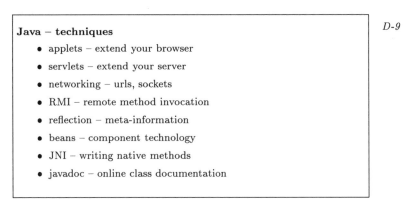

Slide D-9: Java – techniques

example GUI elements, written as beans, can be incorporated at runtime to add the desired functionality to a user interface.

Another well-designed and powerful feature of Java is its *native interface*, which enables the experienced programmer to embed native code in Java applications. No need to say that from a purists' point of view one should avoid this.

Last but not least, the *javadoc* facility must be mentioned. The *javadoc* tool allows for creating documentation directly from the class definitions, that may be annotated with signature descriptions, and information about its author, possible exceptions and comments.

Summary This section has presented an overview of Java.

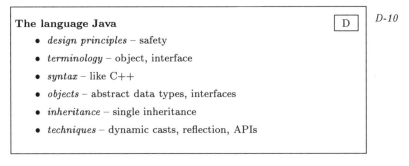

Slide D-10: Java – summary

It gave an outline of its history, and discussed the design principles underlying Java and its possible future as the dial-tone of the Internet.

It described how Java differs from C++, gave an *Hello World* example of an ordinary program, an object that implements an interface and an applet. Also, we discussed briefly the libraries, frameworks and extensions comprising the Java platform.

E

The language DLP

Apart from what may be considered the mainstream languages Smalltalk, Eiffel, C++ and Java, there are numerous other (experimental) languages incorporating the object paradigm in one way or another. See section 5.1.1 and, for example, Davison (1993) for an overview. Of particular interest is the combination of the logic programming paradigm with object orientation, of which the language DLP is an example.

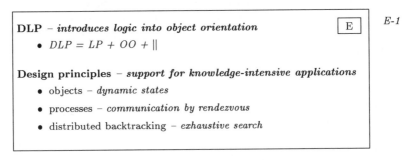

Slide E-1: The language DLP

The DLP language combines logic programming (LP) with object orientation (OO) and parallelism (||). DLP is a (very) high-level language, meant to support the development of knowledge-intensive applications. In addition to the logic programming features, it provides *objects* (that may change their state dynamically), *processes* (such as active objects, that communicate by rendezvous), and it allows for *distributed backtracking* (to enable exhaustive search in a logic programming style). See Eliëns (1992) for a full treatment.

Terminology Syntactically, DLP may be regarded as an extension of Prolog with constructs for parallel object-oriented programming. However, in addition to the familiar Prolog constructs it offers objects as well.

An object definition or object in DLP is a (labeled) collection of (Prolog)

```
Objects – a labeled set of clauses          [ DLP ]     E-2

      object name {
      var variables.

      constructor clauses
      method clauses
      }
```

Slide E-2: DLP – terminology

clauses that define the methods supported by the object, and which in addition may contain non-logical variables that are private to each instance. An active object also contains one or more constructor clauses that defines the object's own activity. See slide E-2.

Expressions The expressiveness of DLP is derived to a large extent from its heritage from Prolog. The basic syntactic units in Prolog are *terms*, which are either *constants* (such as characters, integers, strings, or the empty list []), *variables* (which by convention start with a capital or underscore), or *compound terms* (which may be written as a function symbol with argument terms or as a list of the form [H | T], where H stands for the head of the list and T for its tail). See slide E-3.

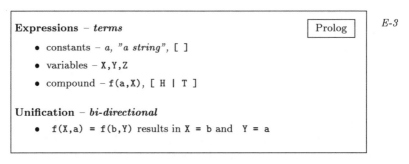

```
Expressions – terms                         [ Prolog ]   E-3

      • constants – a, "a string", [ ]
      • variables – X,Y,Z
      • compound – f(a,X), [ H | T ]

Unification – bi-directional
      • f(X,a) = f(b,Y) results in X = b and  Y = a
```

Slide E-3: DLP – expressions

Terms allow for what is called *unification*, which is an extended form of pattern matching. Unification results in binding variables to terms, in such a way that the two unified terms become syntactically equal. As an example, unifying f(X,a) with f(b,Y) results in binding X to a and Y to b. Unification is the primary mechanism of parameter passing in Prolog. It is essentially bi-directional and satisfies the *one-assignment-only* property, which means that evaluating a goal must result in a consistent binding, otherwise the goal fails.

Control The computation mechanism employed by Prolog may be characterized as goal reduction with unification and backtracking. As an example, look at the Prolog program in slide E-4, consisting of a number of clauses and facts.

Prolog   *E-4*

```
p(X,Y) :- r(Z), b(X).                          clauses
p(X,Y) :- q(Y), b(X).
b(X) :- a(X).
b(0).                                          facts
a(1).
q(2).
```

Query

```
?- p(X,Y).                        results in (X = 1,Y = 2)
                                      and (X = 0, Y = 2)
```

Slide E-4: DLP – control (1)

When we pose our query, it is first attempted to resolve the goal $p(X, Y)$ with the first clause for p (which fails because $r(Z)$ cannot be resolved). Then the second clause is tried, which leads to binding Y to 2 (since $q(2)$ is a fact), and gives us two possible bindings for X, due to the facts $a(1)$ and $b(0)$. (Variables are local to clauses and will be renamed automatically to avoid clashes.) Hence, the evaluation of the goal $p(X, Y)$ leads to two consistent bindings, that may successively be obtained by backtracking.

As an example of somewhat more realistic clauses, look at the list processing predicates *member* and *append* in slide E-5.

List processing – *backtracking*   *E-5*

```
member(X,[X|_]).
member(X,[_|T]) :- member(X,T).

append([],L,L).
append([ H | T ],L,[ H | R ]):- append(T,L,R).
```

Slide E-5: DLP – control (2)

Both predicates are specified in an inductive manner, taking care of all possible cases. For example, the first clause for *member* states as a fact that an element is contained in a list when it is the first element. The second clause prescribes the recursive application of member to the tail of the list if this is not the case. Similarly, the clauses for *append* distiguish between the case of appending a list to an empty list, and the case of appending a list to a non-empty list.

This manner of specification closely adheres to standard practice in mathematical logic and has proven to be a powerful means to develop knowledge-based systems (such as expert systems) that rely on logical reasoning.

Objects The language DLP supports active objects with a state (expressed as the value of non-logical instance variables) and communication by rendezvous (which realizes message passing for active objects). See slide E-6.

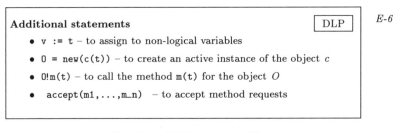

E-6

Additional statements	DLP

- v := t – to assign to non-logical variables
- O = new(c(t)) – to create an active instance of the object *c*
- O!m(t) – to call the method m(t) for the object *O*
- accept(m1,...,m_n) – to accept method requests

Slide E-6: DLP – objects (1)

To support these features we need, in addition to terms and clauses, statements to assign terms to non-logical variables, a statement to create new active instances of an object (class), a statement to call a method for an object (which is essentially the invocation of a goal), and an *accept* statement that allows an active object to interrupt its own activity and accept the request to execute a method. When binding terms to logical variables or assigning terms to non-logical variables, simple rewriting rules are applied. Rewriting includes arithmetic simplification and string manipulation.

Computation model – *distributed logic*   *E-7*

objects – state + methods
processes – to evaluate goals
communication – backtrackable rendezvous

Slide E-7: DLP – objects (2)

The computation model underlying DLP is a model that supports distributed logic, and may be seen as a combination of the models underlying logic programming and parallel object-oriented languages. See slide E-7.

The DLP support system provides, in addition to a Prolog-like evaluation mechanism, support for *objects* (having a state, and methods defined by clauses), *processes* (to realize the object's own activity as well as to evaluate method calls or goals for the object), and a *communication* mechanism (that allows for a backtrackable rendezvous).

As an example of an object in DLP, look at the *travel* agency defined in slide E-8, which has a non-logical instance variable *cities* (containing a number of destinations), a constructor *travel* (which defines the object's own activity) and two methods, *reachable* and *add*.

```
object travel {                                    travel
var cities = [amsterdam, paris, london].

travel() :- accept( all ), travel().

reachable(X) :- member(X, cities).
add(X) :-
        append( cities, [X], R), cities := R.
}
```

Usage

```
?- O = new travel(), O!reachable(X),
   write(X).
```

E-8

Slide E-8: DLP – objects (3)

The *reachable* method may be used to ask whether a particular destination exists or to ask for all possible destinations (which are actually obtained by backtracking). The *add* method may be used to add new destinations to the list of *cities*.

The *travel* constructor merely consists of a (tail-recursive) loop allowing to accept any request, one at a time. By specifying which requests may be accepted at a particular point in the lifetime of the object, the message interface of the object may be dynamically specified. In addition, an explicit *accept* statement is needed to guarantee mutual exclusion between method calls.

Inheritance DLP supports static inheritance, by code sharing, as do Smalltalk, Eiffel, C++ and Java. For a discussion of dynamic inheritance, by delegation, see section 5.4. As an example of inheritance in DLP, look at the refinement of the *travel* object into a veritable *agency*. See slide E-9.

An *agency* offers the user, in addition to the functionality offered by *travel*, the opportunity to *book* for a particular destination and be informed of its price.

Inheritance in DLP conforms to the subsumption relation for logical theories, in that it extends the functionality of a given object in a strict manner. DLP

E-9

```
object agency : travel {                          agency
agency() :- accept( any ), agency().
book(X,Y) :-
        reachable(X),
        price(X,Y).
price(amsterdam,5).
 ...
}
```

Slide E-9: DLP – inheritance

allows for multiple inheritance and even checks for cycles to protect the user from repetitions or cycles in the inheritance chain.

Technology Logic programming offers a wealth of techniques. In particular, the meta programming facilities (which are essentially based on the interpretation of programs as data) allow for very powerful programming techniques. See, for example, Bratko (1990).

E-10

Techniques – *logic*
- meta programming
- active intelligent agents

Slide E-10: DLP – technology

By virtue of being an extension of Prolog, DLP inherits these facilities. In addition, DLP provides the constructs necessary to define what may be called (active) *intelligent agents*, of which the functionality can be specified in a declarative, logic-based fashion. DLP, in other words, is an example of a fruitful combination of paradigms, merging logic with object orientation.

Summary This section has presented an overview of the DLP language. It discussed the design principles underlying DLP and characterized its principal application area as the development of knowledge-based systems.

It gave a brief characterization of Prolog, explained how DLP syntactically extends Prolog with constructs for parallel object-oriented programming, and characterized the computation model of DLP. Some examples were given to illustrate the definition of objects and the use of inheritance.

Knowledge-intensive applications will increasingly become part of mainstream

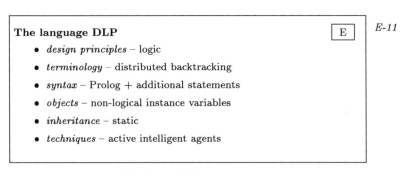

Slide E-11: DLP – summary

IT. Distributed declarative languages and systems, of which DLP is just one example are likely to become the vehicle of choice for such applications.

A language such as DLP is particularly well suited for the realization of so-called agents, software processes that act as an intermediary between the end-user of a system and the system itself.

F

Unified Modeling Language

The Unified Modeling Language (UML) resulted from a joint effort of leading experts in object-oriented analysis and design, Grady Booch, Jim Rumbaugh and Ivar Jacobson, also known as the *three amigos*, all currently employees of Rational.

UML provides (graphical) notations to express functional, structural and behavioral properties of (object-oriented) systems. UML is *not* a method. It does not prescribe the steps to be taken in development. UML may best be regarded as a toolbox, from which the developer can choose a notation or technique as the need occurs.

Unified Modeling Language   UML   *F-1*

- class diagrams – conceptual structure
- use cases – functional requirements
- interaction diagrams – operational characteristics
- package and deployment diagrams – implementation
- state and activity diagrams – dynamic behavior

See http://www.rational.com/uml and UML Distilled, Fowler (1997b)

Slide F-1: UML

In this section we will look at a selection of the notational tools provided in the UML, as indicated in slide F-1. For additional information see Rational's Web site. I also strongly recommend Fowler (1997b).

Class diagrams

Class diagrams represent (ideally) the conceptual structure of the system. Class diagrams typically consist of class descriptions and relations or associations between these. Class descriptions may be given as types, interfaces or actual classes, including attributes, methods and even visibility specifications. There is considerable liberty in how much detail is provided in either class descriptions or relations. As a rule of thumb, omit details as much as possible.

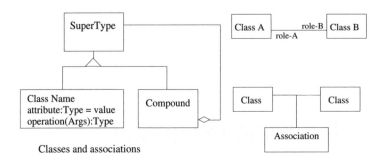

Slide F-2: Class diagrams

Special relations between classes are *generalization* or *inheritance* (indicated with the triangle in the diagram left in slide F-2) and *aggregation* or *containment* (indicated with the diamond). In this example, just think of a *compound* as containing a number of instances of the type of which the compound is derived. The aggregation relation is often referred to as a *has-a* relation, which is, however, not appropriate when the object contained is actually used for delegation as discussed in chapter **??**.

The diagrams on the right indicate how to depict arbitrary associations. Think for example of the relation between *Employer* and *Employee* classes. Clearly, in this case the role each class has with respect to the other class follows from the class name itself. In other cases it may be helpful to indicate the role explicitly.

When the association between classes is more complex, an explicit association class may be introduced, for example a class specifying a work contract, to describe the association in more detail.

Class diagrams may be refined further by adding annotations to the class descriptions and the relations. For example, relations may be more precisely defined by adding *multiplicities* (1,*,0..1,m..n, to indicate respectively one, many, optional or bounded). Class descriptions may be refined by adding *notes*, drawn as a box with a flattened edge, containing descriptive text.

The UML also allows for adding constraints, between curly brackets, and for the definition of so-called stereotypes, indicated by angular brackets as in <<stereotype>>, which represent generic constraints.

Use cases

Use cases define typical interactions between the user and the system. In other words, use cases define the boundaries between a system and its users. Use cases are critical in eliciting the functional requirements a system must satisfy.

A typical use case consists of an actor or role and a more or less detailed description of the actions that an actor performs to accomplish some task. A task may for example be the insertion of text, or the creation of a particular figure in

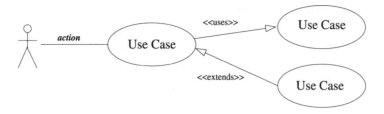

Slide F-3: Use cases

a drawing editor. A distinction must be made between the overall goals of a user, like making a decent drawing, and the actions that must be performed to satisfy these goals. Only the latter can be the subject of use cases.

When defining a use case, other use cases can be (re)used, either through the *extends* or through the *uses* relation. The *extends* relation is similar to the inheritance relation for classes. The extending use case may override aspects of the extended use case. The *uses* relation is used to factor out common parts.

Interaction diagrams

Interaction diagrams are needed to clarify the actual behavior of a system, in particular the interaction between objects (or classes of objects) that result when executing a use case.

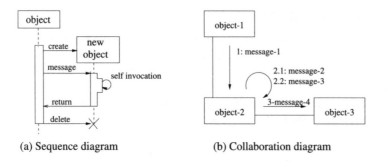

(a) Sequence diagram   (b) Collaboration diagram

Slide F-4: Interaction diagrams

Interaction diagrams come in two forms, *sequence* diagrams and *collaboration* diagrams.

Sequence diagrams depict objects and their lifelines. When an object becomes active, the lifeline may be widened to a rectangle for the period of activity.

Collaboration diagrams depict the objects and their relations in a more static manner. Messages between objects, indicated by arrows, may be specified in greater or lesser detail. Also here, as a rule of thumb, details are given only when needed. To indicate message sequencing in collaboration diagrams numbering may be used, increasing or, as illustrated in slide F-4(b), branching.

Package and component diagrams

Although classes may be considered the building blocks of object-oriented applications and frameworks, they are usually not the units of deployment nor the units of reuse. See Szyperski (1997). Rather, packages and components may be considered as such.

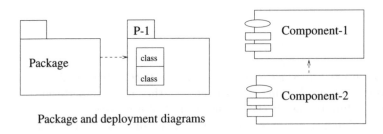

Package and deployment diagrams

Slide F-5: Package and deployment diagrams

A package diagram, depicted left, indicates the dependencies between packages, and possibly classes. Component or deployment diagrams depict the components, their exported interfaces and the dependency between components.

Although package and component diagrams are usually implementation-level diagrams, it seems advisable to take clustering and component packaging into consideration in the early stages of design.

State and activity diagrams

The characterization of behavior given by interaction diagrams primarily concerns, as the name says, the interaction between objects. The dynamic behavior of the objects themselves and the global activity can only be inferred from such diagrams.

An explicit characterization of the dynamic behavior of an individual object may be given by a state transition diagram.

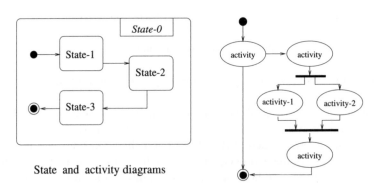

State and activity diagrams

Slide F-6: State diagrams

A state transition diagram consists of states and transitions between states, indicated by arrows. The arrows may be indicated by expressions of the form

```
event(arguments)[conditions]/action
```

indicating that a transition can take place when a particular event occurs and certain conditions are satisfied. The transition will then result in an action, which may possibly modify state/instance variables.

Individual states may contain the specification of actions in response to particular events and the entry and exit of the state. States may be grouped to form a single (super)state, such as *state-0* in the diagram on the left in slide F-6.

To characterize the overall activity of a system, or parts thereof, *activity diagrams* may be used. Activity diagrams consist of nodes indicating activities.

Since activity diagrams are rather unspecific with respect to the actual objects involved, such diagrams are most appropriate in analysing aspects of workflow. In contrast, state diagrams are usually tied to the implementation of objects, such as event-schedulers, with complex dynamic behavior.

Both state diagrams and activity diagrams allow for parallelism. In activity diagrams, parallel activity may be assigned to so-called *swim-lanes*, activity falling under the responsibility of a particular role, an actor or a part of the system.

Discussion

As said before, the UML provides a generic toolbox for analysis and design. It offers no method, so the question remains: *when to use what?* The answer to that question may be very simple. Just use what you need to convey the properties of the system in a clear and understandable way. The answer may also be very complex, since 'clear and understandable' are somewhat elusive notions. Following Fowler (1997b), I would say: *don't overdo.* Use UML to clarify critical aspects of the system and highlights of design, and leave it at that. Never continue modeling when you experience it as a useless, or worse, boring activity.

The UML toolbox is very rich. It allows you to model every conceivable aspect of the system. Nevertheless, to my mind, graphical models are not always appropriate. But, on the other hand, most people like them and they often make a good impression, suggesting clarity ...

As concerns the use of UML, to some extent one can delineate a subset as core UML. Class diagrams lie at the heart of most object models. Depending on the level of abstraction and the amount of detail, they may be regarded as either a domain model, concrete class design, or anything in between. Use cases delimit the functional requirements, and are essential for negotiating these requirements and also for phasing the delivery of the system. Most interesting, I think, is where combined modeling efforts lead to an indication of the validation and verification spots of the system. In particular, the combination of class diagrams, use cases and interaction (sequence) diagrams allows for spotting the high-risk parts of the system and, accordingly, for specifying test procedures to verify whether the system meets its requirement specifications.

G

Interface Definition Language – IDL

The Interface Definition Language (IDL) that accompanies CORBA-2.0 provides the constructs needed to specify interfaces only.

IDL allows for specifying modules, consisting of interfaces. An interface specification may contain (read only) attributes and operations. Operations are synchronous, unless annotated as *oneway*. Operations may raise exceptions upon failure.

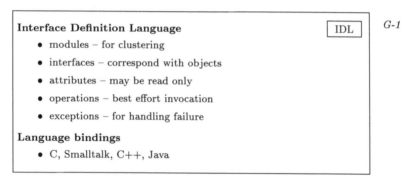

Slide G-1: Interface Definition Language – IDL

Although IDL is syntactically very similar to C++ or Java, it completely lacks the algorithmic constructs of these languages. Objects specified in IDL must be realized in one of the languages for which an official IDL language binding exists, such as C, Smalltalk, C++ or Java, or an unofficial binding, such as Python, Perl and Prolog.

Example

As an example, look at the definition of a module *universe* below. It contains an interface named *world* which provides a method *hello* and two additional methods *ask* and *tell*.

```
module universe {                                        universe

  interface world {
            void hello();

        void ask(in string x);
        string tell();

        oneway void halt();
        };
  };
```

The *ask* method has a string input parameter and the *tell* method has a string result type.

All methods supported by the *world* interface are synchronous, except for the *halt* method, which is annotated as *oneway*.

The realization of the *universe* module is given in Appendix H.

Types and values

The operations specified in an interface may result in a value and may take particular values as arguments. The type of a value must either exist as a basic type or be specified in IDL.

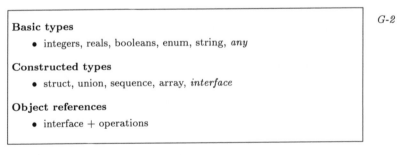

                                                                    G-2

Slide G-2: Types and values

Basic types encompass integers, reals, booleans, enumerations and strings. There is also a generic type, *any*, which allows for checking the actual type dynamically. Constructed types include record structures (*struct*), tagged unions, sequences and arrays.

Interfaces specify object types. However, a value that identifies an object is always a reference to the object. In CORBA 2.0 it is not possible to send objects by value. As a workaround, one may send records by value and then locally instantiate an object.

Operations and exceptions

An operation or method specifies a service that a client may request of an object. Operations may result in a value. Each parameter of an operation has a type and a modifier indicating whether it is an input, output, or combined *inout* parameter.

Operations   *G-3*

> • in, out, inout – parameter attributes

Exceptions

```
exception out_of_range { long count; }

interface writer {
   void position(in long pos)
    raises(out_of_range);
   }
```

Slide G-3: Operations and exceptions

The signature or type of an operation may also include one or more exceptions that may be raised. Exceptions may contain data fields.

The signature of operations may also be assembled dynamically, through the *dynamic invocation interface* of the ORB. The semantics for such requests are the same as for requests via the operation stub generated from the interface specification.

Interfaces and inheritance

Interfaces define polymorphic object types. An interface may be realized by any object that supports the operations specified in the interface.

Interfaces and inheritance   *G-4*

> • no overriding, no overloading

Multiple (interface) inheritance

```
interface A {  };
interface B {  };
interface C : A { };
interface D : B, A { };
```

Slide G-4: Interfaces and inheritance

Interfaces can inherit from other interfaces. This results in augmenting the interfaces with the attributes and operations of the inherited interface. However, in contrast to class inheritance in C++, IDL does not allow for operations to be overridden, nor for overloading operations, that is different signatures for the same operation.

Multiple (interface) inheritance is supported however, provided that no clashes or overloading occurs.

The Object interface Each object type defined in IDL may be assumed to be derived from the interface *Object*. For example, when defining an *iterator* type the interface may look as follows:

```
interface iterator {
            Object next();
            };
```
iterator

It is the responsibility of the implementation to downcast the object type to its actual type.

Language bindings

A language binding for IDL must satisfy a number of requirements.

G-5

Language bindings

 • types, references, access, ORB and BOA support

The *Object* interface

```
interface Object {
            InterfaceDef get_interface();
            Object duplicate();
            ...
}
```
PIDL

Slide G-5: Language bindings

Naturally, the mapping must support IDL basic and constructed types, references to objects and constants, and access to attributes and operations.

In addition it must provide the signatures for operations defined by the Object Request Broker (which transmits requests over the network) and the Basic Object Adaptor (which translates method requests to actual object method or function invocations).

Access to the ORB and BOA is usually provided by means of so-called pseudo-objects, objects described by interfaces in IDL which are not necessarily implemented as ordinary objects. As an example, the *Object* interface describes the functionality that each IDL-defined object has.

H

Hello (CORBA) Universe

CORBA is an impressive technology. It allows for writing heterogeneous platform-independent and language-independent client/server object systems. Most software developers, including those trained in object orientation, are unfamiliar with developing distributed applications. As a consequence, writing a CORBA application may seem to be beyond reach.

This example is meant to break that barrier, and to show the elementary steps to be taken in writing a CORBA application. To complicate matters a bit, we write a three-language system, consisting of three servers and three clients, written respectively in C++, Java and Prolog.

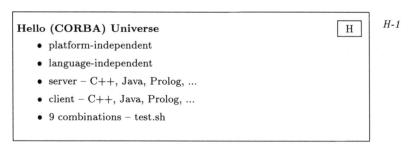

Slide H-1: Hello (CORBA) Universe

Admittedly, the *Hello Universe* example presented here is slightly more complex than the *Hello World* example given in the appendix on Java.

In the example, it is shown in complete detail how to write clients and servers in the three respective languages, how to write a test program to test all possible combinations and how to manage the configuration of a CORBA application.

The example is based on the original *Hello World* example that came with Orbacus 3.1 from Object-Oriented Concepts and examples from the experimental SWI-Prolog CORBA binding for Orbacus 3.1.

The interface – IDL

An *interface* written in IDL is the point of reference for every CORBA application. It informs the client what to expect from a server, and it tells the server what services it is to deliver.

The definition below defines a module *universe* that contains an interface named *world*. The *world* interface provides the method *hello* and two additional methods *ask* and *tell*.

```
module universe {                                        universe.idl

interface world {                                        ┌─────────┐
        void hello();                                    │  world  │
        void ask(in string x);                           └─────────┘
        string tell();

        oneway void halt();
        };

};
```

The *ask* and *tell* methods were introduced to show how CORBA deals with *in* and *out* or result parameters.

In addition, the *world* interface supports a method *halt*, which was introduced to stop the world on the client's demand. In actual applications, you do not want to provide such a method without ensuring that the client has the right to stop the *world*.

C++ realization

The C++ realization consists of a *broker* that gives access to the ORB for the *client* and to both the *ORB* and the *BOA* for the *server*. Apart from a *client* and *server*, we need an implementation for the *world*, which is given in respectively the *world-srv.h* and *world-srv.c* files.

C++ realization   *H-2*
* broker – access to ORB and BOA
* client – needs ORB only
* server – needs access to BOA
* implementation – world-srv.h world-srv.c

Slide H-2: C++ realization

Broker The *broker* class in C++ provides a constructor, an initialization method, the *operator* that starts the server's event loop, and methods to convert strings to object references and methods to read and write object identifiers.

```
class broker {                                        broker.h
public:

broker();

void init(int& argc, char**& argv, int fl=0);         1 = client

int operator()();                                   to run the server

char* ref(corba::object* x);                        object_to_string
corba::object* ref(const char* s);                  string_to object

corba::object* object(const char* file);           get object IOR file
void refout(const char* f, corba::object* x);            IOR to file
};
```

Below, the implementation is given of the constructor, which needs to do nothing, the *init* method, that initializes the ORB, and the BOA in the case of a server.

```
broker::broker() { }                                  broker.c

void broker::init(int& argc, char**& argv, int fl=0) {
   _orb = CORBA_ORB_init(argc, argv);
   if (!fl) _boa = _orb -> BOA_init(argc, argv);
   }
}

int broker::operator()() {
   _boa -> impl_is_ready(CORBA_ImplementationDef::_nil());
   }
```

As said before, the broker class provides only shorthands and abstractions from vendor-specific code.

Client The code snippet below shows how the client creates and initializes a *broker* object, how it obtains an object reference, and also some calls to the *world* server, including *hello* and a request to be informed about Clinton's affairs, which certainly had some relevance at the time of writing this.

```
int main(int argc, char* argv[], char*[]) {           client.c

broker* _broker = new broker();                     get yourself a broker
try
```

```
{
    _broker->init(argc,argv);                              initialize broker

    corba::object* obj = _broker->object("world.ref");
    universe_world_var world = universe_world::_narrow(obj);

    {                                                  some object invocations
        world -> hello();
        world -> ask("How are Clinton's affairs?");
        cout << "client:" << world->tell() << endl;
    }
} catch(corba::exception ex) { ... }
}
```

Note that the object that is obtained from `world.ref` must be dynamically downcasted to its actual type.

Server The server code is similar as far as the creation and initialization of the *broker* is concerned, but instead of creating an object from a string identifier, it writes the identity of the server object created to the file `world.ref`.

```
int main(int argc, char* argv[], char*[])                    server.c
{
    broker* _broker = new broker();                    get yourself a broker

    try
    {
        _broker->init(argc,argv);                  initialize orb and boa
        universe_world_var p = new universe_world_srv;

        _broker->refout("world.ref", p);                    write identity

        _broker->operator()();                          run the the world
    }
    catch(corba::exception& ex) { ... }
}
```

The C++ class that implements the *world* interface might appear disappointingly trivial. It is left to the student to think of something less trivial.

```
void universe_world_srv::hello() {                       world_srv.c
        cout << "Hello World!" << endl;
    }

void universe_world_srv::ask(const char* s) {
        cout << "Asking: " << s << endl;
    }
```

```
char* universe_world_srv::tell() {
        char result[] = "ok";
        CORBA_String_var s = (const char*) result;
        return s._retn();
        }

void  universe_world_srv::halt() {
        exit(0);
        }
```

Discussion Writing a CORBA application might indeed be simpler than you thought. Follow the steps taken in this example as a recipe, and you master the art of writing CORBA applications instantly.

Java realization

The Java realization of the *Hello Universe* example has the same structure as the C++ realization. See slide H-3.

Java realization   *H-3*

- broker – contact ORB and BOA

- client – connect to server

- server – announce server object

- implementation – world_srv.java

Slide H-3: Java realization

Broker The IDL-Java binding seems to be somewhat better standardized, possibly because it is of a later date. So the advantage of using a *broker* abstraction lies primarily in the shorthands it provides, and the similarity with the C++ realization.

```
import org.omg.CORBA.*;                                    broker.java
import java.io.*;


public class broker {
boolean _fl = false;
java.applet.Applet _applet = null;

public broker() { }
public broker(boolean fl) { _fl = fl; }
```

```
public broker(java.applet.Applet x) {
      _applet = x;
      init(null);
      }

public void init(String[] args) {
if (_applet == null) {
            _orb = ORB.init(args,new java.util.Properties());
            if (!_f1)
          _boa = _orb.BOA_init(args,new java.util.Properties());
} else
      _orb = ORB.init(_applet, null);
}


public int operator() {                            run – server-only
      if (!_f1) _boa.impl_is_ready(null);
      return 0; // OK
      }

 ....
};
```

The only (real) difference with the C++ broker class is the possible existence of an *applet*. Somewhat unfortunately, when the (client) object is an applet, the initialization of the ORB must be done in a different way.

Client The client in Java must, also, create and initialize a *broker* object, and create a reference to the *world* server object.

```
package universe;

import org.omg.CORBA.*;                            client.java
import java.io.*;
import hush.broker;                                see broker.java

public class client
{
    public static void main(String args[])
    {
        broker _broker = new broker(true); // true means client only
        try
        {
            _broker.init(args);                       init orb

            org.omg.CORBA.Object obj = _broker.object("world.ref");
            world world = worldHelper.narrow(obj);
            if (world == null)
                throw new RuntimeException();
```

```
                System.out.println("Enter 'h' (hello) or 'x' (exit):");
                ... // do some requests to the world
          } catch(...)   { ... }
      }
};
```

In Java, an extra object *interface*Helper is created to allow for casting the object that is created from a string object identifier to its actual object type, *world* in this case.

Server The server provides access to the (server) object that implements the *world* interface. After creating and initializing a *broker* object, it creates an instance of a *world* server and writes its object identifier to the file `world.ref`. In addition it writes a HTML file that contains an applet that has a (string) reference to the server. See the online version or the Orbacus documentation for details.

```
package universe;                                    ┌─────────────┐
                                                     │ server.java │
                                                     └─────────────┘
import org.omg.CORBA.*;
import java.io.*;
import hush.broker;   // see broker.java

public class server
{
    public static void main(String args[])
    {
        broker _broker = new broker();
        try
        {
            _broker.init(args);                   create orb en boa;

            world_srv p = new world_srv();        create impl object

            _broker.refout("world.ref",p);            write ref

                                                  create world.htm
            _broker.html("world.htm",p,
                " code=universe/applet.class "
                       + "width=500 height=300");


            _broker.operator(); // run  == boa.impl_is_ready(null);

        } catch(SystemException ex) {
            _broker.print(ex);
            System.exit(1);
```

```
        }
            System.exit(0);
    }
}
```

After creating the object and its reference files, the server invokes the method impl_is_ready, through the broker's *operator*.

The implementation of the actual *world* server is as simple as its C++ peer.

world_srv.java

```
package universe;

import org.omg.CORBA.*;

public class world_srv extends _worldImplBase
{
public void hello() {
        System.out.println("Hello World!");
        }

public void ask(String msg) {
        System.out.println(msg);
        }

public String tell() {
        String s = new String("ok");
        return s;
        }

public void halt() {
        System.exit(0);
        }
}
```

Note that dealing with strings is significantly simpler in Java, because of Java's higher-level built-in String.

Discussion Observe that the Java and C++ realizations are very similar in structure and also very similar in code. Nevertheless, what does not become evident in this small example is the bookkeeping that needs to be done in C++ for managing the objects created. Since Java supports garbage collection, the programmer needs to do no such bookkeeping, whereas in C++ one has to use either reference counting or the special _var type, that acts as a smart pointer which does the reference counting automatically. See any CORBA documentation for details.

Prolog realization

Although Prolog is not a mainstream programming language in IT, it is interesting to look at the realization of the *Hello Universe* example in Prolog, if only to observe that its structure is very similar to the realization in Java and C++. In this example, that is implemented with the SWI-Prolog CORBA stubber, which generates most of the code, we will primarily look at the implementation of the server object itself. The relevance of this example may be motivated by the observation that many knowledge-intensive IT applications are realized by imperative (object-oriented) languages such as Java and C++ which are obviously not suited for that.

Prolog realization   *H-4*

- broker – mediating service
- client – get object reference
- server – provide implementation
- implementation – universe.pl

Slide H-4: Prolog realization

For those that do not know Prolog it is sufficient to know that in Prolog so-called predicate definitions act as procedures, that may be invoked by trying to satisfy a goal. A special, very powerful, feature of Prolog is that

```
broker(client(M:F))  :-                                    broker.pl
        ...
        corba_initialize_orb([], _),
        factory(F).                        gives a handle to the server object


broker(server(M:I))  :-
        ...
        corba_initialize_server([server,server(test),
                        timeout(infinite)],Server),
        ...                                create server object
        G =.. [_Create,_Server,Self],
        call(G),
        corba_object_to_string(Self,IOR),
        open(IORFile,write,Fd),            write reference to file
        format(Fd,'string',[IOR]),
        close(Fd),
        corba_main_loop(Server).           enter main loop
```

Obviously, when looking at this code, some standardization of a CORBA binding for Prolog is desirable.

Client The client makes a connection with the broker, gets a binding to the server object and calls some methods of that object.

```
:- use_module(universe).
:- [broker].
```

client.pl
see universe.pl
include broker

```
main :-
        broker(client(universe:F)),                    initialize the broker
        assert(client(factory(F))),
        run.

run :-
        h,
        ask('What is the state of Clinton s affairs?'),
        write('Type h to say hallo, x to quit.'),nl.

ask(X) :-
        client(factory(F)),
        write(client(ask(X))),nl,
        world_ask(F,X),
        world_tell(F,R),
        write(client(ans(R))),nl.

h :- client(factory(F)), world_hello(F).
q :- client(factory(F)), world_halt(F), halt.
x :- halt.
```

Server The server is significantly simpler, due to the fact that all ugly details have been hidden in the broker.

```
:- [broker].
```

server.pl

```
main :-
        broker(server(universe:world)).
```

The implementation of the server object consists of a collection of predicate definitions (procedures), that have the interface or class name as a prefix.

```
:- module('universe',[]).
```

universe.pl

```
world_hello(_Self) :-
        write('Hello World'),nl.
```

```
world_ask(_Self, X) :-
        write(asking(X)), nl.

world_tell(_Self,Y) :-
        Y = 'logically, ok',
        write(telling(Y)),nl.

world_halt(_Self) :-
        halt.
```

As in the previous examples, the actual realization is admittedly simple.

Discussion Prolog, also in its standard (that is, non-object-oriented form) is a powerful language for implementing knowledge-intensive applications. This example shows that CORBA applications can be realized also by using Prolog technology. I would welcome seeing real-life applications in which the knowledge programming part was written in Prolog or an object-oriented extension thereof (such as the language DLP).

Configure, make and test

Still a difficult aspect of CORBA programming, when you are not using an IDE, is to manage the creation and configuration of object files and executables. In the online version of the book you'll find all the details of the `Makefile`, the settings used for Orbacus, and a simple test shell, which allows for testing all nine possible combinations of clients and servers.

Testing CORBA applications is significantly more difficult than testing stand-alone applications. This is due on the one hand to the fact that it concerns a distributed application, involving communication over a network, and on the other hand to the indirection that must take place within both the client and the server to invoke and answer methods over the object request broker software bus.

Conclusions

This concludes our simple CORBA example. It shows that CORBA is ripe to be exploited, on a small scale in practical student assignments, but, as testified by the literature, also on a large scale in business-critical applications.

H-5

- CORBA is ripe to be exploited in OO – the practicum
- the broker is a useful abstraction
- forget about the wiring - concentrate on application logic

Slide H-5: Conclusions

In a multi-lingual, and possibly multi-orb, environment the *broker* abstraction may act as an intermediary, providing a short-hand for common operations and abstracting from the details in which the language bindings and ORBs may differ.

As in other areas, in CORBA programming it is good advice to start small and grow incrementally. Develop your system in such a way that you can gradually forget about the wiring, and concentrate on the application logic instead.

I

Software development projects

An object-oriented approach to software development requires an attitude that must be formed by experience with a practical programming task, employing object-oriented technology. In slide ??, a number of projects are listed that have served as programming assignments at the Vrije Universiteit, Amsterdam.

I-1

Software development projects	$\boxed{\text{I}}$
• gambling machine	
• interactive video game	Coplien (1992)
• simple hypermedia system	Meyrowitz (1986)
• direct manipulation score editor	Pope (1991)
• an object-oriented expert system	Hu (1989)
• 3D animation editor	Ammeraal (1992)
• a simple case tool	Coad and Yourdon (1991b)
• route planner	

Slide I-1: Software development projects

The programming language (mandatorily) employed was C++. The *hush* library was used for developing graphical user interfaces. Students were allowed to work in groups of two. Before starting a project, students were required to write a synopsis giving a global outline of the intended functionality of their system.

The minimal design documentation required was a description of each class interface in the style of CRC cards. Students were encouraged to make documentation and help available online, preferably in a hypertext format.

The programming projects are based on suggestions found in the literature, with the exception of the *gambling machine* and the *routeplanner*. The *gambling machine* seemed nice to allow students to experiment with animation techniques.

The projects A typical example of a *gambling machine* is a *one armed bandit* with three columns of fruit. It is important to offer a realistic interface. Further, one must employ stochastic techniques to determine the chance of winning.

An example of an *interactive video game* is a volley or tennis game for one or two players. One must allow for an option to determine the speed of the ball and an option for replay. See Coplien (1992).

A *simple hypermedia* system must be capable of presenting text and graphics and must allow for the traversal of links between such items. An important aspect of this project is the development of an adequate object model for the items supported, including links. See Meyrowitz (1986) and Conklin (1987).

A *direct manipulation score editor* allows for editing musical fragments interactively. Some musical knowledge is required for such a project. The layout of music notation appears to be a difficult issue, because it is essentially two-dimensional and involves many special symbols. See Pope (1991).

The notion of an *object-oriented expert system* is quite open-ended. An approach one may take is to implement a traditional rule-based expert system in an object-oriented way, using C++. Take care to include an example knowledge-base to test the functionality of the system. See Hu (1989). A more general approach to employing object-oriented technology for the development of knowledge-based systems is described in Eliëns (1992).

A *3D animation editor* supports the creation of (simple) 3D figures and must minimally allow for some basic manipulations in 3D space, such as rotations and translations. As an additional requirement, there must be a facility to replay a series of manipulations. See Ammeraal (1992).

A *simple case tool* allows for the interactive development of a simple object model, including the description of attributes of objects and the inheritance relations between object types. For an example of such tools, see Coad and Yourdon (1991b) and Rumbaugh *et al.* (1991).

A *routeplanner* allows the user to indicate a starting location and an end location. The system then calculates an appropriate route, for example the fastest or cheapest. As an additional requirement, the system must allow for the user to ask additional information about the route and the intermediate locations situated along the selected route. This information should preferably be in multimedia format.

Comments The *routeplanner* has successfully been used as an assignment as part of a CS2 Software Engineering course. Students, indeed, took the opportunity to experiment with the multimedia facilities of *hush*. Some of the other project assignments, such as the *score editor* and the *3D editor*, have led to quite remarkable results. For example, the *3D editor* project led students to develop a system to wander in 3D virtual space. Somewhat disappointingly, however, the *object-oriented expert system* project has not been chosen thus far. Perhaps it is regarded as too difficult or as not interesting enough.

Since the assignments were meant primarily as a means to gain experience with practical aspects of object-oriented programming, students were left free to choose a particular design method. The use of CRC-style documentation, however, was mandatory. Quite often, students developed a design employing OMT notation, which did not necessarily lead to a better result.

To gain experience with object-oriented design and analysis, a practical course focusing on modeling and requirements analysis is advisable. Any of the assignments above may be used in such a course. Other suggestions may be found in Coleman *et al.* (1994) and Sanden (1994) (which may be obtained by anonymous ftp at ftp://isse.gmu.edu/pub/techrep/94_102_sanden.ps.gz).

J

Answers to questions

Chapter 1

1. Object-oriented programming stands for an approach to structure programs using the object metaphor as an abstraction device. See slide 1-2. It is motivated by the need to manage the complexity of software.

2. An exhaustive overview is given in slide 1-4 and slide 1-5. The most important features are, obviously, data abstraction and polymorphism due to inheritance.

3. The complexity referred to is not the structural complexity of the computation, that is the space and time needed to solve a problem, but the conceptual complexity of programming, the organization of the software.

4. Contracts are a means to specify the obligations of the client and the services an object is to provide, in case these obligations are met, in a formal way.

5. From a historical perspective, OOP is a paradigm of programming. See slide 1-15. However, from a software engineering perspective, OOP is increasingly becoming important for design and analysis as well. See slide 1-9.

6. These include imperative languages, functional languages and logic programming languages. The essential features of OOP encapsulation and inheritance. These may be realized in a variety of language settings.

7. An object-oriented approach blurs the distinction between analysis, design and implementation. See slide 1-19. Moreover, it allows for different software development models, such as prototyping. See slide 1-21. What is your opinion? As concerns maintenance, corrective maintenance is facilitated by the localization due to encapsulation. Adaptive maintenance is quite

another matter. Polymorphism helps, but only if extensibility has been an explicit design goal.

8. Aspects of software quality include correctness, robustness and extendibility. In particular, with regard to the cost of maintenance, a valid criterion would be *maintainability*. OOP contributes to maintainability by supporting a strong notion of *locality*.

9. See slide 1-26.

10. See the discussion in section 1.4.

Chapter 2

1. The *letter/envelope* idiom is a means to separate interface aspects of a class from implementation aspects. An advantage is that implementations may be dynamically changed.

2. Polymorphism may be characterized as the ability to be of a different type, dependent upon circumstances. For object-oriented languages, the best-known form is (inclusion) polymorphism by inheritance. However, (ad hoc) polymorphism, due to function overloading, is a facility found in many languages.

3. See section 2.1.4.

4. See section 2.2.

5. We can distinguish between *creational, structural* and *behavioral* patterns. For a discussion of their relevance see section 2.3.

6. See section 2.3.3.

7. The *Reactor* pattern describes how to deal with events, in particular when multiple event loops are involved. See section 2.4.1.

8. See section 2.4.2.

Chapter 3

1. The Fusion method is typically a second-generation development method, containing ingredients of many other (first-generation) methods. See section 3.1.2. In comparison with other methods, it strongly focuses upon process aspects. See section 3.1.3.

2. According to Booch, (1) identify the objects and their attributes, (2) identify the operations associated with objects, and (3) establish the interfaces of object.

   Most of the heuristics for identifying objects are based on a linguistic analysis of the requirements document. See section 3.2.1.

3. Criteria to eliminate spurious classes essentially come down to avoiding classes that provide no information. See slide 3-14.

4. The CRC method consists of defining, for each class, its responsibilities and its collaborators, that is the classes that are needed to function properly. See slide 3-15.

5. A contract defines the behavior of an object by means of an invariant and assertions characterizing the pre- and post-conditions of the methods supported by an object. See slide 3-19.

6. Contracts may help to decide who is responsible for software failures. See slide 3-21.

7. Refining a contract amounts to strengthening the invariant and, for each method, weakening the pre-conditions and strengthening the post-conditions. Also, methods may be added. See slide 3-22.

8. Contracts may be used to establish runtime consistency characteristics. Testing runtime consistency amounts to checking object invariants and pre- and post-conditions of object methods.

9. A formal specification must characterize the requirements of a system and must also provide guidelines for its validation. Contracts may be used to specify invariant consistency properties that may be tested at runtime.

Chapter 4

1. I suggest taking the example described in section 4.1, but you are encouraged to find a different example.

2. See slide 4-12.

3. Class invariants may be disrupted by refining methods that introduce hidden modifications to the value(s) of instance variables. See section 4.2.2.

4. The intuition underlying the Law of Demeter is essentially that ignorance of how a class is implemented is beneficial for understanding and maintenance. See section 4.2.3.

5. See slide 4-16.

6. Semantic modeling is mostly concerned with defining the attributes of objects and the relation between object classes. Object-oriented modeling, in contrast, is more concerned with characterizing the behavioral properties of objects. However, the two approaches are converging.

7. Abstract systems may be regarded as the characterization of the functionality offered by a collection of abstract data types. It specifies the repertoire of methods available to the user of such a collection.

8. Classes corresponding to actual events specify the interactions which must occur between objects. The resources which are needed when the event occurs are specified when creating the event. Protection is offered by hiding the interaction between the objects in the definition of the event activation operator.

Chapter 5

1. Object-oriented languages generally offer a facility for creating objects, the capability of message passing, classes and inheritance. See slide 5-4.

2. A classification of object-oriented languages may distinguish between hybrid languages, frame-based languages as employed in artificial intelligence, parallel/distributed languages and languages supporting prototypes. See slide 5-4.

3. Characteristic for the object model supported by C++ is the unification of classes with the *struct* record type. See slide 5-6.

4. Friends may be classes or functions. They are allowed access to the private parts of an object. They may be necessary for reasons of efficiency. Friends are a relatively safe feature, since they must explicitly be declared by the class itself. They are not inherited. Neither is it possible for a class or function to declare itself as a friend of a class. Nevertheless, friends may jeopardize the integrity of an object. Treat friends with care.

5. Object-based implies support for encapsulation, whereas object-oriented implies support for encapsulation and inheritance. See slide 5-11.

6. As orthogonal dimensions along which to describe the design of object-oriented languages you may distinguish between objects, types, delegation and abstraction. See slide 5-12.

7. Active objects are, basically, objects with threads. Synchronous active objects, as supported by sC++, support method call by rendez-vous, protecting the object from unsafe access. Active objects may be used instead of event-loops and callbacks, thus avoiding the need to merge multiple event-loops. See section 5.3.4.

8. Prototype-based languages support an object model based on exemplars. Their most characteristic feature is support for dynamic delegation.

9. Inheritance is static; it amounts to creation-time sharing, whereas delegation supports lifetime sharing. See slide 5-16.

   Both C++ and Java support the forwarding of member function calls. Forwarding does not, however, allow for binding self-reference to the forwarding object.

10. In classical object-oriented languages, the notion of class stands for object generator and interface description. A class may further be a repository for sharing resources and act as an object capable of answering (class) methods. See slide 5-20.

11. See slide 5-21.

12. The first three postulates given in slide 5-22 pertain to Smalltalk. With some minor modifications, these postulates hold for other classical languages. The fourth postulate of slide 5-22 specifies the constraint that must be met by a reflective architecture: class variables of an object must be instance variables of the class of the object (when considering the class as an object).

Chapter 6

1. The major characteristic of a component is that it is a unit of independent deployment. In contrast, an object is simply a unit of instantiation. There may be many objects in a component. In addition, components must satisfy much stricter requirements than objects. For example, components may not have persistent state, which transcends the boundaries of a transaction. See slide 6-2.

2. See slide 6-3.

3. These are all, in some way, standards for interoperability. There is an obvious commonality since they all use some form of an Interface Definition Language. There are, however, many differences. For example, Microsoft (D)COM is being enforced as a de facto standard for the Windows platform, whereas both CORBA and the ODMG standard are developed by a consortium to arrive at a vendor-independent standard, encompassing multiple platforms. See section 6.2.

4. A number of perspectives relevant to the evaluation of the Java platform are mentioned in slide 7-12, among which are the *software engineering* and *system development* perspectives. In brief, the Java platform is very promising as it provides numerous APIs. There may be some doubt, however, about its efficiency. Also, questions have been raised about issues such as the maintainability of Java code.

5. See section 6.4.

6. One of the problems that occurs is how to integrate the (remote) object types with the types provided by the library. In section 6.5 the notion of *client adaptors* has been introduced as a solution to this problem.

Chapter 7

1. As elements in a software architecture, we can distinguish between *processing elements*, *data elements* and *connections*. See slide 7-2. A software

architecture description may serve to verify critical properties of the system, including properties such as availability, throughput, and interoperability.

2. See the discussion in section 7.1, in particular the definition from Bass *et al.* (1998).

3. Patterns for distributed object architectures range over various levels: framework, application, system, enterprise, and the intra/Internet level. In particular the latter levels require an effort of standardization and agreement on protocols. Patterns on the lower levels are important to make good use of the technology, for example CORBA.

4. A possible example is the architecture for a multimedia information system, of which a sketch is given in section 7.2,

5. Simply, the separation of knowledge-level and system-level aspects. For example, business logic would be a suitable candidate. See section 7.3.1.

6. The issues that play a role are listed in slide 7-10. The actual solution will, naturally, depend on the language for which the extension is made.

7. The JNI allows for the coupling of functions to (native) object methods. However, the JNI does not provide a standard way to associate Java objects with native C++ objects. See section 7.3.3.

8. The choice for an architectural style is determined by both technological constraints and application requirements. See section 7.4.

Chapter 8

1. Control abstractions primarily affect the flow of control. Control abstractions were introduced to support a structured approach to algorithm design. A structured approach avoids the use of goto's, and instead employs if-statements and explicit while-statements. In contrast, data abstraction pertains to data structures and information hiding. Abstract data types may be realized as a collection of functions. Object-oriented languages, however, provide far better support for data abstraction. See slide 8-2.

2. The most obvious interpretation of objects (as algebras) is to regard each object state as an algebra. A state change for the object, then, results in a different algebra. Mathematically, the object may then be considered to live in a different world. See slide 8-28.

3. Types contribute primarily to the reliability of systems. See slide 8-4.

4. A data abstraction matrix, as shown in slide 8-23, provides a powerful way to specify the properties of an abstract data type. Its realization by modules or objects reflects a choice for a particular decomposition, sacrificing the generality of the original matrix.

5. The realization of an abstract data type as a module results in organizing the functionality of the type around the observers. For each observer, the result for the various generators is specified as a separate case. In contracts, objects may be regarded as specifying for each generator the value for the observer operation. As trade-offs we have that objects behave comparatively better when extending the abstract data type with new generators, whereas the reverse seems to hold for extending an abstract data type with new observers.

6. Types have a formal interpretation as the specification of constraints. Classes may be taken as templates for object creation, which is a far more pragmatic interpretation.

   Types may be specified in a syntactic way, semantically or purely pragmatically. In the latter case, the notion of types coincides with the notion of classes. Classes, clearly, may be regarded as an over-specification of the properties of a type. When regarded from a syntactic point of view, types specify too little. However, a purely syntactic specification allows for rigid type checking. The behavioral specification of types must be regarded as an ideal. Contracts as supported by Eiffel are one possible approximation of this ideal. See slide 8-34 and slide 8-35.

7. Behaviorally compatible modifications are refinements that fully meet the substitutability requirement. Alternatives are signature compatible modifications, that are constrained only by syntactic requirements, and name compatible modifications that rely only on the method search algorithm employed, imposing even weaker constraints.

Chapter 9

1. In knowledge representation, inheritance is primarily applied to describe taxonomic structures in a declarative way. Employing exceptions in inheritance networks leads to non-monotony. Non-monotonic inheritance networks may give rise to inconsistencies. See slide 9-2.

2. The meaning of an inheritance lattice may be expressed as a first-order logic formula. An example is given in slide 9-3.

3. A type denotes a set of individuals. The subtyping relation is essentially the set inclusion relation, with some additional constraints. However, the subtype relation is best defined by means of subtype refinement rules.

4. See slide 9-5.

5. The contravariant nature of the function subtype refinement rule may be explained by relying on the business service metaphor: refining a service means better work for less money. Or, put differently, refining a function means imposing less constraints on the client, yet delivering a result that is more tightly defined. See slide 9-7.

6. The notion of *objects as records* is introduced simply to justify the interpretation of objects as records or tuples of values and functions. Again
employing a business metaphor, regarding an object as a collection of services, improving such a collection means offering more, and possibly better,
services. See slide 9-8.

7. Typed formalisms provide protection against errors. Yet, untyped formalisms are generally more flexible. In the practice of computer science
and mathematics, untyped formalisms are surprisingly popular.

8. A first distinction may be made between universal polymorphism and *ad
hoc* polymorphism, which accounts for overloading and coercion. Universal
polymorphism may be subdivided into parametric polymorphism, which
covers template classes, and inclusion polymorphism, which results from
derivation by inheritance. See slide 9-12.

9. Inheritance allows for the incremental development of object descriptions.
A child class may be regarded as modifying the parent base class, as it
may include additional attributes and methods and may refine inherited
attributes or methods.

10. See slides slide 9-19, slide 9-22 and slide 9-26.

11. (a) $\{a : Int, f : Int \rightarrow Int\}$, (b) $Int \rightarrow Int$, (c) $\{a : Bool, f : Bool \rightarrow Int\} \rightarrow$
Int.

12. (a) No, since $1..4 \not\leqslant 2..5$. (b) No, since $f : Bool \rightarrow Int \not\leqslant f : Int \rightarrow Int$,
because $Int \not\leqslant Bool$. (c) Yes, since $\{a : Bool, f : Bool \rightarrow Int\} \leqslant \{a : Bool\}$.

13. To give an example, if you have a record x of type $\exists \alpha.\{val : \alpha.op : \alpha \rightarrow Int\}$
then you do not need to know the precise nature of the (hidden) type α to
be able to type the expression $x.op(x.val)$ as Int. See slide 9-33.

14. A possible realization is given by the record $\{a = 0, f = \lambda x.E\}$, for
$E = if\ even(x)\ then\ true\ else\ false$. The corresponding package is given by
the expression $pack[\alpha = Int\ in\ \{a : \alpha, f : \alpha \rightarrow Bool\}](0, \lambda x.E)$. Another
realization is given by the record type $\{a : R, f : R \rightarrow Bool\}$ where R stands
for $\{x : Int, y : Int\}$.

15. The proof involves unrolling. Let $T_1 = \mu\alpha.\{c : \alpha, b : \alpha \rightarrow \alpha\}$ and $T_2 =
\mu\alpha.\{b : \alpha \rightarrow \alpha\}$. Now suppose that $T_1 \leqslant T_2$ then, by unrolling, we would
have that $\{c : T_1, b : T_1 \rightarrow T_1\} \leqslant \{b : T_2 \rightarrow T_2\}$, and hence, by the
function subtyping rule, that $T_2 \leqslant T_1$ and $T_1 \leqslant T_2$. This would only hold
if $T_1 = T_2$, which is obviously not the case.

16. Let $\sigma = \mu\alpha.\{c : \alpha, b : \tau \rightarrow \alpha\}$ and assume that $\sigma \leqslant \tau$, then by unrolling
we have that $\{c : \sigma, b : \tau \rightarrow \sigma\} \leqslant \{b : \tau \rightarrow \tau\}$ which clearly holds since
$b : \tau \rightarrow \sigma \leqslant b : \tau \rightarrow \tau$. And, by applying the refinement rule for recursive
types (given in slide 9-35), we indeed have that $\sigma \leqslant \tau$.

Chapter 10

1. Conformance not only involves syntactic properties, but behavioral properties as well. Behavioral properties include invariant properties and history
   properties. See slide 10-2.

2. See slide 10-3.

3. Static constraints may be expressed directly in the signature, but also by
   means of pre- and post-conditions. To a certain, but definitely lesser, extent,
   the reverse is also true. See slide 10-4.

4. States may be modeled as functions and state transformations as function
   modifications. See slide 10-6 and slide 10-5.

5. There are two ways to verify the behavior of a program: (a) prove for each
   possible transition that the formula holds; and (b) employ the correctness
   calculus given in slide 10-7.

6. For each syntactical kind of statement allowed by the language, a transition
   system specifies a corresponding execution step, or series of such steps, by
   means of a transition derivation rule. An example transition system for
   a simple object-based language, supporting object creation and message
   passing, is given in section 10.3.

7. To prove that a realization is correct with respect to its abstract specification, one must prove that each concrete operation satisfies the constraints
   imposed on the abstract level. See slide 10-12.

8. See slide 10-13, slide 10-14 and slide 10-15.

9. Correspondence between subtypes involves syntactic constraints, defined by
   the subtyping rules given in chapter 9, behavioral constraints, as characterized by the refinement relation for pre- and post-conditions and invariants,
   and constraints for the extensions, as expressed by the diamond rule. See
   slide 10-16 and slide 10-17.

10. See slide 10-18, slide 10-19 and slide 10-20.

11. Invariance properties of objects cannot completely be checked locally, within
    the confines of a single object. See slide 10-21. Checking invariants explicitly
    for each object, however, is likely to be too expensive.

12. Formal methods to specify the interaction between objects include model-
    based specification methods, the specification of contracts as behavioral
    compositions, the specification of cooperating actors by means of scripts,
    the specification of multi-party interactions, and the specification of joint
    action systems. See slide 10-22.

Chapter 11

1. Business objects give access to corporate data. For the end-user, flexibility in manipulating these data is what counts. For management, business objects may provide a handle to define business processes that make optimal use of IT resources.

2. The SanFrancisco framework gives development companies the foundation for developing added-value products. It is meant to be a reusable framework of business process and business object components, that provides a generic solution for the realization of (IT support for) business processes.

3. See slide 11-5.

4. Logistics-based modeling is concerned with quantitative aspects of business processes, such as throughput and workload. Discrete event simulation provides the tools to model such aspects.

5. The *request for loans* process, discussed in section 11.2.3, is such an example.

6. See slide 11-12.

7. As requirements we may mention support for interaction, support for multiple views, and powerful modeling or visualization primitives. See slide 11-17 for an example architecture.

8. One of the issues to decide upon is whether a two-tier or three-tier architecture is chosen. Another issue is how to make the legacy information available, and how to incorporate additional business logic in (for example middle-tier) objects. For actual solutions, see section 11.5.

Chapter 12

1. The Web is essentially a *client/server* architecture. Objects play an increasingly important role, to extend client-side applications, server-side application and to enhance the technological infrastructure for the Web itself.

2. See section 12.1.2 for a description. As an advantage one may mention that it is a powerful environment, with a large installed user base. A clear disadvantage is that the proposed architecture is tightly connected with one particular platform, Windows 95/NT.

3. Java and CORBA may be used for a smooth extension of Web applications with (distributed) object facilities, as illustrated in slide 12-4 and slide 12-5.

4. Computation on the Web is much more indeterminate than computation in traditional object systems. In comparison with LAN client/server systems delay and response times are far less predictable.

5. See slide 12-11.

6. See section 12.2.1

7. See section 12.2.2.

8. Two basic issues arise: (1) syntactic issues, that is how to incorporate new media into Web documents, (2) semantic/operational issues, that is how to provide the operational support fort the new media. With the introduction of XML and XSL (a powerful stylesheet formalism for XML) there seems to be generic support for tackling these issues. Another way to provide such operational support is to write a plugin for the various browsers and (client) platforms. As an example, see section 12.3.

References

Abadi M. and Cardelli L. (1996), *A Theory of Objects*, Springer-Verlag

Agha G. (1990), The structure and semantics of actor languages. In de Bakker *et al.* (1990), pp. 1-59

Agha G., Wegner P. and Yonezawa A. (eds) (1993), *Research directions in concurrent object-oriented programming*, MIT Press

America P. (1987), POOL-T: a parallel object-oriented language. In *Object-oriented concurrent systems* (Yonezawa A. and Tokoro M., eds), MIT Press, pp. 199-220

America P. (1990), A behavioral approach to subtyping in object-oriented programming languages. In Lenzerini *et al.* (1990), pp. 173-190

America P. and de Boer F. (1993), Reasoning about dynamically evolving process structures, *Formal Aspects of Computing* 3, pp. 1-53

America P., de Bakker J.W., Kok J.N. and Rutten J.J.N.N. (1989), Denotational semantics of a parallel object-oriented language, *Information and Computation*, 83(2), pp. 152-205

Ammeraal L. (1992), *Programming Principles in Computer Graphics*, Wiley, 2nd edn

Andrews G.R. (1991), *Concurrent programming – principles and practice*, Benjamin/Cummings

Apt K.R. and Olderog E-R. (1991), *Verification of Sequential and Concurrent Programs*, Springer

Backhouse R. (1986), *Program Construction and Verification*, Prentice-Hall

Bal H.E. and Grune D. (1994), *Programming Language Essentials*, Addison-Wesley

Bar-David T. (1992), Practical consequences of formal definitions of inheritance, *JOOP* (July/August), pp. 43-49

479

Barendrecht H.P. (1984) , *The Lambda Calculus – Its Syntax and Semantics*, North-Holland, rev. edn

Barnes J.G.P. (1994), *Programming in Ada, Plus an Overview of Ada 9X*, Addison-Wesley, 4th edn

Bass L., Clements P. and Kazman R. (1998), *Software Architecture in Practice*, SEI Series in Software Engineering. Addison-Wesley

Beck K. and Cunningham W. (1989), A laboratory for teaching object-oriented thinking. In *Proc. OOPSLA'89*, ACM Sigplan Notices 17(4), pp. 1-6

Bennett J.K. (1987), The design and implementation of Distributed Smalltalk. In *Proc. OOPSLA'87*, pp. 318-330

Bersoff E.H. and Davis A.M. (1991), Impacts of life cycle models on software configuration management, *CACM* 34(8), pp. 105-117

Bezem M. and Grootte J.F. (eds) (1993), *Typed lambda calculi and applications*, *Proc. Int. Conf. on typed lambda calculi and applications*, *TCLA'93*, Springer LNCS 664

Bigelow J. (1988), Hypertext and CASE, *IEEE Software* (March), pp. 23-26

Black A. and Hutchinson N. (1986), Object structure in the Emerald system. In *Proc. OOPSLA'86*, pp. 78-86

Blaschek G., Pomberger G. and Stritzinger A. (1989), A comparison of object-oriented programming languages, *Structured Programming* 10(4), pp. 187-197

Bobrow D.G. and Winograd T. (1977), An overview of KRL – a knowledge representation language, Technical Report R76/581 Stanford University

Bolier D. and Eliëns A. (1994), Sim – a C++ simulation library, IR-367, Vrije Universiteit

Boncz P.A. and Kersten M.L. (1995), Monet – an impressionist sketch of an advanced database system. In *Proc. Basque Int. Workshop on Information Technology*, San Sebastian, Spain

Booch G. (1986), Object-oriented development, *IEEE Transactions on Software Engineering* 12(2), pp. 211-221

Booch G. (1991), *Object-Oriented Design with Applications*, Benjamin Cummings

Booch G. (1994), *Object-Oriented Analysis and Design with Applications*, Benjamin Cummings, 2nd edn

Bratko I. (1990), *Prolog Programming for Artificial Intelligence*, Addison-Wesley, 2nd edn

Bundy A. (ed) (1990), *Catalogue of Artificial Intelligence tools*, Springer, 3rd edn.

Caglayan A. and Harrison C. (1997), *Agent Source Book – a Complete Guide to Desktop, Internet and Intranet Agents*, Wiley

Cardelli L. (1984), A semantics of multiple inheritance. In *Semantics of Data Types*, Springer LNCS 173, pp. 51-68

Cardelli L. and Wegner P. (1985), On understanding types, data abstraction and polymorphism, *ACM Computing Surveys* 17(4), pp. 472-522

Cardelli L., Donahue J., Jordan M., Kalsow B. and Nelson G. (1989), The Modula-3 Type System. In *Proc. ACM Symposium on Principles of Programming Languages*, Austin, Texas, pp. 202-212

Castagna G., Ghelli G. and Longo G. (1993), A semantics for λ-*early*: a calculus with overloading and early binding. In Bezem en Grootte (1993), pp. 107-123

Cattell R. (ed) (1994), *The Object Database Standard: ODMG-93*, Morgan-Kaufmann

Champeaux D., Lea D. and Faure P. (1993), *Object-Oriented System Development*, Addison-Wesley

Chennupati K. and Saiedian H. (1997), An evaluation of object store management and naming schemes in persistent object systems, *JOOP* 10(6), pp. 20-27

Cheong F-C. (1996), *Internet Agents: Spiders, Wanderers, Brokers and Bots*, New Riders

Cline M. and Lea D. (1990), The behavior of C++ classes. In *Proc. Symp. on Object-Oriented Programming*, Marist College

Coad P. and Yourdon E. (1991a), *Object-Oriented Analysis*, Prentice Hall, 2nd edn

Coad P. and Yourdon E. (1991b), *Object-Oriented Design*, Prentice Hall

Cockburn A. (1997), *Surviving Object-Oriented Projects: A Manager's Guide*, Addison-Wesley

Cointe P. (1987), Metaclasses are first class: the ObjVLisp Model. In *Proc. OOPSLA'87, ACM Sigplan Notices* 22(12), pp. 156-167

Coleman D., Arnold P., Bodoff S., Dollin C., Gilchrist H., Hayes F. and Jeremaes P. (1994) , *Object-Oriented Development – The Fusion Method*, Prentice Hall

Conklin J. (1987), Hypertext: An Introduction and Survey, *IEEE Computer* 20(9), pp. 17-41

Cook W., Hill W. and Canning P. (1990), Inheritance is not subtyping. In *Proc. ACM Symp. on Principles of Programming Languages*

Cook W.R. (1990), Object-oriented programming versus abstract data types. In de Bakker *et al.* (1990), pp. 151-178

Coplien J. (1992), *Advanced C++ Programming Styles and Idioms*, Addison-Wesley

Coplien J.O. and Schmidt D.C. (1995), *Pattern Languages of Program Design*, Addison-Wesley

Coplien J.O. and Schmidt D.C. (eds) (1995), *Pattern Languages of Program Design (1)*, Addison-Wesley

Cox B.J. (1986), *Object-Oriented Programming – An Evolutionary Approach*, Addison-Wesley

Craig I. (1991), *The formal specification of advanced AI architectures*, Ellis Horwood

Dahl O-J. (1992), *Verifiable Programming*, Prentice Hall

Dahl O-J. and Nygaard K. (1966), Simula – an algol-based simulation language, *CACM* 9, pp. 671-678

Danforth S. and Tomlinson C. (1988), Type theories and object-oriented programming, *ACM Computing Surveys* 20(1), pp. 30-72

Davenport and Short J.E. (1995), The new industrial engineering: information technology and business process redesign, *Summer Sloan Management Review*

Davis A.M., Bersoff E.H. and Comer E.R. (1988), A strategy for comparing alternative software development life cycle models, *IEEE Trans. on Software Engineering* 14(10), pp. 1453-1461

Davison A. (1993), A survey of logic programming based object-oriented languages. In Agha *et al.* (1993), pp. 43-106

de Bakker J.W., de Roever W.P. and Rozenberg G. (eds) (1990), *Foundations of Object-Oriented Languages*, Springer LNCS 489

Dijkstra E.W. (1976), *A Discipline of Programming*, Prentice Hall

Diller A. (1994), *Z: An Introduction to Formal Methods*, Wiley, 2nd edn

Dony C., Malenfant J. and Cointe P. (1992), Prototype-based languages: from a new taxonomy to constructive proposals and their validation. In *Proc. OOPSLA'92*, pp. 201-217

Eliëns A. (1992), *DLP – A Language for Distributed Logic Programming*, Wiley

Eliëns A. (1995), Hush – a C++ API for Tcl/Tk, *The X Resource*, Issue 14, April, pp. 111-155

Eliëns A. (1998), Hypermedia support for software engineering, *Workshop: Hypertext functionality and the WWW*, at the 7th WWW Conference, Brisbane University, 1-4 April, Brisbane, Australia

Eliëns A., de Bra P., Treur J., Brazier F., van Vliet J.C. (1997a), Web Agent Support Program, *Workshop: Logic Programming and the Web*, 6th Int WWW Conference, http://www.cs.vu.nl/~eliens/WWW6

Eliëns A., van Ossenbruggen J.R. and Schönhage S.P.C. (1997b), Animating the Web — an SGML-based approach . In: *The Internet in 3D – Information, Images and Interaction*, Academic Press, pp. 75-96

Eliëns A., van Welie M., van Ossenbruggen J. and Schönhage B. (1997c), Jamming (on) the Web. In: *Proc. of the 6th Int. World Wide Web Conference — Everyone, Everything Connected*, 7-11 April, Santa Clara, California USA, O'Reilly and Associates Inc., pp. 419-426

Ellis M. and Stroustrup B. (1990), *The Annotated C++ Reference Manual*, Addison-Wesley

Evangelist M., Francez N. and Katz S. (1989), Multiparty interactions for interprocess communication and synchronization, *IEEE Trans. on Software Engineering* 15(11), pp. 1417-1426

Fichman R.G. and Kemerer C.F. (1992), Object-oriented and conventional analysis and design methodologies, *IEEE Computer* 25(10), pp. 22-39

Fikes R. and Kehler T. (1985), The role of frame-based representation in reasoning, *CACM* 28, pp. 904-920

Fowler M. (1997a), *Analysis Patterns – Reusable Object Models*, Addison Wesley Longman

Fowler M., with Scott K. (1997b), *UML Distilled – Applying the Standard Object Modeling Language*, Addison Wesley Longman

Francez N., Hailpern B. and Taubenfeld R. (1989), Script: a communication abstraction mechanism and its verification, *Science of Computer Programming* 6(1), pp. 35-88

Fukanaga K. (1986), An experience with a Prolog-based object-oriented language. In *Proc. OOPSLA'86*, pp. 224-234

Gamma E., Helm R., Johnson R. and Vlissides J. (1994), *Design Patterns – Elements of Reusable Object-Oriented Software*, Addison-Wesley

Gerrits J.W.M (1995), Towards information logistics – an exploratory study of logistics in information production, PhD thesis, Vrije Universiteit

Ghelli G. and Orsini R. (1990), Types and subtypes as partial equivalence relations. In Lenzerini *et al.* (1990), pp. 191-209

Goguen J.A. and Meseguer J. (1986), Extensions and foundations of object-oriented programming, *ACM SIGPLAN Notices* (October), pp. 153-162

Gosling J. and McGilton H. (1995), The Java(tm) Language Environment: A White Paper, Sun Microsystems

Gries D. (1981), *The Science of Programming*, Springer

Halbert D. and O'Brien P. (1987), Using types and inheritance in object-oriented programming, *IEEE Software* 4(5), pp. 71-79

Hammer M. (1990), Reengineering work: don't automate, obliterate, *Harvard Business Review*, July/August

Hammer M. and McLeod D. (1978), The semantic data model: a modeling mechanism for database applications. In *Proc. ACM SIGMOD Int. Conf. on Management of Data*, pp. 26-35

Harel D. (1987), Statecharts: a visual formalism for complex systems, *Science of Computer Programming* 8, pp. 231-274

Harmon P. and Taylor D.A. (1993), *Objects in Action – Commercial Applications of Object-Oriented Technologies*, Addison-Wesley

Hayes F. and Coleman D. (1991), Coherent models for object-oriented analysis. In *Proc. OOPSLA'91, ACM Sigplan Notices* 26(4), pp. 171-183

Hayes I. (1992), *Specification Case Studies*, Prentice Hall, 2nd edn

Headington M.R. and Riley D.D. (1994), *Data abstraction and structures using C++*, D.C. Heath and Company

Helm R., Holland I.M. and Gangopadhyay D. (1990), Contracts: specifying behavioral compositions in object-oriented systems. In *Proc. ECOOP/OOPSLA'90*, pp. 169-180

Henderson P. (1993), *Object-oriented specification and design with C++*, McGraw-Hill

Henderson-Sellers B. (1992), *A book of Object-Oriented Knowledge*, Prentice-Hall

Henderson-Sellers B. and Edwards J.M. (1990), The object-oriented system's life
cycle, *CACM* 33(9), pp. 143-159

Hill D.R.C. (1996), *Object-Oriented Analysis and Simulation*, Addison-Wesley

Hoare C.A.R. (1969), An axiomatic basis for computer programming, *CACM* 12,
pp. 576-580, 583

Hoare C.A.R. (1972), Proof of correctness of data representation, *Acta
Informatica* 1, pp. 271-281

Hopcroft J.E. and Ullman J.D. (1979), *Introduction to automata theory,
languages and computation*, Addison-Wesley

Hu D. (1989), *C/C++ for Expert Systems*, MIS Press

ISO (1992), *Information Technology – Hypermedia/Time-based Structuring
Language (HyTime)*. International Standard 10744

ISO (1996), *Standard Music Description Language (SMDL)*, Draft International
Standard ISO/IEC 10743

ISO (1997), VRML97. International Standard

Jackson D. (1998), *Business Objects Companion*, Prentice Hall

Jacobson I., Christeron M., Jonsson P. and Övergaard G. (1992),
Object-Oriented Software Engineering – A Use Case Driven Approach,
Addison-Wesley

Janssen W.C. Jr. (1999), A next generation architecture for HTTP, *IEEE
Internet Computing* 3(1), pp. 69-73

Johnson R.E. and Foote B. (1988), Designing reusable classes, *JOOP* 1(2), pp.
22-35

Jones G.W. (1990), *Software Engineering*, Wiley

Kahn K., Tribble E.D., Miller M.S. and Bobrow D.G. (1986), Objects in
concurrent logic programming languages. In *Proc. OOPSLA'86*, pp.
242-257

Kersten M.L., Nes M., Windhouwer M.A. (1998), A feature database for
multimedia objects, CWI Report INS-R9807, July 1998

Kim W. and Lochovsky F. (eds) (1989), *Object-Oriented Concepts, Databases
and Applications*, Addison-Wesley

King R. (1989), My cat is object-oriented. In Kim and Lochovsky (1989), pp.
23-30

Kiniry J. and Zimmerman D. (1997), A hands-on look at Java mobile agents, *IEEE Internet Computing* 1(4)

Knudsen J.L. and Madsen O.L. (1988), Teaching object-oriented programming is more than teaching object-oriented programming languages. In *Proc. ECOOP'88*, Springer LNCS 276, pp. 21-40

Knuth D. (1992), *Literate Programming*, CSLI Lecture Notes 27, Stanford

Krasner G.E. and Pope S.T. (1988), A cookbook for using the Model-View-Controller user interface paradigm in Smalltalk-80, *JOOP* (August), pp. 26-49

Kruchten P.B. (1995), The 4+1 view model of architecture, *IEEE Software*, 12(6), pp. 42-50

Kunz J.C., Kehler T.P. and Williams M.D. (1984), Applications development using a hybrid AI development system, *AI Magazine*, September 1984, pp. 41-54

Kurki-Suonio R. and Jarvinen H.M. (1989), Action system approach to the specification and design of distributed systems. In *Proc. 5th Int. Workshop on Software Specification and Design, ACM Software Engineering Notes* 14(3), pp. 34-40

Kurtz B., Woodfield S.N. and Embley D.W. (1990), *Object-Oriented System Analysis – A Model-Driven Approach*, Prentice Hall

Lenzerini M., Nardi D. and Simi M. (eds) (1990), *Inheritance Hierarchies in Knowledge Representation and Programming Languages*, Wiley

Levy H.M. (1984), *Capability-Based Computer Systems*, Digital Press, Bedford Massachusetts

Lewis T. (1997), If Java is the Answer, *IEEE Computer*, March, pp. 136, 133-135

Lieberherr K. and Holland I. (1989), Assuring good style for object-oriented programs, *IEEE Software* 6(5), pp. 38-48

Lieberman H. (1986), Using prototypical objects to implement shared behavior in object-oriented systems. In *Proc. OOPSLA'86*, pp. 214-223

Lilypond Documentation, http://www.cs.uu.nl/people/hanwen/lilypond

Linton M., Vlissides J. and Calder P. (1989), Composing user interfaces with Interviews, *IEEE Computer* 22(2), pp. 8-22

Lippman S. (1991), *A C++ Primer*, Addison-Wesley, 2nd edn.

Liskov B. and Wing J.L. (1993), A new definition of the subtype relation. In *Proc. ECOOP'93*, Springer LNCS 707, pp. 119-141

Liskov B.H. and Zilles S.N. (1974), Programming with abstract data types, *ACM Sigplan Notices* 9, pp. 50-59

Maes P. (1997), Humanizing the global computer. Interview in: *IEEE Internet Computing* 1(4)

Malenfant J., Lapalme G. and Vaucher J. (1989), ObjVProlog: Metaclasses in Logic. In *Proc. ECOOP'89*, Cambridge University Press, pp. 257-269

Martin R.C., Riehle D. and Buschmann F. (eds) (1997), *Pattern Languages of Program Design (3)*, Addison-Wesley

McGregor J. and Sykes D. (1992), *Object-Oriented Software Development: Engineering Software for Reuse*, Van Nostrand Reinhold

Meyer B. (1988), *Object-Oriented Software Construction*, Prentice Hall

Meyer B. (1992a), *Eiffel: the Language*, Prentice Hall

Meyer B. (1992b), Applying Design by Contract, *IEEE Computer* 25(10), pp. 40-51

Meyer B. (1993), Systematic concurrent object-oriented programming, *CACM* 36(9), pp. 56-80

Meyer B. (1997), *Object-Oriented Software Construction*, Prentice Hall, 2nd edn

Meyrowitz N. (1986), Intermedia: the architecture and construction of an object-oriented hypermedia system and applications framework. In *Proc. OOPSLA'86*, pp. 186-201

Milner R., Tofte M. and Harper R. (1990), *The definition of Standard ML*, MIT Press

Minsky M. (1975), A framework for representing knowledge. In *The Psychology of Computer Vision*, Winston P. (ed), McGraw-Hill, New York, pp. 211-277

Moon D.A. (1986), Object-oriented programming with Flavors. In *Proc. OOPSLA'86*, pp. 1-8

Mowbray T.J. and Malveau R.C. (1997), *CORBA Design Patterns*, Wiley

Negroponte N. (1995), *Being Digital*, New Riders

Nierstrasz O. (1987), Active objects in Hybrid. In *Proc. OOPSLA'87*, pp. 243-253

Nierstrasz O. (1993), Composing active objects – the next 700 concurrent object-oriented languages. In Agha *et al.* (1993)

Noffsinger W.B., Niedbalski R., Blanks M. and Emmart N. (1998), Legacy
     object modeling speeds software integration, *CACM* 41(12), pp. 80-89

ObjectSpace (1997), Voyager, http://www.objectspace.com

Orbacus (1998), JThreads++, Java threads for C++, http://www.orbacus.com

Orfali R., Harkey D., Edwards J. (1999), *Object Web Survival Guide*, Wiley

Ousterhout J.K. (1991), An X11 Toolkit based on the Tcl language. In *Proc.
     USENIX Winter Conference*, pp. 105-115

Paepcke A. (ed) (1993), *Object-oriented programming – The CLOS perspective*,
     MIT Press

Palsberg J. and Schwartzback M.I. (1994), *Object-oriented type systems*, Wiley

Parnas D.L. (1972a), A technique for software module specification, *CACM* 15,
     pp. 330-336

Parnas D.L. (1972b), On the criteria to be used in decomposing systems into
     modules, *CACM* 15, pp. 1052-1058

PetitPierre C. (1998), Synchronous C++, a language for interactive applications,
     IEEE Computer 31(9), pp. 65-72

PetitPierre C. (1999), Synchronous Active Objects – a new concurrent
     object-oriented programming paradigm, http://ltiwww.epfl.ch/sCxx

Petrie C. (1997), What's an agent ... and what's so intelligent about it?,
     WebWord column, *IEEE Internet Computing* 1(4)

Pierce B.C. (1993), Intersection types and bounded polymorphism. In Bezem en
     Grootte (1993), pp. 346-359

Pierce B.C., Remy D. and Turner D.N. (1993), A typed higher-order
     programming language based on the pi-calculus, Report University of
     Edinburgh (available at ftp://ftp.dcs.ed.ac.uk:pub/bcp/pilang.ps)

Pinson L. and Wiener R. (eds) (1990), *Applications of Object Oriented
     Programming*, Addison-Wesley

Plotkin G.D. and Abadi M. (1993), A logic for parametric polymorphism.
     In Bezem en Grootte (1993), pp. 361-375

Pokkunuri B. (1989), Object-oriented programming, *ACM Sigplan Notices*
     24(11), pp. 96-101

Pope S. (1991), *The Well-Tempered Object: Musical Applications of
     Object-Oriented Software Technology*, MIT Press

Rabin M.O. (1974), The computational complexity of Artificial Intelligence, IEEE Symposium

Rumbaugh J., Blaha M., Premerlani W., Eddi F. and Lorensen W. (1991), *Object-Oriented Modeling and Design*, Prentice Hall

Sanden B. (1994), A graduate course in object-oriented analysis based on student-generated projects, Technical Report ISSE-TR-94-102, George Mason University, Fairfax, USA

Saunders J. (1989), A survey of object-oriented programming languages, *JOOP* (March/April), pp. 5-11

Schildt H. (1999), *STL Programming from the ground up*, Osborne/McGraw-Hill

Schmidt D.C. (1995), Experience using design patterns to develop reusable object-oriented communication software, *CACM* 38(10), pp 65-74

Schönhage B. and Eliëns A. (1999), Dynamic and mobile VRML gadgets. In *Proc. VRML99*, 23-26 February, Paderborn, Germany

Schönhage B., Bakker P.P. and Eliëns A. (1998) , So many users - so many perspectives, *IFIP 12.2 Working Conference on Designing Effective and Usable Multimedia Systems*, Fraunhofer Institute, Stuttgart Germany, 9-10 September, Kluwer Academic, pp. 159-172

Shapiro E. and Takeuchi A. (1983), Object-oriented programming in Concurrent Prolog, *New Generation Computing* 1(2), pp. 5-48

Shaw M. (1984), Abstraction techniques in modern programming languages, *IEEE Software*, October, pp. 10-26

Shaw M. and Gorlan D. (1996), *Software Engineering Architectures – Perspectives on an Emerging Discipline*, Prentice Hall

Shimberg D. and Barnes L-A. (1997), *Client/Server and Beyond – Strategies for the 21st Century*, Prentice Hall

Shlaer S. and Mellor S.J. (1988), *Object-Oriented Analysis: Modeling the World in Data*, Yourdon Press, Englewood Cliffs, NJ

Siegel J. (1996), *CORBA Fundamentals and Programming*, OMG

SMIL W3C Recommendation (1999), Synchronized Multimedia Integration Language, http://www.w3.org/AudioVideo

Stefik M. and Bobrow D.G. (1986), Object-oriented programming: themes and variations, *AI Magazine*, December, pp. 40-62

Stepney S., Barden R. and Cooper D. (eds) (1992), *Object Orientation in Z*, Springer

Stroustrup B. (1988), What is 'object-oriented programming'?, *IEEE Software* 5(3), pp. 10-20

Stroustrup B. (1991), *The C++ Programming Language*, Addison-Wesley, 2nd edn

Stroustrup B. (1997), *The Design and Evolution of C++*, Addison-Wesley, 2nd edn

Stroustrup B. (1998), *The C++ Programming Language*, Addison-Wesley Longman, 3rd edn

Subrahmanian V.S. (1998), *Principles of Multimedia Databases*, Morgan Kaufmann

Szyperski C. (1997), *Component Software: Beyond Object-Oriented Programming*, Addison-Wesley Longman

Taivalsaari A. (1993), On the notion of object, *J. Systems Software* 21, pp. 3-16

Touretsky S. (1986), *The Mathematics of Inheritance Systems*, Pitman London

Ungar D. and Smith R.B. (1987), Self: The power of simplicity. In *Proc. OOPSLA'87, ACM Sigplan Notices* 4(8), pp. 227-242

Ungar D., Smith B.S., Chambers C. and Hölze U. (1992), Object, message and performance: How they coexist in Self, *IEEE Computer* 25(10), pp. 53-63

van Doorn M. and Eliëns A. (1995), Integrating WWW and applications, *3d Int. World Wide Web Conf. – Technology, Tools and Applications*, 10-14 April, Darmstadt

van Ossenbruggen J.R. and Eliëns A. (1995), Bringing music to the Web, *Proc. of the 4th Int. World Wide Web Conf. – The Web Revolution*, World Wide Web Journal, December, O'Reilly and Associates, Inc., pp. 309-314

van Rossum G. (1998), Java and Python: a perfect couple, http://www.developer.com/journal/techfocus/081798_jpython.html

van Welie M. and Eliëns A. (1996), Chatting on the Web, *Proc. ERCIM W4G Workshop on CSCW and the Web*, 7-9 Februari, GMD St Augustin, Germany

Visible Decisions (1997), The In3D Programmers Manual, Documentation with In3D Toolkit

Vlissides J.M., Coplien J.O. and Kerth N.L. (eds) (1996), *Pattern Languages of Program Design (2)*, Addison-Wesley

Walker D. (1990), Pi-calculus semantics of object-oriented programming languages, Report ECS-LFCS-90-122, University of Edinburgh

Wasserman A., Pircher P. and Muller R.J. (1989), An object-oriented structured design method for code generation, *Software Engineering Notes* 14(1), pp. 32-55

Wastell D.G., White P. and Kawalek P. (1994), A methodology for business process redesign: experiences and issues, *J. of Strategic Information Systems*, 3(1), pp. 23-40

Watkins K. (1993), *Discrete Event Simulation in C*, McGraw-Hill

Watson M. (1996), *AI Agents in Virtual Reality Worlds – Programming Intelligent VR in C++*, Wiley

Webster D. (1988), Mapping the Design Information Representation Domain, *IEEE Computer*, December, pp. 8-23

Wegner P. (1987), Dimensions of object-based language design, *ACM Sigplan Notices* 23(11), pp. 168-182

Wegner P. (1992), Dimensions of object-oriented modeling, *IEEE Computer* 25(10), pp. 12-19

Wegner P. and S. Zdonik S. (1988), Inheritance as an incremental modification mechanisms or what like is and isn't like. In *Proc. ECOOP'88*, Springer, pp. 56-77

Weinand A., Gamma E. and Marty R. (1988), ET++, an object-oriented application framework in C++. In *Proc. OOPSLA'88*, pp. 46-57

Weiss M.A. (1993), *Data Structures and Algorithm Analysis in C++*, Addison-Wesley

Wielemaker J. (1999), SWI Prolog, http://www.psy.uva.nl/projects/SWI-Prolog

Wiggins M. (1999), Object-orienting the Web, *IEEE Internet Computing* 3(1), pp. 36-37

Wirfs-Brock R. (1989), Object-oriented design: a responsibility-driven approach. In *Proc. OOPSLA'89*, pp. 71-75

Wirfs-Brock R., Wilkerson B. and Wiener L. (1990), *Designing Object-Oriented Software*, Prentice Hall

Wirth N. (1983), *Programming in Modula-2*, Springer

Wolf P. and Perry D. (1992), Foundations for the study of software architecture, *ACM Sigsoft - Software Engineering Notes*, 17(4), October, pp. 40-52

Wooldridge M. and Jennings N.R. (1995), Agent theories, architectures and languages: a survey. In: Wooldridge, M. and Jennings, N.R. (eds) *Intelligent Agents, Lecture Notes in AI*, Vol. 890, pp. 1-39, Springer-Verlag

Yonezawa A. and Tokoro M. (eds) (1987), *Object-oriented concurrent systems*, MIT Press

Yourdon E. and Constantine L. (1979), *Structured Design: Fundamentals of a Discipline of Computer Programming and Design*, Prentice Hall

Index